U0488741

本系列图书为国家社会科学基金重大项目"中国古代经典英译本汇释汇校"(项目编号:10&ZD108)结项成果。

[The books in this series are supported by the project "A Selected Anthology of English Translations and Commentaries on Chinese Classics," National Social Sciences Foundation of China (Project No.: 10 & ZD108).]

《论语》英译本汇释汇校丛书
丛书主编　杨慧林

A Selected Anthology of English
Translations and Commentaries
on *The Analects*

4

# 《论语》英译本术语引得

张靖　徐建委　主编

# Index to Key Terms in English Translations of *The Analects*

南京大学出版社

# 序言

　　《论语》是孔子及其弟子嘉言的记录①。关于《论语》的编者，时代愈后，结论愈清晰②。《论语》始编于孔子卒后，最初参与者应为孔子弟子，郑玄称有仲弓、子游、子夏等人，这或是汉人常识，延续的大约是战国以来的说法，似可信据。初编之后，《论语》应该又经数次增补或删销③，至战国中期（即孟子时代），其规模大体形成。但此时已是孔子卒后一百多年，各地孔门已形成了不同的学派，而他们手中的《论语》，自然会有不同，特别是在汉代学术的主要供给地：齐和鲁。据《汉书·艺文志》《张禹传》《儒林传》的记载，西汉初年，齐、鲁两地的《论语》已具各自面目，说明至迟在战国末年，不同地区的《论语》文本已经相对稳定，并形成了地域差异。汉成帝河平三年（公元前26年），刘向奉命开始整理西汉未央宫藏书。他对《论语》各写本的描述被何晏《论语集解序》所征引。其中说到《齐论语》④相比于《鲁论语》有两个

---

① 关于《论语》一书的内容或性质，古今均无异议。诸家皆认为《论语》乃是记录孔子及诸弟子善言之书。何晏《论语集解序》引刘向曰："《鲁论语》二十篇，皆孔子弟子记诸善言也。"《汉书·艺文志》曰："《论语》者，孔子应答弟子时人及弟子相与言而接闻于夫子之语也。"赵岐《孟子题辞》："七十子之畴，会集夫子所言，以为《论语》。"刘熙《释名》曰："《论语》，记孔子与诸弟子所语之言也。"

② 《汉书·艺文志》曰："当时弟子各有所记。夫子既卒，门人相与辑而论纂，故谓之《论语》。"郑玄《论语序》则称"仲弓、子游、子夏等撰定"。到了唐代，柳宗元《论语辩》论到《论语》述及曾参老死，且曾子、有子称子，故此书应由曾参弟子乐正子春、子思等人编成。宋代程颐、朱熹进一步认为《论语》成于有子、曾子之门人。郑玄所据当为先师之说，后来讨论《论语》编纂者，则主要依据《论语》文本，做出合理之推测。故此问题实无继续讨论的必要。

③ 曾子、有子的部分言语应该就是后来增补进去的。

④ 2015年12月，江西海昏侯墓出土简牍中的《论语》简被发现，其中有《智道》篇，无疑刘贺墓中的这套《论语》简属于《齐论语》系统。此外，还有一枚木牍或木简，乃是日常抄写的几条《论语》，文字与今本几无差异。木简的抄写者很可能就是海昏侯刘贺。

明显的特点：

1. 多出了《问王》(即《问玉》)①、《知道》两篇。
2. 其章、句多于《鲁论语》。②

这是未央宫所藏《论语》的"整理报告"。因此上述特点是皇家藏书中的两个文本系统之间的比较。而皇家藏书并不能完全反映日常社会的一般性知识状况。事实上，西汉中期以后，在普通知识与教育领域，《论语》写本的地域性因素在减弱，文本变异的个体特征开始增强。或者说此时《齐论语》《鲁论语》的地域文化界限渐趋模糊。但大体上二者还是具备了各自面目的文本系统。

今本《论语》编定于西汉末年，时称《张侯论》，属于《鲁论语》系统。张侯，即安昌侯张禹。《汉书·张禹传》对《张侯论》的来历记载颇详：

> 初，禹为师，以上难，数对己问经，为《论语章句》献之。始鲁扶卿及夏侯胜、王阳、萧望之、韦玄成皆说《论语》，篇第或异。禹先事王阳，后从庸生，采获所安，最后出而尊贵。

张禹在汉元帝时(公元前48—前33年)出任太子少傅。《论语章句》大约就是他给时为太子的汉成帝所编的教材。此书后出尊贵，遂成后世《论语》的祖本。在此之前，《论语》尚未出现一个通行本，汉宣帝、元帝时期儒生

---

① 王、玉古写法相似易混。
② 何晏《论语集解序》所言最为详细，也比较可靠："汉中垒校尉刘向言：'《鲁论语》二十篇，皆孔子弟子记诸善言也，太子太傅夏侯胜、前将军萧望之、丞相韦贤及子玄成等传之；《齐论语》二十二篇，其二十篇中，章句颇多于《鲁论》，琅邪王卿及胶东庸生、昌邑中尉王吉皆以教授，故有《鲁论》，有《齐论》。鲁共王时，尝欲以孔子宅为宫，坏，得古文《论语》。《齐论》有《问王》《知道》，多于《鲁论》二篇。《古论》亦无此二篇，分《尧曰》下章"子张问"以为一篇，有两《子张》，凡二十一篇，篇次不与齐、鲁《论》同。'安昌侯张禹本受《鲁论》，兼讲《齐说》，善者从之，号曰《张侯论》，为世所贵，包氏、周氏章句出焉。《古论》唯博士孔安国为之训解，而世不传。至顺帝时，南郡太守马融亦为之训说。汉末大司农郑玄就《鲁论》篇章，考之《齐》《古》，为之注。近故司空陈群、太常王肃、博士周生烈，皆为义说。"

扶卿、夏侯胜、王吉、萧望之、韦玄成诸辈手中的传本"篇第或异",并不相同。三国时代何晏主纂《论语集解》,所用底本即《张侯论》,自两晋以来流传至今。①

汉代还有《古论语》,出于孔子老宅的屋壁,是战国时代孔子后人的藏书,秦末焚书时被埋入墙中。这是一个竹简本的《论语》,用鲁国文字写成,故称《古论语》。这个文本因与西汉流传的《鲁论语》属于同一地区,因此二者大体相同,仅把《尧曰》篇"子张问"一章独立成篇,亦作《子张》,故《古论语》有两个《子张》篇,总计二十一篇。但这个本子的篇序与《张侯论》很不一样,《学而》第一,《乡党》第二,《雍也》第三。②

《张侯论》虽属《鲁论》,但兼收齐说。张禹曾分别受教于《鲁论语》大师夏侯建和《齐论语》大师王吉、庸生。故其《论语》学,在传、说、训、义方面应兼收齐、鲁之长。③ 东汉时代,郑玄又据《古论语》《齐论语》校订《鲁论》(即《张侯论》),所以后来的《张侯论》已非原初面貌,文字上更是三家皆有。④ 今本或可称为何晏集解本《张侯论》。

唐文宗开成二年(837)石壁九经刻成,并附《论语》《孝经》《尔雅》及《五

---

① 《汉志》小序曰:"汉兴,有齐、鲁之说。传《齐论》者,昌邑中尉王吉、少府宋畸、御史大夫贡禹、尚书令五鹿充宗、胶东庸生,唯王阳名家。传《鲁论语》者,常山都尉龚奋、长信少府夏侯胜、丞相韦贤、鲁扶卿、前将军萧望之、安昌侯张禹,皆名家。张氏最后而行于世。"皇侃《论语义疏序》曰:"今日所讲,即是《鲁论》,为张侯所学,何晏所集者也。"

② 《隋书·经籍志》又称《古论》"章句烦省,与《鲁论》不异,唯分《子张》为二篇,故为二十一篇",似《鲁论》跟《古论》除了篇次不同外,差异很小。《古论语》《齐论语》与《鲁论语》的文字差异还有数斑可窥。桓谭《新论》曰:"《古论语》二十一卷,与《齐》《鲁》文异六百四十余字。"不唯文字有异同,《古论语》篇序亦与《齐》《鲁》不同。皇侃《论语集解义疏序》曰:"《古论》分《尧曰》下章'子张问'更为一篇,合二十一篇。篇次以《乡党》为第二篇,《雍也》为第三篇,内倒错不可具说。……《齐论》题目与《鲁论》大体不殊,而长有《问王》《知道》二篇,合二十二篇,篇内亦微有异。"

③ 《经典释文叙录》云:"安昌侯张禹受《鲁论》于夏侯建,又从庸生、王吉受《齐论》。"吴承仕《经典释文叙录疏证》据皇侃《论语义疏·发题》认为《经典释文叙录》本于刘向《别录》:"晚有安昌侯张禹,就建学《鲁论》,兼讲《齐》说,择善而从,号曰《张侯论》,为世所贵。"参吴承仕《经典释文叙录疏证》(秦青点校),中华书局1984年版。

④ 这一情况《隋书·经籍志》有记载:"汉末,郑玄以《张侯论》为本,参考《齐论》、古《论》而为之注。魏司空陈群、太常王肃、博士周生烈,皆为义说。吏部尚书何晏,又为集解。是后诸儒多为之注,《齐论》遂亡。"

经文字》《九经字样》五种著作。开成石经《论语》即用何晏集解本。五代后唐长兴三年(932)冯道动议将《九经》雕版刊印,这是中国历史上政府主导的雕版刊印书籍之始。这次刊印经文依照开成石经。《论语》虽不在九经之列,但一如唐石经例,亦被刊印。北宋时虽然有多次对九经版刻的校改,但长兴雕版并未被废弃,一直使用到北宋末,后被金人掠去。故北宋监本九经其实就是修订过的长兴版本,两宋诸经的印本绝大多数都源出于此。它们又是今日版本之上源。

这大约就是《论语》文本的源流。

基于此,我们就不应抱有这样的期待:以《论语》为基础文献建立与孔子的思想对话。这种思考是一座建立在流沙上的房子。尤其不可取的是,依据《论语》中的某一两句表述来洞见孔子的心思。《论语》中的某些条目,很可能是删裁战国秦汉之间的杜撰故事而成,如《述而》篇的"三月不知肉味"章即属此种类型。① 此前的研究对《论语》材料的审查还很不够,因此《论语》中"孤证式"表述的学术有效性值得怀疑。但是,作为资料的整体——这应是处理《论语》材料的首要方法论,《论语》依然具有无可替代的价值,孔子晚年的不少言行借此得以留存下来。由此帮助我们在《春秋》之外,窥见孔子思想的丰富世界。

同时,不同于《春秋》和《诗》,《论语》在早期文献中很少被引用,战国文献中只有《孟子》引述最多。此书有近30处征引了孔子的话,也就只有8条可以与《论语》建立关联,且文本差异过大,故《孟子》的"作者们"恐怕没有见

---

① 《说苑·修文》篇保存了这个故事的早期样式:
孔子至齐郭门之外,遇一婴儿挈一壶相与俱行。其视精,其心正,其行端。孔子谓御曰:"趣驱之,趣驱之! 韶乐方作。"孔子至彼闻韶,三月不知肉味。故乐非独以自乐也,又以乐人;非独以自正也,又以正人矣哉! 于此乐者,不图为乐至于此。
类似的《论语》变体在战国秦汉文献中还有一些,如《修文》篇还保存了与《泰伯》"曾子有疾"章、《雍也》"雍也可使南面"章相关的两章,其文字差异度与"三月不知肉味"章的两个版本近似。这些故事虽然不排除真实发生的可能,但其讲述颇具传奇色彩,很难让人相信这是真实的记录。

过《论语》一书①。在《礼记·坊记》中已经征引了《论语》②，但孤证，不立。虽然我们根据《论语》文本的内部信息及结构，可以判断至迟到孟子时代，《论语》已经大体成形，但在早期文献中罕被征引，只能说明此书并不被战国时代的士人视作经典。

直到汉武帝时代，文士们才开始征引《论语》。董仲舒的奏议中已经将《论语》视作与《诗》《春秋》一样的经典资源来使用了③。董仲舒之后，史籍文献中《论语》的引据逐渐增多。天子的诏书中，也开始强调《论语》作为经典的重要性④。到汉昭帝、宣帝时期，《论语》已经成为汉代小学的主要经典

---

① 如《公孙丑上》：
"昔者子贡问于孔子曰：'夫子圣矣乎？'孔子曰：'圣则吾不能，我学不厌而教不倦也。'子贡曰：'学不厌，智也；教不倦，仁也。仁且智，夫子既圣矣！'"
《论语·述而》作：
子曰："若圣与仁，则吾岂敢？抑为之不厌，诲人不倦，则可谓云尔已矣。"公西华曰："正唯弟子不能学也。"
《吕氏春秋·尊师》则引作：
子贡问孔子曰："后世将何以称夫子？"孔子曰："吾何足以称哉！勿已者，则好学而不厌，好教而不倦，其惟此邪。"
翟灏《孟子考异》据此云："《论语》'为之不厌，诲人不倦'，是向公西华言之，此向子贡言之。《日知录》谓孟子书所引孔子之言，其载于《论语》者，'我学不厌，而教不倦'，一也。今据《吕氏春秋》，则此实别一时语。"
② 《礼记·坊记》：论语曰："三年无改于父之道，可谓孝矣。"
③ 《汉书·董仲舒传》载董仲舒元光元年举贤良对策曰："臣闻《论语》曰：'有始有卒者，其唯圣人虖！'"略早于董仲舒，韩婴所编《韩诗外传》三引《论语》曰，卷二《论语》曰：'色斯举矣，翔而后集。'"卷五引《论语》曰："必也正名乎！"卷六《论语》曰："君子于其言，无所苟而已矣。"三处引用均无后人插入痕迹。韩婴主要活动于文帝、景帝时期和武帝初年。
④ 如《汉书·昭帝纪》载始元五年六月《诏》曰：
朕以眇身获保宗庙，战战栗栗，夙兴夜寐，修古帝王之事，通《保傅传》《孝经》《论语》《尚书》，未云有明。其令三辅、太常举贤良各二人，郡国文学高第各一人。赐中二千石以下至吏民爵各有差。
《汉书·宣帝纪》载霍光曰：
礼，人道亲亲故尊祖，尊祖故敬宗。大宗毋嗣，择支子孙贤者为嗣。孝武皇帝曾孙病已，有诏掖庭养视，至今年十八，师受《诗》《论语》《孝经》，操行节俭，慈仁爱人，可以嗣孝昭皇帝后，奉承祖宗，子万姓。

之一①。但在南宋之前,《论语》一直被视作初学者的基础读本,并不被视作"经",只被视作经书的附庸。

《论语》有一个漫长的经典化过程,直到"四书"的组合出现,这部早期文献才到达了与《诗》《书》相侔的位置。二十世纪以来,《论语》成为儒学研究中最重要的典籍之一,被视为孔子思想最主要的文献,这大概是一百多年来儒学研究最大的误判。离开了《春秋》谈孔子思想或儒家思想,就像丢掉土豆来炒土豆丝一样让人不可理解。

为什么会出现这样的奇怪局面呢?或许是因为现代意义上的中国哲学研究所使用的基础方法和基本概念来自西方,使用这样的方法和概念,只能从《论语》《孟子》中发现与之相适合的建筑材料,并可以依据"进口图纸"把这些材料建造成型。而《诗》《书》《春秋》乃至《公羊传》《穀梁传》中,却找不到足够的此类材料。也是由于被这些方法和概念潜在掌控,许多研究者对实际发生过的思想史,近乎无视。

有鉴于此,一个更加有趣的问题是,西方人如何来理解中国的早期思想呢?他们会使用什么样的"规矩"来度量中国文本,他们期待发现什么,又会"发现出"什么呢?事实上,自传教士时代开始,中国古代经典便不断被译介,促成了"西学东渐"与"中学西传"的典型互动。譬如,白晋(Joachim Bouvet, 1656—1730)译介《易经》并将之视为与柏拉图、亚里士多德一样合理而完美的哲学;马礼逊(Robert Morrison, 1782—1834)在翻译出版《圣经》的同时也翻译过《三字经》和《大学》等古代经典;卫礼贤(Richard Wilhelm, 1873—1930)通过翻译《老子》《庄子》和《列子》来深入发掘"中国心灵";曾在香港生活 30 年,又在牛津大学担任汉学教授 21 年的理雅各(James Legge, 1815—1897)更是一个最具代表性的例证,他不仅系统研究和翻译了"四书五经",还积极参与文本讨论,他的《论语》译本"主要参照八

---

① 汉元帝时期史游《急就》篇已有"宦学讽诵《孝经》《论》"之语,东汉崔寔《四民月令》曰:"十一月冬至之日……命幼童读《孝经》《论语》篇章,入小学。"《急就》篇是日常识字之书,《四民月令》是当时人四时生活的参考指南,因此二者所述内容乃是一个较长时段的历史信息。

大资源,包括三国魏何晏,宋代朱熹、邢昺,清代王引之、汪廷机的注释和康熙等人的评论。在这些人当中,引用的最多的是何晏、朱熹和邢昺"①。因此,理雅各的《论语》译本不仅给出中文原本及自己的英译,还在其西方思想传统理解背景下用"了解之同情"(sympathetic reading)的比较方法撰写了大量注释,帮助外国读者理解文本。他的翻译加注释的学术范式一度成为后人仿效的榜样。自理雅各始,《论语》英译本已经超过100多种。我们以1861和1893年的理雅各译本为底本,以1910年的苏慧廉译本(Edward William Soothill,1861—1935)、1938年的韦利译本(Arthur Waley,1889—1966)、1979年的刘殿爵译本(D. C. Lau,1921—2010)、1997年的李克曼译本(Pierre Ryckmans,笔名 Simon Leys,1935—2014)及 1998年的安乐哲(Roger Ames,1942— )和罗思文(Henry Rosemont, Jr. , 1934—2017)合译本为参照本②,采用平行集注的方式,列六家译本及注释于《论语》经文之下,仿效汉唐间经史集注,广搜精取,比类见义,但终不以释义为归旨,而是一种平行并置和比较中的互现。

这六个译本都有比较详细的导论或序言,在本丛书的前三卷中已经翻译和介绍,从中可以约略看出译本的底色。相较而言,理雅各、苏慧廉译本的导论多依据清代有关孔子与《论语》的一般知识,理雅各还重点参考了江永的《乡党图考》,但两人的叙述中似是而非的错误特别多,显然是采纳了一些后来逐渐产生的乡闻琐语,是一种奇妙的杂烩。韦利的译本重视学术性,

---

① 张西平、费乐仁:《理雅各〈中国经典〉绪论》,载理雅各:《中国经典》(卷一),上海:华东师范大学出版社,2011年,第22页。按:所谓汪廷机注,实为吴宗昌《四书经注集证》,乃汪廷机三益斋刻本。

② James Legge, trans., *The Chinese Classics with a Translation, Critical and Exegetical Notes Prolegomena, and Copious Indexes*, Vol. 1 (Oxford: The Clarendon Press, 1893); William Edward Soothill, trans., *The Analects of Confucius* (Yokohama: The Presbyterian Mission Press, 1910); Arthur Waley, *The Analects of Confucius* (London: George Allen & Unwin Ltd, 1938); D. C. Lau, trans., *The Analects* (Hong Kong: The Chinese University of Hong Kong, 1992); Simon Leys, trans., *The Analects of Confucius* (New York: W. W. Norton & Company, 1997); Roger T. Ames & Henry Rosement, Jr., trans., *The Analects of Confucius: A Philosophical Translation* (New York: The Random House Publishing Group, 1998).

他受到了"古史辨"的影响,在导论中有许多理性的质疑,也看不到一些明显的知识错误,是西方学术界颇为流行的一个译本。刘殿爵、李克曼、安乐哲/罗思文三个译本都偏重思想性或哲学性的理解。安乐哲/罗思文译本最为晚出,还特别参考了时代为西汉中期的定县汉简《论语》,因此颇有特点。

理雅各译本附有原文,因此可以知道他的底本是朱熹的《论语集注》,安乐哲/罗思文译本部分使用定县汉简《论语》作底本。除此之外,我们并不知道其他四家的底本是什么。但大体可以判断,这四个译本参考的应是某个通俗的《论语》文本,并没有做底本的遴选、校勘。① 但是,《论语》在十三经之中,异文、分章等问题要较其他诸经复杂。阮元《十三经注疏校勘记》录有异文五百多处,有一些直接关系到意义的理解。如《学而》篇"鲜矣仁",皇侃《论语义疏》作"鲜矣有仁";"与朋友交而不信乎",皇侃《义疏》及日本正平本作"与朋友交言而不信乎"。《里仁》篇"里仁为美",皇侃《义疏》作"里仁为善"。在文字的分章方面,情况更是复杂。如《乡党》篇邢昺《论语注疏》分作22小节,皇侃《义疏》不分节,朱熹《集注》分作17节,今人杨伯峻《论语译注》则细分为27节,黄怀信《论语汇校集释》更进一步,分作32节;《先进》篇邢昺《注疏》为24章,皇侃《义疏》23章,朱熹《集注》25章,杨伯峻《译注》26章。一段文字独立为一章,还是与其他文字合成一章,意义自然会有不同。

当然,我们不能苛求译者的版本知识,但早期的异文以及晚期不同版本的分章,必然会对文本意义的形成造成影响。译者们所据底本不同,我们在做平行并置时,也就只能按照底本的分章,对译文进行分拆,所幸这样的地方并不是很多。因此,在必要的地方,我们做了脚注,对重要异文或分章问题进行了说明。

《论语》刻本的祖本是《唐石经》,这也是目前《论语》传世最早的完整文

---

① 安乐哲、罗思文选择定县汉简《论语》作为底本,也不是一个很好的选择。我们今天的读本是一个汉代大师们经过数次校勘整理的版本,相对来说是一个更加优善的版本。首先,定州本不是一个完足的文本,存世仅7576字,不到今本的一半。其次,定州本虽然是汉宣帝时期的《鲁论语》系统的传本,但据残存文字判断文字和分章明显多于今本,是一个与皇家传本有许多差异的文本。今本主要继承了皇家本的特征,总体上是一个比定州本更好的文本。用今本去补足定州本,也显得别扭。

本。但《唐石经》存在后来改刻的情况，故不宜作为底本。《论语》刻本很多，诸宋刻诸经本经文部分大同小异，异文较少，唯廖莹中世彩堂本《九经》参考《唐石经》等多种传本校勘重印，颇具价值。其书虽佚，但尚存两种元代翻印本，皆忠实翻刻。其中相台岳氏本藏国家图书馆，收入《中华再造善本》，甚便使用。故本书采用此本为底本。

如果我们将《论语》材料作为一个整体来使用，那么其中的关键词对理解儒家思想有着举重若轻的作用，因此对关键词的翻译分析不仅必要，也更能凸显中外思想对话的逻辑轨迹。比如"仁"究竟是"reciprocity, perfect virtue"还是"benevolence"？"义"究竟是"righteousness"还是"justice"？"道"究竟是"The Way, The Divine Law, The Nature"还是"The Tao"？不同译本对这些关键语的选用都指向西方概念系统的某个含义，选择的差异也暗示着微妙的思维区别。另一方面，如果说译者将中国思想所固有的词汇，如"天""帝""仁"等重要术语用西方语言命名，意味着中国思想以一种他者的异质姿态进入西方概念系统，那么译者将"道"以音译"Tao"的方式直接译入西方文本，就保留了中国"道"的独一性和陌生性。众所周知，中国经典文本中的关键字词不仅自身深具意蕴，更隐含着中国庞大的传统文化语境的"基因"。我们希望学者们可以通过对这些关键字词翻译的研究，发现中国思想与西方思想的深层次对话，以及西方对中国思想的理解和诠释轨迹。

因此我们参照杨伯峻《论语译注》所附《论语词典》，选择了与孔子生平和思想密切相关的 250 个关键词，以中文词的拼音为序，后附该词在《论语》中出现的次数，但标题中的字词未计数（如"述而"之"述"），地名（如"达巷"之"达"）、人名（如"公权"之"公"）、国名（如"齐景公"之"齐"）等亦未计数。在关键词下我们依次注出上述六个译本所用的英文概念。此外，我们用星号标注多音字和多义字，列出读音差别（如"乘"A/chéng, B/shèng）、声调差异（如"道"A/dǎo, B/dào）和字义区别（如"辞"A/B），并将出现的例句翻译按照读音、声调或含义分别归类。读者可以根据翻译看出译者是否注意到了这些差异，这无疑是一个有趣的比较。此外，有些字在句子中与其他字构成词组，因而译文中没有对应的英文，如"同"字条目下有例句"道不同"，此处"不同"被翻译为"different"，我们在词条里加了"[not]"，以便与基本含义一致。又如，条目"兴"下有例句"礼乐不兴"，大部分译者选择"flourish"，与基本词义一致，但有一位将"不兴"放在一起，选择了"wither"，我们加入"[not]"以示区别。为方便检索，我们编辑了两套索引，第一部分在词目下按照《论语》的章节序号编排，第二部分在词目下按照六个译本的译者姓氏编排。为方便读者查阅和分析比对，《译注汇编》及《术语引得》还专门制作了数据库，可以在线阅读和使用。需要特别说明的是，在最后付梓之前，因版权问题我们不得不取出《译注汇编》卷中的李克曼译本和安乐哲/罗思文译本，但《术语引得》卷依然保留了六个译本的翻译选择。

《译注汇编》涉及的内容非常庞大，有些译本中包含了其他文字，有些版本模糊不清，为文字录入工作带来了诸多挑战。前期的输入劳动了大量学生志愿者，后期又经过五轮校对，其中谬误依然难免。数据库为此提供在线纠错功能，希望能在各位读者的帮助之下进一步更新，更加准确。

是为序。

目 录

001　序　言
001　以章节序号索引
398　以译者姓名索引

# 以章节序号索引

## 爱(9)

1.5 节用而爱人

love (Legge, Soothill, Lau, Leys, Ames/Rosemont)

affection (Waley)

1.6 泛爱众,而亲仁

love (Legge, Soothill, Lau, Leys, Ames/Rosemont)

kindly feeling (Waley)

3.17 尔爱其羊,我爱其礼

love (Legge, Leys)

care for (Soothill)

be loath to (Lau)

grudge (Waley, Ames/Rosemont)

12.10 爱之欲其生

love (Legge, Soothill, Waley, Lau, Leys, Ames/Rosemont)

12.22 樊迟问仁。子曰:"爱人。"

love (Legge, Soothill, Waley, Lau, Leys, Ames/Rosemont)

14.7 爱之,能勿劳乎?

love (Legge, Soothill, Waley, Lau, Leys, Ames/Rosemont)

17.3 君子学道则爱人

love (Legge, Soothill, Lau, Leys, Ames/Rosemont)

be all the tenderer towards (Waley)

17.19 予也有三年之爱于其父母乎

  love (Legge, Lau, Leys)

  affection (Soothill)

  darling (Waley)

  loving care (Ames/Rosemont)

# 安(17)

1.14 居无求安

  appliances of ease (Legge)

  solicitous of comfort (Soothill)

  comfort (Waley, Leys)

  comfortable (Lau)

  comfort and contentment (Ames/Rosemont)

2.10 察其所安

  rest (Legge)

  rest (Soothill)

  content (Waley)

  feel at home (Lau)

  peace (Leys)

  content (Ames/Rosemont)

4.2 仁者安仁

  rest (Legge, Leys)

  at rest (Soothill)

  content (Waley, Ames/Rosemont)

  attract (Lau)

5.26　老者安之

　　　rest（Legge）

　　　comfort（Soothill）

　　　comfort（Waley）

　　　peace（Lau，Leys）

　　　peace and contentment（Ames/Rosemont）

7.38　恭而安

　　　easy（Legge，Soothill，Waley）

　　　at ease（Lau，Ames/Rosemont）

　　　easy to approach（Leys）

11.26　安①见方六七十如五六十而非邪也者

　　　*adv.*（Legge，Soothill，Lau，Waley，Leys，Ames/Rosemont）

14.42　修己以安人……修己以安百姓。修己以安百姓

　　　give rest to（Legge）

　　　ease（Soothill，Waley）

　　　bring peace and security（Lau）

　　　spread one's peace（Leys）

　　　bring accord to（Ames/Rosemont）

16.1　不患贫当作寡而患不安。……安无倾。既来之,则安之

　　　repose（Legge）

　　　contented and tranquil（Legge）

　　　contentment reign（Soothill）

　　　make them contented（Soothill）

　　　content（Waley）

　　　stability（Lau）

　　　make them content（Lau）

　　　peace（Leys）

---

①　副词。

make them enjoy（Leys）

secure（Ames/Rosemont）

17.19 "……于女安乎？"曰："安。""女安，则为之！……居处不安……今女安……"

feel at ease（Legge，Soothill，Waley，Leys）

enjoy（Lau）

comfort（Lau，Leys，Ames/Rosemont）

comfortable（Soothill，Waley，Ames/Rosemont）

comfortably（Legge）

# 霸(1)

14.17 霸诸侯

make leader of（Legge）

make the duke leader of（Soothill）

become leader of（Waley，Ames/Rosemont）

become the leader of（Lau）

impose one's authority over（Leys）

# 百姓(5)

12.9 百姓足……百姓不足

people（Legge，Soothill，Lau，Leys）

the hundred families（Waley）

household（Ames/Rosemont）

14.42 修己以安百姓……修己以安百姓

all the people (Legge，Leys)

people (Soothill，Waley，Lau，Ames/Rosemont)

20.1　百姓有过

people (Legge，Soothill，Waley，Lau，Leys，Ames/Rosemont)

many families (Waley)

# 邦(48)

1.10　夫子至于是邦也

country (Legge，Waley，Leys)

state (Soothill，Lau，Ames/Rosemont)

3.22　邦君树塞门,……邦君为两君之好

state (Legge，Soothill，Waley，Lau，Leys，Ames/Rosemont)

5.2　邦有道……邦无道

country (Legge，Soothill，Waley，Leys)

state (Lau)

land (Ames/Rosemont)

5.19　至于他邦……之一邦

state (Legge，Soothill，Lau，Ames/Rosemont)

country (Waley，Leys)

5.21　邦有道……邦无道

country (Legge，Waley，Leys)

state (Soothill，Lau)

land (Ames/Rosemont)

8.13　危邦不入,乱邦不居……邦有道……邦无道

state (Legge，Soothill，Waley，Lau，Leys，Ames/Rosemont)

country (Legge)

land（Waley）

10.9　问人于他邦

state（Legge，Soothill，Lau，Ames/Rosemont）

country（Waley）

abroad（Leys）

11.24　"唯求则非邦也与？""安见方六七十如五六十而非邦也者？""唯赤则非邦也与？"

state（Legge，Soothill，Lau，Leys，Ames/Rosemont）

kingdom（Waley）

12.2　在邦无怨

country（Legge）

public（Soothill，Leys）

state（Waley，Lau）

political（Ames/Rosemont）

12.20　在邦必闻……在邦必达……在邦必闻

state（Legge，Waley，Lau）

country（Legge）

abroad（Soothill）

public（Leys，Ames/Rosemont）

13.11　善人为邦百年

country（Legge，Soothill，Waley，Leys）

state（Lau）

govern（Ames/Rosemont）

13.15　一言而可以兴邦……不几乎一言而兴邦乎；一言而丧邦……不几乎一言而丧邦乎

country（Legge，Soothill，Waley，Leys）

state（Lau，Ames/Rosemont）

14.1　邦有道，谷；邦无道，谷，耻也

state (Legge，Lau，Leys，Ames/Rosemont)

country (Soothill，Waley)

14.3　邦有道,危言危行;邦无道

state (Legge，Lau，Leys)

land (Soothill，Waley，Lau，Leys)

15.6　虽蛮貊之邦

tribe (Legge)

land (Soothill，Lau)

barbarian (Waley，Leys，Ames/Rosemont)

15.7　邦有道,如矢;邦无道,如矢……邦有道,则仕;邦无道,则可卷而怀之

government (Legge，Leys)

country (Soothill)

land (Waley)

state (Lau，Ames/Rosemont)

15.10　居是邦也

state (Legge，Soothill，Waley，Lau，Ames/Rosemont)

country (Leys)

15.11　颜渊问为邦

country (Legge)

state (Soothill，Waley，Lau，Leys，Ames/Rosemont)

16.1　且在邦域之中矣;邦分崩离析,而谋动干戈于邦内

state (Legge，Soothill，Waley，Lau，Ames/Rosemont)

territory (Legge，Leys)

own land (Waley)

boundary (Lau)

land (Leys)

province (Leys)

16.14　邦君之妻;邦人称之曰君夫人;称诸异邦曰寡小君;异邦人称之亦

曰君夫人

state（Legge，Soothill，Waley，Lau，Ames/Rosemont）

country（Waley）

17.1 怀其宝而迷其邦

country（Legge，Soothill，Waley，Leys，Ames/Rosemont）

state（Lau）

17.16 恶利口之覆邦家者

kingdom（Legge，Waley，Leys）

state（Soothill，Lau，Ames/Rosemont）

18.2 何必去父母之邦

country（Legge，Lau）

land（Soothill，Waley，Leys）

state（Ames/Rosemont）

19.25 夫子之得邦家者

state（Legge，Waley，Lau，Ames/Rosemont）

country（Soothill，Leys）

# 报(4)

14.34 "以德报怨，何如？"子曰："何以报德？以直报怨，以德报德。"

recompense（Legge）

reward（Soothill）

meet（Waley）

repay（Lau，Leys，Ames/Rosemont）

# 本(5)

1.2　君子务本,本立而道生；其为仁之本与

　　　what is radical（Legge）

　　　root（Legge，Lau，Leys，Ames/Rosemont）

　　　fundamental（Soothill）

　　　foundation（Soothill）

　　　trunk（Waley）

3.4　林放问礼之本

　　　the first thing（Legge）

　　　chief principle（Soothill）

　　　main principles（Waley）

　　　basis（Lau）

　　　root（Leys，Ames/Rosemont）

19.12　本之则无

　　　what is essential（Legge）

　　　radical principles（Soothill）

　　　anything important（Waley）

　　　what is basic（Lau）

　　　fundamental matter（Leys）

　　　root（Ames/Rosemont）

## \*辟(10)(bì, pì)

A. bì

3.2　辟公
　　　　prince (Legge)
　　　　prince and nobleman (Soothill)
　　　　ruler and lord (Waley)
　　　　great lord (Lau)
　　　　feudal lord (Leys)
　　　　various nobles (Ames/Rosemont)

14.37　贤者辟世,其次辟地,其次辟色,其次辟言
　　　　retire from (Legge)
　　　　withdraw (Soothill, Waley)
　　　　shun (Lau)
　　　　avoid (Leys, Ames/Rosemont)

18.5　趋而辟之
　　　　hasten away (Legge)
　　　　avoid (Soothill, Lau, Ames/Rosemont)
　　　　get away (Waley)
　　　　away and disappear (Leys)

18.6　且而与其从辟人之士也,岂若从辟世之士哉
　　　　withdraw (Legge)
　　　　flee (Soothill, Waley)
　　　　run away (Lau)
　　　　forsake (Leys)
　　　　avoid (Ames/Rosemont)

B. pì

11.18　师也辟

　　specious (Legge)

　　surface (Soothill)

　　formal (Waley)

　　onesided (Lau)

　　extreme (Leys)

　　biased (Ames/Rosemont)

16.4　友便辟

　　specious (Legge)

　　plausible (Soothill)

　　obsequious (Waley)

　　ingratiate (Lau, Ames/Rosemont)

　　devious (Leys)

# 蔽(9)

2.2　一言以蔽之

　　embrace (Legge)

　　cover (Soothill, Waley, Ames/Rosemont)

　　sum up (Lau, Leys)

17.7　女闻六言六蔽矣乎;其蔽也愚;其蔽也荡;其蔽也贼;共蔽也绞;其蔽也乱;其蔽也狂

　　becloud (Legge)

　　obscure (Soothill)

　　degeneration (Waley, Leys)

　　attendant fault (Lau)

20.1　帝臣不蔽

　　　Keep in obscurity（Legge，Soothill）

　　　slay（Waley）

　　　hide（Leys）

　　　shield（Ames/Rosemont）

# 博(7)

6.27　君子博学于文

　　　extensively（Legge）

　　　widely（Soothill，Waley，Lau）

　　　enlarge（Leys）

　　　broadly（Ames/Rosemont）

6.30　如有博施于民而能济众

　　　extensively（Legge，Lau）

　　　far and wide（Soothill）

　　　wide（Waley）

　　　broadly（Ames/Rosemont）

9.2　博学而无所成名

　　　extensive（Legge）

　　　vast（Soothill，Leys）

　　　vastly（Waley）

　　　wide（Lau）

　　　broad（Ames/Rosemont）

9.11　博我以文

　　　enlarge（Legge）

　　　broaden（Soothill，Waley，Lau，Ames/Rosemont）

stimulate (Leys)

12.15 博学于文
extensively (Legge)
widely (Soothill, Lau)
enlarge (Leys)
broadly (Ames/Rosemont)

17.20 不有博奕者乎
chessplayer (Legge, Soothill)
po (Lau)
play chess (Lau)

19.6 博学而笃志
extensively (Legge)
broad (Soothill)
widely (Waley, Lau)
extend (Leys)
broadly (Ames/Rosemont)

# 才(7)

8.11 如有周公之才之美
ability (Legge)
gift (Soothill, Waley)
gifted (Lau)
talent (Leys, Ames/Rosemont)

8.20 才难,不其然乎
talent (Legge, Soothill, Lau, Leys, Ames/Rosemont)
right material (Waley)

9.11 既竭吾才

　　ability (Legge, Ames/Rosemont)

　　power (Soothill)

　　resource (Waley, Leys)

　　all I can (Lau)

11.8 才不才,亦各言其子也

　　talent (Legge, Lau, Leys, Ames/Rosemont)

　　gifted (Soothill, Waley)

13.2 赦小过,举贤才……焉知贤才而举之

　　man of virtue and talent (Legge)

　　those who are worthy and capable (Soothill)

　　man of superior capacity (Waley)

　　man of talent (Lau, Leys)

　　those with superior character and ability (Ames/Rosemont)

# 藏(2)

7.11 舍之则藏

　　lie retired (Legge)

　　dwell in retirement (Soothill)

　　hide (Waley, Leys)

　　stay out of sight (Lau)

　　hold oneself in reserve (Ames/Rosemont)

9.13 韫椟而藏诸

　　keep (Legge, Soothill)

　　wrap it up (Waley)

　　put it away safely (Lau)

hide it safely（Leys）

safekeep（Ames/Rosemont）

# 彻(3)

3.2　三家者以《雍》彻

while the vessels are being removed, at the conclusion of the sacrifice（Legge）

at the removal of the sacrifices（Soothill）

during the removal of the sacrificial vessels（Waley）

when the sacrificial offerings are being cleared away（Lau）

at the end of their ancestral sacrifices（Leys）

at the conclusion of their sacrifices as the implements are gathered（Ames/Rosemont）

12.9　盍彻乎……如之何其彻也

tithe（Legge, Soothill, Waley, Leys）

tax the people one part in ten（Lau）

levy a tithe（Ames/Rosemont）

# *乘(9)(chéng, shèng)

A. chéng

5.7　乘桴浮于海

get upon（Legge, Soothill, Waley）

put to sea（Lau）

take（Leys, Ames/Rosemont）

6.4　赤之适齐也，乘肥马

　　　have ... to carriage (Legge)

　　　drive (Soothill, Waley, Ames/Rosemont)

　　　in a carriage drawn by (Lau)

　　　(travel) with (Leys)

15.11　乘殷之辂

　　　ride (Legge, Soothill, Lau, Leys, Ames/Rosemont)

　　　use (Waley)

15.26　有马者借人乘之

　　　ride (Legge, Soothill, Ames/Rosemont)

　　　drive (Waley, Lau)

　　　test (Leys)

B.　shèng

1.5　道千乘之国

　　　chariot (Legge, Soothill, Waley, Lau, Ames/Rosemont)

5.8　千乘之国……百乘之家

　　　chariot (Legge, Soothill, Lau, Ames/Rosemont)

　　　war chariot (Waley)

5.19　陈文子有马十乘

　　　horse (Legge, Lau)

　　　chariot (Soothill, Ames/Rosemont)

　　　war chariot (Waley)

11.24　千乘之国

　　　chariot (Legge, Soothill, Lau, Ames/Rosemont)

　　　war chariot (Waley)

# 耻(17)

1.13 远耻辱也

  shame (Legge，Soothill，Leys)

  dishonor (Waley)

  disgrace (Lau，Ames/Rosemont)

2.3 民免而无耻；有耻且格

  shame (Legge，Soothill，Lau，Leys，Ames/Rosemont)

4.9 而耻恶衣恶食者

  be ashamed of (Legge，Soothill，Waley，Lau，Leys，Ames/Rosemont)

4.22 耻躬之不逮也

  fear (Legge)

  out of shame (Soothill)

  disgrace (Waley)

  shameful (Lau)

  fear (Leys)

  be ashamed (Ames/Rosemont)

5.15 不耻下问

  ashamed (Legge，Soothill，Waley，Lau，Leys，Ames/Rosemont)

5.25 左丘明耻之，丘亦耻之。……左丘明耻之，丘亦耻之

  ashamed (Legge，Soothill)

  incapable of stooping (Waley)

  never stoop (Waley)

  shameful (Lau)

  despise (Leys)

shameless（Ames/Rosemont）

8.13 邦有道,贫且贱焉,耻也……耻也

be ashamed of（Legge）

ashamed（Soothill）

disgrace（Waley,Ames/Rosemont）

shamefull（Lau,Leys）

9.27 而不耻者

ashamed（Legge,Lau）

abashed（Soothill,Waley）

shame（Ames/Rosemont）

13.20 行己有耻

shame（Legge）

dishonour（Soothill）

disgrace（Waley,Leys）

shame（Lau,Ames/Rosemont）

14.1 宪问耻……邦无道,谷,耻也

shameful（Legge,Lau,Ames/Rosemont）

dishonour（Soothill）

compunction（Waley）

shame（Leys）

14.27 君子耻其言而过其行

modest（Legge,Soothill）

ashamed（Waley,Lau,Leys）

feel shame（Ames/Rosemont）

## *辞(5)

A.

6.5　与之粟九百,辞

　　　decline (Legge, Soothill, Waley, Lau, Leys)

　　　refuse (Ames/Rosemont)

6.9　善为我辞焉

　　　decline (Legge, Soothill, Lau, Ames/Rosemont)

　　　regret (Leys)

17.18　孔子辞以疾

　　　decline (Legge, Lau, Leys, Ames/Rosemont)

　　　excuse (Soothill, Waley)

B.

15.41　辞达而已矣

　　　language (Legge, Soothill, Lau)

　　　official speech (Waley)

　　　word (Leys)

　　　express oneself (Ames/Rosemont)

16.1　欲之而必为之辞

　　　explanation (Legge)

　　　excuse (Soothill, Leys, Ames/Rosemont)

　　　condone (Waley)

　　　plausible pretext (Lau)

# 辞气(1)

8.4 出辞气
　　　words and tone (Legge)
　　　tone of conversation (Soothill)
　　　every word he utters (Waley)
　　　speak in proper tone (Lau)
　　　speech (Leys)
　　　language (Ames/Rosemont)

# 慈(1)

2.20 孝慈则忠
　　　kind (Legge, Soothill, Ames/Rosemont)
　　　kindness (Waley, Lau)
　　　kind father (Leys)

# 达(18)

6.8 赐也达
　　　fit (Legge)
　　　suitable (Soothill)
　　　capable (Waley)
　　　good enough (Lau)

sagacious（Leys）

talented（Ames/Rosemont）

6.30　己欲达而达人

enlarge（Legge）

develop（Soothill）

turn one's own merits to account（Waley）

get there（Lau，Ames/Rosemont）

obtain（Leys）

promote（Ames/Rosemont）

10.10　丘未达，不敢尝

know（Legge，Lau，Ames/Rosemont）

well acquainted（Soothill）

acquaint（Waley，Leys）

12.20　士何如斯可谓之达矣……尔所谓达者……是闻也，非达也。夫达也者……在邦必达，在家必达

distinguished（Legge）

distinction（Legge）

general estimation（Soothill）

esteem（Soothill）

influential（Waley）

get through（Lau）

perception（Leys）

prominent（Ames/Rosemont）

12.22　樊迟未达

understand（Legge，Waley，Leys，Ames/Rosemont）

comprehend（Soothill）

grasp（Lau）

13.5　授之以政，不达

know (Legge)

practical ability (Soothill)

turn one's merits to account (Waley)

exercise one's own initiative (Lau)

up to the task (Leys)

perform effectively (Ames/Rosemont)

13.17 欲速,则不达

do thoroughly (Legge)

accomplish (Soothill)

come into play (Waley)

reach your goal (Lau, Leys)

achieve your end (Ames/Rosemont)

14.23 君子上达,小人下达

influence (Waley)

get through (Lau)

reach up (Leys)

road (Ames/Rosemont)

14.35 下学而上达

rise (Legge)

soar (Soothill)

feel (Waley)

get through (Lau)

hear (Leys)

aspire (Ames/Rosemont)

15.41 辞达而已矣

convey the meaning (Legge)

perspicuity (Soothill)

get one (Waley)

get the point across (Lau)

merely for communication (Leys)

get the point across (Ames/Rosemont)

16.11 行义以达其道

carry out (Legge)

extend (Soothill, Waley, Ames/Rosemont)

realize (Lau)

reach (Leys)

# 党(12)

4.7 各于其党

the class to which they belong (Legge)

one's type of mind (Soothill)

belong to a set (Waley)

type (Lau)

fall into group (Ames/Rosemont)

5.22 吾党之小子狂简

school (Legge)

at home (Soothill, Waley, Lau, Ames/Rosemont)

6.5 以与尔邻里乡党乎

village (Legge, Soothill, Waley, Leys)

neighborhood (Lau)

neighbors (Ames/Rosemont)

7.31 吾闻君子不党,君子亦党乎

partizan (Legge)

partisan (Soothill, Ames/Rosemont)

partial (Waley，Leys)

partiality (Lau)

9.2　达巷党人曰

village (Legge，Soothill，Waley，Lau，Ames/Rosemont)

10.1　孔子于乡党

village (Legge，Soothill，Waley，Leys，Ames/Rosemont)

community (Lau)

13.18　吾党有直躬者……吾党之直者异于是

us (Legge)

part of the country (Soothill)

country (Waley)

village (Lau，Ames/Rosemont)

one's people (Leys)

13.20　乡党称弟焉

fellow villagers and neighbours (Legge)

neighbours (Soothill)

fellow villagers (Waley，Ames/Rosemont)

in the village (Lau)

of his village (Leys)

14.44　阙党童子将命

village (Legge，Soothill，Waley，Leys，Ames/Rosemont)

Tang (Lau)

15.22　群而不党

partizan (Legge)

enter any clique (Soothill)

party (Waley)

form clique (Lau)

partisan (Leys)

clique (Ames/Rosemont)

# 祷(4)

3.13 无所祷也

 pray (Legge，Ames/Rosemont)

 prayer (Soothill，Lau，Leys)

 expiation (Waley)

7.35 子路请祷……祷尔于上下神祇……丘之祷久矣

 pray (Legge，Soothill，Lau，Leys，Ames/Rosemont)

 prayer (Legge)

 have prayers offered (Soothill)

 perform the rite of expiation (Waley)

 offer a prayer (Lau)

# *道(90)(dǎo, dào)

A. dǎo

1.5 道千乘之国

 rule (Legge)

 conduct (Soothill)

 administer (Waley)

 guide (Lau)

 govern (Leys)

 the way to lead (Ames/Rosemont)

2.3 道之以政……道之以德

lead (Legge, Leys, Ames/Rosemont)

govern (Soothill, Waley)

guide (Lau)

12.23 忠告而善道之

lead (Legge, Ames/Rosemont)

guide (Soothill, Waley, Lau, Leys)

19.25 道之斯行

lead (Legge, Soothill, Waley, Leys, Ames/Rosemont)

guide (Lau)

B. dào

1.2 本立而道生

all practical courses (Legge)

right courses (Soothill)

Way (Waley, Lau, Leys, Ames/Rosemont)

1.11 三年无改于父之道

way (Legge, Soothill, Lau, Leys, Ames/Rosemont)

household (Waley)

1.12 先王之道斯为美

way (Legge, Waley, Lau, Leys, Ames/Rosemont)

regulation (Soothill)

1.14 就有道而正焉

principle (Legge)

high-principled (Soothill)

way (Waley, Lau, Ames/Rosemont)

virtuous (Leys)

1.15 未若贫而乐道

way (Waley, Lau)

3.16 古之道也

way（Legge，Waley，Lau，Ames/Rosemont）

rule（Soothill）

view（Leys）

3.24　天下之无道也久矣

principles of truth and right（Legge）

light and leading（Soothill）

way（Waley，Lau，Leys，Ames/Rosemont）

4.5　不以其道得之……不以其道得之

proper way（Legge）

right way（Soothill）

way（Waley，Ames/Rosemont）

right way（Lau）

principle（Leys）

4.8　朝闻道

right way（Legge）

truth（Soothill）

way（Waley，Lau，Leys，Ames/Rosemont）

4.9　士志于道

truth（Legge）

wisdom（Soothill）

way（Waley，Lau，Leys，Ames/Rosemont）

4.15　吾道一以贯之……夫子之道

doctrine（Legge，Leys）

teaching（Soothill）

way（Waley，Lau，Ames/Rosemont）

doctrine（Leys）

4.20　三年无改于父之道

way（Legge，Soothil，Lau，Leys，Ames/Rosemont）

household（Waley）

5.2 邦有道……邦无道

　　govern（Legge，Soothill）

　　way（Waley，Lau，Leys，Ames/Rosemont）

5.7 道不行

　　doctrine（Legge，Soothill）

　　way（Waley，Lau，Leys，Ames/Rosemont）

5.13 夫子之言性与天道

　　way（Legge，Waley，Lau，Leys，Ames/Rosemont）

　　laws（Soothill）

5.16 有君子之道四焉

　　characteristic（Legge，Soothill）

　　virtue（Waley）

　　way（Lau，Leys，Ames/Rosemont）

5.21 邦有道……邦无道

　　order（Legge，Soothill）

　　way（Waley，Lau，Leys，Ames/Rosemont）

6.12 非不说子之道……中道而废

　　doctrine（Legge）

　　teaching（Soothill）

　　way（Waley，Lau，Leys，Ames/Rosemont）

6.17 何莫由斯道也

　　way（Legge，Soothill，Waley，Lau，Leys，Ames/Rosemont）

6.24 至于道

　　true principle（Legge）

　　way（Soothill，Waley，Lau，Leys，Ames/Rosemont）

7.6 志于道

　　path（Legge）

right way（Soothill）

way（Waley，Lau，Leys，Ames/Rosemont）

8.4　君子所贵乎道者三

principle（Legge）

rule（Soothill）

way（Waley，Lau，Ames/Rosemont）

thing（Leys）

8.7　任重而道远

course（Legge）

road（Soothill，Lau）

journey（Waley，Leys）

way（Ames/Rosemont）

8.13　守死善道……天下有道则见,无道则隐。邦有道,贫且贱焉,耻也。邦无道

principles（Legge）

law and order（Soothill）

way（Waley，Lau，Leys，Ames/Rosemont）

9.12　予死于道路乎

road（Legge）

roadside（Soothill，Waley，Ames/Rosemont）

wayside（Lau，Leys）

9.27　是道也,何足以臧

mean（Legge）

point（Soothill）

wisdom（Waley）

way（Lau）

line（Leys）

remark（Ames/Rosemont）

9.30　未可与适道；可与适道
　　　principle (Legge)
　　　truth (Soothill)
　　　way (Waley, Lau, Leys)
　　　path (Ames/Rosemont)

11.19　子张问善人之道
　　　characteristics (Legge)
　　　characterise the way (Soothill)
　　　way (Waley, Lau, Leys, Ames/Rosemont)

11.22　以道事君
　　　right (Legge, Soothill)
　　　way(Waley, Lau, Leys, Ames/Rosemont)

12.19　如杀无道，以就有道何如
　　　principle (Legge)
　　　law (Soothill)
　　　way (Waley, Lau, Ames/Rosemont)

13.25　说之不以道……说之虽不以道
　　　way (Legge, Soothill, Waley, Lau, Ames/Rosemont)
　　　mean (Leys)

14.1　邦有道……邦无道
　　　govern (Legge, Soothill)
　　　way (Waley, Lau, Leys, Ames/Rosemont)

14.3　邦有道……邦无道
　　　govern (Legge)
　　　law and order (Soothill)
　　　way (Waley, Lau, Leys, Ames/Rosemont)

14.19　子言卫灵公之无道也
　　　principle (Legge, Soothill, Lau, Leys)

way (Waley, Ames/Rosemont)

14.28　君子道者三

　　way (Legge)

　　characteristic (Soothill)

　　way (Waley)

　　thing (Lau)

　　principle (Leys)

　　path (Ames/Rosemont)

14.28　夫子自道也

　　say (Legge, Soothill)

　　Way (Waley)

　　quote (Lau)

　　draw (Leys)

　　path (Ames/Rosemont)

14.36　道之将行也与……道之将废也与

　　principle (Legge, Soothill)

　　way (Waley, Lau, Ames/Rosemont)

　　truth (Leys)

15.7　邦有道……邦无道……邦有道……邦无道

　　govern (Legge, Soothill, Leys)

　　way (Waley, Lau, Ames/Rosemont)

15.25　三代之所以直道而行也

　　path (Legge, Lau, Ames/Rosemont)

　　course (Soothill, Leys)

　　way (Waley)

15.29　人能弘道,非道弘人

　　principle (Legge, Soothill)

　　way (Waley, Lau, Leys, Ames/Rosemont)

15.32 君子谋道不谋食……君子忧道不忧贫

　　　truth（Legge）

　　　duty（Soothill）

　　　way（Waley，Lau，Leys，Ames/Rosemont）

15.40 道不同,不相为谋

　　　course（Legge）

　　　way（Soothill，Waley，Lau，Leys，Ames/Rosemont）

15.42 与师言之道与？……固相师之道也

　　　rule（Legge）

　　　proper thing（Soothill）

　　　way（Waley，Lau，Leys，Ames/Rosemont）

16.2 天下有道……天下无道；天下有道……天下无道

　　　govern（Legge，Soothill）

　　　way（Waley，Lau，Leys，Ames/Rosemont）

16.5 乐道人之善

　　　speak of（Legge）

　　　discuss（Soothill，Waley）

　　　sing the praise（Lau）

　　　praise（Leys）

　　　talk about（Ames/Rosemont）

16.11 行义以达其道

　　　principle（Legge，Soothill）

　　　way（Waley，Lau，Leys，Ames/Rosemont）

17.3 君子学道则爱人,小人学道则易使也

　　　instruct（Legge）

　　　wisdom（Soothill）

　　　way（Waley，Lau，Leys，Ames/Rosemont）

17.12 道听而涂说

way (Legge)

road (Soothill)

highroad (Waley)

streets and alleyway (Ames/Rosemont)

18.2 直道而事人……枉道而事人

way (Legge, Waley, Lau)

public service (Soothill)

conscious (Leys)

path (Ames/Rosemont)

18.6 天下有道

right principle (Legge)

right rule (Soothill)

way (Waley, Lau, Leys, Ames/Rosemont)

18.7 道之不行

right principle (Legge, Soothill)

way (Lau, Leys, Ames/Rosemont)

19.2 信道不笃

right (Legge)

truth (Soothill)

way (Waley, Lau, Leys, Ames/Rosemont)

19.4 虽小道

studies and employment (Legge)

art (Soothill, Lau)

walk (Waley)

discipline (Leys)

byway (Ames/Rosemont)

19.7 君子学以致其道

principle (Legge)

wisdom (Soothill)

way (Waley, Lau, Ames/Rosemont)

truth (Leys)

19.12 君子之道……君子之道

way (Legge, Waley, Lau)

teaching (Soothill)

doctrine (Leys)

path (Ames/Rosemont)

19.19 上失其道

duty (Legge)

principle (Soothill)

way (Waley, Lau, Leys, Ames/Rosemont)

19.22 文武之道……莫不有文武之道焉

doctrine (Legge, Soothill)

way (Waley, Lau, Leys, Ames/Rosemont)

# 盗(3)

12.18 季康子患盗

thief (Legge, Lau, Ames/Rosemont)

robber (Soothill)

burglar (Waley, Leys)

17.10 其犹穿窬之盗也与

thief (Legge, Soothill)

burglar (Lau)

cutpurse (Leys)

house burglar (Ames/Rosemont)

17.21　小人有勇而无义为盗

　　　robbery（Legge）

　　　robber（Soothill）

　　　thief（Waley）

　　　brigand（Lau）

　　　bandit（Leys）

　　　thief（Ames/Rosemont）

# 德(38)

1.9　民德归厚矣

　　　virtue（Legge，Lau，Leys，Ames/Rosemont）

　　　moral（Soothill）

　　　moral force（Waley）

2.1　为政以德

　　　virtue（Legge，Lau，Leys）

　　　moral（Soothill）

　　　moral force（Waley）

　　　excellence（Ames/Rosemont）

2.3　道之以德

　　　virtue（Legge，Lau，Leys）

　　　moral excellence（Soothill）

　　　moral force（Waley）

　　　excellence（Ames/Rosemont）

4.11　君子怀德

　　　virtue（Legge，Leys）

　　　one's character（Soothill）

moral force (Waley)

benign rule (Lau)

justice (Leys)

excellence (Ames/Rosemont)

fairness (Ames/Rosemont)

4.25 德不孤

virtue (Legge, Soothill, Lau, Leys)

moral force (Waley)

excellent person (Ames/Rosemont)

6.29 中庸之为德也

virtue (Legge, Soothill)

moral power (Waley, Leys)

moral virtue (Lau)

excellence (Ames/Rosemont)

7.3 德之不修

virtue (Legge, Lau)

character (Soothill)

moral power (Waley, Leys)

excellence (Ames/Rosemont)

7.6 据于德

good (Legge)

moral character (Soothill)

power (Waley)

virtue (Lau)

moral power (Leys)

excellence (Ames/Rosemont)

7.23 天生德于予

virtue (Legge, Soothill, Lau)

power (Waley)

moral power (Leys)

excellence (Ames/Rosemont)

8.1 泰伯,其可谓至德也已矣

virtuous (Legge)

noblest (Soothill)

moral (Waley, Leys)

the highest virtue (Lau)

excellence (Ames/Rosemont)

8.20 周之德,其可谓至德也已矣

virtue (Legge, Soothill, Lau)

moral (Waley, Leys)

excellence (Ames/Rosemont)

9.18 吾未见好德如好色者也

virtue (Legge, Soothill, Lau, Leys)

moral power (Waley)

excellence (Ames/Rosemont)

12.10 子张问崇德辨惑……徙义,崇德也

virtue (Legge)

character (Soothill)

moral (Waley, Leys)

virtue (Lau)

excellence (Ames/Rosemont)

12.19 君子之德风,小人之德草

moral character (Soothill)

character (Soothill)

essence (Waley)

nature (Lau)

moral（Leys）

excellence（Ames/Rosemont）

12.21　敢问崇德……非崇德与

virtue（Legge）

character（Soothill）

moral（Waley，Leys）

virtue（Lau）

excellence（Ames/Rosemont）

13.22　不恒其德

virtue（Legge，Lau）

moral character（Soothill）

te（Waley）

moral（Leys）

character（Ames/Rosemont）

14.4　有德者必有言，有言者不必有德

virtuous（Legge，Leys）

principle（Soothill）

moral power（Waley）

virtue（Lau）

excellence（Ames/Rosemont）

14.5　尚德哉若人

virtue（Legge，Soothill，Waley，Lau，Leys）

excellence（Ames/Rosemont）

14.33　称其德也

good quality（Legge）

character（Soothill）

inner quality（Waley）

strength（Lau）

inner force（Leys）

excellence（Ames/Rosemont）

14.34　以德报怨……何以报德……以德报德

kindness（Legge，Soothill，Leys）

inner power（Waley）

good turn（Lau）

beneficence（Ames/Rosemont）

gratitude（Ames/Rosemont）

15.4　知德者鲜矣

virtue（Legge，Soothill，Lau）

moral force（Waley）

moral power（Leys）

excellence（Ames/Rosemont）

15.13　吾未见好德如好色者也

virtue（Legge，Soothill，Lau，Leys）

moral power（Waley）

excellence（Ames/Rosemont）

15.27　巧言乱德

virtue（Legge，Lau，Leys）

moral（Soothill）

moral force（Waley）

excellence（Ames/Rosemont）

16.12　民无德而称焉

virtue（Legge，Soothill）

good deed（Waley）

sense of gratitude（Ames/Rosemont）

17.11　德之贼也

virtue（Legge，Lau，Leys）

moral (Soothill)

true virtue (Waley)

excellence (Ames/Rosemont)

17.12 德之弃也

virtue (Legge，Soothill，Lau，Leys)

excellence (Ames/Rosemont)

18.5 何德之衰

virtue (Legge，Lau)

power (Waley)

excellence (Ames/Rosemont)

19.2 执德不弘

virtue (Legge，Soothill，Lau，Leys)

moral force (Waley)

excellence (Ames/Rosemont)

19.11 大德不逾闲,小德出入可也

virtue (Legge，Soothill)

moral (Waley)

principle (Leys)

excellence (Ames/Rosemont)

# 德行(1)

11.3 德行:颜渊,闵子骞

virtuous principles and practice (Legge)

moral character (Soothill)

moral power (Waley)

virtuous conduct (Lau)

virtue（Leys）

excel in conduct（Ames/Rosemont）

# *弟(15)(dì, tì)

A. dì

1.6 弟子入则孝

youth（Legge，Soothill）

young man（Lau，Leys，Waley）

young brother（Ames/Rosemont）

2.8 弟子服其劳

the young（Legge，Soothill，Lau，Ames/Rosemont）

young people（Waley，Leys）

2.21 友于兄弟

brotherly（Legge，Leys）

brethren（Soothill）

brother（Waley，Lau，Ames/Rosemont）

11.5 人不间于其父母昆弟之言

brother（Legge，Soothill，Waley，Lau，Leys）

sibling（Ames/Rosemont）

12.5 人皆有兄弟……皆兄弟也。君子何患乎无兄弟也

brother（Legge，Soothill，Waley，Lau，Leys，Ames/Rosemont）

13.7 鲁、卫之政，兄弟也

young brother（Legge，Soothill，Waley，Lau，Leys，Ames/Rosemont）

13.28 兄弟怡怡

brethren（Legge）

brother (Sooothill, Waley, Lau, Leys, Ames/Rosemont)

B. tì

1.2 其为人也孝弟……孝弟也者

fraternal (Legge)

respect (Soothill)

respectful (Soothill)

behave well (Waley)

proper behaviour (Waley)

obedient (Lau)

respect (Leys)

xiaodi (孝弟, filial and fraternal responsibility) (Ames/Rosemont)

1.6 弟子入则孝……出则弟

respectful (Legge, Soothill)

behave well (Waley)

obedient (Lau)

respect (Leys)

deferential (Ames/Rosemont)

13.20 乡党称弟焉

fraternal (Legge)

brotherly (Soothill)

deference to one's elder (Waley)

respectful young man (Lau)

respect the elder (Leys)

deferential to their elder (Ames/Rosemont)

14.43 幼而不孙弟

befit a junior (Legge)

respect (Leys, Soothill, Waley)

deferential (Lau)

respectful (Ames/Rosemont)

# 帝(3)

20.1　敢昭告于皇皇后帝……帝臣不蔽,简在帝心

　　　god (Legge, Soothill, Waley, Leys)

　　　lord (Lau)

　　　ancestor (Ames/Rosemont)

# 禘(2)

3.10　禘自既灌而往者

　　　great sacrifice (Legge)

　　　quinquennial sacrifice (Soothill)

　　　ancestral sacrifice (Waley)

　　　ti sacrifice (Lau)

　　　the sacrifice to the ancestor of the dynasty (Leys)

　　　di imperial ancestral sacrifice (Ames/Rosemont)

3.11　或问禘之说

　　　great sacrifice (Legge)

　　　quinquennial sacrifice (Soothill)

　　　ancestral sacrifice (Waley)

　　　ti sacrifice (Lau)

　　　the sacrifice to the ancestor of the dynasty (Leys)

　　　di imperial ancestral sacrifice (Ames/Rosemont)

## 独(3)

12.5　我独亡
　　　only (Legge)
　　　alone (Soothill, Waley, Lau, Leys)

16.13　尝独立……又独立
　　　alone (Legge, Soothill, Waley, Leys, Ames/Rosemont)
　　　by himself (Lau)

## 笃(7)

8.2　君子笃于亲
　　　perform well all their duties (Legge)
　　　pay generous regard (Soothill)
　　　deal generously with (Waley)
　　　feel profound affection for (Lau)
　　　treat generously (Leys)
　　　earnestly commit to (Ames/Rosemont)

8.13　笃信好学
　　　sincere (Legge)
　　　sincerity (Soothill)
　　　unwavering (Waley)
　　　firm (Lau)
　　　uphold (Leys)
　　　earnest (Ames/Rosemont)

11.19　论笃是与

　　solid and sincere（Legge）

　　solid and reliable（Soothill）

　　sound（Waley）

　　tenacious（Lau）

　　sound（Leys）

　　earnest（Ames/Rosemont）

15.6　行笃敬……行不笃敬

　　honourable（Legge）

　　trustworthy（Soothill）

　　serious（Waley）

　　single minded（Lau）

　　dedication（Leys）

　　earnest（Ames/Rosemont）

19.2　信道不笃

　　sincerity（Legge）

　　steadfastness（Soothill）

　　hold on（Lau）

　　determination（Leys）

　　earnest（Ames/Rosemont）

19.6　博学而笃志

　　firm and sincere（Legge）

　　earnest（Soothill）

　　earnestly（Waley）

　　steadfast（Lau）

　　hold fast to（Leys）

　　focus（Ames/Rosemont）

# 端(3)

2.16 攻乎异端
   doctrine (Legge，Ames/Rosemont)
   speculation (Soothill)
   strand (Waley)
   end (Lau, Leys)

9.8 我叩其两端而竭焉
   end (Legge，Ames/Rosemont)
   pros and cons (Soothill，Waley)
   side (Lau, Leys)

11.24 如会同，端章甫
   dress (Legge，Lau)
   in (gown) (Soothill，Waley，Lau)
   wear (Leys)
   don (Ames/Rosemont)

# 夺(5)

8.6 临大节而不可夺也
   drive (Legge)
   shake (Soothill)
   upset (Waley)
   deflect (Lau)
   perturb (Ames/Rosemont)

9.26　三军可夺帅也,匹夫不可夺志也
　　　be carried off (Legge)
　　　rob (Soothill, Waley)
　　　be deprived of (Lau, Ames/Rosemont)
　　　deprive (Leys)
14.9　夺伯氏骈邑三百
　　　take (Legge, Lau, Leys)
　　　despoil (Soothill)
　　　seize (Waley, Ames/Rosemont)
17.16　恶紫之夺朱也
　　　take away (Legge)
　　　rob (Soothill)
　　　kill (Waley)
　　　displace (Lau)
　　　replace (Leys)
　　　steal the place of (Ames/Rosemont)


\* 恶(39)(è,wù)


A. è
4.4　无恶也
　　　wickedness (Legge)
　　　evil (Soothill, Lau, Leys)
　　　dislike (Waley)
　　　wrong (Ames/Rosemont)
4.9　而耻恶衣恶食者
　　　bad (Legge)

shabby (Soothill, Waley, Leys)

poor (Soothill, Lau)

coarse (Waley, Leys, Ames/Rosemont)

rude (Ames/Rosemont)

5.23 叔齐不念旧恶

wickedness (Legge)

ill (Soothill, Waley)

score (Lau)

grievance (Leys)

grudge (Ames/Rosemont)

8.21 恶衣服

poor (Legge)

shabby (Soothill)

plainest (Waley)

coarse (Lau, Leys, Ames/Rosemont)

10.6 色恶,不食。

dis(color)(Legge, Soothill, Waley)

off(color)(Lau, Leys, Ames/Rosemont)

10.6 恶臭,不食。

bad (Legge, Waley, Lau, Leys)

smell (Soothill)

strange (Ames/Rosemont)

12.16 不成人之恶

bad quality (Legge)

evil (Soothill)

defect (Waley)

bad (Lau, Leys)

worst (Ames/Rosemont)

12.21 攻其恶，无攻人之恶
  wickedness（Legge）
  fail（Soothill）
  evil（Waley，Lau，Leys）
  depravity（Ames/Rosemont）

17.22 人之恶者
  evil（Legge，Lau）
  misdeed（Soothill）
  hateful（Waley，Leys）
  detestable（Ames/Rosemont）

19.20 天下之恶皆归焉
  evil（Legge，Soothill）
  filth（Waley，Leys，Ames/Rosemont）
  sordid（Lau）

20.2 屏四恶……何谓四恶
  bad（Legge，Soothill）
  ugly（Waley）
  wicked（Lau）
  evil（Leys）
  vice（Ames/Rosemont）

B. wù

4.3 能恶人
  hate（Legge，Soothill，Leys）
  dislike（Waley，Lau）
  discriminate（Ames/Rosemont）

4.5 是人之所恶也……恶乎成名
  dislike（Legge，Lau）
  detest（Soothill，Waley）

hate (Leys)

avoid (Ames/Rosemont)

4.6　恶不仁者……恶不仁者

hate (Legge, Soothill, Leys)

abhor (Waley, Ames/Rosemont)

repulsive (Lau)

11.23　是故恶夫佞者

hate (Legge, Soothill, Waley, Leys, Ames/Rosemont)

dislike (Lau)

12.10　恶之欲其死

hate (Legge, Soothill, Waley, Lau, Leys, Ames/Rosemont)

13.24　乡人皆恶之……其不善者恶之

hate (Legge, Soothill, Waley)

dislike (Lau, Leys)

despise (Ames/Rosemont)

15.28　众恶之

hate (Legge, Soothill)

dislike/disliked (Waley, Lau, Leys)

despise (Ames/Rosemont)

17.16　恶紫之夺朱也,恶郑声之乱雅乐也,恶利口之覆邦家者

hate (Legge, Soothill, Waley)

detest (Lau, Leys, Ames/Rosemont)

17.22　"君子亦有恶乎?"子曰:"有恶:恶称人之恶者,恶居下流而讪上者,恶勇而无礼者,恶果敢而窒者。"曰:"赐也亦有恶乎?""恶徼以为知者,恶不孙以为勇者,恶讦以为直者。"

hatred (Legge, Waley, Leys)

hate (Legge, Waley, Leys)

detest (Soothill, Ames/Rosemont)

dislike (Lau)

17.24 年四十而见恶焉

dislike (Legge, Soothill, Waley, Lau, Leys, Ames/Rosemont)

19.20 是以君子恶居下流

hate (Legge, Waley, Lau, Leys, Ames/Rosemont)

abhor (Soothill)

# 法度(1)

20.1 审法度

the body of the laws (Legge)

laws and regulations (Soothill)

statutes and laws (Waley)

government measures (Lau)

authority of the government (Leys)

laws and statutes (Ames/Rosemont)

# 法语(1)

9.24 法语之言

words of strict admonition (Legge)

words of just admonition (Soothill)

words of the far (Waley)

exemplary word (Lau)

words of admonition (Leys)

model saying (Ames/Rosemont)

# 方(14)

1.1 　　有朋自远方来
　　　　quarter (Legge)

4.19 　　游必有方
　　　　fixed place (Legge)
　　　　stated destination (Soothill)
　　　　where (Waley)
　　　　whereabouts (Lau)
　　　　address (Leys)
　　　　specific destination (Ames/Rosemont)

6.30 　　可谓仁之方也已
　　　　art (Legge)
　　　　rule (Soothill)
　　　　direction (Waley)
　　　　method (Lau, Ames/Rosemont)
　　　　recipe (Leys)

11.24 　且知方也……方六七十……安见方六七十如五六十而非邦也者
　　　　righteous conduct (Legge)
　　　　right course (Soothill)
　　　　right conduct (Waley)
　　　　a sense of direction (Lau)
　　　　set back on one's feet (Leys)
　　　　sure direction (Ames/Rosemont)
　　　　square (Legge, Soothill, Lau, Ames/Rosemont)
　　　　league (Waley, Leys)

13.4　则四方之民襁负其子而至矣

　　quarter（Legge，Soothill，Lau，Ames/Rosemont）

　　side（Waley）

13.5　使于四方

　　quarter（Legge，Ames/Rosemont）

　　anywhere（Soothill）

　　far parts（Waley）

　　foreign states（Lau）

　　abroad（Leys）

13.20　使于四方

　　quarter（Legge，Ames/Rosemont）

　　wheresoever（Soothill）

　　far lands（Waley）

　　abroad（Lau）

　　corner of the world（Leys）

14.29　子贡方人

　　compare（Legge）

　　make comparison（Soothill）

　　criticize（Waley，Leys）

　　grade（Lau）

　　judge（Ames/Rosemont）

16.7　及其壮也，血气方①刚

　　*adv.*（Legge, Soothill, Lau, Waley, Leys, Ames/Rosemont）

20.1　无以万方；万方有罪……四方之政行焉

　　myriad regions（Legge）

　　country（Soothill）

　　land（Waley）

---

① 副词。

state (Lau, Ames/Rosemont)

fief (Leys)

government of the kingdom (Legge)

universal (Soothill)

quarter (Waley)

everywhere (Lau, Leys, Ames/Rosemont)

## *放(3)(fǎng, fàng)

A. fǎng

4.12 放于利而行

a constant view to (Legge)

work for (Soothill)

dictate by (Waley)

guide by (Lau)

act out of (Leys)

act with an eye to (Ames/Rosemont)

B. fàng

15.11 放郑声,远佞人

banish (Legge, Soothill, Lau)

do away (Waley)

proscribe (Leys)

abolish (Ames/Rosemont)

18.8 隐居放言

give licence to (Legge)

immoderate (Soothill)

refrain (Waley)

give free rein (Lau)

give up (Leys)

say (Ames/Rosemont)

# 富(17)

1.15 富而无骄……富而好礼者也

rich (Legge, Soothill, Waley, Leys, Ames/Rosemont)

wealthy (Lau)

4.5 富与贵

rich (Legge, Leys)

wealth (Soothill, Waley, Lau, Ames/Rosemont)

6.4 君子周急不继富

rich (Legge, Soothill, Waley, Lau, Leys, Ames/Rosemont)

7.12 富而可求也

rich (Legge)

wealth (Soothill, Lau, Leys, Ames/Rosemont)

7.16 不义而富且贵

rich (Legge, Leys)

wealth (Soothill, Waley, Lau, Ames/Rosemont)

8.13 富且贵焉

rich (Legge, Waley, Lau, Leys)

affluence (Soothill)

wealthy (Ames/Rosemont)

11.17 季氏富于周公

richer (Legge, Soothill, Waley, Leys)

greater (Lau)

wealthy（Ames/Rosemont）

12.5 富贵在天

rich（Legge, Leys）

wealth（Soothill, Waley, Lau, Ames/Rosemont）

12.10 诚不以富

rich（Legge, Lau）

wealth（Soothill, Waley, Leys）

fortune（Ames/Rosemont）

12.22 富哉言乎

rich（Legge, Soothill, Lau, Leys, Ames/Rosemont）

wealth（Waley）

13.8 富有

rich（Legge, Waley）

have amassed plenty（Soothill）

sumptuous（Lau）

considerable（Leys）

prospered（Ames/Rosemont）

13.9 曰："富之。"曰："既富矣……"

enrich（Legge, Soothill, Waley, Leys）

improve（Lau）

prosperous（Ames/Rosemont）

14.10 富而无骄易

rich（Legge, Soothill, Waley, Lau, Leys）

wealthy（Ames/Rosemont）

19.23 百官之富

rich array（Legge）

richness（Soothill）

wealth（Waley, Leys）

sumptuousness (Lau)

lavishness (Ames/Rosemont)

20.1　善人是富

enrich (Legge, Soothill, Waley, Lau, Ames/Rosemont)

prosper (Leys)

# 刚(5)

5.11　吾未见刚者……焉得刚

firm and unbending (Legge)

of strong character (Soothill)

steadfast (Waley)

unbending strength (Lau)

steadfast (Leys, Ames/Rosemont)

13.27　刚、毅、木、讷近仁

firm (Legge)

firm of spirit (Soothill)

imperturbable (Waley)

unbending strength (Lau)

firmness (Leys)

firm (Ames/Rosemont)

16.7　血气方刚

full of vigour (Legge)

mature strength (Soothill)

hardened (Waley)

unyielding (Lau)

at its full (Leys)

at its height (Ames/Rosemont)

17.7 好刚不好学

firmness (Legge)

strength of character (Soothill)

courage (Waley)

unbending strength (Lau)

force (Leys)

firmness (Ames/Rosemont)

# 格(1)

2.3 有耻且格

good (Legge)

standard (Soothill)

accord (Waley)

reform (Lau)

participation (Leys)

order (Ames/Rosemont)

# *公(38)

A.

2.19 哀公问曰

duke (Legge, Soothill, Waley, Lau, Leys, Ames/Rosemont)

3.2 相维辟公

prince (Legge)

prince and nobleman (Soothill)

ruler and lord (Waley)

great lord (Lau)

feudal lord (Leys)

noble (Ames/Rosemont)

3.19 定公问

duke (Legge, Soothill, Waley, Lau, Leys, Ames/Rosemont)

3.21 哀公

duke (Legge, Soothill, Waley, Lau, Leys, Ames/Rosemont)

6.3 哀公问

duke (Legge, Soothill, Waley, Lau, Leys, Ames/Rosemont)

7.5 久矣吾不复梦见周公

duke (Legge, Soothill, Waley, Lau, Leys, Ames/Rosemont)

7.19 叶公问孔子于子路

duke (Legge, Soothill, Leys, Ames/Rosemont)

governor (Waley, Lau)

7.31 陈司败问:"昭公知礼乎?"

duke (Legge, Soothill, Waley, Lau, Leys, Ames/Rosemont)

8.11 如有周公之才之美

duke (Legge, Soothill, Waley, Lau, Leys, Ames/Rosemont)

10.3 入公门

palace (Legge, Soothill, Waley)

Lord's (Lau)

duke (Leys, Ames/Rosemont)

10.6 祭于公

prince (Legge)

ducal (Soothill, Waley)

lord (Lau)

state（Leys）

public（Ames/Rosemont）

11.17　季氏富于周公

duke（Legge，Soothill，Waley，Lau，Leys，Ames/Rosemont）

12.9　哀公问于有若曰

duke（Legge，Soothill，Waley，Lau，Leys，Ames/Rosemont）

12.11　齐景公问政于孔子……公曰

duke（Legge，Soothill，Waley，Lau，Leys，Ames/Rosemont）

13.8　子谓卫公子荆

ducal（Legge，Soothill）

grandee（Waley）

prince（Lau，prince Leys）

duke（Ames/Rosemont）

13.15　定公问

duke（Legge，Soothill，Waley，Lau，Leys，Ames/Rosemont）

13.16　叶公问政

duke（Legge，Soothill，Waley，Lau，Leys，Ames/Rosemont）

13.18　叶公语孔子曰

duke（Legge，Soothill，Waley）

governor（Lau,Leys，Ames/Rosemont）

14.15　晋文公谲而正，齐桓公正而不谲

duke（Legge，Soothill，Waley，Lau，Leys，Ames/Rosemont）

14.16　桓公杀公子纠……桓公九合诸侯

duke（Legge，Soothill，Waley，Lau，Leys，Ames/Rosemont）

14.17　桓公杀公子纠……管仲相桓公

duke（Legge，Soothill，Waley，Lau，Leys，Ames/Rosemont）

14.18　公叔文子之臣大夫僎与文子同升诸公

duke（Legge，Soothill，Waley，Lau，Leys，Ames/Rosemont）

14.19 子言卫灵公之无道也

　　duke（Legge，Soothill，Waley，Lau，Leys，Ames/Rosemont）

14.21 陈成子弑简公……告于哀公曰……公曰

　　duke（Legge，Soothill，Waley，Lau，Leys，Ames/Rosemont）

15.1 卫灵公问陈于孔子

　　duke（Legge，Soothill，Waley，Lau，Leys，Ames/Rosemont）

16.3 禄之去公室五世矣

　　ducal（Legge，Soothill，Waley，Lau，Leys，Ames/Rosemont）

16.12 齐景公有马千驷

　　duke（Legge，Soothill，Waley，Lau，Leys，Ames/Rosemont）

18.3 齐景公待孔子曰

　　duke（Legge，Soothill，Waley，Lau，Leys，Ames/Rosemont）

18.10 周公谓鲁公曰

　　duke（Legge，Soothill，Waley，Lau，Leys，Ames/Rosemont）

B.

6.14 非公事

　　public（Legge，Soothill，Waley，Ames/Rosemont）

　　official（Lau，Leys）

20.1 公则说

　　justice（Legge，Soothill，Leys）

　　just（Waley）

　　impartial（Lau，Ames/Rosemont）

# 恭(13)

1.10 温、良、恭、俭、让

　　courteous（Legge，Soothill，Waley，Leys）

respectful（Lau）

deferential（Ames/Rosemont）

1.13 恭近于礼

respect（Legge，Soothill）

obeisance（Waley）

respectful（Lau）

conform（Leys）

deferential（Ames/Rosemont）

5.16 其行己也恭

humble（Legge）

serious（Soothill）

courteous（Waley）

respectful（Lau）

dignified（Leys）

gracious（Ames/Rosemont）

5.25 巧言、令色、足恭

respect（Legge，Soothill）

reverence（Waley）

servility（Lau）

obsequiousness（Leys）

solicitude（Ames/Rosemont）

7.38 恭而安

respectful（Legge，Lau）

courteous（Soothill）

polite（Waley）

dignified（Leys）

deferential（Ames/Rosemont）

8.2 恭而无礼则劳

respectfulness（Legge）

courtesy（Soothill，Waley，Leys）

spirit（Lau）

deference（Ames/Rosemont）

12.5 与人恭而有礼

respectful（Legge）

courteous（Soothill）

courtesy（Waley，Leys）

respectful（Lau）

deferential（Ames/Rosemont）

13.19 居处恭

sedately grave（Legge）

courteous（Soothill，Waley，Leys）

respectful attitude（Lau）

deferential（Ames/Rosemont）

15.5 恭己正南面而已矣

reverently（Legge，Waley，Ames/Rosemont）

seriousness（Soothill）

respectful posture（Lau）

hold（Leys）

16.10 貌思恭

respectful（Legge，Soothill，Waley，Lau）

deferential（Leys）

deference（Ames/Rosemont）

17.5 恭,宽,信,敏,惠。恭则不侮

gravity（Legge）

grave（Legge）

respect（Soothill）

　　　　courtesy（Waley，Leys）

　　　　courteous（Waley，Leys）

　　　　respectfulness（Lau）

　　　　respectful（Lau）

　　　　deference（Ames/Rosemont）

　　　　deferential（Ames/Rosemont）

19.25　子为恭也

　　　　modest（Legge，Soothill，Leys）

　　　　modesty（Waley）

　　　　respectful（Lau）

　　　　deferential（Ames/Rosemont）

# 躬(11)

4.22　耻躬之不逮也

　　　　one's action（Legge）

　　　　deed（Soothill）

　　　　one's deed（Leys）

7.33　躬行君子

　　　　carry out in one's conduct（Legge）

　　　　live（Soothill，Leys）

　　　　carry out the duties（Waley）

　　　　practice（Lau）

　　　　live the life（Ames/Rosemont）

10.3　鞠躬如也……鞠躬如也

　　　　bend one's body（Legge）

　　　　stoop（Soothill）

shrink (Waley)

double up (Waley)

draw in (Lau)

discreetly (Leys)

bow (Leys，Ames/Rosemont)

bend (Ames/Rosemont)

10.4　鞠躬如也

bend one's body (Legge)

bend (Soothill)

double up (Waley)

draw in (Lau)

bow (Leys，Ames/Rosemont)

13.18　吾党有直躬者

conduct (Legge)

Kung (Waley)

body (Lau)

integrity (Leys)

14.5　禹稷躬稼而有天下

personally (Legge，Ames/Rosemont)

take a personal interest in (Soothill)

devote themselves to (Waley)

take (Lau)

drive (Leys)

15.15　躬自厚而薄责于人

oneself (Legge, Leys，Soothill，Waley，Lau，Ames/Rosemont)

20.1　天之历数在尔躬……朕躬有罪……罪在朕躬

person (Legge, Soothill，Waley，Lau，Ames/Rosemont)

# 古(12)

3.16 古之道也

　　　old (Legge)

　　　yore (Soothill)

　　　ancient (Waley, Leys, Ames/Rosemont)

　　　antiquity (Lau)

4.22 古者言之不出

　　　ancient (Legge, Leys, Ames/Rosemont)

　　　old (Soothill)

　　　old day (Waley)

　　　antiquity (Lau)

7.1 信而好古

　　　ancient (Legge, Waley, Ames/Rosemont)

　　　antiquity (Soothill, Lau)

　　　past (Leys)

7.15 古之贤人也

　　　ancient (Legge)

　　　old (Soothill, Waley, Lau, Leys)

　　　bygone day (Ames/Rosemont)

7.20 好古,敏以求之者也

　　　antiquity (Legge, Soothill, Lau, Ames/Rosemont)

　　　past (Waley, Leys)

12.7 自古皆有死

　　　old (Legge, Soothill, Waley)

　　　the beginning of time (Lau)

ancient (Ames/Rosemont)

14.24 古之学者为己

　　ancient time (Legge)

　　old (Soothill, Ames/Rosemont)

　　old day (Waley, Leys)

　　antiquity (Lau)

14.40 古之人皆然

　　ancient (Legge, Leys, Ames/Rosemont)

　　man of old (Soothill, Waley)

　　man of antiquity (Lau)

17.14 古者民有三疾……古之狂也肆,今之狂也荡;古之矜也廉,今之矜也忿戾;古之愚也直

　　anciently (Legge)

　　antiquity (Legge, Lau)

　　in olden time (Soothill)

　　old (Soothill, Waley, Ames/Rosemont)

　　old day (Waley, Ames/Rosemont)

　　ancient (Leys)

* 固(10)

A.

1.8 学则不固

　　solid (Legge)

　　stability (Soothill)

　　firm ground (Waley)

　　inflexible (Lau, Ames/Rosemont)

[not] shallow (Leys)

7.36 俭则固。与其不孙也，宁固

 meanness (Legge，Waley)

 narrow (Soothill)

 shabbiness (Lau)

 stinginess (Leys)

 miserliness (Ames/Rosemont)

9.4 毋必，毋固

 obstinacy (Legge)

 obduracy (Soothill)

 obstinate (Waley)

 inflexible (Lau，Ames/Rosemont)

14.32 疾固也

 obstinacy (Legge，Waley)

 obstinately immovable (Soothill)

 inflexibility (Lau，Ames/Rosemont)

 pigheadedness (Leys)

16.1 固而近于费

 strong (Legge)

 fortified (Soothill)

 strongly fortified (Waley，Lau)

 have strong defense (Leys)

 heavy fortified (Ames/Rosemont)

B.

9.6 固天纵之将圣

 certainly (Legge，Waley)

 of a truth (Soothill)

 true (Lau)

indeed（Leys）

definitely（Ames/Rosemont）

14.36　夫子固有惑志于公伯寮

certainly（Legge，Soothill，Ames/Rosemont）

greatly unsettled（Waley）

definite（Lau）

15.2　君子固穷

may indeed（Legge）

withstand（Waley）

come as no surprise（Lau）

indeed（Leys）

steadfast（Ames/Rosemont）

15.42　固相师之道也

certainly（Legge，Waley）

undoubtedly（Soothill）

indeed（Ames/Rosemont）

# 寡(12)

2.18　则寡尤……则寡悔。言寡尤,行寡悔

few（Legge，Lau，Ames/Rosemont）

little（Soothill）

seldom（Waley）

8.5　以多问于寡

little（Legge）

few（Soothill，Lau）

less（Waley，Ames/Rosemont）

talentless (Leys)

14.25 夫子欲寡其过而未能也

few (Legge, Soothill, Leys)

diminish (Waley)

reduce (Lau, Ames/Rosemont)

16.1 不患寡当作贫而患不均,不患贫当作寡而患不安……和无寡

few (Legge, Soothill, Ames/Rosemont)

scarcity (Legge)

lack of people (Soothill)

poor (Waley)

lack of men (Waley)

underpopulation (Lau)

lack of population (Leys)

16.14 称诸异邦曰寡小君

K'WA (Legge)

Kua (Soothill)

lonely (Waley)

little (Lau, Leys, Ames/Rosemont)

19.23 得其门者或寡矣

few (Legge, Soothill, Waley, Leys, Ames/Rosemont)

20.2 君子无众寡

few (Legge, Soothill, Waley, Leys, Ames/Rosemont)

# 怪(1)

7.21 子不语怪

extraordinary thing (Legge)

prodigy（Soothill，Waley，Lau）

miracle（Leys）

strange happening（Ames/Rosemont）

# 官(4)

3.22　官事不摄

officer（Legge）

staff member（Soothill，Ames/Rosemont）

state officer（Waley）

staff（Lau）

14.40　百官总己以听于冢宰三年

officer（Legge，Soothill）

minister（Waley，Ames/Rosemont）

official（Lau，Leys）

19.23　百官之富

officer（Legge，Soothill）

ministrant（Waley）

official buildings（Lau）

apartment（Leys）

estate（Ames/Rosemont）

20.1　修废官

officer（Legge）

office（Soothill，Waley，Leys，Ames/Rosemont）

official post（Lau）

# 贯(3)

4.15　吾道一以贯之

　　　all pervade (Legge, Soothill)

　　　run through (Waley, Leys)

　　　bind together (Lau, Ames/Rosemont)

11.14　仍旧贯如之何

　　　style (Legge)

　　　line (Waley, Leys)

　　　likeness (Ames/Rosemont)

15.3　予一以贯之

　　　all pervade (Legge)

　　　connect (Soothill)

　　　string all (Waley, Leys)

　　　bind together (Lau)

　　　pull together (Ames/Rosemont)

# *归(11)(guī, kuì)

A. guī

1.9　民德归厚矣

　　　resume (Legge)

　　　restoration (Soothill)

　　　reach (Waley)

　　　incline (Lau)

3.22 管氏有三归

　　　kwei (Legge)

　　　kuei palace (Soothill)

　　　lots of wives (Waley)

　　　establishment (Lau)

　　　palace (Leys)

　　　residence (Ames/Rosemont)

5.22 归与！归与

　　　return (Legge, Soothill)

　　　go back (Waley)

　　　go home (Lau, Leys)

　　　homeward (Ames/Rosemont)

10.16 无所归

　　　depend on (Legge)

　　　fall back upon (Soothill)

　　　fall back on (Waley)

　　　kin (Lau)

11.24 咏而归

　　　return home (Legge, Soothill, Ames/Rosemont)

　　　go home (Waley, Lau, Leys)

12.1 天下归仁焉

　　　ascribe (Legge)

　　　accord (Soothill)

　　　respond (Waley)

　　　consider (Lau)

　　　rally (Leys)

　　　defer (Ames/Rosemont)

19.20 天下之恶皆归焉

flow in (Legge, Soothill)

accumulate (Waley)

find its way (Lau, Ames/Rosemont)

drift (Leys)

20.1 天下之民归心焉

turn toward (Legge)

give (Soothill, Waley)

turn to (Lau)

win (Leys, Ames/Rosemont)

B. kuì

17.1 归孔子豚

send a present (Legge)

send (Soothill, Waley, Lau, Leys, Ames/Rosemont)

18.4 齐人归女乐

send (Legge, Soothill, Waley, Leys)

make a present (Lau)

make a gift (Ames/Rosemont)

# 鬼(5)

2.24 非其鬼而祭之

spirit (Legge, Ames/Rosemont)

spirit of an ancestor (Soothill, Lau)

ancestor (Waley)

god (Leys)

6.22 敬鬼神而远之

spiritual being (Legge)

spirit (Soothill, Waley, Lau)

ghosts (Leys, Ames/Rosemont)

8.21 而致孝乎鬼神

spirit (Legge, Soothill, Waley, Lau, Ames/Rosemont)

the ghosts and spirit (Leys)

11.12 季路问事鬼神……焉能事鬼

spirit (Legge, Leys, Ames/Rosemont)

the dead (Soothill)

ghost (Waley)

spirit of the dead (Lau)

# 贵(8)

1.12 和为贵

prize (Legge, Waley)

be of value (Soothill)

valuable (Lau)

matter most (Leys)

most valuable (Ames/Rosemont)

4.5 富与贵

honour (Legge)

rank (Soothill, Waley, Leys)

high station (Lau)

honor (Ames/Rosemont)

7.16 不义而富且贵

honour (Legge, Soothill, Leys)

rank (Waley, Lau)

position（Ames/Rosemont）

8.4 君子所贵乎道者三

consider specially important（Legge）

place（Soothill）

place above all the rest（Waley）

value（Lau）

pay special attention（Leys）

utmost（Ames/Rosemont）

8.13 富且贵焉

honour（Legge，Soothill，Waley，Leys）

noble（Lau，Ames/Rosemont）

9.24 改之为贵……绎之为贵

valuable（Legge）

value（Soothill）

matter（Waley）

important（Lau）

main（Leys）

value（Ames/Rosemont）

12.5 富贵在天

honour（Legge，Soothill，Lau，Leys，Ames/Rosemont）

rank（Waley）

# 国(10)

1.5 道千乘之国

country（Legge，Waley）

government of a state（Soothill）

state (Lau, Leys, Ames/Rosemont)

4.13　能以礼让为国乎……不能以礼让为国

　　　kingdom (Legge)

　　　country (Soothill, Waley, Leys)

　　　state (Lau, Ames/Rosemont)

5.8　千乘之国

　　　kingdom (Legge, Soothill)

　　　country (Waley, Leys)

　　　state (Lau, Ames/Rosemont)

11.24　千乘之国,摄乎大国之间……为国以礼

　　　state (Legge, Waley, Lau, Leys, Ames/Rosemont)

　　　kingdom (Soothill)

　　　power (Soothill)

　　　country (Soothill, Waley)

16.1　丘也闻有国有家者

　　　state (Legge, Waley, Lau, Leys, Ames/Rosemont)

　　　kingdom (Soothill)

16.2　陪臣执国命

　　　state (Legge, Lau, Ames/Rosemont)

　　　kingdom (Soothill)

　　　country (Waley, Leys)

20.1　兴灭国

　　　state (Legge, Soothill, Waley, Lau, Leys, Ames/Rosemont)

# 过(32)

1.8 过则勿惮改
　　　fault（Legge，Leys）
　　　wrong（Soothill）
　　　mistake（Waley，Lau）
　　　err（Ames/Rosemont）

4.7 人之过也……观过
　　　fault（Legge，Soothill，Waley，Leys）
　　　error（Lau）
　　　astray（Ames/Rosemont）
　　　divergency（Ames/Rosemont）

5.7 也好勇过我
　　　more...than（Legge，Soothill，Lau，Leys）
　　　far too much（Waley）
　　　exceed（Ames/Rosemont）

5.27 吾未见能见其过而内自讼者也
　　　fault（Legge，Soothill，Waley，Leys）
　　　error（Lau）
　　　excess（Ames/Rosemont）

6.3 不贰过
　　　fault（Legge，Soothill，Waley）
　　　mistake（Lau，Leys，Ames/Rosemont）

7.17 可以无大过矣
　　　fault（Legge）
　　　error（Soothill，Waley，Lau）

mistake (Leys)

oversight (Ames/Rosemont)

7.31 苟有过

error (Legge)

mistake (Soothill, Waley, Lau, Leys)

go astray (Ames/Rosemont)

9.10 过之,必趋

pass by (Legge)

pass (Soothill, Lau, Ames/Rosemont)

past (Waley)

9.25 过则勿惮改

fault (Legge)

wrong (Soothill)

mistake (Waley, Lau, Leys)

astray (Ames/Rosemont)

10.3 过位,色勃如也

pass (Legge, Soothill, Leys, Ames/Rosemont)

go through (Waley)

past (Lau)

11.16 师也过……过犹不及

go beyond (Legge)

exceed (Soothill)

go too far (Waley)

overshoot the mark (Lau)

overshoot (Leys)

overstep the mark (Ames/Rosemont)

13.2 赦小过,举贤才

fault (Legge)

error（Soothill）

offence（Waley）

offender（Lau）

mistake（Leys）

offense（Ames/Rosemont）

14.13 以告者过也

beyond the truth（Legge）

exaggeration（Soothill）

exaggerate（Waley，Lau，Leys，Ames/Rosemont）

14.25 夫子欲寡其过而未能也

fault（Legge，Soothill，Ames/Rosemont）

fail（Waley）

error（Lau）

mistake（Leys）

14.27 君子耻其言而过其行

exceed（Legge）

surpass（Soothill）

outrun（Waley）

outstrip（Lau）

match（Leys）

better（Ames/Rosemont）

14.39 有荷蒉而过孔氏之门者

pass（Legge，Soothill，Waley，Lau，Leys，Ames/Rosemont）

15.30 过而不改,是谓过矣

fault（Legge，Waley，Leys）

err（Soothill，Lau）

error（Soothill）

go astray（Ames/Rosemont）

fail (Ames/Rosemont)

16.1 无乃尔是过与……且尔言过矣……是谁之过与

in fault (Legge)

fault (Legge，Soothill，Waley，Lau)

misdeed (Soothill)

wrong (Soothill，Lau，Leys)

hold responsible for (Waley)

false (Waley)

blame (Leys，Ames/Rosemont)

accountable (Leys)

16.13 鲤趋而过庭……鲤趋而过庭

pass (Legge)

across (Soothill，Ames/Rosemont)

past (Waley)

cross (Lau)

cross (Leys)

18.5 楚狂接舆歌而过孔子曰

pass (Legge，Ames/Rosemont)

past (Soothill，Waley，Lau，Leys)

18.6 孔子过之

pass (Legge，Soothill，Waley，Leys，Ames/Rosemont)

past (Lau)

19.8 小人之过也必文

fault (Legge)

mistake (Soothill，Lau，Leys)

go wrong (Waley)

go astray (Ames/Rosemont)

19.12 言游过矣

wrong (Legge)

astray (Soothill)

mistake (Waley, Lau, Leys, Ames/Rosemont)

19.21 君子之过也,如日月之食焉:过也……

fault (Legge, Waley)

transgression (Soothill)

error (Lau)

mistake (Leys)

go astray (Ames/Rosemont)

20.1 百姓有过

blame (Legge)

grievance (Soothill)

wrong (Waley, Leys)

transgress (Lau)

go astray (Ames/Rosemont)

## *行(79)(háng, xíng)

A. háng

11.13 子路,行行如也

bold and soldierly (Legge)

full of energy (Soothill)

impatient energy (Waley)

unbending (Lau)

keen (Leys)

intent (Ames/Rosemont)

B. xíng

1.6 行有余力

　　performance（Legge）

　　act（Soothill）

　　do（Waley，Leys）

　　activity（Lau）

　　behave（Ames/Rosemont）

1.11 父没，观其行

　　conduct（Legge，Soothill）

　　carry one out（Waley）

　　do（Lau，Ames/Rosemont）

　　action（Leys）

1.12 有所不行……亦不可行也

　　observe（Legge）

　　do（Legge，Leys）

　　permissible（Soothill）

　　go（Waley）

　　work（Lau，Ames/Rosemont）

　　go well（Ames/Rosemont）

2.13 先行其言

　　act（Legge）

　　practice（Soothill，Waley，Leys）

　　deed（Lau）

　　accomplish（Ames/Rosemont）

2.18 慎行其余……行寡悔

　　practice（Legge，Lau）

　　act（Soothill，Waley，Ames/Rosemont）

　　apply（Leys）

2.22　其何以行之哉

　　　go (Legge, Soothill, Waley, Lau)

　　　pull (Leys)

　　　drive (Ames/Rosemont)

4.12　放于利而行

　　　act with (Legge)

　　　work for (Soothill)

　　　measure (Waley)

　　　action (Lau)

　　　act (Leys, Ames/Rosemont)

4.24　子欲讷于言而敏于行

　　　conduct (Legge)

　　　act (Soothill, Leys, Ames/Rosemont)

　　　deed (Waley)

　　　action (Lau)

5.7　道不行,乘桴浮于海

　　　way (Legge)

　　　progress (Soothill, Waley)

　　　prevail (Lau, Leys, Ames/Rosemont)

5.10　听其言而信其行……听其言而观其行

　　　conduct (Legge)

　　　deed (Soothill)

　　　what they do (Soothill, Waley, Leys, Ames/Rosemont)

　　　carry out one's word (Waley)

　　　deed (Lau)

　　　act accordingly (Leys)

5.14　未之能行

　　　carry into practice (Legge)

put into practice (Soothill, Waley, Lau)

practice (Leys)

act upon it (Ames/Rosemont)

5.16 其行己也恭

conduct (Legge, Soothill, Waley, Lau, Leys)

deport (Ames/Rosemont)

5.20 季文子三思而后行

act (Legge, Soothill, Waley, Leys)

take action (Lau)

take action (Ames/Rosemont)

6.2 居敬而行简……居简而行简

business (Legge)

practice (Legge)

conduct (Soothill)

dealing (Waley)

measure (Lau)

act (Ames/Rosemont)

6.14 行不由径

walk (Legge, Soothill, Waley)

7.7 自行束修以上

bring (Legge, Soothill, Waley)

give (Lau)

offer (Leys)

afford (Ames/Rosemont)

7.11 用之则行……子行三军

undertake (Legge)

conduct (Legge, Soothill)

require (Legge)

go (Waley)

command (Waley, Lau, Leys, Ames/Rosemont)

go forward (Lau)

come out (Leys)

advance (Ames/Rosemont)

7.22 三人行

walk (Legge, Soothill, Waley, Lau)

stroll (Ames/Rosemont)

7.24 吾无行而不与二三子者

do (Legge, Soothill, Waley, Lau, Leys, Ames/Rosemont)

7.25 文,行,忠,信

ethic (Legge)

conduct (Soothill, Waley)

moral conduct (Lau)

life (Leys)

proper conduct (Ames/Rosemont)

7.33 躬行君子

carry out (Legge, Waley)

live ... life (Soothill, Ames/Rosemont)

practice (Lau)

live (Leys)

9.12 由之行诈也

act (Legge, Soothill, Lau)

go in for (Waley)

organize (Leys)

serve (Ames/Rosemont)

10.3 行不履阈

pass (Legge)

go through (Soothill, Waley)

walk (Lau)

10.14 不俟驾行矣

go (Legge, Leys)

stare (Soothill)

go straight (Waley)

set off (Lau, Ames/Rosemont)

11.8 吾不徒行以为之椁……不可徒行也

walk (Legge)

walk on foot (Soothill)

go on foot (Waley, Lau, Leys, Ames/Rosemont)

11.20 闻斯行诸……如之何其闻斯行之……闻斯行诸……闻斯行之……由也问闻斯行诸……求也问闻斯行诸……闻斯行之

carry into practice (Legge)

put into practice (Soothill, Waley, Lau)

practice (Leys)

act (Ames/Rosemont)

12.6 不行焉……不行焉

successful (Legge)

moved (Soothill)

influenced (Waley, Lau)

waver (Ames/Rosemont)

12.14 行之以忠

practise (Legge)

carry (Soothill, Waley, Leys, Ames/Rosemont)

action (Lau)

12.20 色取仁而行违

action (Legge, Soothill)

conduct (Waley, Ames/Rosemont)

deed (Lau)

behave (Leys)

13.3 言之必可行也

carry out (Legge)

carry into practice (Soothill)

carry into effect (Waley)

practicable (Lau)

do (Leys)

act upon (Ames/Rosemont)

13.6 不令而行

effective (Legge)

do one's duty (Soothill)

go well (Waley)

obedience (Lau)

work out (Leys)

follow (Ames/Rosemont)

13.20 行己有耻……行必果

conduct (Legge, Soothill, Lau, Ames/Rosemont)

behave (Leys)

14.1 克、伐、怨、欲不行焉

[not] repress (Legge)

[not] refrain (Soothill, Ames/Rosemont)

Good (Waley)

stand firm (Lau)

[not] shed (Leys)

14.3 危言危行……危行言孙

action (Legge, Soothill, Waley)

act（Lau，Leys）

conduct（Ames/Rosemont）

14.27 君子耻其言而过其行

action（Legge）

do（Soothill）

deed（Waley，Lau，Leys，Ames/Rosemont）

14.36 道之将行也与

advance（Legge）

prevail（Soothill，Waley，Lau，Leys，Ames/Rosemont）

14.44 见其与先生并行也

walk（Legge，Soothill，Waley，Lau，Leys，Ames/Rosemont）

15.2 明日遂行

departure（Legge，Soothill）

travel（Waley）

depart（Lau）

leave（Leys，Ames/Rosemont）

15.6 子张问行……行笃敬……行矣……行不笃敬……行乎哉……夫然后行

conduct（Legge，Leys，Ames/Rosemont）

action（Legge）

get on with other（Soothill）

what you do（Soothill）

get on（Soothill，Waley）

get on with people（Waley）

do（Waley）

go forward without obstruction（Lau）

deed（Lau）

go forward（Lau）

act (Leys)

proper conduct (Ames/Rosemont)

15.11 行夏之时

follow (Legge，Lau)

adopt (Soothill)

go by (Waley)

observe (Leys)

introduce (Ames/Rosemont)

15.17 好行小慧

carry out (Legge)

deed (Soothill)

perform (Waley)

act (Lau)

display (Leys)

occupy (Ames/Rosemont)

15.18 礼以行之

perform (Legge)

practice (Soothill，Waley，Lau)

enact (Leys)

develop (Ames/Rosemont)

15.24 有一言而可以终身行之者乎

serve as a rule of practice (Legge)

conduct (Soothill)

act upon (Waley，Ames/Rosemont)

guide to conduct (Lau)

guide (Leys)

15.25 三代之所以直道而行也

pursue (Legge，Soothill)

follow (Waley)

keep to (Lau)

steer (Leys)

continue (Ames/Rosemont)

16.11 行义以达其道

practise (Legge, Soothill)

deed (Waley)

practice (Lau)

walk (Leys)

act (Ames/Rosemont)

17.5 能行五者于天下为仁矣

practice (Legge)

carry into practice (Soothill, Ames/Rosemont)

put into practice (Waley, Lau)

spread (Leys)

17.17 天何言哉？四时行焉

pursue (Legge)

run (Soothill, Waley)

go (Lau)

follow (Leys)

turn (Ames/Rosemont)

18.3 孔子行

take one's departure (Legge)

depart (Soothill)

leave (Waley, Leys)

depart (Lau)

take one's leave (Ames/Rosemont)

18.4 三日不朝,孔子行

take one's departure (Legge, Soothill)

leave (Waley, Leys)

depart (Lau)

take one's leave (Ames/Rosemont)

18.6 子路行以告

go (Legge, Soothill, Waley, Lau, Leys)

come back (Ames/Rosemont)

18.7 子路行以告……则行矣……行其义也。道之不行已知之矣……

go (Legge, Leys)

go on one's way (Legge, Waley)

perform (Legge)

make progress (Legge, Soothill)

go one's way (Soothill)

fulfil (Soothill)

go away (Waley)

service (Waley)

do (Lau)

put into practice (Lau)

resume one's journey (Lau, Leys)

depart (Lau)

serve (Leys)

prevail (Waley, Leys, Ames/Rosemont)

take one's leave (Ames/Rosemont)

leave (Ames/Rosemont)

effect (Ames/Rosemont)

18.8 言中伦,行中虑

action (Legge)

do (Soothill, Ames/Rosemont)

deed (Waley, Lau, Leys)

19.25 道之斯行

follow (Legge, Soothill, Ames/Rosemont)

go (Waley)

walk (Lau)

march (Leys)

20.1 四方之政行焉

take its course (Legge)

prevail (Soothill)

give (Waley)

enforce (Lau)

reach (Leys)

carry out (Ames/Rosemont)

# 和(8)

1.12 和为贵……知和而和

natural ease (Legge)

ease (Legge)

manifest (Legge)

naturalness (Soothill)

natural (Soothill)

harmony (Waley, Lau, Leys, Ames/Rosemont)

attune (Waley)

7.32 而后和之

accompany (Legge)

join (Soothill)

join in (Waley, Lau, Leys, Ames/Rosemont)

13.23　君子和而不同,小人同而不和
　　　　affable (Legge)
　　　　friendly (Soothill)
　　　　conciliatory (Waley)
　　　　agree with other (Lau)
　　　　in agreement (Lau)
　　　　harmony (Leys, Ames/Rosemont)

16.1　和无寡,安无倾
　　　　harmony prevail (Legge)
　　　　concord prevail (Soothill)
　　　　[not] divided (Waley)
　　　　harmony (Lau, Leys)
　　　　harmonious (Ames/Rosemont)

19.25　动之斯和
　　　　harmonious (Legge)
　　　　harmony (Soothill, Lau, Ames/Rosemont)
　　　　harmoniously (Waley)
　　　　peace (Leys)

# 恒(4)

7.26　得见有恒者……难乎有恒矣
　　　　constancy (Legge, Lau)
　　　　constant purpose (Soothill)
　　　　fixed principle (Waley)
　　　　principled (Leys)

constant（Ames/Rosemont）

13.22　人而无恒……不恒其德

　　　constancy（Legge，Soothill，Lau，Leys，Ames/Rosemont）

　　　constant（Legge，Soothill，Ames/Rosemont）

　　　stability（Waley）

　　　stabilize（Waley）

　　　steadfastness（Leys）

# 弘(4)

8.7　士不可以不弘毅

　　　breadth of mind（Legge）

　　　capacity（Soothill）

　　　broad shouldered（Waley）

　　　strong（Lau，Leys，Ames/Rosemont）

15.29　人能弘道，非道弘人

　　　enlarge（Legge，Soothill，Waley，Leys）

　　　broaden（Lau，Ames/Rosemont）

19.2　执德不弘

　　　enlarge（Legge，Soothill）

# 厚(5)

1.9　民德归厚矣

　　　proper excellence（Legge）

　　　abundant（Soothill）

　　　　highest point (Waley)

　　　　fullness (Lau)

　　　　fullest (Leys)

　　　　thrive (Ames/Rosemont)

10.5　狐貉之厚以居

　　　　thick (Legge, Soothill, Lau, Leys, Ames/Rosemont)

　　　　thicker (Waley)

11.11　门人欲厚葬之……门人厚葬之

　　　　great (Legge)

　　　　imposing (Soothill)

　　　　sumptuously (Soothill)

　　　　grand (Waley, Leys)

　　　　lavish (Lau, Ames/Rosemont)

15.15　躬自厚而薄责于人

　　　　much (Legge, Soothill, Waley, Leys, Ames/Rosemont)

　　　　strict standard (Lau)

# 怀(9)

4.11　君子怀德,小人怀土;君子怀刑,小人怀惠

　　　　think of (Legge, Soothill, Waley)

　　　　set one's heart upon (Waley)

　　　　cherish (Lau, Ames/Rosemont)

　　　　seek (Leys)

5.26　少者怀之

　　　　treat tenderly (Legge)

　　　　cherish (Soothill, Waley, Lau, Leys)

love and protect (Ames/Rosemont)

14.2 　士而怀居

cherish (Legge, Ames/Rosemont)

regard (Soothill)

think (Waley)

attach (Lau)

care for (Leys)

15.7 　则可卷而怀之

keep in one's breast (Legge)

keep in one's bosom (Soothill)

hide in the folds of one's dress (Waley)

put away (Lau)

fold up in one's heart (Leys)

tuck away (Ames/Rosemont)

17.1 　怀其宝而迷其邦

keep in one's bosom (Legge)

hide in one's bosom (Soothill, Waley)

hoard (Lau)

keep (Leys)

hoard (Ames/Rosemont)

17.19 　然后免于父母之怀

arm (Legge, Soothill, Waley)

nurse (Lau)

bosom (Leys, Ames/Rosemont)

# 悔(3)

2.18　则寡悔……行寡悔
　　　repentance（Legge）
　　　regret（Soothill，Lau，Leys，Ames/Rosemont）
　　　undo（Waley）

7.11　死而无悔者
　　　regret（Legge，Soothill，Lau，Ames/Rosemont）
　　　fear（Leys）

# 诲(5)

2.17　诲女知之乎
　　　teach（Legge，Soothill，Waley，Leys，Ames/Rosemont）
　　　tell（Lau）

7.2　诲人不倦
　　　instruct（Legge，Ames/Rosemont）
　　　instruction（Soothill）
　　　teach（Waley，Lau，Leys）

7.7　吾未尝无诲焉
　　　instruction（Legge，Soothill，Waley，Lau）
　　　teach（Leys）
　　　instruct（Ames/Rosemont）

7.34　诲人不倦
　　　teach（Legge，Soothill，Waley，Lau，Leys）

instruct（Ames/Rosemont）

14.7 能勿诲乎

instruction（Legge）

admonition（Soothill）

admonish（Waley，Leys）

educate（Lau）

instruct（Ames/Rosemont）

# 惠(8)

4.11 小人怀惠

favour（Legge，Soothill，Leys）

exemption（Waley）

generous treatment（Lau）

think of gain（Ames/Rosemont）

5.16 其养民也惠

kind（Legge）

beneficent（Soothill）

more than one's due（Waley）

generous（Lau，Leys，Ames/Rosemont）

14.9 惠人也

kind（Legge，Ames/Rosemont）

kindly（Soothill，Waley）

generous（Lau，Leys）

17.5 恭，宽，信，敏，惠……惠则足以使人

kindness（Legge，Soothill）

kind（Legge）

clemency (Waley)

clement (Waley)

generosity (Lau, Leys, Ames/Rosemont)

generous (Lau, Ames/Rosemont)

20.2 君子惠而不费……何谓惠而不费……斯不亦惠而不费乎

beneficent (Legge, Soothill)

beneficence (Soothill)

benefaction (Soothill)

bounteous (Waley)

generous (Lau, Leys, Ames/Rosemont)

# 货殖(1)

11.18 而货殖焉

good (Legge, Soothill)

enrich oneself (Waley)

money making (Lau)

go into business (Leys)

have taken to hoarding and speculations (Ames/Rosemont)

# 继(3)

2.23 其或继周者

follow (Legge)

succeed (Soothill, Ames/Rosemont)

successor (Waley, Lau, Leys)

6.4  君子周急不继富

　　　add to（Legge，Soothill）

20.1  兴灭国,继绝世

　　　restore（Legge，Soothill）

　　　re-establish（Waley）

　　　revive（Lau，Leys）

　　　continue（Ames/Rosemont）

# 祭(14)

2.5  祭之以礼

　　　sacrifice（Legge，Soothill，Waley，Leys，Ames/Rosemont）

　　　bury（Lau）

2.24  非其鬼而祭之

　　　sacrifice（Legge，Soothill，Waley，Lau，Ames/Rosemont）

　　　worship（Leys）

3.12  祭如在,祭神如神在……吾不与祭,如不祭

　　　sacrifice（Legge，Soothill，Waley，Lau，Leys，Ames/Rosemont）

10.6  祭于公……祭肉不出三日

　　　sacrifice（Legge，Soothill，Waley，Lau，Leys，Ames/Rosemont）

10.6  虽疏食菜羹,瓜祭

　　　offer in sacrifice（Legge，Soothill）

　　　offering（Waley，Lau，Ames/Rosemont）

10.12  君祭,先饭

　　　sacrifice（Legge，Soothill，Ames/Rosemont）

　　　sacrificial（Waley）

　　　offer（Lau）

10.17　非祭肉,不拜

　　　sacrifice (Legge)

　　　sacrificial (Soothill，Waley，Lau，Leys，Ames/Rosemont)

12.2　使民如承大祭

　　　sacrifice (Legge，Soothill，Waley，Lau，Ames/Rosemont)

　　　ceremony (Leys)

19.1　祭思敬,丧思哀

　　　sacrifice (Legge, Soothill，Waley, Lau, Leys, Ames/Rosemont)

20.1　所重:民、食、丧、祭

　　　sacrifice (Legge, Soothill，Waley，Lau，Leys，Ames/Rosemont)

# 家(11)

3.2　三家者以《雍》彻……奚取于三家之堂

　　　family (Legge，Soothill, Lau, Leys，Ames/Rosemont)

　　　great house (Soothill)

5.8　百乘之家

　　　clan (Legge)

　　　household (Soothill)

　　　baronial family (Waley)

　　　noble family (Lau)

　　　family (Ames/Rosemont)

12.2　在家无怨

　　　family (Legge，Waley，Lau)

　　　private (Soothill，Leys)

　　　personal (Ames/Rosemont)

12.20　在家必闻……在家必达……在家必闻

clan（Legge）

home（Soothill）

ruling family（Waley，Ames/Rosemont）

family（Lau）

private（Leys）

16.1　丘也闻有国有家者

family（Legge，Waley，Lau，Leys）

house（Soothill）

household（Ames/Rosemont）

17.16　恶利口之覆邦家者

family（Legge，Soothill，Ames/Rosemont）

clan（Waley，Leys）

noble family（Lau）

19.23　窥见室家之好

apartment（Legge）

home（Soothill）

house（Waley，Lau）

building inside（Leys，Ames/Rosemont）

19.25　夫子之得邦家者

family（Legge，Waley，Lau）

clan（Ames/Rosemont）

# 俭（6）

1.10　夫子温、良、恭、俭、让以得之

temperate（Legge，Soothill，Waley，Leys）

frugal（Lau，Ames/Rosemont）

3.4 礼,与其奢也,宁俭

　　　　spear (Legge)

　　　　simple (Soothill)

　　　　spare (Waley)

　　　　frugality (Lau)

　　　　simplicity (Leys)

　　　　modest (Ames/Rosemont)

3.22 管仲俭乎……焉得俭

　　　　parsimonious (Legge)

　　　　economical (Soothill)

　　　　frugality (Waley)

　　　　frugal (Lau, Leys, Ames/Rosemont)

7.36 俭则固

　　　　parsimony (Legge)

　　　　frugal (Soothill)

　　　　frugality (Waley, Lau, Leys, Ames/Rosemont)

9.3 今也纯,俭,吾从众

　　　　economical (Legge)

　　　　save expense (Soothill)

　　　　economical (Waley)

　　　　frugal (Lau)

　　　　convenient (Leys)

　　　　frugality (Ames/Rosemont)

# 贱(3)

4.5　贫与贱
　　meanness (Legge)
　　obscurity (Soothill, Waley, Leys)
　　low station (Lau)
　　disgrace (Ames/Rosemont)

8.13　贫且贱焉
　　mean (Legge)
　　of no account (Soothill)
　　obscure (Waley, Leys)
　　humble (Lau)
　　without rank (Ames/Rosemont)

9.6　吾少也贱
　　low (Legge)
　　humble (Soothill, Waley, Lau)
　　poor (Leys, Ames/Rosemont)

# 教(7)

2.20　举善而教不能则劝
　　teach (Legge, Soothill)
　　train (Waley, Leys)
　　instruct (Lau, Ames/Rosemont)

7.25　子以四教

teach（Legge，Soothill，Waley，Leys，Ames/Rosemont）

instruct（Lau）

13.9 教之

teach（Legge，Ames/Rosemont）

educate（Soothill，Leys）

instruct（Waley）

train（Lau）

13.29 善人教民七年

teach（Legge，Leys）

train（Soothill，Lau）

instruct（Waley，Ames/Rosemont）

13.30 以不教民战

instruct（Legge，Waley）

teach（Leys）

train（Soothill，Lau，Ames/Rosemont）

15.39 有教无类

teach（Legge，Soothill，Leys）

instruction（Waley，Lau，Ames/Rosemont）

20.2 不教而杀谓之虐

instruct（Legge）

teach（Soothill，Waley）

reform（Lau）

educate（Ames/Rosemont）

# *节(6)

A.

1.5 节用而爱人

  economy（Legge，Soothill）

  economical（Waley）

  keep expenditure under proper regulation（Lau）

  thrifty（Leys）

  frugal（Ames/Rosemont）

1.12 不以礼节之

  regulate（Legge，Lau，Ames/Rosemont）

  restraint（Soothill）

  modulate（Waley）

  subordinate（Leys）

8.6 临大节而不可夺也

  emergency（Legge，Soothill，Waley）

  crisis（Lau）

  test（Leys）

  matter（Ames/Rosemont）

16.5 乐节礼乐

  discriminating study（Legge）

  refinement（Soothill）

  due ordering（Waley）

  correct regulation（Lau）

  perform（Leys）

  attune（Ames/Rosemont）

18.7　长幼之节

　　relation (Legge)

　　regulation (Soothill, Lau)

　　law (Waley)

　　difference (Leys)

　　differentiation (Ames/Rosemont)

B.

5.18　山节藻棁

　　pillar (Legge, Lau, Leys)

　　pillar top (Soothill, Waley)

　　column divider (Ames/Rosemont)

# 矜(5)

15.22　君子矜而不争

　　dignified (Legge)

　　dignity (Soothill)

　　proud (Waley, Leys)

　　conscious of one's own superiority (Lau)

　　self possessed (Ames/Rosemont)

17.14　古之矜也廉,今之矜也忿戾

　　stern dignity (Legge)

　　dignity (Soothill)

　　proud (Waley, Ames/Rosemont)

　　conceited (Lau)

　　pride (Leys)

19.3　嘉善而矜不能

pity (Legge, Waley)

commiserate (Soothill)

take pity on (Lau)

have compassion for (Leys)

sympathetic (Ames/Rosemont)

19.19 则哀矜而勿喜

pity (Legge, Waley)

commiserate (Soothill)

compassion (Lau, Leys)

take pity on and show sympathy (Ames/Rosemont)

# 谨(3)

1.6 谨而信

earnest (Legge)

circumspect (Soothill)

cautious (Waley)

spare of speech (Lau)

talk little (Leys)

cautious (Ames/Rosemont)

10.1 唯谨尔

cautiously (Legge)

a measure of reserve (Soothill)

choose one's words with care (Waley)

speak lightly (Lau)

circumspect (Leys)

deliberation (Ames/Rosemont)

20.1 谨权量

　　carefully attended (Legge)

　　careful attention (Soothill)

　　pay strict attention (Waley)

　　decide on standard (Lau)

　　set standard (Leys)

　　carefully calibrate (Ames/Rosemont)

# 敬(21)

1.5 敬事而信

　　reverent attention (Legge)

　　religious attention (Soothill)

　　attend strictly (Waley)

　　reverence (Lau)

　　dignity (Leys)

　　respectfully (Ames/Rosemont)

2.7 不敬,何以别乎

　　reverence (Legge, Soothill, Lau)

　　respect (Waley, Leys, Ames/Rosemont)

2.20 使民敬……临之以庄则敬

　　reverence (Legge)

　　respect (Soothill)

　　respectful (Waley, Leys, Ames/Rosemont)

　　reverent (Lau)

3.26 为礼不敬

　　reverence (Legge, Soothill, Waley, Lau, Leys)

respectful (Ames/Rosemont)

4.18 又敬不违

reverence (Legge)

respectful (Soothill, Leys, Ames/Rosemont)

deference (Waley)

reverent (Lau)

5.16 其事上也敬

respectful (Legge, Leys)

deferential (Soothill)

punctilious (Waley)

reverent (Lau)

deferential (Ames/Rosemont)

5.17 久而敬之

respect (Legge)

consideration (Soothill)

scrupulous courtesy (Waley)

reverence (Lau)

never turn to familiarity (Leys)

treat with respect (Ames/Rosemont)

6.2 居敬而行简

reverential (Legge)

strict (Soothill, Leys)

scrupulous (Waley)

reverence (Lau)

respect (Ames/Rosemont)

6.22 敬鬼神而远之

respect (Legge, Soothill, Waley, Leys, Ames/Rosemont)

reverence (Lau)

11.15 门人不敬子路

    respect（Legge，Soothill，Waley，Leys）

    treat with respect（Lau，Ames/Rosemont）

12.5 君子敬而无失

    reverentially（Legge）

    self respect（Soothill）

    attend to business（Waley）

    reverent（Lau）

    reverence（Leys）

    respectful（Ames/Rosemont）

13.4 则民莫敢不敬

    reverent（Legge，Lau）

    respectful（Soothill，Waley，Ames/Rosemont）

    obedient（Leys）

13.19 执事敬

    reverently attentive（Legge）

    serious（Soothill）

    diligent（Waley）

    reverent（Lau，Leys）

    respectful（Ames/Rosemont）

14.42 修己以敬

    reverential carefulness（Legge）

    unfailingly respectful（Soothill）

    diligent（Waley）

    reverence（Lau）

    dignity（Leys）

    respectful（Ames/Rosemont）

15.6 行笃敬……行不笃敬

    careful（Legge，Waley）

    circumspect（Soothill）

    reverent（Lau）

    good faith（Leys）

    respectful（Ames/Rosemont）

15.33 则民不敬

    respect（Legge，Soothill，Waley，Leys）

    reverent（Lau）

    respectful（Ames/Rosemont）

15.38 敬其事而后其食

    reverently（Legge）

    careful attention（Soothill）

    intent（Waley）

    reverence（Lau）

    devotion（Leys）

    full attention（Ames/Rosemont）

16.10 事思敬

    careful（Legge）

    earnest（Soothill）

    diligent（Waley）

    reverent（Lau）

    respectful（Leys）

    respect（Ames/Rosemont）

19.1 祭思敬

    reverential（Legge）

    reverence（Soothill，Waley，Lau）

    piety（Leys）

    respect（Ames/Rosemont）

## 静(1)

6.23　仁者静

　　　still (Waley, Lau, Ames/Rosemont)

　　　tranquil (Legge)

　　　quiet (Leys)

　　　calm (Soothill)

## 举(14)

2.19　举直错诸枉……举枉错诸直

　　　advance (Legge)

　　　promote (Soothill)

　　　raise up (Waley)

　　　raise (Lau, Leys, Ames/Rosemont)

2.20　举善而教不能则劝

　　　advance (Legge)

　　　promote (Soothill, Waley)

　　　raise (Lau, Leys, Ames/Rosemont)

7.8　举一隅不以三隅反

　　　present (Legge)

　　　demonstrate (Soothill)

　　　hold (Waley)

　　　point (Lau)

　　　lift (Leys)

show (Ames/Rosemont)

10.21 色斯举矣

  rise (Legge, Waley, Soothill, Lau, Leys)

  take flight (Ames/Rosemont)

12.22 举直错诸枉……举直错诸枉……举皋陶……举伊尹

  employ (Legge)

  promote (Soothill, Ames/Rosemont)

  raise (Waley, Lau, Leys)

  select (Ames/Rosemont)

13.2 举贤才……焉知贤才而举之……举尔所知

  raise to office (Legge)

  promote (Soothill, Waley, Lau, Leys, Ames/Rosemont)

15.23 君子不以言举人

  promote (Legge, Ames/Rosemont)

  appreciate (Soothill)

  accept (Waley)

  recommend (Lau)

  approve (Leys)

20.1 举逸民

  call (Legge, Soothill)

  summon (Walcy)

  raise (Lau)

  reinstate (Leys)

  lift up (Ames/Rosemont)

## 狷(2)

13.21 必也狂狷乎……狷者有所不为也

  the cautiously decided（Legge）

  the discreet（Soothill）

  the hasty（Waley）

  the over scrupulous（Lau）

  the pure（Leys）

  the timid（Ames/Rosemont）

## 君子(107)

1.1 不亦君子乎

  man of complete virtue（Legge）

  true philosopher（Soothill）

  gentleman（Waley，Leys）

  gentlemanly（Lau）

  exemplary person（Ames/Rosemont）

1.2 君子务本

  superior man（Legge）

  true philosopher（Soothill）

  gentleman（Waley，Lau，Leys）

  exemplary person（Ames/Rosemont）

1.8 君子不重则不威

  scholar（Legge，Soothill）

gentleman (Waley, Lau, Leys)

exemplary person (Ames/Rosemont)

1.14 君子食无求饱

man of complete virtue (Legge)

scholar (Soothill)

gentleman (Waley, Lau, Leys)

exemplary person (Ames/Rosemont)

2.12 君子不器

accomplished scholar (Legge)

higher type of man (Soothill)

gentleman (Waley, Lau, Leys)

exemplary person (Ames/Rosemont)

2.13 子贡问君子

superior (Legge)

nobler type of man (Soothill)

gentleman (Waley, Lau, Leys)

exemplary person (Ames/Rosemont)

2.14 君子周而不比

superior (Legge)

nobler type of (Soothill)

gentleman (Waley, Lau, Leys)

exemplary person (Ames/Rosemont)

3.7 君子无所争……其争也君子

student of virtue (Legge)

Chün tsze (Legge)

gentleman (Soothill, Waley, Lau, Leys)

gentlemanly (Lau)

exemplary person (Ames/Rosemont)

3.24　君子之至于斯也

　　　man of superior virtue（Legge）

　　　man of virtue（Soothill）

　　　gentleman（Waley，Lau，Leys）

　　　distinguished person（Ames/Rosemont）

4.5　君子去仁……君子无终食之间违仁

　　　superior man（Legge）

　　　man of honour（Soothill）

　　　gentleman（Waley，Lau，Leys）

　　　exemplary person（Ames/Rosemont）

4.10　君子之于天下也

　　　superior man（Legge）

　　　wise man（Soothill）

　　　gentleman（Waley，Lau，Leys）

　　　exemplary person（Ames/Rosemont）

4.11　君子怀德……君子怀刑

　　　superior man（Legge）

　　　man of honour（Soothill）

　　　gentleman（Waley，Lau，Leys）

　　　exemplary person（Ames/Rosemont）

4.16　君子喻于义

　　　superior man（Legge）

　　　wise man（Soothill）

　　　gentleman（Waley，Lau，Leys）

　　　exemplary person（Ames/Rosemont）

4.24　君子欲讷于言

　　　superior man（Legge）

　　　wise man（Soothill）

       gentleman（Waley，Lau，Leys）

       exemplary person（Ames/Rosemont）

5.3  君子哉若人！鲁无君子者

       superior virtue（Legge）

       virtuous men（Legge）

       honourable man（Soothill）

       man of honour（Soothill）

       gentleman（Waley，Lau）

       true gentleman（Leys）

       exemplary person（Ames/Rosemont）

5.16  有君子之道四焉

       superior（Legge）

       ideal man（Soothill）

       true gentleman（Waley）

       gentleman（Lau，Leys）

       exemplary person（Ames/Rosemont）

6.4  君子周急不继富

       superior man（Legge）

       wise man（Soothill）

       gentleman（Waley，Lau，Leys）

       exemplary person（Ames/Rosemont）

6.13  女为君子儒

       superior（Legge）

       nobler（Soothill）

       gentleman（Waley，Lau）

       noble scholar（Leys）

       exemplary person（Ames/Rosemont）

6.18  然后君子

man of virtue（Legge）

higher type of man（Soothill）

true gentleman（Waley）

gentlemanliness（Lau）

gentleman（Leys）

exemplary person（Ames/Rosemont）

6.26　君子可逝也

superior（Legge）

higher（Soothill）

gentleman（Waley，Lau，Leys）

exemplary person（Ames/Rosemont）

6.27　君子博学于文

superior man（Legge）

scholar（Soothill）

gentleman（Waley，Lau，Leys）

exemplary person（Ames/Rosemont）

7.26　得见君子者

man of real talent and virtue（Legge）

noble man（Soothill）

gentleman（Waley，Lau，Leys）

exemplary person（Ames/Rosemont）

7.31　吾闻君子不党，君子亦党乎

superior man（Legge）

man of noble（Soothill）

gentleman（Waley，Lau，Leys）

exemplary person（Ames/Rosemont）

7.33　躬行君子

superior（Legge）

noble life（Soothill）

gentleman（Waley，Lau）

exemplary person（Ames/Rosemont）

7.37　君子坦荡荡

superior man（Legge）

nobler man（Soothill）

gentleman（Waley，Lau，Leys）

exemplary person（Ames/Rosemont）

8.2　君子笃于亲

those who are in old stations（Legge）

the highly placed（Soothill）

gentleman（Waley，Lau，Leys）

exemplary person（Ames/Rosemont）

8.4　君子所贵乎道者三

man of high rank（Legge）

man of high rank（Soothill）

gentleman（Waley，Lau，Leys）

exemplary person（Ames/Rosemont）

8.6　君子人与？君子人也

superior man（Legge）

nobler order（Soothill）

gentleman（Waley，Lau，Leys）

exemplary person（Ames/Rosemont）

9.6　君子多乎哉

superior man（Legge）

nobleness（Soothill）

gentleman（Waley，Lau，Leys）

exemplary person（Ames/Rosemont）

9.14 君子居之

　　superior man（Legge）

　　man of noble character（Soothill）

　　true gentleman（Waley）

　　gentleman（Lau，Leys）

　　exemplary person（Ames/Rosemont）

10.5 君子不以绀緅饰

　　superior（Legge）

　　he（Soothill）

　　gentleman（Waley，Lau，Leys）

　　persons of nobility（Ames/Rosemont）

11.1 后进于礼乐，君子也

　　accomplished gentleman（Legge）

　　cultured gentleman（Soothill）

　　gentleman（Waley，Lau）

　　nobleman（Leys）

　　nobility（Ames/Rosemont）

11.19 君子者乎

　　superior man（Legge）

　　man of the higher type（Soothill）

　　true gentleman（Waley）

　　gentleman（Lau，Leys）

　　exemplary person（Ames/Rosemont）

11.24 以俟君子

　　superior man（Legge）

　　nobler man（Soothill）

　　real gentleman（Waley）

　　abler gentleman（Lau）

true gentleman（Leys）

exemplary person（Ames/Rosemont）

12.4　司马牛问君子……君子不忧不惧……斯谓之君子已乎

superior man（Legge）

man of noble mind（Soothill）

noble man（Soothill）

gentleman（Waley，Lau，Leys）

exemplary person（Ames/Rosemont）

12.5　君子敬而无失……君子何患乎无兄弟也

superior man（Legge）

man of noble mind（Soothill）

chün tzǔ（Soothill）

gentleman（Waley，Lau，Leys）

exemplary person（Ames/Rosemont）

12.8　君子质而已矣……夫子之说君子也

superior man（Legge）

man of high character（Soothill）

chün tzǔ（Soothill）

gentleman（Waley，Lau，Leys，Ames/Rosemont）

exemplary person（Ames/Rosemont）

12.16　君子成人之美

superior man（Legge）

man of noble（Soothill）

gentleman（Waley，Lau，Leys）

exemplary person（Ames/Rosemont）

12.19　君子之德风

superior（Legge）

those in high position（Soothill）

gentleman（Waley，Lau，Leys）

exemplary person（Ames/Rosemont）

12.24 君子以文会友

superior man（Legge）

wise man（Soothill）

gentleman（Waley，Lau，leys）

exemplary person（Ames/Rosemont）

13.3 君子于其所不知……故君子名之必可言也……君子于其言

superior（Legge）

wise man（Soothill）

gentleman（Waley，Lau，Leys）

exemplary person（Ames/Rosemont）

13.23 君子和而不同

superior man（Legge）

true gentleman（Soothill，Waley）

gentleman（Lau，Leys）

exemplary person（Ames/Rosemont）

13.25 君子易事而难说也

superior man（Legge）

true gentleman（Soothill，Waley）

gentleman（Lau，Leys）

exemplary person（Ames/Rosemont）

13.26 君子泰而不骄

superior man（Legge）

well bred（Soothill）

gentleman（Waley，Lau，Leys）

exemplary person（Ames/Rosemont）

14.5 君子哉若人

superior man (Legge)

scholar (Soothill)

true gentleman (Waley)

gentlemanly (Lau, Leys)

exemplary person (Ames/Rosemont)

14.6 君子而不仁者有矣夫

superior (Legge)

man of the higher type (Soothill)

true gentleman (Waley)

gentleman (Lau, Leys)

exemplary (Ames/Rosemont)

14.23 君子上达

superior man (Legge)

nobler minded man (Soothill)

gentleman (Waley, Lau, Leys)

exemplary person (Ames/Rosemont)

14.26 君子思不出其位

superior man (Legge)

true gentleman (Soothill)

gentleman (Waley, Lau, Leys)

exemplary person (Ames/Rosemont)

14.27 君子耻其言而过其行

superior man (Legge)

higher type of man (Soothill)

gentleman (Waley, Lau, Leys)

exemplary person (Ames/Rosemont)

14.28 君子道者三

superior man (Legge)

noble man（Soothill）

true gentleman（Waley）

gentleman（Lau，Leys）

exemplary person（Ames/Rosemont）

14.42　子路问君子

superior man（Legge）

nobler order（Soothill）

true gentleman（Waley）

gentleman（Lau，Leys）

exemplary person（Ames/Rosemont）

15.2　君子亦有穷乎……君子固穷

superior man（Legge，Soothill）

man of superior order（Soothill）

gentleman（Waley，Lau，Leys）

exemplary person（Ames/Rosemont）

15.7　君子哉蘧伯玉

superior man（Legge）

noble man（Soothill）

gentlemanly（Lau）

gentleman（Waley，Leys）

exemplary person（Ames/Rosemont）

15.18　君子义以为质……君子哉

superior man（Legge）

noble man（Soothill）

gentleman（Waley，Lau，Leys）

exemplary person（Ames/Rosemont）

15.19　君子病无能焉

superior man（Legge）

noble man (Soothill)

gentleman (Waley, Lau, Leys)

exemplary person (Ames/Rosemont)

15.20 君子疾没世而名不称焉

superior man (Legge)

nobler man (Soothill)

gentleman (Waley, Lau, Leys)

exemplary person (Ames/Rosemont)

15.21 君子求诸己

superior man (Legge)

noble man (Soothill)

gentleman (Waley, Lau, Leys)

exemplary person (Ames/Rosemont)

15.22 君子矜而不争

superior man (Legge)

noble man (Soothill)

gentleman (Waley, Lau, Leys)

exemplary person (Ames/Rosemont)

15.23 君子不以言举人

superior man (Legge)

wise man (Soothill)

gentleman (Waley, Lau, Leys)

exemplary person (Ames/Rosemont)

15.32 君子谋道不谋食……君子忧道不忧贫

superior man (Legge)

wise man (Soothill)

gentleman (Waley, Lau, Leys)

exemplary person (Ames/Rosemont)

15.34　君子不可小知而可大受也

　　superior man（Legge）

　　man of the higher type（Soothill）

　　gentleman（Waley，Lau，Leys）

　　exemplary person（Ames/Rosemont）

15.37　君子贞而不谅

　　superior man（Legge）

　　wise man（Soothill）

　　gentleman（Waley，Lau，Leys）

　　exemplary person（Ames/Rosemont）

16.1　君子疾夫舍曰欲之而必为之辞

　　superior man（Legge）

　　man of honour（Soothill）

　　true gentleman（Waley）

　　gentleman（Lau，Leys）

　　exemplary person（Ames/Rosemont）

16.6　侍于君子有三愆

　　man of virtue（Legge）

　　superior（Soothill）

　　gentleman（Waley，Lau，Leys）

　　one's lord（Ames/Rosemont）

16.7　君子有三戒

　　superior man（Legge）

　　higher type of man（Soothill）

　　gentleman（Waley，Lau，Leys）

　　exemplary person（Ames/Rosemont）

16.8　君子有三畏

　　superior man（Legge）

man of noble mind (Soothill)

gentleman (Waley, Lau, Leys)

exemplary person (Ames/Rosemont)

16.10 君子有九思

superior man (Legge)

wise man (Soothill)

gentleman (Waley, Lau, Leys)

exemplary person (Ames/Rosemont)

16.13 又闻君子之远其子也

superior man (Legge)

wise man (Soothill)

gentleman (Waley, Lau, Leys)

exemplary person (Ames/Rosemont)

17.3 君子学道则爱人

man of high station (Legge)

man of rank (Soothill)

gentleman (Waley, Lau, Leys)

exemplary person (Ames/Rosemont)

17.6 君子不入也

superior man (Legge)

man of honour (Soothill)

gentleman (Waley, Lau, Leys)

exemplary person (Ames/Rosemont)

17.19 君子三年不为礼……夫君子之居丧

superior man (Legge)

well-bred man (Soothill)

gentleman (Waley, Lau, Leys)

exemplary person (Ames/Rosemont)

17.21 君子尚勇乎……君子义以为上……君子有勇而无义为乱

　　　　superior man (Legge)

　　　　man in superior situation (Legge)

　　　　man of the superior class (Soothill)

　　　　gentleman (Waley, Lau, Leys)

　　　　exemplary person (Ames/Rosemont)

17.22 君子亦有恶乎

　　　　superior man (Legge)

　　　　man of superior order (Soothill)

　　　　gentleman (Waley, Lau, Leys)

　　　　exemplary person (Ames/Rosemont)

18.7 君子之仕也

　　　　superior man (Legge)

　　　　wise man (Soothill)

　　　　gentleman (Waley, Lau, Leys)

　　　　exemplary person (Ames/Rosemont)

18.10 君子不施其亲

　　　　virtuous prince (Legge)

　　　　wise prince (Soothill)

　　　　gentleman (Waley, Lau, Leys)

　　　　exemplary person (Ames/Rosemont)

19.3 君子尊贤而容众

　　　　superior man (Legge)

　　　　wise man (Soothill)

　　　　gentleman (Waley, Lau, Leys)

　　　　exemplary person (Ames/Rosemont)

19.4 是以君子不为也

　　　　superior man (Legge)

wise man (Soothill)

gentleman (Waley, Lau, Leys)

exemplary person (Ames/Rosemont)

19.7　君子学以致其道

superior man (Legge)

wise man (Soothill)

gentleman (Waley, Lau, Leys)

exemplary person (Ames/Rosemont)

19.9　君子有三变

superior man (Legge)

wise man (Soothill)

gentleman (Waley, Lau, Leys)

exemplary person (Ames/Rosemont)

19.10　君子信而后劳其民

superior man (Legge)

wise man (Soothill)

gentleman (Waley, Lau, Leys)

exemplary person (Ames/Rosemont)

19.12　君子之道……君子之道

superior man (Legge)

wise man (Soothill)

gentleman (Waley, Lau, Leys)

exemplary person (Ames/Rosemont)

19.20　是以君子恶居下流

superior man (Legge)

wise man (Soothill)

gentleman (Waley, Lau, Leys)

exemplary person (Ames/Rosemont)

19.21 君子之过也

  superior man (Legge)

  wise man (Soothill)

  gentleman (Waley, Lau, Leys)

  exemplary person (Ames/Rosemont)

19.25 君子一言以为知

  man (Legge)

  educated man (Soothill)

  gentleman (Waley, Lau, Leys)

  exemplary person (Ames/Rosemont)

20.2 君子惠而不费……君子无众寡……君子正其衣冠

  person in authority (Legge)

  wise ruler (Soothill)

  gentleman (Waley, Lau, Leys)

  exemplary person (Ames/Rosemont)

20.3 无以为君子也

  superior man (Legge)

  noble man (Soothill)

  gentleman (Waley, Lau, Leys)

  exemplary person (Ames/Rosemont)

# 克(3)

12.1 克己复礼为仁。一日克己复礼

  subdue (Legge)

  denial (Soothill)

  deny (Soothill)

   submit (Waley)

   overcome (Lau)

   tame (Leys)

   discipline (Ames/Rosemont)

14.1 克、伐、怨、欲不行焉

   superiority (Legge)

   ambition (Soothill，Leys)

   mastery (Waley)

   press one's advantage (Lau)

   intimidation (Ames/Rosemont)

## 宽(4)

3.26 居上不宽

   generosity (Legge，Leys)

   magnanimity (Soothill)

   [not] narrow (Waley)

   tolerance (Lau)

   tolerant (Ames/Rosemont)

17.5 恭，宽，信，敏，惠……宽则得众

   generosity (Legge)

   magnanimity (Soothill)

   breadth (Waley)

   tolerance (Lau，Leys，Ames/Rosemont)

20.1 宽则得众

   generosity (Legge)

   magnanimity (Soothill)

broad (Waley)

tolerant (Lau, Ames/Rosemont)

generosity (Leys)

# 狂(7)

8.16 狂而不直

ardent (Legge)

impulsive (Soothill)

impetuous (Waley)

reject (Lau)

impetuous (Leys, Ames/Rosemont)

13.21 必也狂狷乎,狂者进取

ardent (Legge)

ambitious (Soothill)

impetuous (Waley)

undisciplined (Lau)

crazy (Leys)

rash (Ames/Rosemont)

17.7 其蔽也狂

extravagant conduct (Legge)

intractability (Soothill)

recklessness (Waley)

indiscipline (Lau)

anarchy (Leys)

rashness (Ames/Rosemont)

17.14 古之狂也肆,今之狂也荡

　　　　high mindedness（Legge）

　　　　high spirit（Soothill）

　　　　impetuous（Waley）

　　　　wild（Lau）

　　　　pride（Leys）

　　　　proud（Ames/Rosemont）

18.5　楚狂接舆歌而过孔子曰

　　　　madman（Legge，Waley，Lau，Leys，Ames/Rosemont）

　　　　eccentric man（Soothill）

# 狂简(1)

5.22　吾党之小子狂简

　　　　ambitious and hasty（Legge，Soothill）

　　　　headstrong and careless（Waley）

　　　　wildly ambitions（Lau）

　　　　full of fire（Leys）

　　　　rash and ambitious（Ames/Rosemont）

# 劳(10)

2.8　弟子服其劳

　　　　toil（Legge）

　　　　burden（Soothill，Lau）

　　　　hard work（Waley）

　　　　service（Leys）

energy（Ames/Rosemont）

4.18　劳而不怨

punish（Legge）

deal hardly with（Soothill）

discouraged（Waley）

distressed（Lau）

efforts（Leys）

concerned（Ames/Rosemont）

5.26　无施劳

meritorious deeds（Legge）

merits（Soothill）

trouble（Waley）

onerous tasks（Lau）

good deeds（Leys）

accomplishment（Ames/Rosemont）

8.2　恭而无礼则劳

laborious bustle（Legge）

labour efforts（Soothill）

tiresome（Waley，Leys）

wear out（Lau）

lethargy（Ames/Rosemont）

13.1　先之劳之

laborious（Legge）

work（Soothill）

encourage（Waley，Leys）

work（Lau）

urge（Ames/Rosemont）

14.7　能勿劳乎

strictness (Legge)

exacting (Soothill)

exact effort (Waley)

work hard (Lau)

[not] spare (Leys)

urge on (Ames/Rosemont)

19.10　君子信而后劳其民

impose labour (Legge)

impose burden (Soothill)

put burden (Waley)

work (Lau, Ames/Rosemont)

mobilize (Leys)

20.2　劳而不怨……择可劳而劳之

task (Legge, Leys)

labour (Legge)

service (Soothill)

work (Soothill, Waley, Lau, Leys, Ames/Rosemont)

perform (Waley)

burden (Lau)

project (Ames/Rosemont)


\* 乐(48)(lè, yuè)


A. lè

1.1　不亦乐乎

delightful (Legge, Soothill, Waley)

joy (Lau)

delight（Leys）

enjoyment（Ames/Rosemont）

1.15　未若贫而乐道

cheerful（Legge）

happy（Soothill）

delighting（Waley，Lau）

cheerful（Leys）

enjoy the way（Ames/Rosemont）

3.20　乐而不淫

enjoyment（Legge）

passionate（Soothill）

pleasure（Waley）

joy（Lau）

gay（Leys）

pleasing（Ames/Rosemont）

4.2　不可以长处乐

enjoyment（Legge）

happiness（Soothill）

prosperity（Waley）

easy circumstance（Lau）

joy（Leys）

happy circumstance（Ames/Rosemont）

6.11　回也不改其乐

joy（Legge，Lau，Leys）

cheerfulness（Soothill，Waley）

enjoyment（Ames/Rosemont）

6.20　好之者不如乐之者

delight（Legge，Soothill，Waley）

　　　　find-joy (Lau)

　　　　rejoice (Leys)

　　　　enjoy (Ames/Rosemont)

6.23　知者乐水,仁者乐山……知者乐,仁者寿

　　　　pleasure (Legge)

　　　　joyful (Legge)

　　　　delight (Soothill, Waley)

　　　　enjoy (Soothill, Ames/Rosemont)

　　　　happy (Waley)

　　　　joy (Lau, Leys)

　　　　joyful (Lau, Leys)

　　　　enjoyment (Ames/Rosemont)

7.16　乐亦在其中矣

　　　　joy (Legge, Lau)

　　　　happy (Soothill, Leys)

　　　　happiness (Waley)

　　　　pleasure (Ames/Rosemont)

7.19　乐以忘忧

　　　　joy (Legge, Lau, Leys)

　　　　happy (Soothill, Waley)

　　　　enjoy oneself (Ames/Rosemont)

11.13　子乐

　　　　pleased (Legge, Waley, Leys, Ames/Rosemont)

　　　　gratified (Soothill)

　　　　happy (Lau)

13.15　予无乐乎为君

　　　　pleasure (Legge, Waley, Leys, Ames/Rosemont)

　　　　gratification (Soothill)

enjoy（Lau）

14.13　乐然后笑

　　　joyful（Legge）

　　　pleased（Soothill）

　　　delighted（Waley）

　　　feeling happy（Lau）

　　　merry（Leys）

　　　happy（Ames/Rosemont）

16.5　益者三乐,损者三乐。乐节礼乐,乐道人之善,乐多贤友……乐骄乐,乐佚游,乐晏乐

　　　enjoyment（Legge，Waley，Ames/Rosemont）

　　　pleasure（Soothill，Waley，Lau，Leys）

17.9　……闻乐不乐

　　　pleasure（Legge，Lau，Ames/Rosemont）

　　　enjoy（Soothill）

　　　please（Waley）

　　　enjoyment（Leys）

B. yuè

3.3　如乐何

　　　music（Legge，Soothill，Waley，Lau，Leys）

　　　play of music（Ames/Rosemont）

3.23　子语鲁大师乐……乐其可知也

　　　music（Legge，Soothill，Waley，Lau，Leys，Ames/Rosemont）

7.14　不图为乐之至于斯也

　　　music（Legge，Soothill，Waley，Lau，Leys，Ames/Rosemont）

8.8　成于乐

　　　music（Legge，Soothill，Waley，Lau，Leys，Ames/Rosemont）

9.15　然后乐正

music（Legge，Soothill，Waley，Lau，Leys）

Book of Music（Ames/Rosemont）

11.1　先进于礼乐,后进于礼乐

　　music（Legge，Waley，Lau，Leys，Ames/Rosemont）

　　arts of civilization（Soothill）

11.24　如其礼乐

　　music（Legge，Waley，Lau，Ames/Rosemont）

　　arts of civilization（Soothill）

　　spiritual wellbeing（Leys）

13.3　则礼乐不兴;礼乐不兴

　　music（Legge，Waley，Lau，Leys）

　　harmony（Soothill）

　　playing of music（Ames/Rosemont）

14.12　文之以礼乐

　　music（Legge，Waley，Lau，Leys）

　　harmony（Soothill）

　　play music（Ames/Rosemont）

15.11　乐则韶、舞

　　music（Legge，Waley，Lau，Leys，Ames/Rosemont）

　　civil ordinances（Soothill）

16.2　则礼乐征伐自天子出……则礼乐征伐自诸侯出

　　music（Legge，Soothill，Waley，Lau，Leys，Ames/Rosemont）

17.9　乐云乐云

　　music（Legge，Soothill，Waley，Lau，Leys，Ames/Rosemont）

17.16　恶郑声之乱雅乐也

　　song（Legge）

　　music（Soothill，Waley，Lau，Leys）

　　court music（Ames/Rosemont）

17.19　三年不为乐，乐必崩……闻乐

　　　music (Legge, Soothill, Waley, Lau, Ames/Rosemont)

　　　musical performance (Leys)

18.4　齐人归女乐

　　　musician (Legge, Soothill, Waley)

　　　singing and dancing (Lau, Leys, Ames/Rosemont)

# 类(1)

15.39　有教无类

　　　distinction of class (Legge)

　　　class distinction (Soothill)

　　　kind (Waley)

　　　grade into category (Lau)

　　　all (Leys)

　　　such thing as social class (Ames/Rosemont)

# 礼(75)

1.12　礼之用……不以礼节之

　　　rules of propriety (Legge)

　　　decorum (Soothill)

　　　ritual (Waley, Leys)

　　　rite (Lau)

　　　ritual propriety (Ames/Rosemont)

1.13　恭近于礼

what is proper (Legge)

good taste (Soothill)

ritual (Waley, Leys)

observant of the rite (Lau)

ritual propriety (Ames/Rosemont)

1.15　富而好礼者也

rules of propriety (Legge)

courtesy (Soothill)

ritual (Waley)

rite (Lau)

considerate (Leys)

ritual propriety (Ames/Rosemont)

2.3　齐之以礼

rules of propriety (Legge)

decorous conduct (Soothill)

ritual (Waley, Leys)

rite (Lau)

ritual propriety (Ames/Rosemont)

2.5　事之以礼……葬之以礼,祭之以礼

propriety (Legge)

decorum (Soothill)

ritual (Waley, Leys)

rite (Lau)

ritual propriety (Ames/Rosemont)

2.23　殷因于夏礼……周因于殷礼

regulation (Legge)

civilization (Soothill)

ritual (Waley, Leys)

rite (Lau)

observances of ritual propriety (Ames/Rosemont)

3.3 如礼何

the rites of propriety (Legge)

worship (Soothill)

ritual (Waley, Leys)

rite (Lau)

observe ritual propriety (Ames/Rosemont)

3.4 林放问礼之本……礼，与其奢也

ceremony (Legge)

ceremonial observance (Soothill)

ritual (Waley, Leys)

rite (Lau)

observe ritual propriety (Ames/Rosemont)

3.8 礼后乎

ceremony (Legge)

manner (Soothill)

ritual (Waley, Leys)

practice of the rites (Lau)

observe ritual propriety (Ames/Rosemont)

3.9 夏礼……殷礼

ceremony (Legge)

civilisation (Soothill)

ritual (Waley, Leys)

rite (Lau)

ritual propriety (Ames/Rosemont)

3.15 孰谓鄹人之子知礼乎……是礼也

rules of propriety (Legge)

   correct form (Soothill)

   ritual (Waley, Leys)

   rite (Lau)

   observe ritual propriety (Ames/Rosemont)

3.17 我爱其礼

   ceremony (Legge, Soothill, Leys)

   ritual (Waley, Ames/Rosemont)

   rite (Lau)

3.18 事君尽礼

   rules of property (Legge)

   homage (Soothill)

   ritual (Waley, Leys)

   rite (Lau, Ames/Rosemont)

3.19 君使臣以礼

   rules of propriety (Legge)

   courtesy (Soothill, Leys)

   prescriptions of ritual (Waley)

   rite (Lau)

   observe ritual propriety (Ames/Rosemont)

3.22 然则管仲知礼乎……氏而知礼,孰不知礼

   rules of propriety (Legge)

   etiquette (Soothill)

   ritual (Waley, Leys, Ames/Rosemont)

   rite (Lau)

3.26 为礼不敬

   ceremony (Legge)

   religious observance (Soothill)

   ritual (Waley)

rite (Lau)

ceremony (Leys)

ritual propriety (Ames/Rosemont)

4.13 能以礼让为国乎？何有？不能以礼让为国，如礼何

rules of propriety (Legge)

forms of courtesy (Soothill)

ritual (Waley, Leys)

rite (Lau)

rules are able to effect order (Ames/Rosemont)

ritual propriety (Ames/Rosemont)

6.27 约之以礼

rules of propriety (Legge)

bounds of good taste (Soothill)

ritual (Waley, Leys)

rite (Lau)

ritual propriety (Ames/Rosemont)

7.18 《诗》、《书》、执礼

rules of propriety (Legge)

observances of decorum (Soothill)

ritual (Waley)

rite (Lau)

ceremony (Leys)

observe ritual propriety (Ames/Rosemont)

7.31 陈司败问昭公知礼乎，孔子曰："知礼……君而知礼，孰不知礼？"

propriety (Legge)

regulation (Soothill)

rite (Waley, Lau)

ritual (Leys)

observe ritual propriety (Ames/Rosemont)

8.2 恭而无礼则劳,慎而无礼则葸,勇而无礼则乱,直而无礼则绞

the rules of propriety (Legge)

law (Soothill)

prescription (Waley)

respectful (Lau)

ritual (Waley, Leys)

ritual propriety (Ames/Rosemont)

8.8 立于礼

rules of propriety (Legge)

law (Soothill)

ritual (Waley, Leys)

rite (Lau)

ritual propriety (Ames/Rosemont)

9.3 麻冕,礼也……拜下,礼也

rule (Legge)

rules of ceremony (Soothill)

ritual (Waley)

rite (Lau)

ritual (Leys)

propriety (Ames/Rosemont)

9.11 约我以礼

propriety (Legge)

reverence (Soothill)

ritual (Waley)

rite (Lau)

ritual (Leys)

ritual propriety (Ames/Rosemont)

10.4 享礼,有容色
  present (Legge, Soothill)

  gift (Waley, Lau, Leys)

  credential (Ames/Rosemont)

11.1 先进于礼乐,野人也;后进于礼乐,君子也
  ceremony (Legge)

  arts of civilization (Soothill)

  ritual (Waley)

  rite (Lau)

  knowledge of rite (Leys)

  ritual propriety (Ames/Rosemont)

11.24 如其礼乐……为国以礼
  propriety (Legge, Ames/Rosemont)

  arts of civilization (Soothill)

  right bearing (Soothill)

  rite (Waley, Lau)

  ritual (Waley)

  spiritual wellbeing (Leys)

  ritual restraint (Leys)

  ritual propriety (Ames/Rosemont)

12.1 克己复礼为仁。一日克己复礼……非礼勿视,非礼勿听,非礼勿言,非礼勿动
  propriety (Legge)

  right and proper (Soothill)

  ritual (Waley)

  rite (Lau, Leys)

  ritual propriety (Ames/Rosemont)

12.5 与人恭而有礼

propriety (Legge)

well behaved (Soothill)

ritual (Waley)

rite (Lau)

courtesy (Leys)

ritual propriety (Ames/Rosemont)

12.15 约之以礼

propriety (Legge)

good taste (Soothill)

rules of ritual (Waley)

rite (Lau)

ritual (Leys)

propriety (Ames/Rosemont)

13.3 则礼乐不兴；礼乐不兴

propriety (Legge)

order (Soothill)

rite (Waley, Lau, Leys)

observances of ritual propriety (Ames/Rosemont)

13.4 上好礼

propriety (Legge)

good manner (Soothill)

ritual (Waley)

rite (Lau, Leys)

observances of ritual propriety (Ames/Rosemont)

14.12 文之以礼乐

rules of propriety (Legge)

arts of courtesy (Soothill)

ritual (Waley)

rite (Lau, Leys)

ritual propriety (Ames/Rosemont)

14.41 上好礼

rules of propriety (Legge)

orderly behaviour (Soothill)

ritual (Waley)

rite (Lau)

civility (Leys)

ritual propriety (Ames/Rosemont)

15.18 礼以行之

rules of propriety (Legge)

courtesy (Soothill)

ritual (Waley, Leys)

rite (Lau)

ritual propriety (Ames/Rosemont)

15.33 动之不以礼

rules of propriety (Legge)

manner (Soothill)

ritual (Waley, Leys)

rite (Lau)

ritual propriety (Ames/Rosemont)

16.2 则礼乐征伐自天子出……则礼乐征伐自诸侯出

ceremony (Legge)

civil ordinances (Soothill)

orders concerning ritual (Waley)

the rite (Lau)

rite (Leys)

ritual propriety (Ames/Rosemont)

16.5　乐节礼乐

　　ceremony（Legge）

　　manner（Soothill）

　　ritual（Waley）

　　rite（Lau，Leys）

　　ritual propriety（Ames/Rosemont）

16.13　学礼乎……不学礼……鲤退而学礼……闻诗,闻礼

　　rules of propriety（Legge）

　　rules of ceremony（Soothill）

　　ritual（Waley，Leys）

　　rite（Lau，Ames/Rosemont）

17.9　礼云礼云

　　rule of propriety（Legge）

　　offering（Soothill）

　　ritual（Waley）

　　rite（Lau，Leys）

　　ritual propriety（Ames/Rosement）

17.19　君子三年不为礼,礼必坏

　　observance of propriety（Legge）

　　observance（Legge）

　　manner（Soothill）

　　rite（Waley，Lau，Ames/Rosemont）

　　ritual practice（Leys）

　　ritual propriety（Ames/Rosemont）

17.22　恶勇而无礼者

　　observant of propriety（Legge）

　　manner（Soothill，Leys）

　　ritual（Waley）

rite (Lau)

ritual propriety (Ames/Rosemont)

20.3 不知礼,无以立也

rule of propriety (Legge)

law of right demeanour (Soothill)

rite (Waley, Lau, Leys)

ritual propriety (Ames/Rosemont)

# 历数(1)

20.1 天之历数在尔躬

order of succession (Legge)

lineage (Soothill)

succession (Waley, Lau, Leys)

lines of succession (Ames/Rosemont)

# 厉(5)

7.38 子温而厉

dignified (Legge, Soothill)

firm (Waley)

stern (Lau, Leys)

serious (Ames/Rosemont)

14.39 深则厉

cross with the clothes on (Legge)

strip up to the waist (Soothill)

　　　　use the stepping stone (Waley)

　　　　go across by wading (Lau)

　　　　wade through it with one's cloth (Leys)

　　　　take the plunge (Ames/Rosemont)

17.10　色厉而内荏

　　　　stern firmness (Legge, Soothill, Ames/Rosemont)

　　　　fierceness (Waley)

　　　　brave (Lau)

　　　　fierce (Leys)

19.9　听其言也厉

　　　　firm and decided (Legge)

　　　　decided (Soothill)

　　　　incisive (Waley, Leys)

　　　　stern (Lau, Ames/Rosemont)

19.10　则以为厉己也

　　　　oppress (Legge, Soothill)

　　　　exploit (Waley, Ames/Rosemont)

　　　　ill-used (Lau, Leys)


# 立(26)

1.2　本立而道生

　　　　establish (Legge, Soothill, Lau)

　　　　set up (Waley)

　　　　secure (Leys)

　　　　take hold (Ames/Rosemont)

2.4　三十而立

stand firm (Legge, Soothill)

plant one's feet firm upon the ground (Waley)

take one's stand (Lau, Leys)

take one's stance (Ames/Rosemont)

4.14 患所以立

fit oneself for one (Legge)

fit one to occupy it (Soothill)

qualities that entitle one to office (Waley)

what would earn one a position (Lau)

deserve a position (Leys)

what it takes to have one (Ames/Rosemont)

5.8 束带立于朝

stand (Legge, Soothill, Waley, Leys)

take one's place (Lau, Ames/Rosemont)

6.30 己欲立而立人

establish (Legge, Ames/Rosemont)

maintain (Soothill)

sustain (Soothill)

stand (Waley)

take stand (Lau)

achieve (Leys)

8.8 立于礼

establish (Legge, Soothill)

give a firm footing (Waley)

stand (Lau, Ames/Rosemont)

steady (Leys)

9.11 如有所立卓尔

stand (Legge, Soothill, Waley)

rise sheer (Lau)

tower right above (Leys)

rise up (Ames/Rosemont)

9.27 与衣狐貉者立

stand (Legge, Lau, Soothill, Waley, Leys, Ames/Rosemont)

9.30 未可与立；可与立

establish (Legge)

stand (Soothill, Lau, Ames/Rosemont)

take one's stand (Waley)

commitment (Leys)

10.2 揖所与立

stand (Legge, Soothill, Leys, Ames/Rosemont)

10.3 立不中门

stand (Legge, Soothill, Lau, Leys, Ames/Rosemont)

halt (Waley)

10.8 朝服而立于阼阶

stand (Legge, Soothill, Waley, Lau, Leys, Ames/Rosemont)

10.20 必正立

stand (Legge, Soothill, Waley, Lau, Leys, Ames/Rosemont)

12.7 民无信不立

stand (Legge, Soothill, Lau, Leys)

endure (Ames/Rosemont)

15.6 立则见其参于前也

stand (Legge, Lau, Soothill, Waley, Leys, Ames/Rosemont)

15.14 知柳下惠之贤而不与立也

stand (Legge)

appoint (Soothill)

have one as one's colleague (Waley)

give one an appropriate position (Lau)

share one's position (Leys)

give one a place (Ames/Rosemont)

16.13　尝独立……又独立……无以立

stand (Legge, Soothill, Waley, Lau, Leys, Ames/Rosemont)

establish (Legge)

take one's stand (Waley, Lau, Leys)

17.8　其犹正墙面而立也与

stand (Legge, Soothill, Waley, Lau)

stick (Leys)

take stand (Ames/Rosemont)

18.7　子路拱而立

stand (Legge, Soothill, Waley, Lau, Ames/Rosemont)

19.25　所谓立之斯立

plant (Legge)

stand (Legge, Soothill, Waley, Lau, Leys)

raise (Waley, Leys)

take stand (Ames/Rosemont)

20.3　无以立也

establish (Legge)

form one's character (Soothill)

stand (Waley, Ames/Rosemont)

take one's stand (Lau, Leys)

# 利(11)

4.2　知者利仁

desire（Legge）

covet（Soothill）

persue（Waley）

advantage（Lau）

profit（Leys）

flourish（Ames/Rosemont）

4.12　放于利而行

advantage（Legge）

interest（Soothill）

expediency（Waley）

profit（Lau，Ames/Rosemont）

interest（Leys）

4.16　小人喻于利

gain（Legge）

pay（Soothill）

right（Waley）

profitable（Lau）

expedient（Leys）

advantage（Ames/Rosemont）

9.1　子罕言利与命与仁

profitableness（Legge）

profit（Soothill，Waley，Lau，Leys）

advantage（Ames/Rosemont）

13.17　无见小利……见小利

advantage（Legge，Soothill，Leys）

consideration（Waley）

gain（Lau）

opportunity（Ames/Rosemont）

14.12 见利思义

　　gain (Legge, Waley)

　　advantage (Soothill)

　　profit (Lau, Leys, Ames/Rosemont)

15.10 必先利其器

　　sharpen (Legge, Soothill, Waley, Lau, Leys, Ames/Rosemont)

17.16 恶利口之覆邦家者

　　sharp (Legge, Soothill, Waley)

　　clever (Lau)

　　glib (Leys)

　　glib tongued (Ames/Rosemont)

20.2 因民之所利而利之

　　beneficial (Legge, Lau, Leys, Ames/Rosemont)

　　benefit (Legge, Soothill, Ames/Rosemont)

　　natural resource (Soothill)

　　advantage (Waley)

　　advantageous (Waley)

　　take advantage of (Lau)

# 廉(1)

17.14 今之狂也荡；古之矜也廉

　　grave reserve (Legge)

　　reserve (Soothill)

　　stiff and formal (Waley)

　　uncompromising (Lau)

　　blunt (Leys)

smug（Ames/Rosemont）

# 谅(3)

14.17 岂若匹夫匹妇之为谅也

　　　 fidelity（Legge，Soothill）

　　　 true constancy（Waley）

　　　 petty faithfulness（Lau）

　　　 wits' end（Leys）

　　　 earnestness（Ames/Rosemont）

15.37 君子贞而不谅

　　　 firm merely（Legge）

　　　 blindly loyal（Soothill）

　　　 blind fidelity（Waley）

　　　 inflexible（Lau）

　　　 rigid（Leys）

　　　 fastidious（Ames/Rosemont）

16.4 友直, 友谅

　　　 sincere（Legge）

　　　 faithful（Soothill）

　　　 true to death（Waley）

　　　 trustworthy（Lau, Leys）

　　　 make good on one's word（Ames/Rosemont）

# 陋(3)

6.11　在陋巷
　　　mean narrow（Legge）
　　　mean（Soothill，Waley，Lau）
　　　a hovel for one's shelter（Leys）
　　　hovel（Ames/Rosemont）

9.14　陋，如之何……何陋之有
　　　rude（Legge）
　　　rudeness（Legge）
　　　uncivilized（Soothill）
　　　lack of civilization（Soothill）
　　　lack of refinement（Waley）
　　　uncouth（Lau）
　　　uncounthness（Lau）
　　　wild（Leys）
　　　crudeness（Ames/Rosemont）

# 禄(5)

2.18　子张学干禄……禄在其中矣
　　　official emolument（Legge）
　　　preferment（Soothill）
　　　han lu（Waley）
　　　reward（Waley）

official career（Lau）

official position（Leys）

career（Leys）

take office（Ames/Rosemont）

15.32　禄在其中矣

emolument（Legge，Soothill）

high pay（Waley）

salary of an official（Lau）

career（Leys）

official salary（Ames/Rosemont）

16.3　禄之去公室五世矣

revenue of the state（Legge）

revenue（Soothill）

power over the exchequer（Waley）

patronage（Lau）

authority（Leys）

ranks and emolument（Ames/Rosemont）

20.1　天禄永终

revenue（Legge）

bounty（Soothill）

gift（Waley，Leys）

honour（Lau）

charge（Ames/Rosemont）

# 乱(15)

1.2　而好作乱者

confusion (Legge)

disorder (Soothill)

revolution (Waley)

rebellion (Lau, Leys, Ames/Rosemont)

7.21 子不语怪,力,乱,神

disorder (Legge, Waley, Lau, Leys, Ames/Rosemont)

lawlessness (Soothill)

8.2 勇而无礼则乱

insubordination (Legge)

recklessness (Soothill)

timidity (Waley)

timid (Lau)

quarrelsome (Leys)

rowdiness (Ames/Rosemont)

8.10 好勇疾贫,乱也……乱也

insubordination (Legge, Lau)

desperate deed (Soothill)

[not] law abiding (Waley)

rebel (Waley, Leys)

trouble (Ames/Rosemont)

8.13 乱邦不居

disorganized (Legge)

rebellious (Soothill)

rebel (Waley)

in danger (Lau)

in turmoil (Leys)

in revolt (Ames/Rosemont)

8.15 《关雎》之乱

magnificent（Legge）

closing strains（Soothill）

flood（Waley）

come to its end（Lau）

finale（Leys）

crescendo（Ames/Rosemont）

8.20　予有乱臣十人

able（Legge，Soothill）

capable（Lau）

10.6　不及乱

confuse（Legge，Lau）

confusion（Soothill）

disorderly（Waley）

[not] clear（Leys）

drunk（Ames/Rosemont）

15.27　巧言乱德……则乱大谋

confound（Legge，Soothill，Waley）

ruin（Lau，Leys）

undermine（Ames/Rosemont）

come to naught（Ames/Rosemont）

17.7　其蔽也乱

insubordination（Legge，Soothill，Lau）

into turbulence（Waley）

degenerate（Leys）

unruliness（Ames/Rosemont）

17.16　恶郑声之乱雅乐也

confound（Legge）

pervert（Soothill）

corrupt (Waley, Lau, Leys, Ames/Rosemont)

17.21　君子有勇而无义为乱

　　　　insubordination (Legge)

　　　　rebel (Soothill, Leys)

　　　　turbulent (Waley)

　　　　make trouble (Lau)

　　　　unruly (Ames/Rosemont)

18.7　而乱大伦

　　　　confusion (Legge, Lau)

　　　　subvert (Soothill, Waley)

　　　　discard (Leys)

　　　　turmoil (Ames/Rosemont)

# 伦(2)

18.7　而乱大伦

　　　　relation (Legge)

　　　　principle (Soothill)

　　　　relationship (Waley, Ames/Rosemont)

　　　　human relationship (Lau, Leys)

18.8　言中伦

　　　　reason (Legge)

　　　　social order (Soothill)

　　　　relationship (Waley)

　　　　station (Lau)

　　　　decency (Leys)

　　　　reasonable (Ames/Rosemont)

# 慢(3)

8.4　斯远暴慢矣
　　heedlessness（Legge）
　　remissness（Soothill）
　　arrogance（Waley，Leys）
　　rancorous conduct（Ames/Rosemont）

20.2　无敢慢……慢令致期谓之贼
　　disrespect（Legge）
　　without urgency（Legge）
　　slight（Soothill，Waley）
　　remissness（Soothill）
　　dilatory（Waley）
　　neglect（Lau）
　　tardy（Lau）
　　neglect（Ames/Rosemont）
　　slow（Ames/Rosemont）

# 貌(3)

8.4　动容貌
　　deportment and manner（Legge）
　　bear（Soothill）
　　attitude（Waley，Leys）
　　countenance（Lau）

demeanor (Ames/Rosemont)

10.19 必以貌

　　ceremonious manner (Legge)

　　respect (Soothill, Lau, Leys, Ames/Rosemont)

　　attitude (Waley)

16.10 貌思恭

　　demeanour (Legge, Lau)

　　manner (Soothill, Waley)

　　attitude (Leys)

　　bearing and attitude (Ames/Rosemont)

# 美(14)

1.12 先王之道斯为美

　　excellent quality (Legge)

　　admirable feature (Soothill)

　　beauty (Waley, Leys)

　　beautiful (Lau)

　　elegant (Ames/Rosemont)

3.8 美目盼兮

　　pretty (Legge)

　　bewitching (Soothill)

　　lovely (Waley)

　　beautiful (Lau, Leys)

　　dazzling (Ames/Rosemont)

3.25 尽美矣……尽美矣

　　beautiful (Legge, Soothill, Lau, Leys, Ames/Rosemont)

beauty (Waley)

4.1 里仁为美

excellence (Legge, Soothill)

beauty (Waley)

beautiful (Lau, Leys)

greatest attraction (Ames/Rosemont)

6.16 而有宋朝之美

beauty (Legge, Soothill, Waley, Leys)

good look (Lau)

countenance (Ames/Rosemont)

8.11 如有周公之才之美

admirable (Legge, Soothill, Ames/Rosemont)

wonderful (Waley)

gifted (Lau)

splendid (Leys)

8.21 而致美乎黻冕

elegance (Legge, Soothill)

magnificence (Waley, Leys)

sacrificial (Lau)

admirable (Ames/Rosemont)

9.13 有美玉于斯

beautiful (Legge, Lau)

lovely (Soothill, Waley)

precious (Leys)

exquisite (Ames/Rosemont)

12.16 君子成人之美

admirable quality (Legge)

good (Soothill, Waley, Lau, Leys)

best（Ames/Rosemont）

13.8　苟美矣

admirable（Legge）

fine（Soothill）

beautiful（Waley）

grand（Lau）

splendid（Leys）

luxurious（Ames/Rosemont）

19.23　不见宗庙之美

beauty（Legge，Soothill，Waley）

magnificence（Lau，Ames/Rosemont）

splendor（Leys）

20.2　尊五美……何谓五美

excellent（Legge）

excellent thing（Legge）

good（Soothill）

lovely thing（Waley）

excellent practice（Lau）

treasure（Leys）

virtue（Ames/Rosemont）

# 猛(3)

7.38　威而不猛

fierce（Legge，Lau）

overbearing（Soothill，Leys）

harsh（Waley）

severe (Ames/Rosemont)

20.2　威而不猛……斯不亦威而不猛乎

　　　fierce (Legge, Lau, Leys, Ames/Rosemont)

　　　domineering (Soothill)

　　　ferocious (Waley)

　　　ferocity (Waley)

# 民(48)

1.5　使民以时

　　　people (Legge)

　　　public work (Soothill)

　　　peasantry (Waley)

　　　labour of the common people (Lau)

　　　people (Leys)

　　　common people (Ames/Rosemont)

1.9　民德归厚矣

　　　people (Legge, Soothill, Waley, Leys)

　　　common people (Lau, Ames/Rosemont)

2.3　民免而无耻

　　　people (Legge, Soothill, Waley, Leys, Ames/Rosemont)

　　　common people (Lau)

2.19　何为则民服……则民服……则民不服

　　　people (Legge, Soothill, Leys, Ames/Rosemont)

　　　common people (Waley, Lau)

2.20　使民敬

　　　people (Legge, Soothill, Leys, Ames/Rosemont)

common people (Waley, Lau)

3.21 使民战栗

people (Legge, Soothill, Leys, Ames/Rosemont)

common people (Waley, Lau)

5.16 其养民也惠,其使民也义

people (Legge, Soothill, Waley, Leys)

common people (Lau, Ames/Rosemont)

6.2 以临其民

people (Legge, Soothill, Waley, Leys, Ames/Rosemont)

common people (Lau)

6.22 务民之义

man (Legge)

humanity (Soothill)

subject (Waley)

common people (Lau)

people (Leys, Ames/Rosemont)

6.29 民鲜久矣

people (Legge, Soothill, Leys, Ames/Rosemont)

common people (Waley, Lau)

6.30 如有博施于民而能济众

people (Legge, Soothill, Leys, Ames/Rosemont)

common people (Waley, Lau)

8.1 民无得而称焉

people (Legge, Soothill, Waley, Leys, Ames/Rosemont)

common people (Lau)

8.2 则民兴于仁……则民不偷

people (Legge, Soothill, Waley, Lau, Leys, Ames/Rosemont)

8.9 民可使由之

people (Legge，Soothill，Waley，Lau，Leys，Ames/Rosemont)

8.19　民无能名焉

people (Legge，Soothill，Waley，Lau，Leys，Ames/Rosemont)

11.24　可使足民

people (Legge，Soothill，Leys，Ames/Rosemont)

common people (Waley)

population (Lau)

12.2　使民如承大祭

people (Legge，Soothill，Leys)

common people (Waley，Lau，Ames/Rosemont)

12.7　民信之矣……民无信不立

people (Legge，Soothill，Leys)

common people (Waley，Lau，Ames/Rosemont)

12.19　子欲善而民善矣

people (Legge，Soothill，Waley，Leys，Ames/Rosemont)

common people (Lau)

13.3　则民无所错手足

people (Legge，Soothill，Waley，Leys，Ames/Rosemont)

common people (Lau)

13.4　则民莫敢不敬……则民莫敢不服……则民莫敢不用情……则四方之民襁负其子而至矣

people (Legge，Soothill，Leys)

common people (Waley，Lau，Ames/Rosemont)

13.29　善人教民七年

people (Legge，Soothill，Waley，Leys，Ames/Rosemont)

common people (Lau)

13.30　以不教民战

people (Legge，Soothill，Waley，Leys，Ames/Rosemont)

common people (Lau)

14.17 民到于今受其赐

people (Legge, Soothill, Waley, Leys, Ames/Rosemont)

common people (Lau)

14.41 则民易使也

people (Legge, Soothill, Waley, Leys)

common people (Lau, Ames/Rosemont)

15.25 斯民也

people (Legge, Soothill, Leys, Ames/Rosemont)

common people (Waley, Lau)

15.33 则民不敬

people (Legge, Soothill, Leys)

common people (Waley, Lau, Ames/Rosemont)

15.35 民之于仁也

man (Legge, Soothill, Leys)

people (Waley)

common people (Lau, Ames/Rosemont)

16.9 民斯为下矣

people (Legge)

man (Soothill)

common people (Waley, Lau, Leys)

they (Ames/Rosemont)

16.12 民无德而称焉……民到于今称之

people (Legge, Soothill, Waley, Leys)

common people (Lau, Ames/Rosemont)

17.14 古者民有三疾

man (Legge)

people (Soothill)

common people（Waley，Lau，Ames/Rosemont）

ancient（Leys）

18.8　逸民

man（Legge，Soothill，Lau）

subject（Waley）

world（Leys）

people（Ames/Rosemont）

19.10　君子信而后劳其民

people（Legge，Soothill，Leys）

common people（Lau，Ames/Rosemont）

19.19　民散久矣

people（Legge，Soothill，Leys）

common people（Waley，Lau，Ames/Rosemont）

20.1　举逸民,天下之民归心焉……民、食、丧、祭……信则民任焉

people（Legge，Soothill，Waley，Leys）

the common people（Lau，Ames/Rosemont）

20.2　因民之所利而利之

people（Legge，Soothill，Waley，Leys）

common people（Lau，Ames/Rosemont）

# 民人(1)

11.23　有民人焉

common people and officer（Legge）

people and officer（Soothill）

peasant（Waley）

common people and one（Lau）

local people (Leys)

people (Ames/Rosemont)

# 敏(9)

1.14 敏于事而慎于言

　　earnest (Legge)

　　diligent (Soothill, Waley, Leys)

　　quick (Lau)

　　action (Ames/Rosemont)

4.24 讷于言而敏于行

　　earnest (Legge)

　　quick (Soothill, Lau, Ames/Rosemont)

　　prompt (Waley, Leys)

5.15 敏而好学

　　active nature (Legge)

　　clever (Soothill)

　　diligent (Waley, Ames/Rosemont)

　　quick (Lau)

　　agile mind (Leys)

7.20 敏以求之者也

　　earnest (Legge, Ames/Rosemont)

　　diligent (Soothill, Waley, Leys)

　　quick (Lau)

12.1 回虽不敏

　　intelligence and vigour (Legge)

　　clever (Soothill, Waley, Leys, Ames/Rosemont)

quick（Lau）

12.2　雍虽不敏

　　　intelligence and vigour（Legge）

　　　clever（Soothill，Waley，Leys，Ames/Rosemont）

　　　quick（Lau）

17.5　恭,宽,信,敏,惠……敏则有功

　　　earnestness（Legge，Soothill）

　　　diligence（Waley，Ames/Rosemont）

　　　quickness（Lau）

20.1　敏则有功

　　　earnest（Legge）

　　　diligence（Soothill）

　　　diligent（Waley，Ames/Rosemont）

　　　quick（Lau）

　　　industriousness（Leys）

# 名(8)

4.5　恶乎成名

　　　name（Legge，Soothill，Waley，Lau，Leys，Ames/Rosemont）

8.19　民无能名焉

　　　name（Legge，Waley，Lau）

　　　express（Soothill）

　　　bounty（Leys）

　　　accomplishment（Ames/Rosemont）

9.2　博学而无所成名

　　　name（Legge，Lau，Leys）

reputation (Soothill, Waley)

renowned (Ames/Rosemont)

13.3 必也正名乎……名不正……故君子名之必可言也

name (Legge, Lau, Leys, Ames/Rosemont)

term (Soothill)

denominate (Soothill)

language (Waley)

conceive of (Leys)

put a name to (Ames/Rosemont)

15.20 君子疾没世而名不称焉

name (Legge, Soothill, Lau, Leys, Ames/Rosemont)

reputation (Waley)

17.8 多识于鸟兽草木之名

name (Legge, Soothill, Waley, Lau, Leys)

# 命(22)

2.4 五十而知天命

decree (Legge, Lau)

law (Soothill)

bidding (Waley)

will (Leys)

propensity (Ames/Rosemont)

6.3 不幸短命死矣

appointed time (Legge)

life (Soothill)

span of life (Waley)

allotted span (Lau, Leys)

6.10 命矣夫

appointment of Heaven (Legge)

will of heaven (Soothill)

ordained (Waley)

destiny (Lau)

fate (Leys)

8.6 可以寄百里之命

authority (Legge)

command (Soothill)

sovereignty (Waley)

fate (Lau)

government (Leys)

commission (Ames/Rosemont)

9.1 子罕言利与命与仁

appointment of Heaven (Legge)

ordering of providence (Soothill)

fate (Waley, Leys)

destiny (Lau)

propensity of circumstances (Ames/Rosemont)

10.2 必复命曰

report (Legge, Waley, Lau, Ames/Rosemont)

announce (Leys)

10.14 君命召

call (Legge)

command (Soothill, Waley)

summon (Lau, Leys, Ames/Rosemont)

11.7 不幸短命死矣

appointed time (Legge)

life (Soothill, Leys)

allotted span (Waley, Lau)

11.18 赐不受命

appointment of Heaven (Legge)

lot (Soothill, Waley, Lau, Leys, Ames/Rosemont)

12.5 死生有命

determined appointment (Legge)

divine dispensation (Soothill)

heaven (Waley)

destiny (Lau)

fate (Leys)

lot (Ames/Rosemont)

13.20 不辱君命

commission (Legge, Soothill, Waley, Lau, Ames/Rosemont)

14.8 为命,裨谌草创之

governmental notification (Legge)

state document (Soothill)

ducal mandate (Waley)

text of a treaty (Lau)

edict (Leys)

diplomatic treaty (Ames/Rosemont)

14.12 见危授命

life (Legge, Soothill, Waley, Lau, Leys)

live (Ames/Rosemont)

14.36 命也……命也……公伯寮其如命何

order (Legge)

fated (Soothill)

will of heaven (Waley)

destiny (Lau)

heaven (Leys)

circumstance (Ames/Rosemont)

14.44 阙党童子将命

carry the message (Legge)

act as messenger (Soothill)

message (Waley)

visitor (Lau)

messenger (Leys)

carry message (Ames/Rosemont)

16.2 陪臣执国命

order (Legge)

command (Soothill, Ames/Rosemont)

commission (Waley)

prerogative to command (Lau)

affair (Leys)

17.18 将命者出户

message (Legge, Soothill, Waley, Lau, Leys, Ames/Rosemont)

19.1 士见危致命

life (Legge, Soothill, Waley, Lau, Leys, Ames/Rosemont)

20.1 舜亦以命禹

charge (Legge, Soothill, Waley)

command (Lau)

pass the message (Leys)

cede throne (Ames/Rosemont)

20.3 不知命

ordinances of heaven (Legge)

divine (Soothill)

will of heaven (Waley)

destiny (Lau)

fate (Leys)

circumstance (Ames/Rosemont)

# 末(6)

9.11　末由也已

　　no way (Legge, Waley, Lau)

　　never (Soothill)

　　cannot (Leys)

　　no road (Ames/Rosemont)

9.24　吾末如之何也已矣

　　do nothing (Legge, Soothill, Waley, Lau)

　　do not (Leys, Ames/Rosemont)

14.39　末之难矣

　　not (Legge, Soothill)

　　no (Lau)

15.16　吾末如之何也已矣

　　can indeed do nothing (Legge)

　　nothing whatever one can do (Soothill)

　　no possibility of one's doing anything (Waley)

　　nothing one can do (Lau)

　　do not (Leys)

　　nothing that one can do (Ames/Rosemont)

17.4　末之也

not (Legge)

nowhere (Soothill, Lau, Leys, Ames/Rosemont)

19.12 抑末也

branch (Legge, Soothill)

minor matter (Waley)

trifling matter (Lau)

trifle (Leys)

tip of the branch (Ames/Rosemont)

## *难 (22) (nán, nàn)

A. nán

2.8 色难

difficulty (Legge, Soothill)

difficult (Waley, Lau)

matter (Leys)

6.16 难乎免于今之世矣

difficult (Legge, Lau, Ames/Rosemont)

not enough (Leys)

hard (Soothill, Waley)

7.26 难乎有恒矣

difficult (Legge, Ames/Rosemont)

hard (Soothill, Lau, Leys)

content (Leys)

7.29 互乡难与言

difficult (Legge, Waley, Lau, Ames/Rosemont)

hard (Soothill)

deaf（Leys）

8.20  才难，不其然乎

difficult（Legge，Lau）

hard（Soothill，Waley）

12.3  为之难

difficulty（Legge）

difficult（Soothill，Waley，Lau，Leys，Ames/Rosemont）

13.15  为君难……如知为君之难也

difficult（Legge，Lau，Leys，Ames/Rosemont）

difficulty（Legge，Soothill，Lau，Leys，Ames/Rosemont）

hard（Soothill，Waley）

13.25  君子易事而难说也……小人难事而易说也

difficult（Legge，Soothill，Waley，Lau，Ames/Rosemont）

hard（Soothill）

[not] easy（Leys）

14.1  可以为难矣

difficult（Legge，Soothill，Waley，Lau，Leys）

hard（Ames/Rosemont）

14.10  贫而无怨难

difficult（Legge，Soothill，Lau，Leys，Ames/Rosemont）

hard（Waley）

14.20  则为之也难

difficult（Legge，Lau）

difficulty（Soothill）

beyond one's power（Waley）

hard（Leys，Ames/Rosemont）

14.39  末之难矣

difficult（Legge，Soothill）

15.17　难矣哉

　　hard（Legge，Soothill，Ames/Rosemont）

　　difficult（Waley）

　　difficulty（Lau）

17.20　难矣哉

　　hard（Legge，Soothill）

　　difficult（Waley）

　　difficulty（Lau）

　　problem（Ames/Rosemont）

17.23　唯女子与小人为难养也

　　difficult（Legge，Lau，Leys，Ames/Rosemont）

　　hard（Soothill，Waley）

19.15　吾友张也为难能也

　　hard（Legge，Waley）

　　hardly possible（Soothill）

　　difficult（Lau）

　　rare ability（Leys）

　　laudable in ability（Ames/Rosemont）

19.16　难与并为仁矣

　　difficult（Legge，Lau，Ames/Rosemont）

　　hard（Soothill，Waley）

　　not easy（Leys）

19.18　是难能也

　　difficult（Legge，Lau，Ames/Rosemont）

　　hardly possible（Soothill）

　　hard（Waley）

B. nàn

6.22　仁者先难而后获

difficulty (Legge, Lau, Ames/Rosemont)

difficult (Soothill, Waley)

trials (Leys)

16.10 忿思难

question other (Legge)

seek information (Soothill)

ask for information (Waley)

in doubt (Lau)

question (Leys)

questions to ask (Ames/Rosemont)

# 佞(10)

5.5 雍也仁而不佞……焉用佞……焉用佞

ready with the tongue (Legge)

readiness of the tongue (Legge)

ready of speech (Soothill)

ready speech (Soothill)

good talker (Waley)

facile tongue (Lau)

eloquence (Leys, Ames/Rosemont)

6.16 不有祝鮀之佞

smooth tongue (Lau)

agile tongue (Leys)

authoritative conduct (Ames/Rosemont)

11.23 是故恶夫佞者

glib tongued (Legge)

glib（Soothill，Waley，Ames/Rosemont）

plausible（Lau）

wit（Leys）

14.32 无乃为佞乎……非敢为佞也

insinuating talker（Legge）

adcaptandum talker（Soothill）

clever talker（Waley）

flattery（Lau）

clever tongue（Leys）

eloquent talker（Ames/Rosemont）

15.11 远佞人……佞人殆

specious talker（Legge）

specious man（Soothill）

clever talker（Waley，Leys）

plausible man（Lau）

glib talker（Ames/Rosemont）

16.4 友便佞

glib-tongued（Legge）

glib（Soothill，Leys）

clever at talk（Waley）

plausible in speech（Lau）

glib talker（Ames/Rosemont）

# 怒(1)

6.3 不迁怒

anger（Legge, Soothill, Lau, Ames/Rosemont）

wrath (Waley)

frustration (Leys)

## 虐(1)

20.2　不教而杀谓之虐
　　　cruelty (Legge，Soothill)
　　　savagery (Waley)
　　　cruel (Lau，Ames/Rosemont)
　　　terror (Leys)

## 朋(1)

1.1　有朋自远方来
　　　friend (Legge，Waley，Leys，Ames/Rosemont)
　　　man of kindred spirit (Soothill)
　　　like minded friend (Lau)

## 朋友(8)

1.4　与朋友交而不信乎
　　　friend (Legge, Soothill, Waley, Lau, Leys, Ames/Rosemont)
1.7　与朋友交言而有信
　　　friend (Legge, Soothill, Waley, Lau, Leys)
　　　colleague and friend (Ames/Rosemont)

4.26　朋友数

　　friend（Legge，Soothill，Lau）

　　friendship（Waley，Ames/Rosemont）

　　friendly（Leys）

5.26　与朋友共敝之而无憾……朋友信之

　　friend（Legge，Soothill，Waley，Lau，Leys，Ames/Rosemont）

10.16　朋友死

　　friend（Legge，Soothill，Waley，Lau，Leys，Ames/Rosemont）

10.17　朋友之馈

　　friend（Legge，Soothill，Waley，Lau，Leys，Ames/Rosemont）

13.28　朋友切切偲偲

　　friend（Legge，Soothill，Waley，Lau，Leys，Ames/Rosemont）

# 贫(9)

1.15　贫而无谄……未若贫而乐道

　　poor（Legge，Soothill，Waley，Lau，Leys，Ames/Rosemont）

4.5　贫与贱

　　poverty（Legge，Soothill，Waley，Lau，Leys，Ames/Rosemont）

8.10　好勇疾贫

　　poverty（Legge，Soothill，Waley，Lau，Leys，Ames/Rosemont）

8.13　贫且贱焉

　　poverty（Legge）

　　needy（Soothill，Waley）

　　poor（Lau，Leys，Ames/Rosemont）

14.10　贫而无怨难

　　poor（Legge，Soothill，Waley，Lau，Leys，Ames/Rosemont）

15.32 君子忧道不忧贫

　　　　poverty（Legge，Soothill，Waley，Lau，Ames/Rosemont）

　　　　poor（Leys）

16.1　不患寡而患不均，不患贫而患不安。盖均无贫

　　　　poverty（Legge，Soothill，Waley，Lau，Leys，Ames/Rosemont）

　　　　few（Waley）

　　　　poor（Ames/Rosemont）

\* 齐(10)（qí，zhāi，zī）

A. qí

2.3　齐之以刑……齐之以礼

　　　　uniformity（Legge）

　　　　keep in order（Soothill）

　　　　keep order（Waley）

　　　　keep in line（Lau）

　　　　restrain（Leys）

　　　　keep orderly（Ames/Rosemont）

4.17　见贤思齐焉

　　　　equal（Legge）

　　　　rise to one's level（Soothill）

　　　　equal（Waley）

　　　　as good as（Lau）

　　　　emulate（Leys）

　　　　stand shoulder to shoulder with（Ames/Rosemont）

10.6　必齐如也

　　　　grave（Legge）

solemnity (Soothill, Ames/Rosemont)

solemnly (Waley, Lau)

devoutly (Leys)

B. zhāi

7.13 齐,战,疾

fasting (Legge, Soothill, Lau, Leys, Ames/Rosemont)

purification before sacrifice (Waley)

10.5 齐,必有明衣

fasting (Legge, Soothill)

prepare oneself for sacrifice (Waley)

purification (Lau)

abstinence (Leys)

purification (Ames/Rosemont)

10.6 齐,必变食

fasting (Legge, Soothill)

prepare oneself for sacrifice (Waley)

purification (Lau)

abstinence (Leys)

purification (Ames/Rosemont)

C. zī

9.10 子见齐衰者

mourn (Legge, Soothill, Waley, Lau, Leys, Ames/Rosemont)

10.3 摄齐升堂

robe (Legge, Lau)

skirt (Soothill, Waley)

hem of gown (Leys)

hem of skirt (Ames/Rosemont)

10.19 见齐衰者

mourn (Legge，Soothill，Waley，Lau，Leys，Ames/Rosemont)

## 祇(1)

7.35　祷尔于上下神祇
　　　spirits (Legge，Soothill，Waley，Leys)
　　　gods (Lau，Ames/Rosemont)

## 器(6)

2.12　君子不器
　　　utensil (Legge)
　　　machine (Soothill)
　　　implement (Waley)
　　　vessel (Lau，Ames/Rosemont)
　　　pot (Leys)

3.22　管仲之器小哉
　　　capacity (Legge，Waley，Lau，Ames/Rosemont)
　　　calibre (Soothill，Leys)

5.4　女,器也……何器也
　　　utensil (Legge)
　　　vessel (Soothill，Waley，Lau，Ames/Rosemont)
　　　pot (Leys)

13.25　及其使人也,器之
　　　according to one's capacity (Legge)
　　　regard to one's capacity (Soothill)

what one is capable of performing (Waley)

within the limits of one's capacity (Lau)

never demand anything that is beyond one's capacity (Leys)

according to one's ability (Ames/Rosemont)

15.10 必先利其器

tool (Legge, Soothill, Waley, Lau, Leys, Ames/Rosemont)

# 亲(9)

1.6 而亲仁

cultivate the friendship (Legge)

ally (Soothill)

intimacy (Waley)

cultivate the friendship (Lau)

associate (Leys)

intimate (Ames/Rosemont)

1.13 因不失其亲

intimate (Legge)

friend (Soothill)

kin (Waley)

kinsman (Lau, Leys)

close (Ames/Rosemont)

8.2 君子笃于亲

relation (Legge)

family (Soothill)

kin (Waley, Leys)

parent (Lau, Ames/Rosemont)

10.20 不亲指

  one's (Legge, Soothill, Waley)

12.21 以及其亲

  parent (Legge, Lau, Ames/Rosemont)

  relative (Soothill)

  kith and kin (Waley)

  kin (Leys)

17.6 亲于其身为不善者

  in one's own person (Legge, Waley, Lau)

  personally (Soothill, Leys, Ames/Rosemont)

18.10 君子不施其亲

  relation (Legge)

  relative (Soothill)

  kinsmen (Waley)

  those closely related to (Lau)

  relative (Leys)

  family relation (Ames/Rosemont)

19.17 必也亲丧乎

  parent (Legge, Soothill, Lau, Leys, Ames/Rosemont)

  father or mother (Waley)

20.1 虽有周亲

  relative (Legge)

  closely related (Soothill)

  kinsman (Waley, Lau)

  closely relatives (Leys)

  immediate relatives (Ames/Rosemont)

# 清(2)

5.19　子曰:"清矣。"
　　　　pure (Legge, Lau, Leys)
　　　　clean handed (Soothill)
　　　　scrupulous (Waley)
　　　　incorruptible (Ames/Rosemont)

18.8　身中清
　　　　purity (Legge, Soothill, Lau)
　　　　integrity (Waley)
　　　　pure (Leys)
　　　　flawless (Ames/Rosemont)

# 情(2)

13.4　则民莫敢不用情
　　　　sincere (Legge, Soothill)
　　　　[not] depart from facts (Waley)
　　　　true colour (Lau)
　　　　[not] mendacious (Leys)
　　　　[not] duplicitous (Ames/Rosemont)

19.19　如得其情
　　　　truth (Legge, Lau)
　　　　discovery (Soothill)
　　　　evidence (Waley)

what really happens（Ames/Rosemont）

# 穷(4)

15.2　君子亦有穷乎……君子固穷……小人穷斯滥矣

want（Legge，Soothill）

in want（Legge，Soothill）

strait（waley）

hardship（Waley）

extreme strait（Lau）

distress（Leys）

adversity（Ames/Rosemont）

20.1　四海困穷

want（Legge）

lean（Soothill）

dry（Waley）

strait（Lau，Ames/Rosemont）

penury（Leys）

# 权(3)

9.30　未可与权

weigh occurring event（Legge）

associate in judgment（Soothill）

join in counsel（Waley）

exercise of moral discretion（Lau）

share counsel（Leys）

weigh things up（Ames/Rosemont）

18.8　废中权

exigency of the times（Legge）

weighty cause（Soothill）

due balance（Waley）

measure（Lau）

self-effacement（Leys）

discretion（Ames/Rosemont）

20.1　谨权量

weight（Legge，Soothill，Waley，Lau，Leys）

scale（Ames/Rosemont）

# 群(4)

15.17　群居终日

a number of people（Legge）

associate together（Soothill）

together（Waley，Lau，Leys）

get together（Ames/Rosemont）

15.22　群而不党

sociable（Legge，Soothill，Leys）

ally（Waley）

come together（Lau）

gather together（Ames/Rosemont）

17.8　可以群

sociability（Legge）

social intercourse (Soothill)

live in a community (Lau)

communion (Leys)

get on with others (Ames/Rosemont)

18.6　鸟兽不可与同群

associate with (Legge, Lau, Leys)

herd with (Soothill, Waley)

run with (Ames/Rosemont)

# 让(7)

1.10　温、良、恭、俭、让以得之

complaisant (Legge)

deferential (Soothill, Waley, Lau, Leys)

unassuming (Ames/Rosemont)

3.7　揖让而升

complaisantly (Legge)

yield (Soothill)

make way for (Waley, Lau, Ames/Rosemont)

exchange civility (Leys)

4.13　能以礼让为国乎……不能以礼让为国

deference (Stoothill, Lau, Leys)

yield (Waley)

defer to other (Ames/Rosemont)

8.1　三以天下让

decline (Legge)

leave (Soothill)

　　　　renounce (Waley, Leys, Ames/Rosemont)

　　　　abdicate (Lau)

11.24　其言不让

　　　　humble (Legge)

　　　　modesty (Soothill, Lau)

　　　　cession (Waley)

　　　　[not] swagger (Leys)

　　　　deference (Ames/Rosemont)

15.36　不让于师

　　　　yield (Legge, Lau, Ames/Rosemont)

　　　　give way (Soothill)

　　　　avoid competing with (Waley)

　　　　be afraid to (Leys)

# 仁(109)

1.2　其为仁之本与

　　　　benevolent action (Legge)

　　　　unselfish life (Soothill)

　　　　goodness (Waley)

　　　　character (Lau)

　　　　humanity (Leys)

　　　　authoritative conduct (Ames/Rosemont)

1.3　鲜矣仁

　　　　true virtue (Legge)

　　　　virtue (Soothill)

　　　　good (Waley)

benevolent（Lau）

goodness（Leys）

authoritative conduct（Ames/Rosemont）

1.6 而亲仁

good（Legge，Soothill，Waley）

one's fellow man（Lau）

virtuous（Leys）

conduct（Ames/Rosemont）

3.3 人而不仁……人而不仁

virtue（Legge）

virtuous（Soothill）

good（Waley）

benevolent（Lau）

humanity（Leys）

authoritative（Ames/Rosemont）

4.1 里仁为美。择不处仁

virtuous manner（Legge）

moral character（Soothill）

moral（Soothill）

goodness（Waley）

good（Waley）

benevolence（Lau）

humanity（Leys）

authoritative person（Ames/Rosemont）

4.2 不仁者不可以久处约……仁者安仁,知者利仁

virtuous（Legge, Soothill）

virtue（Legge，Soothill）

good（Waley, Leys）

benevolent (Lau)

benevolence (Lau)

authoritative (Ames/Rosemont)

4.3 唯仁者能好人

virtuous (Legge，Soothill)

good (Waley，Leys)

benevolent (Lau)

authoritative (Ames/Rosemont)

4.4 苟志于仁矣

virtue (Legge，Soothill)

goodness (Waley)

benevolence (Lau)

humanity (Leys)

authoritative conduct (Ames/Rosemont)

4.5 君子去仁……君子无终食之间违仁

virtue (Legge，Soothill)

goodness (Waley)

benevolence (Lau)

principle (Leys)

humanity (Leys)

authoritative conduct (Ames/Rosemont)

4.6 我未见好仁者，恶不仁者。好仁者……恶不仁者，其为仁矣，不使不仁者加乎其身。有能一日用其力于仁矣乎

virtue (Legge，Soothill)

virtuous (Legge，Soothill)

goodness (Waley，Leys)

good (Waley)

benevolence (Lau)

benevolent（Lau）

authoritative（Ames/Rosemont）

4.7　斯知仁矣

virtuous（Legge）

virtue（Soothill）

goodness（Waley）

one's quality（Leys）

authoritative（Ames/Rosemont）

5.5　雍也仁而不佞……不知其仁

truly virtuous（Legge）

virtuous（Soothill）

virtue（Soothill）

good（Waley，Leys）

benevolent（Lau）

authoritative（Ames/Rosemont）

5.8　孟武伯问子路仁乎？……不知其仁也……不知其仁也……不知其仁也

perfectly virtuous（Legge）

virtue（Soothill）

good（Waley，Leys）

benevolent（Lau）

authoritative（Ames/Rosemont）

authoritative person（Ames/Rosemont）

5.19　仁矣乎……焉得仁……仁矣乎……焉得仁

virtuous（Legge）

virtue（Soothill）

good（Waley，Leys）

benevolent（Lau）

authoritative conduct（Ames/Rosemont）

abtoritative（Ames/Rosemont）

6.7　其心三月不违仁

virtue（Legge，Soothill）

goodness（Waley，Leys）

benevolence（Lau）

authoritative（Ames/Rosemont）

6.22　问仁。曰："仁者先难而后获,可谓仁矣。"

perfect virtue（Legge）

virtue（Legge，Soothill）

goodness（Waley，Leys）

good（Waley，Leys）

benevolence（Lau）

benevolent（Lau）

authoritative（Ames/Rosemont）

authoritative conduct（Ames/Rosemont）

6.23　仁者乐山。知者动,仁者静。知者乐,仁者寿。

virtuous（Legge，Soothill）

good（Waley，Leys）

benevolent（Lau）

authoritative（Ames/Rosemont）

6.26　仁者……井有仁焉

benevolent（Legge，Lau）

altruist（Soothill）

good（Waley，Leys）

authoritative（Ames/Rosemont）

6.30　可谓仁乎……何事于仁……夫仁者……可谓仁之方也已

virtuous（Legge）

virtue（Legge）

philanthropist（Soothill）

philanthropy（Soothill）

good（Waley，Leys）

goodness（Waley，Leys）

benevolence（Lau）

benevolent（Lau）

authoritative（Ames/Rosemont）

authoritative conduct（Ames/Rosemont）

7.6　依于仁

perfect virtue（Legge）

kindness（Soothill）

goodness（Waley）

benevolence（Lau）

goodness（Leys）

authoritative conduct（Ames/Rosemont）

7.15　求仁而得仁

virtuously（Legge）

virtue（Soothill）

goodness（Waley，Leys）

benevolence（Lau）

authoritative in one's conduct（Ames/Rosemont）

7.30　仁远乎哉？我欲仁，斯仁至矣

virtue（Legge，Soothill，Waley）

benevolence（Lau）

goodness（Leys）

authoritative conduct（Ames/Rosemont）

7.34　若圣与仁

  perfect virtue（Legge）

  virtue（Soothill）

  good（Waley）

  benevolent（Lau）

  human perfection（Leys）

  authoritative（Ames/Rosemont）

8.2 则民兴于仁

  virtue（Legge）

  kindness（Soothill）

  goodness（Waley，Leys）

  benevolence（Lau）

  authoritative conduct（Ames/Rosemont）

8.7 仁以为己任

  perfect virtue（Legge）

  virtue（Soothill）

  goodness（Waley）

  benevolence（Lau）

  humanity（Leys）

  authoritative conduct（Ames/Rosemont）

8.10 人而不仁，疾之已甚

  virtuous（Legge）

  moral character（Soothill）

  truly good（Waley）

  benevolent（Lau）

  morality（Leys）

9.1 子罕言利与命与仁

  perfect（Legge）

  perfection（Soothill）

goodness（Waley）

benevolence（Lau）

humanity（Leys）

authoritative conduct（Ames/Rosemont）

9.29 仁者不忧

virtuous（Legge，Soothill）

good（Waley，Leys）

benevolence（Lau）

authoritative（Ames/Rosemont）

12.1 颜渊问仁……克己复礼为仁……天下归仁焉。为仁由己

perfect virtue（Legge）

virtue（Soothill）

goodness（Waley）

benevolence（Lau）

humanity（Leys）

authoritative（Ames/Rosemont）

12.2 仲问仁

virtue（Legge，Soothill）

goodness（Waley）

benevolence（Lau）

humanity（Leys）

authoritative conduct（Ames/Rosemont）

12.3 司马牛问仁……仁者……斯谓之仁已乎

perfect virtue（Legge）

virtue（Soothill）

goodness（Waley）

good（Waley）

benevolence（Lau）

humanity（Leys）

authoritative conduct（Ames/Rosemont）

12.20　色取仁而行违

virtue（Legge）

magnanimity（Soothill）

goodness（Waley）

benevolence（Lau）

virtue（Leys）

authoritative（Ames/Rosemont）

12.22　樊迟问仁……不仁者远矣……不仁者远矣

benevolence（Legge）

virtue（Soothill）

good（Waley）

benevolence（Lau）

humanity（Leys）

authoritative（Ames/Rosemont）

12.24　以友辅仁

virtue（Legge）

goodness of character（Soothill）

goodness（Waley）

benevolence（Lau）

humanity（Leys）

authoritative conduct（Ames/Rosemont）

13.12　必世而后仁

virtue（Legge，Soothill）

goodness（Waley）

benevolence（Lau）

humanity（Leys）

authoritative conduct（Ames/Rosemont）

13.19　樊迟问仁

perfect virtue（Legge）

virtue（Soothill）

goodness（Waley）

benevolence（Lau）

humanity（Leys）

authoritative conduct（Ames/Rosemont）

13.27　刚、毅、木、讷近仁

virtue（Legge，Soothill）

goodness（Waley）

benevolence（Lau）

humanity（Leys）

authoritative conduct（Ames/Rosemont）

14.1　可以为仁矣……仁则吾不知也

perfect virtue（Legge）

virtue（Soothill）

good（Waley）

benevolent（Lau）

humanity（Leys）

authoritative（Ames/Rosemont）

14.4　仁者必有勇，勇者不必有仁

principle（Legge）

virtuous（Soothill）

good（Waley，Leys）

benevolent（Lau）

authoritative（Ames/Rosemont）

14.6　君子而不仁者有矣夫，未有小人而仁者也

        virtuous（Legge，Soothill）

        goodness（Waley）

        benevolent（Lau）

        humanity（Leys）

        authoritative（Ames/Rosemont）

14.16　未仁乎……如其仁，如其仁

        virtue（Legge，Soothill）

        goodness（Waley）

        benevolence（Lau）

        human quality（Leys）

        authoritative（Ames/Rosemont）

14.17　管仲非仁者与

        virtue（Legge，Soothill）

        good（Waley）

        benevolent（Lau）

        principle（Leys）

        authoritative（Ames/Rosemont）

14.28　仁者不忧

        virtuous（Legge，Soothill）

        good（Waley）

        benevolence（Lau）

        humanity（Leys）

        authoritative（Ames/Rosemont）

15.9　志士仁人，无求生以害仁，有杀身以成仁

        virtue（Legge，Soothill）

        virtuous（Soothill）

        good（Waley）

        goodness（Waley）

benevolence (Lau)

humanity (Leys)

authoritative (Ames/Rosemont)

15.10 子贡问为仁……友其士之仁者

virtue (Legge, Soohtill)

virtuous (Legge, Soothill)

good (Waley)

benevolence (Lau)

benevolent gentlemen (Lau)

humanity (Leys)

gentlemen (Leys)

conduct (Ames/Rosemont)

scholar apprentice (Ames/Rosemont)

15.33 仁不能守之……仁能守之……仁能守之

virtue (Legge)

moral character (Soothill)

goodness (Waley, Leys)

benevolence (Lau)

authoritative (Ames/Rosemont)

15.35 民之于仁也……未见蹈仁而死者也

virtue (Legge, Soothill)

goodness (Waley)

benevolence (Lau)

humanity (Leys)

authoritative conduct (Ames/Rosemont)

15.36 当仁,不让于师

virtue (Legge)

moral duty (Soothill)

goodness (Waley)

benevolence (Lau)

virtue (Leys)

authoritative (Ames/Rosemont)

17.1 可谓仁乎

benevolent (Legge, Lau)

lover of fellow man (Soothill)

good (Waley)

virtuous (Leys)

authoritative (Ames/Rosemont)

17.5 子张问仁于孔子……能行五者于天下为仁矣

perfect virtue (Legge)

virtue (Soothill)

goodness (Waley)

good (Waley)

benevolence (Lau)

benevolent (Lau)

humanity (Leys)

authoritative (Ames/Rosemont)

17.7 好仁不好学

benevolent (Legge)

kindness (Soothill)

goodness (Waley)

benevolence (Lau)

humanity (Leys)

authoritative (Ames/Rosemont)

17.15 巧言令色,鲜矣仁

virtue (Legge, Soothill)

good (Waley)

benevolent (Lau)

goodness (Leys)

authoritative conduct (Ames/Rosemont)

17.19 予之不仁也

virtue (Legge)

feelingness (Soothill)

feeling (Waley)

human (Lau)

humanity (Leys)

perverse (ren) (Ames/Rosemont)

18.1 殷有三仁焉

virtue († Legge, Soothill)

good man (Waley)

benevolent (Lau)

models of humanity (Leys)

authoritative person (Ames/Rosemont)

19.6 仁在其中矣

virtue (Legge, Soothill)

goodness (Waley)

benevolence (Lau)

humanity (Leys)

authoritative conduct (Ames/Rosemont)

19.15 然而未仁

virtuous (Legge)

virtue (Soothill)

good (Waley)

benevolence (Lau)

humanity (Leys)

authoritative (Ames/Rosemont)

19.16　难与并为仁矣

virtue (Legge)

perfect (Soothill)

good (Waley)

benevolence (Lau)

humanity (Leys)

authoritative in one's conduct (Ames/Rosemont)

20.1　不如仁人

virtue (Soothill)

good (Waley)

benevolent (Lau)

virtuous (Leys)

trust (Leys)

authoritative person (Ames/Rosemont)

20.2　欲仁而得仁

benevolent (Legge)

good (Soothill)

goodness (Waley)

benevolence (Lau)

humanity (Leys)

authoritative (Ames/Rosemont)

# 忍(3)

3.1　是可忍也,孰不可忍也

bear (Legge，Soothill)

endure (Waley)

tolerate (Lau)

capable of (Leys)

condone (Ames/Rosemont)

15.27 小不忍

forbearance (Legge)

impatience (Soothill，Waley，Leys)

self restraint (Lau)

impatient (Ames/Rosemont)

# 任(4)

8.7 任重而道远。仁以为己任

burden (Legge，Waley，Lau，Leys)

sustain (Legge)

load (Soothill)

charge (Ames/Rosemont)

17.5 信则人任焉

trust (Legge，Soothill，Waley，Leys)

entrust (Lau)

rely upon (Ames/Rosemont)

20.1 信则民任焉

trust (Legge，Waley，Leys)

confidence (Soothill)

entrust (Lau)

rely upon (Ames/Rosemont)

# 容(6)

8.4 动容貌
　　deportment (Legge)
　　bear (Soothill)
　　attitude (Waley, Leys)
　　countenance (Lau)
　　demeanor (Ames/Rosemont)

10.3 如不容
　　admit (Legge, Soothill, Lau)
　　have room (Waley)
　　high enough (Ames/Rosemont)

10.4 有容色
　　appearance (Legge)
　　look (Soothill)
　　expression (Lau, Leys, Waley)
　　countenance (Ames/Rosemont)

10.18 居不容
　　put on any formal deportment (Legge)
　　wear formal air (Soothill)
　　use ritual attitudes (Waley)
　　sit in the formal manner of a guest (Lau)
　　sit stiffly like a guest (Leys)
　　kneel in a formal posture as though entertaining guests (Ames/Rosemont)

19.3 君子尊贤而容众……于人何所不容

bear with (Legge)

tolerate (Soothill, Leys)

find room (Waley)

tolerant (Lau, Ames/Rosemont)

## 儒(2)

6.13 女为君子儒! 无为小人儒

scholar (Legge, Soothill)

ju (Waley, Lau)

noble scholar (Leys)

counselor (Ames/Rosemont)

## 辱(6)

1.13 远耻辱也

disgrace (Legge, Soothill, Lau, Leys)

dishonor (Waley)

insult (Ames/Rosemont)

4.26 斯辱矣

disgrace (Legge, Soothill, Leys, Ames/Rosemont)

loss of favour (Waley)

humiliation (Lau)

12.23 毋自辱焉

disgrace (Legge, Ames/Rosemont)

humiliation (Soothill, Waley)

snubbed (Lau)

rebuff (Leys)

13.20　不辱君命

disgrace (Legge, Soothill, Waley, Lau, Leys, Ames/Rosemont)

18.8　不辱其身……降志辱身矣

taint (Legge)

abase (Soothill)

bring humiliation upon (Waley)

humiliate (Lau)

insult (Leys)

bring disgrace (Ames/Rosemont)


\* 丧(22)(sāng, sàng)


A. sāng

3.4　丧,与其易也

mourning (Legge, Soothill, Waley, Lau, Ames/Rosemont)

funeral (Leys)

3.26　临丧不哀

mourning (Legge, Soothill, Waley, Lau, Leys)

mourning rite (Ames/Rosemont)

7.9　子食于有丧者之侧

mourner (Legge, Soothill)

mourning (Waley, Leys, Ames/Rosemont)

bereaved (Lau)

9.16　丧事不敢不勉

duties to the dead (Legge)

duties to one's fathers and brethren (Soothill)

mourning (Waley)

funeral (Lau)

bury the dead (Leys)

funerary (Ames/Rosemont)

10.5 去丧，无所不佩

mourning (Legge, Soothill, Waley, Lau)

funeral (Leys, Ames/Rosemont)

17.19 三年之丧……夫君子之居丧……夫三年之丧，天下之通丧也

mourning (Legge, Soothill, Waley, Lau, Leys, Ames/Rosemont)

19.1 丧思哀

mouring (Legge, Soothill, Waley, Lau)

mourn (Leys)

funeral (Ames/Rosemont)

19.14 丧致乎哀而止

mourning (Legge, Soothill, Waley, Lau, Leys, Ames/Rosemont)

19.17 必也亲丧乎

mourning (Legge, Waley, Lau, Leys, Ames/Rosemont)

mourn (Soothill)

20.1 民、食、丧、祭

mourning (Legge, Soothill, Waley, Lau, Leys, Ames/Rosemont)

B. sàng

3.24 二三子何患于丧乎

loss of office (Legge, Soothill, Lau)

failure (Waley)

dismissal (Leys)

loss (Ames/Rosemont)

9.5 天之将丧斯文也，天之未丧斯文也

perish (Legge)

destroy (Soothill, Waley, Lau, Leys, Ames/Rosemont)

disappear (Waley)

11.9 天丧予！天丧予

destroy (Legge, Leys)

bereft (Soothill, Waley, Lau)

ruin (Ames/Rosemont)

13.15 一言而丧邦……不几乎一言而丧邦乎

ruin (Legge, Soothill, Waley, Lau, Leys, Ames/Rosemont)

14.19 奚而不丧……奚其丧

grief (Waley)

lose (Legge, Soothill, Lau, Leys)

ruin (Ames/Rosemont)

## 色(27)

1.3 巧言令色

appearance (Legge, Ames/Rosemont)

demeanour (Soothill)

manner (Waley)

countenance (Lau)

manner (Leys)

1.7 贤贤易色

love of beauty (Legge)

feminine allurement (Soothill)

air of respect (Waley)

countenance (Lau)

look（Leys）

beauty（Ames/Rosemont）

2.8　子曰:色难

countenance（Legge，Ames/Rosemont）

demeanour（Soothill，Waley）

expression（Lau）

attitude（Leys）

5.19　无喜色……无愠色

countance（Legge）

sign（Soothill，Waley）

appearance（Lau）

face（Ames/Rosemont）

5.25　巧言、令色

appearance（Legge）

demeanour（Soothill）

manner（Waley）

countenance（Lau，Ames/Rosemont）

affectation（Leys）

8.4　正颜色

countenance（Legge，Ames/Rosemont）

look（Soothill，Waley）

expression（Lau，Leys）

9.18　吾未见好德如好色者也

beauty（Legge）

woman（Soothill）

sexual desire（Waley）

beauty in woman（Lau）

sex（Leys）

physical beauty（Ames/Rosemont）

10.2　色勃如也

countenance（Legge）

expression（Soothill，Lau）

look（Waley）

countenance（Ames/Rosemont）

10.3　色勃如也……逞颜色

countenance（Legge）

expression（Soothill，Lau，Leys，Ames/Rosemont）

look（Waley）

10.4　勃如战色……有容色

countenance（Legge）

expression（Soothill，Waley，Lau，Leys）

demeanor（Ames/Rosemont）

10.6　色恶,不食

colour（Legge，Soothill，Waley，Lau，Leys，Ames/Rosemont）

10.19　必变色而作

countenance（Legge，Leys）

expression（Soothill，Waley，Lau）

appearance（Ames/Rosemont）

10.21　色斯举矣

countenance（Legge）

face（Soothill）

sign（Waley）

approach（Ames/Rosemont）

11.19　色庄者乎

appearance（Legge，Soothill，Lau）

outward（Waley）

pretense（Leys）

pretend（Ames/Rosemont）

12.20　察言而观色……色取仁而行违

countenance（Legge）

appearance（Legge，Ames/Rosemont）

expression（Soothill，Waley，Lau，Leys）

air（Soothill，Leys）

outward（Waley）

facade（Lau）

demeanor（Ames/Rosemont）

14.8　东里子产润色之

elegance（Legge）

embellish（Soothill，Lau）

colour（Waley）

polish（Leys）

final touches（Ames/Rosemont）

14.37　其次辟色

disrespectful look（Legge）

uncongenial look（Soothill）

look（Waley）

hostile look（Lau）

attitude（Leys）

decadent manner（Ames/Rosemont）

15.13　吾未见好德如好色者也

beauty（Legge，Soothill，Lau）

sexual desire（Waley）

sex（Leys）

physical beauty（Ames/Rosemont）

16.6 未见颜色而言谓之瞽

   countenance（Legge，Ames/Rosemont）

   expression（Soothill，Waley，Lau，Leys）

16.7 戒之在色

   lust（Legge，Soothill，Waley，Leys）

   attraction of feminine beauty（Lau）

   licentiousness（Ames/Rosemont）

16.10 色思温

   countenance（Legge，Ames/Rosemont，Lau）

   appearance（Soothill）

   look（Waley）

   expression（Leys）

17.10 色厉而内荏

   appearance（Legge，Soothill，Ames/Rosemont）

   outward（Waley）

   front（Lau）

   look（Leys）

17.15 巧言令色

   appearance（Legge，Ames/Rosemont）

   demeanour（Soothill）

   manner（Waley，Leys）

   countenance（Lau）

# 杀(9)

10.5 必杀之

   cut（Legge，Lau，Leys）

shape（Soothill）

tailor（Ames/Rosemont）

12.19 如杀无道……焉用杀

kill（Legge，Lau，Ames/Rosemont，Leys）

execute（Soothill）

slay（Waley）

13.11 亦可以胜残去杀矣

capital punishment（Legge，Soothill）

slaughter（Waley）

kill（Lau，Ames/Rosemont）

murder（Leys）

14.16 桓公杀公子纠

kill（Legge，Lau，Leys，Ames/Rosemont）

put to death（Soothill，Waley）

14.17 桓公杀公子纠

kill（Legge，Lau，Leys，Ames/Rosemont）

put to death（Soothill，Waley）

15.9 有杀身以成仁

sacrifice（Legge，Soothill）

give one's life（Waley，Leys）

accept death（Lau）

give up（Ames/Rosemont）

18.7 杀鸡为黍而食之

kill（Legge，Soothill，Waley，Lau，Leys，Ames/Rosemont）

20.2 不教而杀谓之虐

death（Legge，Soothill，Waley）

death penalty（Lau）

murder（Leys）

execute（Ames/Rosemont）

# 善(37)

2.20　举善而教不能则劝

　　　good（Legge，Leys，Lau）

　　　excel（Soothill）

　　　worthy（Waley）

　　　adept（Ames/Rosemont）

3.25　又尽善也……未尽善也

　　　good（Legge，Soothill，Lau，Leys）

　　　goodness（Waley）

　　　felicitous（Ames/Rosemont）

5.17　晏平仲善与人交

　　　know well（Legge）

　　　gifted（Soothill）

　　　good example（Waley）

　　　excel（Lau）

　　　know（Leys）

　　　good（Ames/Rosemont）

5.26　愿无伐善

　　　excellence（Legge）

　　　good（Soothill，Waley，Lau，Leys）

　　　ability（Ames/Rosemont）

6.9　善为我辞焉

　　　polite（Legge，Waley）

　　　courteously（Soothill）

tactfully（Lau）

kindly（Leys）

best（Ames/Rosemont）

7.3 不善不能改

good（Legge，Leys）

perfection（Soothill）

productive（Ames/Rosemont）

7.22 择其善者而从之，其不善者而改之

good quality（Legge，Soothill，Waley）

good point（Lau）

quality（Leys）

strength（Ames/Rosemont）

7.28 择其善者而从之

good（Legge，Soothill，Waley，Lau）

best（Leys）

what works well（Ames/Rosemont）

7.32 子与人歌而善

well（Legge，Ames/Rosemont）

good（Soothill）

attractive（Lau）

like（Waley，Leys）

8.4 其言也善

good（Legge）

worth listening to（Soothill）

be of note（Waley）

good（Lau）

true（Leys）

felicitous（Ames/Rosemont）

8.13　守死善道

　　excellence（Legge，Soothill）

　　good（Waley，Lau，Leys）

　　efficacious（Ames/Rosemont）

9.11　夫子循循然善诱人

　　skillfully（Legge，Soothill，Waley）

　　good at（Lau，Ames/Rosemont）

　　know（Leys）

9.13　求善贾而沽诸

　　good（Legge, Soothill, Lau, Leys, Ames/Rosemont）

　　best（Waley）

12.11　善哉

　　good（Legge）

　　excellent（Soothill，Leys，Ames/Rosemont）

　　true（Waley）

　　splendid（Lau）

12.19　子欲善而民善矣

　　good（Legge，Soothill，Waley，Lau，Leys）

　　adept（Ames/Rosemont）

12.21　善哉问

　　good（Legge）

　　excellent（Soothill，Waley，Leys）

　　splendid（Lau）

　　fine（Ames/Rosemont）

12.23　忠告而善道之

　　skillfully（Legge）

　　discreetly（Soothill，Waley）

　　properly（Lau）

          tactfully（Leys）

          adeptly（Ames/Rosemont）

13.8    善居室

          well（Legge，Soothill）

          laudable（Lau）

          know（Leys）

          make the most of（Ames/Rosemont）

13.15   如其善而莫之违也，不亦善乎？如不善而莫之违也

          good（Legge，Soothill，Waley，Lau）

          right（Leys）

          efficacious（Ames/Rosemont）

13.22   善夫

          good（Legge）

          well（Soothill，Waley，Lau）

          true（Leys）

          apt（Ames/Rosemont）

13.24   不如乡人之善者好之，其不善者恶之

          good（Legge，Soothill，Waley，Lau，Leys）

          best（Ames/Rosemont）

14.5    羿善射

          skillful（Legge）

          excel（Soothill）

          mighty（Waley）

          good at（Lau）

          good（Leys）

          master（Ames/Rosemont）

15.10   工欲善其事

          work well（Legge，Soothill）

do good work (Waley, Leys)

practise one's craft well (Lau)

good at (Ames/Rosemont)

15.33 未善也

excellence (Legge, Soothill)

perfection (Lau)

right sort of power (Leys)

good (Ames/Rosemont)

16.4 友善柔

good at (Waley)

16.5 乐道人之善

goodness (Legge, Lau)

excellence (Soothill)

good point (Waley)

quality (Leys)

what others do well (Ames/Rosemont)

16.11 见善如不及,见不善如探汤

good (Legge, Soothill, Waley, Lau, Leys)

ability (Ames/Rosemont)

17.6 亲于其身为不善者

good (Lau)

19.3 嘉善而矜不能

good (Legge, Soothill, Waley, Lau, Leys)

efficacious (shan) (Ames/Rosemont)

19.20 纣之不善

[not] wickedness (Legge, Soothill, Waley)

[not] iniquity (Soothill)

[not] wicked (Waley, Lau)

[not] evil (Leys)

[not] perversity (Ames/Rosemont)

# 善人(5)

7.26 善人,吾不得而见之矣

good man (Legge, Soothill, Lau)

perfect man (Leys)

faultless man (Waley)

efficacious person (Ames/Rosemont)

11.19 子张问善人之道

good man (Legge, Lau, Leys)

man of natural goodness (Soothill)

good people (Waley)

efficacious person (Ames/Rosemont)

13.11 善人为邦百年

good man (Legge, Soothill, Lau, Leys)

right sort of people (Waley)

efficacious people (Ames/Rosemont)

13.29 善人教民七年

good man (Legge, Soothill, Lau, Leys)

man of the right sort (Waley)

efficacious person (Ames/Rosemont)

20.1 善人是富

the good (Legge, Soothill, Waley)

good man (Lau)

good people (Leys)

efficacious person（Ames/Rosemont）

# 伤(4)

3.20 哀而不伤

    hurtfully excessive（Legge）

    morbid（Soothill）

    self injury（Waley，Lau）

    bitterness（Leys）

    injurious（Ames/Rosemont）

10.11 伤人乎

    hurt（Legge，Soothill，Waley，Lau，Leys，Ames/Rosemont）

11.24 何伤乎

    harm（Legge，Soothill，Waley，Lau，Leys，Ames/Rosemont）

19.24 其何伤于日月乎

    harm（Legge，Soothill，Waley）

    detract（Lau）

    affect（Leys）

    damage（Ames/Rosemont）

# 韶(3)

3.25 子谓《韶》

    Shâo（Legge）

    Shao（Soothill，Lau，Ames/Rosemont）

    hymn of peaceful coronation（Leys）

succession dance (Waley)

7.14 子在齐闻韶

Shâo (Legge)

Shao (Soothill, Lau, Ames/Rosemont)

coronation hymn of shun (Leys)

succession (Waley)

15.11 乐则《韶》、《舞》

Shâo (Legge)

Shao (Soothill, Lau, Ames/Rosemont)

succession (Waley)

coronation Hymn of Shun and Victory Hymn of Wu (Leys)

# 召南(1)

17.8 《召南》……《召南》

Shâo nan (Legge)

Chao Nan (Soothill)

second part of the poem (Leys)

shao nan (Waley, Lau)

shaonan (Ames/Rosemont)

# 摄(3)

3.22 官事不摄

perform (Legge, Soothill, Waley)

service (Leys)

responsibility（Ames/Rosemont）

10.3　摄齐升堂

　　　hold up（Legge，Soothill，Waley）

　　　lift（Lau，Leys，Ames/Rosemont）

11.24　摄乎大国之间

　　　straiten（Legge）

　　　hem（Soothill，Waley）

　　　situate（Lau）

　　　squeeze（Leys）

　　　set（Ames/Rosemont）

# 身(17)

1.4　吾日三省吾身

　　　oneself（Legge，Soothill，Waley，Lau，Leys）

　　　person（Ames/Rosemont）

1.7　事君能致其身

　　　life（Legge，Soothill，Waley，Leys）

　　　oneself（Lau）

　　　one's whole person（Ames/Rosemont）

4.6　不使不仁者加乎其身

　　　one's person（Legge，Lau）

　　　one（Soothill，Waley，Leys）

　　　itself to one（Ames/Rosemont）

9.27　子路终身诵之

　　　continually（Legge，Waley，Leys）

　　　perpetually（Soothill）

constantly (Lau)

over and over again (Ames/Rosemont)

10.5 长一身有半

body (Legge, Soothill, Ames/Rosemont)

man (Waley)

12.21 忘其身

life (Legge)

own (Soothill, Waley, Lau, Ames/Rosemont)

oneself (Leys)

13.6 其身正……其身不正

personal conduct (Legge, Ames/Rosemont)

oneself (Soothill, Waley)

own person (Lau)

one (Lau)

13.13 苟正其身矣……不能正其身

own conduct (Legge, Ames/Rosemont)

oneself (Soothill, Waley, Lau)

own life (Leys)

15.9 有杀身以成仁

one's life (Legge, Soothill, Waley, Leys, Ames/Rosemont)

15.24 有一言而可以终身行之者乎

one (Legge, Lau, Ames/Rosemont)

life (Soothill, Leys)

17.6 亲于其身为不善者

own person (Legge, Waley, Lau)

personally (Soothill, Leys, Ames/Rosemont)

18.7 欲洁其身

personal (Legge, Soothill, Ames/Rosemont)

one's own (Waley)

character (Lau)

one (Leys)

18.8 不辱其身……降志辱身矣……身中清

one's person (Legge)

oneself (Soothill, Waley, Lau)

one's own person (Ames/Rosemont)

# 神(7)

3.12 祭神如神在

spirit (Legge, Waley, Ames/Rosemont)

god (Soothill, Lau, Leys)

6.22 敬鬼神而远之

spiritual being (Legge)

spirit (Soothill, Waley, Ames/Rosemont)

god (Lau, Leys)

7.21 子不语怪,力,乱,神

spiritual being (Legge)

supernatural (Soothill)

god (Lau)

spirit (Waley, Leys, Ames/Rosemont)

7.35 祷尔于上下神祇

spirits of the upper (Legge)

spirits celestial (Soothill)

sky spirit (Waley)

gods above (Lau)

spirit (Leys)

gods of the heaven (Ames/Rosemont)

8.21 而致孝乎鬼神

spirit (Legge, Soothill, Waley, Leys, Ames/Rosemont)

ancestral (Lau)

11.12 季路问事鬼神

spirit (Legge, Soothill, Waley, Lau)

god (Leys, Ames/Rosemont)

# 慎(7)

1.9 慎终追远

careful (Legge)

solicitude (Soothill)

proper respect (Waley)

meticulous care (Lau)

honored (Leys)

circumspect (Ames/Rosemont)

1.14 敏于事而慎于言

careful (Legge)

guarded (Soothill)

cautious (Waley, Lau, Ames/Rosemont)

prudent (Leys)

2.18 慎言其余……慎行其余

cautious (Legge, Waley, Lau, Leys, Ames/Rosemont)

guardedly (Soothill)

7.13 子之所慎

caution (Legge)

solicitude (Soothill)

attention (Waley)

careful (Lau)

circumspection (Leys)

care (Ames/Rosemont)

8.2　慎而无礼则葸

carefulness (Legge)

caution (Soothill, Waley, Ames/Rosemont)

careful (Lau)

prudence (Leys)

19.25　言不可不慎也

careful (Legge, Waley, Lau, Leys, Ames/Rosemont)

heed (Soothill)

# 圣(4)

6.30　必也圣乎

sage (Legge, Soothill, Lau, Ames/Rosemont)

divine sage (Waley)

saint (Leys)

7.34　若圣与仁

sage (Legge, Soothill, Lau, Ames/Rosemont)

divine sage (Waley)

wisdom (Leys)

9.6　夫子圣者与……固天纵之将圣

sage (Legge, Lau, Ames/Rosemont)

inspiration（Soothill）

divine sage（Waley）

saint（Leys）

# 圣人(4)

7.26　圣人,吾不得而见之矣

sage（Legge，Lau，Ames/Rosemont）

inspired man（Soothill）

divine sage（Waley）

saint（Leys）

16.8　畏圣人之言……侮圣人之言

sage（Legge，Soothill，Lau，Ames/Rosemont）

divine sage（Waley）

saint（Leys）

19.12　其惟圣人乎

sage（Legge，Soothill，Lau，Ames/Rosemont）

diving sage（Waley）

saint（Leys）

# 诗(14)

1.15　《诗》云……始可与言《诗》已矣

book of poetry（Legge）

ode（Soothill，Lau）

song（Waley）

poem (Leys)

book of song (Ames/Rosemont)

2.2 《诗》三百

book of poetry (Legge)

ode (Soothill, Lau)

song (Waley)

poem (Leys)

song (Ames/Rosemont)

3.8 始可与言《诗》矣

ode (Legge, Lau)

poet (Soothill)

song (Waley)

poem (Leys)

song (Ames/Rosemont)

7.18 《诗》、《书》、执礼

ode (Legge, Soothill, Lau)

song (Waley)

poem (Leys)

song (Ames/Rosemont)

8.3 《诗》云

book of poetry (Legge)

ode (Soothill, Lau)

song (Waley)

poem (Leys)

book of song (Ames/Rosemont)

8.8 兴于《诗》

ode (Legge, Lau)

poet (Soothill)

song（Waley）

poem（Leys）

song（Ames/Rosemont）

13.5 诵《诗》三百

ode（Legge，Soothill，Lau）

song（Waley，Ames/Rosemont）

poem（Leys）

16.13 学诗乎……不学诗……鲤退而学诗……闻诗

ode（Legge，Soothill，Lau）

song（Waley，Ames/Rosemont）

poem（Leys）

17.8 小子何莫学夫诗？诗,可以兴

book of poetry（Legge）

poetry（Soothill）

song（Waley，Ames/Rosemont）

ode（Lau）

poem（Leys）

\* 识(6)(shí,zhì)

A. shí

17.8 多识于鸟兽草木之名

acquaint（Legge，Soothill）

acquaintance（Waley）

acquire a wide knowledge of（Lau）

learn（Leys）

broad vocabulary of（Ames/Rosemont）

B. zhì

7.2 默而识之

　　treasure up of knowledge (Legge, Soothill)

　　note what is said (Waley)

　　store up knowledge (Lau, Leys)

　　persevere in storing up what is learned (Ames/Rosemont)

7.28 多见而识之

　　keep in memory (Legge)

　　treasure up (Soothill)

　　take due note of (Waley)

　　retain (Lau)

　　keep a record of (Leys)

　　remember (Ames/Rosemont)

15.3 女以予为多学而识之者与

　　keep in memory (Legge)

　　retain all in mind (Soothill)

　　retain in mind (Waley)

　　learn in one's mind (Lau)

　　store all up (Leys)

　　remember (Ames/Rosemont)

19.22 贤者识其大者,不贤者识其小者

　　remember (Legge)

　　keep in mind (Soothill)

　　record (Waley)

　　get hold of (Lau)

　　retain (Leys)

　　grasp (Ames/Rosemont)

# 实(2)

8.5 实若虚

　　full（Legge，Soothill，Waley，Lau，Leys）

　　much（Ames/Rosemont）

9.22 秀而不实者有矣夫

　　fruit（Legge，Soothill，Waley，Lau，Leys，Ames/Rosemont）

# *食(41)(shí,sì)

A. shí

1.14 君子食无求饱

　　food（Legge，Soothill）

　　eat（Waley，Leys）

2.8 有酒食

　　food（Legge，Soothill，Waley，Lau，Leys，Ames/Rosemont）

4.5 君子无终食之间违仁

　　meal（Legge，Soothill，Ames/Rosemont）

　　eat（Lau）

4.9 而耻恶衣恶食者

　　food（Legge，Soothill，Waley，Lau，Leys，Ames/Rosemont）

6.11 一箪食

　　rice（Legge，Waley，Lau，Leys，Ames/Rosemont）

　　millet（Soothill）

7.9 子食于有丧者之侧

eat (Legge, Lau, Leys)

dine (Soothill, Ames/Rosemont)

meal (Waley)

7.16 饭疏食饮水

eat (Legge, Soothill, Waley, Lau, Ames/Rosemont)

food (Leys)

7.19 发愤忘食

food (Legge, Soothill)

hunger (Waley)

eat (Lau, Leys, Ames/Rosemont)

8.21 菲饮食

food (Legge, Soothill, Waley, Ames/Rosemont)

eat (Lau, Leys)

10.6 必变食

food (Legge, Waley)

diet (Soothill, Lau, Leys)

diet (Ames/Rosemont)

10.6 食不厌精……食饐而餲……不食……不食……不食……不食……不食……不食……不使胜食气……不食。不撤姜食,不多食

rice (Legge, Soothill, Waley, Leys)

eat (Legge, Soothill, Waley, Lau, Leys, Ames/Rosemont)

meat (Soothill)

food (Leys, Ames/Rosemont)

meal (Leys)

dish (Ames/Rosemont)

cereal (Ames/Rosemont)

10.6 不食之矣

eat (Legge, Soothill, Waley, Lau, Leys, Ames/Rosemont)

10.6 食不语

eat (Legge, Soothill, Waley, Ames/Rosemont)

meal (Lau, Leys)

10.6 虽疏食菜羹

food (Legge, Soothill)

rice (Waley)

meal (Lau, Leys, Ames/Rosemont)

10.12 君赐食……侍食于君

cook meat (Legge)

food (Soothill, Lau, Waley, Leys, Ames/Rosemont)

12.7 足食……去食

food (Legge, Soothill, Waley, Lau, Leys, Ames/Rosemont)

12.11 吾得而食诸

food (Legge, Soothill, Waley, Lau, Leys, Ames/Rosemont)

14.9 饭疏食

rice (Legge, Lau, Ames/Rosemont)

food (Soothill, Waley, Leys)

15.31 吾尝终日不食

eat (Legge, Ames/Rosemont)

food (Soothill, Waley, Lau, Leys)

15.32 君子谋道不谋食

food (Legge, Lau)

living (Soothill, Leys)

make a living (Waley)

sustenance (Ames/Rosemont)

15.38 敬其事而后其食

emolument (Legge)

pay (Soothill, Waley)

reward（Lau，Leys）

compensation（Ames/Rosemont）

17.6　焉能系而不食

eat（Legge，Soothill，Waley，Lau，Leys，Ames/Rosemont）

17.19　食夫稻……食旨不甘

eat（Legge，Soothill，Waley，Lau，Leys，Ames/Rosemont）

17.20　饱食终日

food（Legge，Soothill，Waley）

19.21　如日月之食焉

eclipse（Legge，Soothill，Waley，Lau，Leys，Ames/Rosemont）

20.1　民、食、丧、祭

food（Legge，Soothill，Waley，Lau，Leys）

sufficient（Ames/Rosemont）

B. sì

18.7　杀鸡为黍而食之

feast（Legge）

eat（Soothill，Lau）

millet（Waley，Leys，Ames/Rosemont）

# 史(3)

6.18　文胜质则史

manners of a clerk（Legge）

clerk（Soothill）

pedantry（Waley，Lau，Leys）

officious scribe（Ames/Rosemont）

15.7　直哉史鱼

    historiographer (Legge)

    recorder (Soothill, Waley)

    shih (Lau)

    shi (Leys)

15.26 吾犹及史之阙文也

    historiographer (Legge)

    recorder (Soothill)

    scribe (Waley, Lau, Leys, Ames/Rosemont)

# 士(18)

4.9  士志于道

    scholar (Legge, Leys)

    student (Soothill)

    knight (Waley)

    gentleman (Lau)

    scholar apprentice (Ames/Rosemont)

7.12  虽执鞭之士

    groom (Legge, Soothill, Ames/Rosemont)

    gentleman (Waley)

    guard (Lau)

    ganitor (Leys)

8.7  士不可以不弘毅

    officer (Legge)

    scholar (Soothill, Leys)

    knight of the way (Waley)

    gentleman (Lau)

scholar apprentices (Ames/Rosemont)

12.20 士何如斯可谓之达矣

officer (Legge)

man (Soothill)

knight (Waley)

gentleman (Lau)

scholar (Leys)

scholar apprentice (Ames/Rosemont)

13.20 何如斯可谓之士矣……可谓士矣

officer (Legge, Soothill)

knight (Waley)

gentleman (Lau, Leys)

scholar apprentice (Ames/Rosemont)

13.28 何如斯可谓之士矣……可谓士矣

scholar (Legge)

educated man (Soothill)

knight of the way (Waley)

gentleman (Lau, Leys)

scholar apprentice (Ames/Rosemont)

14.2 士而怀居,不足以为士矣

scholar (Legge, Soothill, Leys)

knight of the way (Waley)

gentleman (Lau)

scholar apprentice (Ames/Rosemont)

15.9 志士仁人

scholar (Legge, Soothill)

knight (Waley)

gentleman (Lau)

man (Leys)

scholar apprentice (Ames/Rosemont)

15.10 友其士之仁者

scholar (Legge, Soothill)

knight (Waley)

gentleman (Lau, Leys)

scholar apprentice (Ames/Rosemont)

18.2 柳下惠为士师

chief criminal judge (Legge, Soothill)

leader of the Knight (Waley)

judge (Lau)

magistrate (Leys, Ames/Rosemont)

18.6 且而与其从辟人之士也，岂若从辟世之士哉

one (Legge, Waley)

leader (Soothill)

gentleman (Lau, Leys)

teacher (Ames/Rosemont)

18.11 周有八士

officer (Legge)

valiant man (Soothill)

knight (Waley, Leys)

gentleman (Lau)

scholar apprentice (Ames/Rosemont)

19.1 士见危致命

scholar (Legge)

servant of the State (Soothill)

knight (Waley)

gentleman (Lau, Leys)

scholar apprentice (Ames/Rosemont)

19.19 孟氏使阳肤为士师

chief criminal judge (Legge, Soothill)

leader of the Knight (Waley)

judge (Lau, Leys)

magistrate (Ames/Rosemont)

# 世(14)

2.23 十世可知也……虽百世可知也

age (Legge, Soothill)

generation (Waley, Lau, Leys, Ames/Rosemont)

6.16 难乎免于今之世矣

age (Legge, Leys)

generation (Soothill)

world (Ames/Rosemont)

13.12 必世而后仁

generation (Legge, Soothill, Waley, Lau, Leys, Ames/Rosemont)

14.37 贤者辟世

world (Legge, Soothill, Lau, Leys)

generation (Waley)

office (Ames/Rosemont)

15.20 君子疾没世而名不称焉

one's day (Soothill, Waley, Ames/Rosemont)

world (Leys)

16.1 后世必为子孙忧

descendant (Legge, Soothill, Lau)

son or grandson (Waley)

children and grandchildren (Leys)

descendent (Ames/Rosemont)

16.2 盖十世希不失矣……五世希不失矣……三世希不失矣

generation (Legge, Soothill, Waley, Lau, Leys, Ames/Rosemont)

16.3 禄之去公室五世矣,政逮于大夫四世矣

generation (Legge, Soothill, Waley, Lau, Leys, Ames/Rosemont)

18.6 岂若从辟世之士哉

world (Legge, Soothill, Lau, Leys, Ames/Rosemont)

generation (Waley)

20.1 继绝世

families whose line of succession (Legge)

succession (Soothill)

lines of succession (Waley)

lines (Lau)

dynastic line (Leys)

lineage (Ames/Rosemont)

# 仕(8)

5.6 子使漆雕开仕

enter on official employment (Legge)

in office (Soothill)

take office (Waley, Lau)

official position (Leys)

seek office (Ames/Rosemont)

5.19 令尹子文三仕为令尹

take office (Legge，Soothill)

office (Waley)

prime minister (Lau，Leys，Ames/Rosemont)

15.7　邦有道，则仕

in office (Legge)

hold office (Soothill)

serve the state (Waley)

take office (Lau)

display one's talents (Leys)

give of one's service (Ames/Rosemont)

17.1　吾将仕矣

go into office (Legge)

take office (Soothill，Lau)

serve (Waley)

accept the office (Leys)

serve in office (Ames/Rosemont)

18.7　不仕无义……君子之仕也

take office (Legge)

serve one's country (Soothill，Waley)

enter public life (Lau)

public life (Leys)

serve in office (Ames/Rosemont)

19.13　仕而优则学，学而优则仕

officer (Legge)

office (Soothill)

duty to the state (Waley)

take office (Lau)

politics (Leys)

public office (Ames/Rosemont)

# 守(5)

8.13　守死善道
　　　hold (Legge)
　　　keep (Soothill)
　　　attack (Waley)
　　　abide (Lau)
　　　defend (Leys)
　　　steadfast (Ames/Rosemont)

15.33　仁不能守之……仁能守之……仁能守之
　　　hold (Legge)
　　　live up to (Soothill)
　　　secure that power (Waley)
　　　keep (Lau)
　　　retain (Leys)
　　　sustain (Ames/Rosemont)

16.1　而不能守也
　　　preserve (Legge, Soothill, Lau)
　　　save (Waley)
　　　hold it together (Leys)
　　　shore up (Ames/Rosemont)

# 寿(1)

6.23　仁者寿

　　　long lived (Legge, Lau)

　　　prolong life (Soothill)

　　　secure (Waley)

　　　live long (Leys)

　　　long enduring (Ames/Rosemont)

# 述(3)

7.1　述而不作

　　　transmit (Legge, Soothill, Waley, Lau, Leys)

　　　follow the proper way (Ames/Rosemont)

14.43　长而无述焉

　　　worthy of being handed down (Legge)

　　　worthy of mention (Soothill)

　　　worth mentioning (Waley)

　　　worthwhile (Lau)

　　　achieve (Leys)

　　　accomplish (Ames/Rosemont)

17.17　则小子何述焉

　　　record (Legge)

　　　pass on (Soothill)

　　　hand down (Waley, Leys)

transmit (Lau)

find the proper way (Ames/Rosemont)

## 恕(2)

4.15 忠恕而已矣
benevolent (Legge)
consideration (Soothill, Waley)
use oneself as a measure to gauge the likes and dislikes of others (Lau)
reciprocity (Leys)
put oneself in the other's place (Ames/Rosemont)

15.24 其恕乎
reciprocity (Legge, Leys)
sympathy (Soothill)
consideration (Waley)
Shu (Lau, Ames/Rosemont)

## *说(21)(shuō, yuè)

A. shuō

3.11 或问禘之说……不知也;知其说者之于天下也
meaning (Legge, Soothill, Leys)
explanation (Waley, Ames/Rosemont)
theory (Lau)

3.21 成事不说

speak out（Legge）

discuss（Soothill，Waley，Ames/Rosemont）

explain away（Lau）

argue（Leys）

12.8 夫子之说君子也

word（Legge，Soothill）

speak（Waley，Lau，Ames/Rosemont）

say（Leys）

17.12 道听而涂说

tell（Legge，Waley）

proclaim（Soothill）

gossip（Lau）

say（Leys）

repeat（Ames/Rosemont）

B. yuè

1.1 不亦说乎

pleasant（Legge）

pleasure（Soothill，Waley，Lau，Ames/Rosemont）

joy（Leys）

5.6 子说

pleased（Legge，Soothill，Lau，Ames/Rosemont）

delight（Waley，Leys）

6.12 非不说子之道

delight（Legge）

pleasure（Soothill）

pleased（Lau）

enjoy（Leys）

rejoice（Ames/Rosemont）

6.28 子路不说

　　　　pleased（Legge，Lau，Waley，Leys）

　　　　pleasure（Soothill）

　　　　happy（Ames/Rosemont）

9.24 能无说乎……说而不绎

　　　　pleased（Legge，Soothill，Lau）

　　　　approve（Waley）

　　　　delight（Leys）

　　　　pleasure（Ames/Rosemont）

11.4 于吾言无所不说

　　　　delight（Legge）

　　　　satisfied（Soothill）

　　　　accept（Waley）

　　　　pleased（Lau，Leys）

　　　　like（Ames/Rosemont）

13.16 近者说

　　　　happy（Legge，Soothill，Leys）

　　　　approve（Waley）

　　　　pleased（Lau，Ames/Rosemont）

13.25 君子易事而难说也……说之不以道,不说也……小人难事而易说也。说之虽不以道,说也

　　　　pleased（Legge，Soothill，Waley，Lau，Leys，Ames/Rosemont）

17.4 子路不说

　　　　pleased（Legge，Soothill，Lau）

　　　　approve（Waley）

　　　　[not] dismayed（Leys）

　　　　[not] upset（Ames/Rosemont）

20.1 公则说

delighted (Legge)

gratified (Soothill)

joy (Waley, Leys)

pleased (Lau)

happy (Ames/Rosemont)

# 私(2)

2.9 退而省其私

conduct when away from one (Legge)

conduct when not with one (Soothill)

private conduct (Waley)

in private (Lau)

on one's own (Leys, Ames/Rosemont)

10.4 私觌,愉愉如也

private (Legge, Soothill, Waley, Lau, Leys, Ames/Rosemont)

# 思(24)

2.2 思无邪

thought (Legge, Soothill, Waley)

think (Leys)

go (Ames/Rosemont)

2.15 学而不思则罔,思而不学则殆

thought (Legge)

think (Soothill, Waley, Lau, Leys)

reflection（Ames/Rosemont）

4.17　见贤思齐焉

　　　think（Legge，Soothill，Waley，Lau，Ames/Rosemont）

　　　seek to（Leys）

5.20　季文子三思而后行

　　　thought（Legge，Lau，Leys）

　　　think（Soothill，Waley，Ames/Rosemont）

9.30　岂不尔思……未之思也

　　　think（Legge，Soothill，Lau，Leys，Ames/Rosemont）

　　　love（Waley）

14.12　见利思义

　　　think（Legge，Soothill，Waley，Ames/Rosemont）

　　　remember（Lau）

　　　sense（Leys）

14.26　君子思不出其位

　　　thought（Legge，Soothill，Waley，Lau，Ames/Rosemont）

　　　contemplate（Leys）

15.31　以思，无益

　　　think（Legge，Soothill，Lau）

　　　meditate（Waley，Leys）

　　　thought（Ames/Rosemont）

16.10　君子有九思：视思明，听思聪，色思温，貌思恭，言思忠，事思敬，疑思问，忿思难，见得思义

　　　anxious（Legge）

　　　subjects with one of thoughtful consideration（Legge）

　　　think（Legge，Waley）

　　　point of thoughtful care（Soothill）

　　　care（Soothill，Waley）

　　　　careful（Waley）

　　　　turn one's thought to（Lau）

　　　　take care（Leys）

　　　　think about（Ames/Rosemont）

19.1　见得思义,祭思敬,丧思哀

　　　　think of（Legge，Waley）

　　　　thought（Legge，Soothill）

　　　　[not] forget（Lau）

　　　　not make one forget（Leys）

　　　　concern oneself with（Ames/Rosemont）

19.6　切问而近思

　　　　reflect with self application（Legge）

　　　　reflection（Soothill）

　　　　think for oneself（Waley）

　　　　reflect（Lau，Ames/Rosemont）

　　　　meditate（Leys）

# 死(38)

2.5　死,葬之以礼

　　　　dead（Legge，Soothill，Ames/Rosemont）

　　　　die（Waley，Lau，Leys）

4.8　夕死可矣

　　　　die（Legge，Soothill，Waley，Lau，Leys）

　　　　death（Ames/Rosemont）

6.3　不幸短命死矣

　　　　die（Legge，Soothill，Waley，Lau，Ames/Rosemont）

dead (Leys)

7.11 死而无悔者

dying (Legge, Soothill)

die (Waley, Lau)

death (Leys, Ames/Rosemont)

8.4 鸟之将死……人之将死

die (Legge, Waley, Leys)

dying (Soothill, Lau, Ames/Rosemont)

8.7 死而后已

death (Legge, Soothill, Waley, Lau, Leys, Ames/Rosemont)

8.13 守死善道

death (Legge, Soothill, Lau, Ames/Rosemont)

die (Waley)

life (Leys)

9.5 后死者不得与于斯文也

death (Legge)

mortal (Soothill, Waley)

dead (Lau, Leys, Ames/Rosemont)

9.12 且予与其死于臣之手也，无宁死于二三子之手乎……予死于道路乎

die (Legge, Soothill, Waley, Lau, Leys, Ames/Rosemont)

10.16 朋友死

die (Legge, Soothill, Waley, Lau, Leys)

death (Ames/Rosemont)

11.7 不幸短命死矣

die (Legge, Soothill, Waley, Lau, Ames/Rosemont)

dead (Leys)

11.8 颜渊死……鲤也死

die (Legge, Soothill, Waley, Lau, Leys, Ames/Rosemont)

11.9 颜渊死

　　die（Legge, Soothill, Waley, Lau, Leys, Ames/Rosemont）

11.10 颜渊死

　　die（Legge, Soothill, Waley, Lau, Leys, Ames/Rosemont）

11.11 颜渊死

　　die（Legge, Soothill, Waley, Lau, Leys, Ames/Rosemont）

11.12 敢问死……焉知死

　　death（Legge, Soothill, Lau, Leys, Ames/Rosemont）

　　dead（Waley）

11.13 不得其死然

　　death（Legge, Soothill, Lau, Leys, Ames/Rosemont）

　　die（Waley）

11.21 吾以女为死矣……回何敢死

　　die（Legge, Soothill, Waley, Lau, Leys, Ames/Rosemont）

　　dead（Soothill, Waley, Leys, Ames/Rosemont）

12.5 死生有命

　　death（Legge, Soothill, Waley, Lau, Leys, Ames/Rosemont）

12.7 自古皆有死

　　death（Legge, Soothill, Waley, Lau, Leys, Ames/Rosemont）

12.10 恶之欲其死……又欲其死

　　die（Legge, Lau, Leys, Ames/Rosemont）

　　dead（Soothill）

　　perish（Waley）

14.5 俱不得其死然

　　die a natural death（Legge, Soothill, Leys）

　　come to a bad end（Waley）

　　meet violent deaths（Lau）

　　meet an unnatural end（Ames/Rosemont）

14.16 召忽死之，管仲不死

　　　die（Legge，Soothill，Lau，Leys，Ames/Rosemont）

　　　give one's life（Waley）

14.17 不能死

　　　die（Legge，Lau，Ames/Rosemont）

　　　dying（Soothill，Waley）

14.43 老而不死

　　　dying（Soothill）

　　　die（Lau，Ames/Rosemont）

　　　death（Leys）

15.35 吾见蹈而死者矣，未见蹈仁而死者也

　　　die（Legge，Soothill，Lau）

　　　lose one's life（Waley，Leys，Ames/Rosemont）

16.12 死之日

　　　death（Legge，Soothill，Waley，Lau，Leys）

　　　die（Ames/Rosemont）

18.1 比干谏而死

　　　die（Legge）

　　　death（Soothill）

　　　slay（Waley）

　　　lose one's life（Lau，Ames/Rosemont）

　　　execute（Leys）

19.25 其死也哀

　　　die（Legge）

　　　death（Soothill，Waley，Lau，Leys，Ames/Rosemont）

# 四海(2)

12.5 四海之内

　　　four seas（Legge，Soothill，Waley，Lau，Leys）

　　　world（Ames/Rosemont）

20.1 四海困穷

　　　four seas（Legge，Waley，Leys，Ames/Rosemont）

　　　land（Soothill）

　　　empire（Lau）

# 肆(3)

14.36 吾力犹能肆诸市朝

　　　expose（Legge，Soothill，Waley，Lau，Leys）

　　　display（Ames/Rosemont）

17.14 古之狂也肆

　　　disregard of small thing（Legge）

　　　liberty in detail（Soothill）

　　　impatient of small restraint（Waley）

　　　impatient of restraint（Lau）

　　　carefree（Leys）

　　　reckless（Ames/Rosemont）

19.7 百工居肆以成其事

　　　shop（Legge，Ames/Rosemont）

　　　workshop（Soothill，Waley，Lau，Leys）

# 绥(2)

10.20 升车,必正立,执绥

 cord (Legge, Ames/Rosemont)

 mounting cord (Soothill, Waley, Lau)

 handrail (Leys)

19.25 绥之斯来

 make one happy (Legge)

 give one tranquility (Soothill)

 steady one as with a rope (Waley)

 bring peace to (Lau)

 offer one peace (Leys)

 bring peace (Ames/Rosemont)

# 泰(6)

7.26 约而为泰

 at ease (Legge)

 prosperous (Soothill)

 affluence (Waley, Leys)

 comfortable (Lau)

 comfort (Ames/Rosemont)

9.3 今拜乎上,泰也

 arrogant (Legge)

 too far (Soothill)

presumptuous (Waley)

casual (Lau)

rude (Leys)

hubris (Ames/Rosemont)

13.26 君子泰而不骄,小人骄而不泰

dignified ease (Legge)

dignified (Soothill, Waley)

at ease (Lau)

show authority (Leys)

distinguished (Ames/Rosemont)

20.2 泰而不骄……斯不亦泰而不骄乎

dignified ease (Legge)

dignified (Soothill)

proud (Waley, Ames/Rosemont)

at ease (Lau)

authority (Leys)

# 贪(2)

20.2 欲而不贪……又焉贪

covetous (Legge, Waley, Ames/Rosemont)

greedy (Soothill, Lau)

rapacity (Leys)

# 天(22)

3.2　天子穆穆

　　heaven（Legge，Soothill，Waley，Leys）

3.13　获罪于天

　　heaven（Legge，Soothill，Waley，Lau，Leys）

　　tian（Ames/Rosemont）

3.24　天将以夫子为木铎

　　heaven（Legge，Soothill，Waley，Lau，Leys）

　　tian（Ames/Rosemont）

6.28　天厌之！天厌之

　　heaven（Legge，Soothill，Waley，Lau，Leys）

　　tian（Ames/Rosemont）

7.23　天生德于予

　　heaven（Legge，Soothill，Waley，Lau，Leys）

　　tian（Ames/Rosemont）

8.19　唯天为大

　　heaven（Legge，Soothill，Waley，Lau，Leys）

　　tian（Ames/Rosemont）

9.5　天之将丧斯文也……天之未丧斯文也

　　heaven（Legge，Soothill，Waley，Lau，Leys）

　　tian（Ames/Rosemont）

9.6　固天纵之将圣

　　heaven（Legge，Soothill，Waley，Lau，Leys）

　　tian（Ames/Rosemont）

9.12　欺天乎

heaven (Legge, Soothill, Waley, Lau, Leys)

tian (Ames/Rosemont)

11.9　天丧予！天丧予

　　heaven (Legge, Soothill, Waley, Lau, Leys)

　　tian (Ames/Rosemont)

12.5　富贵在天

　　heaven (Legge, Soothill, Waley, Lau, Leys)

　　tian (Ames/Rosemont)

14.35　不怨天……知我者其天乎

　　heaven (Legge, Soothill, Waley, Lau, Leys)

　　tian (Ames/Rosemont)

16.2　则礼乐征伐自天子出

　　heaven (Legge, Waley, Leys)

17.17　天何言哉……天何言哉

　　heaven (Legge, Soothill, Waley, Lau, Leys)

　　tian (Ames/Rosemont)

19.25　犹天之不可阶而升也

　　heaven (Legge)

　　sky (Soothill, Waley, Lau, Leys, Ames/Rosemont)

20.1　天之历数在尔躬……天禄永终

　　heaven (Legge, Soothill, Lau)

　　celestial (Soothill)

　　heavenly (Legge, Waley, Leys)

　　tian (Ames/Rosemont)

# 天道(1)

5.13　夫子之言性与天道

the way of heaven (Legge, Waley, Lau, Leys)

the laws of heaven (Soothill)

the way of tian (Ames/Rosemont)

# 天命(3)

2.4　五十而知天命

decrees of heaven (Legge, Lau)

laws of heaven (Soothill)

biddings of heaven (Waley)

will of heaven (Leys)

propensities of tian (Ames/Rosemont)

16.8　畏天命……小人不知天命而不畏也

ordinances of heaven (Legge)

divine will (Soothill)

will of heaven (Waley, Leys)

decree of heaven (Lau)

propensities of tian (Ames/Rosemont)

# 天下(23)

3.11　知其说者之于天下也

　　　kingdom（Legge）

　　　whole empire（Soothill）

　　　all things under heaven（Waley）

　　　empire（Lau，Ames/Rosemont）

　　　world（Leys）

3.24　天下之无道也久矣

　　　kingdom（Legge）

　　　empire（Soothill，Lau）

　　　world（Waley，Leys）

　　　all under tian（Ames/Rosemont）

4.10　君子之于天下也

　　　world（Legge，Soothill，Waley，Lau，Leys，Ames/Rosemont）

8.1　三以天下让

　　　kingdom（Legge）

　　　imperial（Soothill）

　　　all things under heaven（Waley）

　　　empire（Lau，Ames/Rosemont）

　　　entire world（Leys）

8.13　天下有道则见

　　　kingdom（Legge）

　　　empire（Soothill，Lau）

　　　under heaven（Waley）

　　　world（Leys，Ames/Rosemont）

8.18 舜、禹之有天下也

　　　empire（Legge，Soothill，Lau）

　　　heaven（Waley，Leys）

　　　world（Ames/Rosemont）

8.20 舜有臣五人而天下治……三分天下有其二

　　　empire（Legge，Soothill，Lau）

　　　under heaven（Waley）

　　　entire world（Leys）

　　　world（Ames/Rosemont）

12.1 天下归仁焉

　　　all under heaven（Legge）

　　　everybody（Soothill）

　　　everyone under heaven（Waley）

　　　whole empire（Lau，Ames/Rosemont）

　　　whole world（Leys）

12.22 舜有天下……汤有天下

　　　kingdom（Legge）

　　　empire（Soothill，Lau）

　　　all that is under heaven（Waley）

　　　world（Leys）

　　　land（Ames/Rosemont）

14.5 禹稷躬稼而有天下

　　　kingdom（Legge）

　　　empire（Soothill，Lau）

　　　all that is under heaven（Waley）

　　　world（Leys，Ames/Rosemont）

14.17 一匡天下

　　　whole kingdom（Legge）

empire (Soothill)

all that is under heaven (Waley)

empire (Lau, Ames/Rosemont)

entire world in order (Leys)

16.2 天下有道……天下无道……天下有道……天下有道

empire (Legge, Soothill, Lau)

kingdom (Legge)

under heaven (Waley)

world (Leys, Ames/Rosemont)

17.5 能行五者于天下为仁矣

whole empire (Legge)

everywhere (Soothill)

everywhere under heaven (Waley)

empire (Lau)

everywhere in the world (Leys)

world (Ames/Rosemont)

17.19 天下之通丧也

empire (Legge, Lau, Ames/Rosemont)

everywhere (Soothill)

everywhere under heaven (Waley)

everywhere in the world (Leys)

18.6 滔滔者天下皆是也……天下有道

empire (Legge, Lau)

world (Soothill, Leys, Ames/Rosemont)

under heaven (Waley)

19.20 天下之恶皆归焉

world (Legge, Soothill, Leys, Ames/Rosemont)

under heaven (Waley)

empire(Lau)

world (Leys)

20.1 天下之民归心焉

throughout the kingdom (Legge)

all (Soothill)

under heaven (Waley)

empire (Lau)

all over the world (Leys)

throughout the land (Ames/Rosemont)

# 同(9)

3.16 为力不同科

equal (Legge, Soothill)

even (Leys)

7.31 为同姓

same (Legge, Soothill, Waley, Lau, Ames/Rosemont)

11.24 如会同……宗庙会同

audience (Legge, Soothill)

general gathering (Waley)

gathering (Lau, Leys)

alliance (Ames/Rosemont)

13.23 君子和而不同,小人同而不和

adulatory (Legge)

familiar (Soothill)

accommodating (Waley)

echo (Lau)

conformity（Leys）

sameness（Ames/Rosemont）

14.18 公叔文子之臣大夫僎与文子同升诸公

in company with（Legge，Soothill）

same（Waley）

side by side（Lau）

together（Leys，Ames/Rosemont）

15.40 道不同

[not] different（Legge，Soothill，Waley，Lau，Leys，Ames/Rosemont）

18.6 鸟兽不可与同群

associate with（Legge，Lau，Leys）

herd with（Soothill，Waley）

run with（Ames/Rosemont）

# 偷(1)

8.2 则民不偷

meanness（Legge）

meanly（Soothill）

fickle（Waley，Leys）

shirk obligation（Lau）

indifferent（Ames/Rosemont）

# 退(13)

2.9　退而省其私

　　retire（Legge）

　　withdraw（Soothill，Lau，Ames/Rosemont）

　　when one is not with（Waley）

7.29　不与其退也

　　retire（Legge，Waley，Ames/Rosemont）

　　withdraw（Soothill，Lau）

　　beside（Leys）

7.31　孔子退

　　retire（Legge）

　　withdraw（Soothill，Waley，Leys，Ames/Rosemont）

　　go（Lau）

10.2　宾退，必复命曰

　　retire（Legge，Ames/Rosemont）

　　depart（Soothill，Leys）

　　go（Waley）

　　withdrawal（Lau）

10.11　子退朝

　　return（Legge）

　　come forth from（Soothill）

　　return（Waley，Lau）

　　leave（Leys）

　　back（Ames/Rosemont）

11.20　求也退……故退之

retire and slow (Legge)

keep back (Legge)

lag behind (Soothill)

hold back (Sootill, Waley, Lau, Leys)

backward (Waley)

slow (Leys)

rein in (Ames/Rosemont)

12.22 樊迟退

retire (Legge)

withdraw (Soothill, Waley, Lau, Leys, Ames/Rosemont)

13.14 冉子退朝

return (Legge, Leys)

come from (Soothill)

come back (Waley)

return (Lau, Ames/Rosemont)

16.13 鲤退而学诗……鲤退而学礼……陈亢退而喜曰

retire (Legge, Waley, Lau)

go out (Soothill)

come away (Waley)

withdraw (Leys)

go away (Leys)

take one's leave (Ames/Rosemont)

19.12 当洒扫应对进退

recede (Legge)

retire (Soothill, Waley)

withdraw (Lau)

say goodbye (Leys)

## 万方(2)

20.1 无以万方;万方有罪

the people of the myriad region (Legge)

the country (Soothill)

many lands (Waley)

ten thousand states (Lau)

ten thousand fiefs (Leys)

many states (Ames/Rosemont)

## 罔(3)

2.15 学而不思则罔

labour lost (Legge)

useless (Soothill)

lost (Waley)

bewildered (Lau)

futile (Leys)

perplexity (Ames/Rosemont)

6.19 罔之生也幸而免

lose one's uprightness (Legge)

without (Soothill, Waley, Leys)

dupe (Lau)

crook (Ames/Rosemont)

6.26 不可罔也

befool (Legge)

hoodwink (Soothill)

lead astray (Waley, Leys)

dupe (Lau, Ames/Rosemont)

# 威(4)

1.8　君子不重则不威

veneration (Legge)

respect (Soothill, Waley)

awe (Lau)

authority (Leys)

dignity (Ames/Rosemont)

7.38　威而不猛

majestic (Legge)

command (Soothill, Waley, Ames/Rosemont)

awe inspiring (Lau)

authority (Leys)

20.2　威而不猛……斯不亦威而不猛乎

majestic (Legge)

command (Soothill)

awe (Waley)

awe inspiring (Lau)

stern (Leys)

dignify (Ames/Rosemont)

# 违(14)

2.5 无违……无违

　　disobedient（Legge，Soothill）

　　disobey（Waley，Leys）

　　fail to comply（Lau）

　　contrary（Ames/Rosemont）

2.9 不违

　　objection（Legge，Soothill，Leys，Ames/Rosemont）

　　differ（Waley）

　　disagree（Lau）

4.5 君子无终食之间违仁

　　abandon（Legge，Ames/Rosemont）

　　disregard（Soothill）

　　quit（Waley）

　　forsake（Lau，Leys）

　　go against（Leys）

4.18 又敬不违

　　abandon（Legge）

　　desist（Soothill）

　　thwart（Waley）

　　disobedient（Lau）

　　contradict（Leys）

　　contrary（Ames/Rosemont）

5.19 弃而违之……违之……违之

　　leave（Legge，Soothill，Lau，Leys）

go away（Waley）

take one's leave（Ames/Rosemont）

6.7　其心三月不违仁

contrary（Legge）

depart（Soothill，Ames/Rosemont）

lapse（Lau）

interruption（Leys）

9.3　虽违众

oppose（Legge）

infringe（Soothill）

contrary（Waley，Ames/Rosemont）

against（Lau，Leys）

12.20　色取仁而行违

oppose（Legge）

belie（Soothill，Lau，Waley，Ames/Rosemont）

contrary（Leys）

13.15　唯其言而莫予违也……如其善而莫之违也……如不善而莫之违也

opposition（Legge）

oppose（Soothill，Waley）

against（Lau）

contradiction（Leys）

take exception to（Ames/Rosemont）


* 畏(10)（wéi，wèi）


A.　通"围"，wéi

9.5　子畏于匡

　　　　　put in fear (Legge)

　　　　　intimidate (Soothill)

　　　　　trap (Waley, Leys)

　　　　　meet with danger (Lau)

　　　　　surround (Ames/Rosemont)

11.21　子畏于匡

　　　　　fear (Legge)

　　　　　peril (Soothill)

　　　　　trap (Waley, Leys)

　　　　　meet with danger (Lau)

　　　　　surround (Ames/Rosemont)

B. wèi

9.23　后生可畏……斯亦不足畏也已

　　　　　respect (Legge, Soothill, Waley)

　　　　　awe (Lau, Leys)

　　　　　esteem (Ames/Rosemont)

16.8　君子有三畏：畏天命，畏大人，畏圣人之言。小人不知天命而不畏也

　　　　　awe (Legge, Soothill, Lau, Ames/Rosemont)

　　　　　fear (Waley, Leys)

20.2　俨然人望而畏之

　　　　　awe (Legge, Soothill, Waley, Lau, Leys, Ames/Rosemont)

# 温(5)

1.10　夫子温、良、恭、俭、让

　　　　　benign (Legge, Soothill)

　　　　　cordial (Waley, Lau, Leys, Ames/Rosemont)

2.11　温故而知新

　　　cherish（Legge）

　　　review（Soothill，Ames/Rosemont）

　　　reanimate（Waley）

　　　keep fresh（Lau）

　　　revise（Leys）

7.38　子温而厉

　　　mild（Legge）

　　　affable（Soothill，Waley，Leys）

　　　cordial（Lau）

　　　gracious（Ames/Rosemont）

16.10　色思温

　　　benign（Legge）

　　　kindly（Soothill，Waley）

　　　cordial（Lau）

　　　amiable（Leys）

　　　cordiality（Ames/Rosemont）

19.9　即之也温

　　　mild（Legge，Waley）

　　　gracious（Soothill）

　　　cordial（Lau，Ames/Rosemont）

　　　amiable（Leys）

\* 文(23)(wén, wèn)

A. wén

1.6　则以学文

                polite study (Legge, Soothill)

                polite arts (Waley)

                cultivate (Lau)

                literature (Leys)

                improve oneself (Ames/Rosemont)

3.14    郁郁乎文哉

                regulation (Legge)

                culture (Soothill, Waley, Lau)

                civilization (Leys)

5.15    孔文①子何以谓之"文"也……是以谓之"文"也

                WĂN (Legge)

                cultured (Soothill, Waley)

                wen (Lau)

                civilized (Leys)

                refine (Ames/Rosemont)

6.18    质胜文则野,文胜质则史。文质彬彬

                accomplishment (Legge)

                training (Soothill)

                ornamentation (Waley)

                acquired refinement (Lau)

                culture (Leys)

                refinement (Ames/Rosemont)

6.27    君子博学于文

                all learning (Legge)

                letters (Soothill, Waley)

                culture (Lau, Ames/Rosemont)

---

① 人名。

literature (Leys)

7.25 文,行,忠,信

letters (Legge)

culture (Soothill, Waley, Lau, Ames/Rosemont)

literature (Leys)

7.33 文,莫吾犹人也

letters (Legge, Soothill)

culture († Ames/Rosemont)

9.5 文不在兹乎？天之将丧斯文也,后死者不得与于斯文也；天之未丧斯文也

cause of truth (Legge)

enlightenment (Soothill)

culture (Waley, Lau)

civilization (Leys)

wen (Ames/Rosemont)

9.11 博我以文

learning (Legge)

culture (Soothill, Waley, Lau, Ames/Rosemont)

literature (Leys)

12.8 何以文为……文犹质也,质犹文也

ornamental (Legge)

art (Soothill)

culture (Waley, Leys)

refinement (Lau, Ames/Rosemont)

12.15 博学于文

learning (Legge)

letters (Soothill, Waley)

culture (Lau, Ames/Rosemont)

literature (Leys)

12.24 君子以文会友

culture (Legge, Soothill, Waley, Leys)

cultivate (Lau)

refinement (Ames/Rosemont)

14.18 可以为"文"矣

WǍN (Legge)

culture (Soothill)

wên (Waley)

wen (Lau)

civilized (Leys)

refine (Ames/Rosemont)

15.26 吾犹及史之阙文也

one's text (Legge)

one's record (Soothill)

refinement (Lau)

text (Ames/Rosemont)

B. wèn

14.12 文之以礼乐

add to (Legge)

refine (Soothill, Lau, Ames/Rosemont)

grace (Waley, Leys)

19.8 小人之过也必文

gloss (Legge, Lau, Ames/Rosemont)

embellish (Soothill)

over elaboration (Waley)

cover up (Leys)

## 文德(1)

16.1　则修文德以来之
　　　civil culture and virtue (Legge)
　　　culture and morality (Soothill)
　　　prestige (Waley)
　　　moral quality (Lau)
　　　moral power of civilization (Leys)
　　　refinement (Ames/Rosemont)

## 文献(1)

3.9　文献不足故也
　　　record (Legge, Soothill, Lau, Leys)
　　　document (Waley)
　　　documentation (Ames/Rosemont)

## 文学(1)

11.3　文学:子游,子夏
　　　literary (Legge)
　　　literature and learning (Soothill)
　　　culture and learning (Waley, Lau)
　　　culture (Leys)

study of culture (Ames/Rosemont)

## 文章(2)

5.13　夫子之文章

personal displays of one's principles and ordinary descriptions of them (Legge)

culture and refinement (Soothill)

views concerning culture and the outward insignia of goodness (Waley)

accomplishment (Lau)

view (Leys)

cultural refinement (Ames/Rosemont)

8.19　焕乎其有文章

elegant regulation (Legge)

civilising regulation (Soothill)

culture (Waley)

civilized accomplishment (Lau)

institution (Leys)

cultural achievement (Ames/Rosemont)

## 无道(12)

3.24　天下之无道也久矣

without the principles (Legge)

without light and leading (Soothill)

way no longer prevails（Waley）

without the way（Lau，Leys）

lose one's way（Ames/Rosemont）

5.2　邦无道

ill governed（Legge，Soothill）

not rule according to the way（Waley）

way falls into disuse（Lau）

without the way（Leys）

way does not prevail（Ames/Rosemont）

5.21　邦无道

disorder（Legge，Soothill）

way no longer prevails（Waley，Lau）

lose the way（Leys）

without the way（Ames/Rosemont）

8.13　无道则隐……邦无道

ill governed（Legge）

law and order fail（Soothill）

way does not prevail（Waley，Lau）

lose the way（Leys）

way not prevail（Ames/Rosemont）

12.19　如杀无道

unprincipled（Legge）

lawless（Soothill）

have not the way（Waley）

not follow the way（Lau）

bad（Leys）

abandon the way（Ames/Rosemont）

14.1　邦无道

bad government prevail (Legge)

ill governed (Soothill)

not rule according to the way (Waley)

way not prevail (Lau, Ames/Rosemont)

lose the way (Leys)

14.3 邦无道

bad government prevail (Legge)

lack law and order (Soothill)

way does not prevail (Waley, Lau)

lose the way (Leys)

way not prevail (Ames/Rosemont)

14.19 子言卫灵公之无道也

unprincipled course (Legge)

unprincipled character (Soothill)

no follower of the true way (Waley)

lack of moral principle (Lau)

without principle (Leys)

lose the way (Ames/Rosemont)

15.7 邦无道……邦无道

bad government prevail (Legge)

ill governed (Soothill)

way ceased (Waley)

way falls into disuse (Lau)

bad government (Leys)

way not prevail (Ames/Rosemont)

16.2 天下无道

bad government prevail (Legge)

good government fail (Soothill)

way does not prevail (Waley, Lau, Ames/Rosemont)

lose the way (Leys)

# 武(1)

3.25 谓《武》

    wû (Legge)

    wu (Soothill, Lau, Ames/Rosemont)

    war dance (Waley)

    hymn of military conquest (Leys)

    wu (Soothill, Waley, Lau, Leys, Ames/Rosemont)

# 习(3)

1.1 学而时习之

    application (Legge)

    exercise (Soothill)

    repeat (Waley)

    try out (Lau)

    put into practice (Leys)

    apply (Ames/Rosemont)

1.4 传不习乎

    master and practice (Legge)

    practice (Soothill)

    repeat (Waley)

    practice (Lau, Leys, Ames/Rosemont)

17.2　习相远也

　　practice（Legge，Soothill，Waley）

　　behaviour（Lau）

　　habit（Leys）

　　virtue of one's habit（Ames/Rosemont）

## 贤(25)

1.7　贤贤易色

　　apply as sincerely to the love of（Legge）

　　virtuous（Legge）

　　excel（Soothill）

　　moral excellence（Soothill）

　　treat better（Waley）

　　better（Waley）

　　show deference（Lau）

　　man of excellence（Lau）

　　value（Leys）

　　virtue（Leys）

　　care for（Ames/Rosemont）

　　character（Ames/Rosemont）

4.17　见贤思齐焉，见不贤而内自省也

　　man of worth（Legge，Soothill）

　　good man（Waley）

　　someone better than oneself（Lau）

　　worthy man（Leys）

　　person of exceptional character（Ames/Rosemont）

6.11　贤哉……贤哉

　　admirable（Legge，Lau，Leys）

　　worthy（Soothill）

　　incomparable（Waley）

　　character（Ames/Rosemont）

7.15　古之贤人也

　　worthy（Legge，Soothill）

　　good（Waley）

　　excellent（Lau）

　　virtuous（Leys）

　　character（Ames/Rosemont）

11.16　师与商也孰贤

　　superior（Legge，Lau）

　　better（Soothill，Waley，Leys）

　　superior character（Ames/Rosemont）

13.2　举贤才……焉知贤才而举之

　　man of virtue and talent（Legge）

　　those who are worthy and capable（Soothill）

　　man of superior capacity（Waley）

　　man of talent（Lau，Leys）

　　those with superior character（Ames/Rosemont）

14.29　赐也贤乎哉

　　excellence（Legge）

　　worthy（Soothill）

　　perfect（Waley）

　　superior（Lau）

　　perfection（Leys）

　　superior character（Ames/Rosemont）

14.31 是贤乎

  superior worth（Legge）

  real worth（Soothill）

  sage（Waley）

  superior（Lau）

  sagacity（Leys）

  superior character（Ames/Rosemont）

14.37 贤者辟世

  worth（Legge）

  good（Soothill）

  best of all（Waley）

  highest wisdom（Leys）

  highest character（Ames/Rosemont）

15.10 事其大夫之贤者

  great officer（Legge）

  minister（Soothill）

  officers as are worthy（Waley）

  distinguished counsellor（Lau）

  virtuous minister（Leys）

  ministers who are of the highest character（Ames/Rosemont）

15.14 知柳下惠之贤而不与立也

  virtue（Legge）

  superiority（Soothill）

  best man（Waley）

  excellence（Lau）

  better qualified（Leys）

  superior character（Ames/Rosemont）

16.5 乐多贤友

worthy (Legge, Soothill)

wise (Waley)

excellent (Lau)

talented (Leys)

superior character (Ames/Rosemont)

17.20 犹贤乎已

better (Legge, Soothill, Waley, Lau, Leys, Ames/Rosemont)

19.3 君子尊贤而容众……我之大贤与……我之不贤与

talented and virtuous (Legge)

worth (Soothill)

worthy (Soothill)

excel (Waley)

those that excel (Waley)

better (Lau)

superior (Lau, Ames/Rosemont)

wisdom (Leys)

wise (Leys)

19.22 贤者识其大者，不贤者识其小者

talents and virtue (Legge)

gifted (Soothill)

those of great understanding (Waley)

superior (Lau)

wise (Leys)

superior character (Ames/Rosemont)

19.23 子贡贤于仲尼

superior (Legge, Soothill, Lau)

better (Waley, Leys, Ames/Rosemont)

19.24 他人之贤者

talents and virtue（Legge）

excellence（Soothill，Lau）

good（Waley）

merit（Leys）

superior character（Ames/Rosemont）

19.25　仲尼岂贤于子乎

superior（Legge，Soothill，Waley，Lau，Leys，Ames/Rosemont）

# 小人(24)

2.14　小人比而不周

mean man（Legge）

inferior man（Soothill）

small man（Waley，Lau，Leys）

petty person（Ames/Rosemont）

4.11　小人怀土……小人怀惠

small man（Legge，Lau，Leys）

inferior man（Soothill）

commoner（Waley）

petty person（Ames/Rosemont）

4.16　小人喻于利

mean man（Legge）

inferior man（Soothill）

lesser man（Waley）

small man（Lau，Leys）

petty person（Ames/Rosemont）

6.13　无为小人儒

mean man (Legge)

inferior man (Soothill)

common people (Waley)

petty (Lau)

vulgar man (Leys)

petty person (Ames/Rosemont)

7.37　小人长戚戚

mean man (Legge)

inferior man (Soothill)

small man (Waley, Lau)

vulgar man (Leys)

petty person (Ames/Rosemont)

12.16　小人反是

mean man (Legge)

little minded man (Soothill)

small man (Waley, Lau)

vulgar man (Leys)

petty person (Ames/Rosemont)

12.19　小人之德草

inferior (Legge)

those below (Soothill)

small people (Waley)

small man (Lau)

common man (Leys)

petty person (Ames/Rosemont)

13.4　小人哉

small man (Legge)

little minded man (Soothill)

no gentleman (Waley)

petty (Lau)

vulgar man (Leys)

petty person (Ames/Rosemont)

13.20 硁硁然小人哉

little man (Legge)

man of grit (Soothill)

such a one (Waley)

stubborn petty mindedness (Lau)

vulgar man (Leys)

13.23 小人同而不和

mean man (Legge)

inferior man (Soothill)

common people (Waley)

small man (Lau)

vulgar man (Leys)

petty person (Ames/Rosemont)

13.25 小人难事而易说也

mean man (Legge)

inferior man (Soothill)

common people (Waley)

small man (Lau)

vulgar man (Leys)

petty person (Ames/Rosemont)

13.26 小人骄而不泰

mean man (Legge)

ill bred (Soothill)

common people (Waley)

small man (Lau)

vulgar man (Leys)

petty person (Ames/Rosemont)

14.6 未有小人而仁者也

mean man (Legge)

one of the lower type (Soothill)

not a gentleman (Waley)

small man (Lau, Leys)

petty person (Ames/Rosemont)

14.23 小人下达

mean man (Legge)

inferior man (Soothill)

small man (Waley, Lau)

vulgar man (Leys)

petty person (Ames/Rosemont)

15.2 小人穷斯滥矣

mean man (Legge)

inferior man (Soothill)

small man (Waley, Lau)

vulgar man (Leys)

petty person (Ames/Rosemont)

15.21 小人求诸人

mean man (Legge)

inferior man (Soothill)

small man (Waley, Lau)

vulgar man (Leys)

petty person (Ames/Rosemont)

15.34 小人不可大受而可小知也

small man（Legge，Waley，Lau）

inferior man（Soothill）

vulgar man（Leys）

petty person（Ames/Rosemont）

16.8　小人不知天命而不畏也

mean man（Legge）

baser man（Soothill）

small man（Waley，Lau）

vulgar man（Leys）

petty person（Ames/Rosemont）

17.3　小人学道则易使也

man of low station（Legge）

common people（Soothill）

small man（Waley，Lau）

small people（Leys）

petty person（Ames/Rosemont）

17.10　譬诸小人

small mean people（Legge）

common herd（Soothill）

low walks of life（Waley）

small man（Lau）

coward（Leys）

petty people（Ames/Rosemont）

17.21　小人有勇而无义为盗

one of lower people（Legge）

man of the lower order（Soothill）

small man（Waley，Lau）

vulgar man（Leys）

petty person（Ames/Rosemont）

17.23 唯女子与小人为难养也

 servant（Legge，Soothill）

 people of low birth（Waley）

 small man（Lau）

 underling（Leys）

 petty person（Ames/Rosemont）

19.8 小人之过也必文

 mean man（Legge）

 inferior man（Soothill）

 small man（Waley，Lau）

 vulgar man（Leys）

 petty person（Ames/Rosemont）

# 亵(3)

10.5 红紫不以为亵服……亵裘长

 sleeping dress（Legge）

 undress（Soothill，Waley）

 sleeping garment（Soothill）

 bedcloth（Waley）

 lapels and cuff（Lau）

 night shirt（Lau）

 lapel（Leys）

 nightgown（Leys）

 casual clothing（Ames/Rosemont）

 night coat（Ames/Rosemont）

10.19 虽亵，必以貌

  undress (Legge)

  not in public (Soothill)

  informally (Waley)

  well known to one (Lau)

  low condition (Leys)

  frequent acquaintance (Ames/Rosemont)

心(6)

2.4 七十而从心所欲

  heart (Legge, Soothill, Waley, Lau, Leys)

  heart and mind (Ames/Rosemont)

6.7 其心三月不违仁

  mind (Legge, Waley, Leys)

  heart (Soothill, Lau)

  thoughts and feelings (Ames/Rosemont)

14.39 有心哉

  heart (Legge)

  feeling (Soothill)

  passionately (Waley)

  frustrated purpose (Lau)

  real heart (Leys)

  moving (Ames/Rosemont)

17.20 无所用心

  mind (Legge, Soothill, Waley, Lau, Leys)

  heart and mind (Ames/Rosemont)

20.1 简在帝心……天下之民归心焉
　　mind (Legge)
　　heart (Legge, Soothill, Waley, Lau, Leys)
　　heart and mind (Ames/Rosemont)

## 新(3)

2.11 温故而知新
　　new (Legge, Soothill, Waley, Lau, Leys, Ames/Rosemont)
5.19 必以告新令尹
　　new (Legge, Soothill)
　　successor (Waley, Lau, Leys)
　　incoming (Ames/Rosemont)
17.19 新谷既升
　　new (Legge, Soothill, Waley, Lau, Leys, Ames/Rosemont)

## 信(38)

1.4 与朋友交而不信乎
　　sincere (Legge, Soothill)
　　true to one's word (Waley)
　　trustworthy (Lau)
　　faithful (Leys)
　　make good on one's word (Ames/Rosemont)
1.5 敬事而信
　　sincerity (Legge)

good faith (Soothill)

punctually observe one's promise (Waley)

trustworthy (Lau)

good faith (Leys)

make good on one's word (Ames/Rosemont)

1.6 谨而信

truthful (Legge, Soothill)

punctual (Waley)

trustworthy (Lau)

good faith (Leys)

make good on one's word (Ames/Rosemont)

1.7 与朋友交言而有信

sincere (Legge, Soothill)

true (Waley, Leys)

trustworthy (Lau)

make good on one's word (Ames/Rosemont)

1.8 主忠信

sincerity (Legge, Soothill)

keep promise (Waley)

trustworthy (Lau)

faithfulness (Leys)

make good on one's word (Ames/Rosemont)

1.13 信近于义

agreement (Legge)

promise (Soothill, Waley, Leys)

trustworthy (Lau)

make good on one's word (Ames/Rosemont)

2.22 人而无信

truthfulness (Legge)

good faith (Soothill)

trust (Waley, Leys)

trustworthy (Lau)

make good on one's word (Ames/Rosemont)

5.6 吾斯之未能信

assurance (Legge)

confidence (Soothill)

faith (Waley)

trust oneself (Lau)

up to the task (Leys)

sure (Ames/Rosemont)

5.10 听其言而信其行

give one credit (Legge, Soothill)

take for granted (Waley)

trust (Lau, Leys)

believe (Ames/Rosemont)

5.26 朋友信之

sincerity (Legge)

faithful (Soothill)

faith (Waley)

trust (Lau, Leys)

trust and confidence (Ames/Rosemont)

5.28 必有忠信如丘者焉

sincere (Legge, Soothill)

true (Waley)

trustworthy (Lau)

faithful (Leys)

make good on one's word（Ames/Rosemont）

7.1 信而好古

believe（Legge，Soothill）

faithful（Waley）

truthful（Lau）

trust（Leys）

confidence（Ames/Rosemont）

7.25 文,行,忠,信

truthfulness（Legge）

good faith（Soothill）

keeping of promise（Waley）

trustworthy（Lau）

good faith（Leys）

make good on one's word（Ames/Rosemont）

8.4 斯近信矣

sincerity（Legge，Soothill）

good faith（Waley）

trust（Lau）

faith（Leys）

trust and confidence（Ames/Rosemont）

8.13 笃信好学

faith（Legge，Waley，Lau，Leys）

sincerity（Soothill）

commitment（Ames/Rosemont）

8.16 悾悾而不信

sincere（Legge）

truthful（Soothill）

simple minded（Waley）

trustworthy (Lau)

reliable (Leys)

honesty (Ames/Rosemont)

9.25 主忠信

sincerity (Legge, Soothill)

keep all promise (Waley)

trustworthy (Lau)

trust above everything else (Leys)

make good on one's word (Ames/Rosemont)

12.7 民信之矣……民无信不立

confidence (Legge, Soothill, Waley, Ames/Rosemont)

faith (Legge, Soothill)

trust (Waley, Lau, Leys)

12.10 主忠信

sincerity (Legge, Soothill)

faith (Waley, Leys)

trustworthy (Lau)

make good on one's word (Ames/Rosemont)

12.11 信如君不君

indeed (Legge, Waley, Leys, Ames/Rosemont)

truly (Soothill, Lau)

13.4 上好信

good faith (Legge, Soothill, Waley, Leys)

trustworthiness (Lau)

make good on one's word (Ames/Rosemont)

13.20 言必信

sincere (Legge)

stand by one's word (Soothill, Waley)

keep one's word (Lau)

trust (Leys)

make good on one's word (Ames/Rosemont)

14.13 信乎

true (Legge, Soothill, Lau, Leys)

fact (Waley)

believe (Ames/Rosemont)

14.14 吾不信也

believe (Legge, Soothill, Waley, Lau, Leys, Ames/Rosemont)

14.31 不亿不信

believe (Legge)

[not] doubt one's word (Soothill)

promise (Waley)

faith (Lau, Leys)

honesty (Ames/Rosemont)

15.6 言忠信……言不忠信

truthful (Legge, Soothill)

true (Waley)

trustworthy (Lau)

good faith (Leys)

make good on one's word (Ames/Rosemont)

15.18 信以成之

sincerity (Legge, Soothill)

faithful (Waley)

trustworthy (Lau)

faith (Leys)

make good on one's word (Ames/Rosemont)

17.5 恭,宽,信,敏,惠……信则人任焉

sincerity (Legge，Soothill)

good faith (Waley，Leys)

trustworthiness (Lau)

make good on one's word (Ames/Rosemont)

17.7 好信不好学

sincere (Legge)

honesty (Soothill)

keep promise (Waley)

trustworthiness (Lau)

chivalry (Leys)

make good on one's word (Ames/Rosemont)

19.2 信道不笃

sincerity (Legge)

believe (Soothill，Waley，Lau)

conviction (Leys)

earnest (Ames/Rosemont)

19.10 君子信而后劳其民；未信……信而后谏；未信

confidence (Legge，Soothill，Waley，Ames/Rosemont)

trust (Lau，Leys)

20.1 信则民任焉

make the people repose (Legge)

good faith (Soothill，Leys)

keep one's word (Waley)

trustworthy (Lau)

make good on one's word (Ames/Rosemont)

\* 兴(9)(xīng,xìng)

A. xīng

8.2 则民兴于仁
arouse(Legge)
stir(Soothill,Lau)
incite(Waley)
attract(Leys)
aspire(Ames/Rosemont)

8.8 兴于《诗》
arouse(Legge)
form(Soothill)
incite(Waley)
stimulate(Lau)
draw inspiration(Leys)
inspiration(Ames/Rosemont)

13.3 则礼乐不兴;礼乐不兴
flourish(Legge,Soothill,Waley,Lau,Ames/Rosemont)
[not] wither(Leys)

13.15 一言而可以兴邦……不几乎一言而兴邦乎
prosperous(Legge,Soothill)
save(Waley)
prosper(Lau,Ames/Rosemont)
prosperity(Leys)

15.2 莫能兴
rise(Legge)

stand (Soothill)

drag oneself on to one's feet (Waley)

get to one's feet (Lau)

rise to one's feet (Leys)

stand up (Ames/Rosemont)

20.1 兴灭国,继绝世

revive (Legge)

re-establish (Soothill)

raise up (Waley)

restore (Lau, Leys, Ames/Rosemont)

B. xìng

17.8 诗,可以兴

stimulate the mind (Legge, Soothill)

incite people's emotions (Waley)

stimulate the imagination (Lau)

stimulation (Leys)

arise one's sensibilities (Ames/Rosemont)

# 行人(1)

14.8 行人子羽修饰之

the manager of Foreign intercourse (Legge)

the Foreign Minister (Soothill)

the receriver of Envoys (Waley)

the master of protocol (Lau, Lays)

the diplomat (Ames/Rosemont)

# 省(4)

1.4 　吾日三省吾身
　　　examine (Legge, Soothill, Waley, Lau, Leys, Ames/Rosemont)

2.9 　退而省其私
　　　examine (Legge, Soothill, Ames/Rosemont)
　　　enquire (Waley)
　　　look (Lau)
　　　observe (Leys)

4.17 　见不贤而内自省也
　　　examine (Legge, Soothill, Lau, Leys, Ames/Rosemont)
　　　turn one's gaze within (Waley)

12.4 　内省不疚
　　　examination (Legge)
　　　find (Soothill, Lau)
　　　look (Waley)
　　　conscience (Leys)
　　　examine (Ames/Rosemont)

# 性(2)

5.13 　夫子之言性与天道
　　　man's nature (Legge, Waley)
　　　nature of man (Soothill)
　　　human nature (Lau)

nature of thing (Leys)

natural disposition (Ames/Rosemont)

17.2　性相近也

nature (Legge, Soothill, Waley, Lau, Leys)

natural tendency (Ames/Rosemont)

# 兄弟(6)

2.21　友于兄弟

brotherly (Legge)

brethren (Soothill)

brother (Waley, Lau, Leys, Ames/Rosemont)

12.5　人皆有兄弟……皆兄弟也——君子何患乎无兄弟也

brother (Legge, Soothill, Waley, Lau, Leys, Ames/Rosemont)

13.7　鲁、卫之政,兄弟也

brother (Legge, Soothill, Waley, Lau, Leys, Ames/Rosemont)

13.28　兄弟怡怡

brethren (Legge)

brother (Soothill, Waley, Lau, Leys, Ames/Rosemont)

# 修(11)

7.3　德之不修

cultivation (Legge, Soothill)

tend (Waley)

cultivate (Lau, Leys, Ames/Rosemont)

7.7 自行束修以上
　　　dried flesh (Legge, Soothill, Waley)
　　　dried meat (Lau, Ames/Rosemont)
　　　token (Leys)

12.21 修慝,辨惑……非修慝与
　　　correct (Legge, Soothill)
　　　remedy (Soothill)
　　　repair (Waley)
　　　reformation (Lau)
　　　reform (Lau, Ames/Rosemont)
　　　neutralize (Leys)

14.8 行人子羽修饰之
　　　polish (Legge)
　　　amend (Soothill, Waley)
　　　touch it up (Lau)
　　　edit (Leys)
　　　revise (Ames/Rosemont)

14.42 修己以敬……修己以安人……修己以安百姓。修己以安百姓
　　　cultivation (Legge, Leys)
　　　cultivate (Soothill, Waley, Lau, Ames/Rosemont)

16.1 则修文德以来之
　　　cultivate (Legge, Lau)
　　　promotion (Soothill)
　　　enhance (Waley)
　　　cultivation (Leys, Ames/Rosemont)

20.1 修废官
　　　restore (Legge, Soothill, Waley)
　　　re-establish (Lau, Leys)

revive (Ames/Rosemont)

# 羞(1)

13.22　或承之羞
　　　disgrace (Legge, Soothill, Leys)
　　　evil (Waley)
　　　shame (Lau, Ames/Rosemont)

# 虚(2)

7.26　虚而为盈
　　　empty (Legge, Soothill, Lau)
　　　emptiness (Waley, Leys, Ames/Rosemont)
8.5　实若虚
　　　empty (Legge, Soothill, Waley, Leys, Ames/Rosemont)

# 学(64)

1.1　学而时习之
　　　learn (Legge, Waley, Lau, Leys)
　　　acquire knowledge (Soothill)
　　　study (Ames/Rosemont)
1.6　则以学文
　　　employ (Legge, Soothill)

study（Waley，Leys，Ames/Rosemont）

1.7 虽曰未学,吾必谓之学矣

learn（Legge）

educate（Soothill，Waley，Leys，Ames/Rosemont）

education（Waley）

school（Lau）

1.8 学则不固

learning（Legge，Soothill，Leys）

education（Waley）

study（Lau，Ames/Rosemont）

1.14 可谓好学也已

learn（Legge，Lau）

learning（Soothill，Waley，Leys，Ames/Rosemont）

2.4 吾十有五而志于学

learning（Legge，Waley，Lau，Leys，Ames/Rosemont）

wisdom（Soothill）

2.15 学而不思则罔,思而不学则殆

learning（Legge，Soothill，Ames/Rosemont）

learn（Waley，Lau）

study（Leys）

2.18 子张学干禄

learning（Legge）

studying（Soothill，Waley，Lau，Leys，Ames/Rosemont）

5.15 敏而好学

learning（Legge，Soothill，Waley，Leys，Ames/Rosemont）

learn（Lau）

5.28 不如丘之好学也

learning（Legge，Soothill，Waley，Leys，Ames/Rosemont）

　　　　learn（Lau）

6.3　弟子孰为好学……有颜回者好学……未闻好学者也

　　　　learn（Legge，Lau）

　　　　learning（Soothill，Waley，Leys，Ames/Rosemont）

6.27　君子博学于文

　　　　study（Legge）

　　　　verse（Soothill，Waley，Lau）

　　　　learning（Leys）

　　　　learn（Ames/Rosemont）

7.2　学而不厌

　　　　learning（Legge，Waley，Leys）

　　　　pursuit of wisdom（Soothill）

　　　　learn（Lau）

　　　　studying（Ames/Rosemont）

7.3　学之不讲

　　　　what is learned（Legge）

　　　　study（Soothill）

　　　　learning（Waley）

　　　　what one has learned（Lau，Leys）

　　　　what one learns（Ames/Rosemont）

7.17　五十以学《易》

　　　　study（Legge，Soothill，Waley，Leys，Ames/Rosemont）

　　　　learn（Lau）

7.34　正唯弟子不能学也

　　　　imitate（Legge）

　　　　learn（Soothill，Waley，Lau，Ames/Rosemont）

　　　　emulate（Leys）

8.12　三年学

learn (Legge)

study (Soothill, Waley, Lau, Leys, Ames/Rosemont)

8.13 笃信好学

learning (Legge, Waley, Lau, Leys, Ames/Rosemont)

moral (Soothill)

8.17 学如不及

learn (Legge, Soothill, Waley)

study (Lau, Ames/Rosemont)

learning (Leys)

9.2 博学而无所成名

learning (Legge, Soothill, Lau, Leys, Ames/Rosemont)

learn (Waley)

9.30 可与共学

study (Legge, Soothill, Waley, Ames/Rosemont)

information (Leys)

learn (Lau)

11.7 弟子孰为好学……有颜回者好学

learn (Legge, Lau)

learning (Soothill, Waley, Leys, Ames/Rosemont)

11.23 然后为学

learn (Legge, Lau, Leys, Ames/Rosemont)

learning (Waley)

educate (Soothill)

11.24 愿学焉

learn (Legge, Soothill, Lau, Leys, Ames/Rosemont)

train (Waley)

12.15 博学于文

study (Legge)

verse (Soothill, Waley, Lau)

learning (Leys)

learn (Ames/Rosemont)

13.4　樊迟请学稼……请学为圃

teach (Legge, Soothill, Waley, Lau, Leys)

learn (Ames/Rosemont)

14.24　古之学者为己,今之学者为人

learn (Legge)

study (Soothill, Waley, Lau, Leys)

scholar (Ames/Rosemont)

14.35　下学而上达

study (Legge, Soothill, Waley, Lau, Ames/Rosemont)

learning (Leys)

15.1　未之学也

learn (Legge, Leys)

study (Soothill, Waley, Lau, Ames/Rosemont)

15.3　女以予为多学而识之者与

learn (Legge, Waley, Lau, Leys, Ames/Rosemont)

study (Soothill)

15.31　不如学也

learning (Legge, Lau, Ames/Rosemont)

learn (Soothill, Waley)

study (Leys)

15.32　学也,禄在其中矣

learning (Legge, Waley, Leys)

scholarship (Soothill)

study (Lau)

studying (Ames/Rosemont)

16.9　学而知之者次也；困而学之……困而不学

　　　learn（Legge，Soothill，Ames/Rosemont）

　　　acquire（Soothill）

　　　learning（Waley，Leys）

　　　study（Lau，Ames/Rosemont）

16.13　学诗乎……不学诗……鲤退而学诗……学礼乎……不学礼……鲤退而学礼

　　　learn（Legge）

　　　study（Legge，Soothill，Waley，Lau，Leys，Ames/Rosemont）

17.3　君子学道则爱人，小人学道则易使也

　　　instruct（Legge，Lau）

　　　learn（Soothill）

　　　study（Waley，Ames/Rosemont）

　　　cultivate（Leys）

17.7　好仁不好学……好知不好学……好信不好学……好直不好学……好勇不好学……好刚不好学

　　　learning（Legge，Waley，Lau，Leys，Ames/Rosemont）

　　　learn（Soothill）

17.8　小子何莫学夫诗

　　　study（Legge，Soothill，Waley，Lau，Leys，Ames/Rosemont）

19.5　可谓好学也已矣

　　　learn（Legge，Lau，Leys）

　　　learning（Soothill，Waley，Ames/Rosemont）

19.6　博学而笃志

　　　learning（Legge，Leys）

　　　culture（Soothill）

　　　study（Waley）

　　　learn（Lau，Ames/Rosemont）

19.7　君子学以致其道

　　learn（Legge）

　　study（Soothill，Waley，Ames/Rosemont）

　　learning（Lau，Leys）

19.13　仕而优则学，学而优则仕

　　learning（Legge，Leys）

　　study（Soothill，Waley，Lau，Ames/Rosemont）

19.22　仲尼焉学……夫子焉不学

　　learning（Legge，Soothill）

　　derive one's learning（Waley，Leys）

　　learn（Lau）

　　study（Ames/Rosemont）

# 血气(3)

16.7　血气未定……血气方刚……血气既衰

　　physical power（Legge）

　　physical nature（Soothill）

　　blood and vital humours（Waley）

　　blood and ch'i（Lau）

　　energy of the blood（Leys）

　　vigorous（Ames/Rosemont）

# 雅(4)

7.18　子所雅言……皆雅言也

correct (Waley, Lau, Leys)

proper (Ames/Rosemont)

9.15 《雅》、《颂》各得其所

royal songs (Legge)

secular pieces (Soothill)

court pieces (Waley, Leys)

ya (Lau)

songs of the kingdom (Ames/Rosemont)

17.16 恶郑声之乱雅乐也

ya (Legge)

correct (Soothill)

court music (Waley)

classical (Lau, Leys, Ames/Rosemont)

# 厌(9)

6.28 天厌之！天厌之

reject (Legge, Soothill)

avert (Waley)

curse (Lau)

confound (Leys)

abandon (Ames/Rosemont)

7.2 学而不厌

satiety (Legge)

weary (Soothill)

tired (Waley)

flag (Lau)

respite (Ames/Rosemont)

7.34　抑为之不厌

　　satiety (Legge)

　　weary (Soothill, Waley)

　　tired (Lau)

　　flag (Leys)

　　respite (Ames/Rosemont)

10.6　食不厌精,脍不厌细

　　dislike (Legge)

　　objection (Soothill, Waley)

　　gorge (Leys)

　　object (Ames/Rosemont)

14.13　人不厌其言……人不厌其笑……人不厌其取

　　get tired of (Legge)

　　tire of (Soothill)

　　feel too much (Waley)

　　tired (Lau, Ames/Rosemont)

　　think that one speaks too much (Leys)

# 野(3)

6.18　质胜文则野

　　rusticity (Legge)

　　rustic (Soothill)

　　boorishness of the rustic (Waley)

　　churlishness (Lau)

　　savage (Leys)

boorish (Ames/Rosemont)

11.1 野人也
rustic (Legge, Lau)
uncultivated (Soothill)
common (Waley, Leys)
simple folk (Ames/Rosemont)

13.3 野哉,由也
uncultivated (Legge, Soothill)
boorish (Waley, Lau, Leys)
dense (Ames/Rosemont)

# 疑(3)

2.18 多闻阙疑
doubt (Legge, Soothill)
doubtful (Waley, Lau, Leys)
unsure (Ames/Rosemont)

12.20 居之不疑
doubt (Legge)
misgiving (Soothill, Lau)
[no] self assurance (Waley)
flappable pretense (Leys)
[not] confident (Ames/Rosemont)

16.10 疑思问
doubt (Legge, Soothill, Waley, Lau, Leys, Ames/Rosemont)

# 亿(2)

11.18 亿则屡中
  judgment (Legge, Soothill, Leys)
  calculation (Waley)
  conjecture (Lau)
  venture (Ames/Rosemont)

14.31 不亿不信
  think beforehand (Legge)
  imagine (Soothill)
  reckon (Waley)
  presume (Lau)
  suspect (Leys, Ames/Rosemont)

# 义(24)

1.13 信近于义
  what is right (Legge, Soothill, Waley, Leys)
  moral (Lau)
  appropriate (Ames/Rosemont)

2.24 见义不为
  right (Legge, Soothill, Waley)
  what ought to be done (Lau)
  justice (Leys)
  appropriate (Ames/Rosemont)

4.10 义之与比

　　right (Legge, Waley)

　　what is right (Soothill)

　　what is moral (Lau)

　　justice (Leys)

　　appropriate (Ames/Rosemont)

4.16 君子喻于义

　　righteousness (Legge)

　　what is right (Soothill, Waley)

　　what is moral (Lau)

　　what is just (Leys)

　　what is appropriate (Ames/Rosemont)

5.16 其使民也义

　　just (Legge, Soothill, Waley, Lau, Leys)

　　appropriate (Ames/Rosemont)

6.22 务民之义

　　duty (Legge, Soothill)

　　right (Waley, Lau, Leys)

　　appropriate (Ames/Rosemont)

7.3 闻义不能徙

　　righteousness (Legge)

　　recognised duty (Soothill)

　　righteous (Waley)

　　right (Lau, Leys)

　　appropriate (Ames/Rosemont)

7.16 不义而富且贵

　　righteousness (Legge)

　　worthily (Soothill)

right（Waley）

moral（Lau）

justice（Leys）

appropriate（Ames/Rosemont）

12.10 徙义，崇德也

what is right（Legge）

right（Soothill，Waley）

rightness（Lau）

justice（Leys）

appropriate（Ames/Rosemont）

12.20 质直而好义

righteousness（Legge）

justice（Soothill，Leys）

right（Waley，Lau）

appropriate（Ames/Rosemont）

13.4 上好义

righteousness（Legge）

justice（Soothill，Leys）

right（Waley）

what is right（Lau）

appropriate conduct（Ames/Rosemont）

14.12 见利思义

righteousness（Legge）

right（Soothill，Waley）

what is right（Lau）

justice（Leys）

appropriate conduct（Ames/Rosemont）

14.13 义然后取

righteousness (Legge)

right (Soothill，Waley, Lau)

just (Leys)

appropriate (Ames/Rosemont)

15.17 言不及义

righteousness (Legge)

what is just and right (Soothill)

right (Waley)

subject of morality (Lau)

single truth (Leys)

appropriate conduct (Ames/Rosemont)

15.18 君子义以为质

righteousness (Legge)

right (Soothill，Waley)

morality (Lau)

justice (Leys)

appropriate conduct (Ames/Rosemont)

16.10 见得思义

righteousness (Legge)

right (Soothill，Waley)

what is right (Lau)

if it is fair (Leys)

appropriate conduct (Ames/Rosemont)

16.11 行义以达其道

righteousness (Legge，Waley, Leys)

right (Soothill，Lau)

what is appropriate (Ames/Rosemont)

17.21 君子义以为上,君子有勇而无义为乱,小人有勇而无义为盗

righteousness（Legge）

rectitude（Soothill）

right（Waley）

morality（Lau）

just（Leys）

appropriate conduct（Ames/Rosemont）

sense of appropriateness（Ames/Rosemont）

18.7　不仕无义……君臣之义……行其义也

righteous（Legge）

right（Soothill，Waley，Leys）

duty（Lau）

appropriate（Ames/Rosemont）

19.1　见得思义

righteousness（Legge）

right（Soothill，Waley，Lau，Leys）

appropriate（Ames/Rosemont）

# 艺(4)

6.8　求也艺

various ability（Legge）

proficiency（Soothill）

versatile（Waley）

accomplished（Lau）

talented（Leys）

cultivated and refined（Ames/Rosemont）

7.6　游于艺

art（Legge，Soothill，Waley，Lau，Leys，Ames/Rosemont）

9.7 吾不试,故艺

art（Legge，Soothill，Ames/Rosemont）

handy（Waley）

jack of all trades（Lau）

various skills（Leys）

14.12 冉求之艺

varied talent（Legge）

skill（Soothill，Leys）

dexterity（Waley）

accomplished（Lau）

cultivated（Ames/Rosemont）

# 易(12)

1.7 贤贤易色

withdraw one's mind from（Legge）

transfer（Soothil）

wear（Waley）

put on（Lau）

3.4 与其易也

minute attention to observances（Legge）

observance of detail（Soothill）

be dictated by fear（Waley）

indifference（Lau）

formality（Leys）

formal details（Ames/Rosemont）

7.17　五十以学《易》

　　　Yî (Legge)

　　　the book of change (Soothill)

　　　the changes (Leys)

8.12　不易得也

　　　easy (Legge, Soothill, Waley, Lau, Leys, Ames/Rosemont)

13.15　为臣不易

　　　easy (Legge, Soothill, Waley, Lau, Leys, Ames/Rosemont)

13.25　君子易事而难说也……小人难事而易说也

　　　easy (Legge, Soothill, Waley, Lau, Leys, Ames/Rosemont)

14.10　富而无骄易

　　　easy (Legge, Soothill, Leys)

14.41　则民易使也

　　　readily (Legge)

　　　easily (Soothill, Leys)

　　　easy (Waley, Lau, Ames/Rosemont)

17.3　小人学道则易使也

　　　easily (Legge, Soothill)

　　　easy (Waley, Lau, Leys, Ames/Rosemont)

18.6　而谁以易之……丘不与易也

　　　change (Legge, Lau, Ames/Rosemont)

　　　reform (Soothill)

　　　alter (Waley)

　　　reform (Leys)

# 逸民(2)

18.8  逸民：伯夷、叔齐……

man who has retired to privacy from the world (Legge)

man noted for withdrawal into private life (Soothill)

subjects whose service are lost to the State (Waley)

man who withdraws from society (Lau)

those who withdraw from the world (Leys)

examples of those whose talents are lost to the people (Ames/Rosemont)

20.1  举逸民

those who have retired into obscurity (Legge)

man who has exiled themself (Soothill)

lose subjects (Waley)

man who has withdrawn from society (Lau)

political exile (Leys)

those subjects whose talents have been lost to the people (Ames/Rosemont)

# 意(1)

9.4  子绝四——毋意，毋必，毋固，毋我

foregone conclusion (Legge)

preconceptions (Soothill)

take something for granted (Waley)

entertain conjectures（Lau）

［no］capriciousness（Leys）

speculate（Ames/Rosemont）

## 毅(2)

8.7 士不可以不弘毅

vigorous endurance（Legge）

fortitude（Soothill）

stout of heart（Waley）

resolute（Lau，Leys）

resolve（Ames/Rosemont）

13.27 刚、毅、木、讷近仁

endure（Legge）

resolute in character（Soothill）

resolute（Waley）

resoluteness（Lau，Ames/Rosemont）

resolution（Leys）

## 淫(2)

3.20 乐而不淫

licentious（Legge）

sensual（Soothill）

debauch（Waley）

wantonness（Lau）

lasciviousness (Leys)

excessive (Ames/Rosemont)

15.11 郑声淫

licentious (Legge, Soothill, Waley)

wanton (Lau)

corrupt (Leys)

lewd (Ames/Rosemont)

## 隐(9)

7.24 二三子以我为隐乎？吾无隐乎尔

concealment (Legge)

possess something occult (Soothill)

keep (Waley)

hide (Lau, Leys)

hidden away (Ames/Rosemont)

8.13 无道则隐

keep concealed (Legge)

withdraw (Soothill)

hide (Waley, Leys)

keep out of sight (Lau)

remain hidden away (Ames/Rosemont)

13.18 父为子隐，子为父隐

conceal the misconduct (Legge)

screen (Soothill, Waley)

cover up (Lau, Leys)

cover (Ames/Rosemont)

16.6 言及之而不言谓之隐

concealment (Legge)

reticence (Soothill)

secretiveness (Waley, Leys)

evasive (Lau)

hold back (Ames/Rosemont)

16.11 隐居以求其志

retirement (Legge, Lau)

seclusion (Soothill, Waley, Ames/Rosemont)

withdraw (Leys)

18.7 隐者也

recluse (Legge, Soothill, Waley, Lau, Ames/Rosemont)

hermit (Leys)

18.8 隐居放言

hide (Legge)

seclusion (Soothill, Waley, Ames/Rosemont)

live as recluses (Lau)

hermit (Leys)

# 盈(2)

7.26 虚而为盈

full (Legge, Soothill, Lau)

fullness (Waley, Leys, Ames/Rosemont)

8.15 洋洋乎盈耳哉

fill (Legge, Soothill, Waley, Lau, Ames/Rosemont)

fullness (Leys)

# 勇(16)

2.24 见义不为，无勇也

    courage（Legge，Lau，Ames/Rosemont）

    [not] cowardice（Soothill，Waley，Leys）

5.7 由也好勇过我

    fonder of daring（Legge，Soothill）

    feats of physical daring（Waley）

    foolhardy（Lau）

    bold（Leys）

    boldness（Ames/Rosemont）

8.2 勇而无礼则乱

    boldness（Legge，Soothill，Ames/Rosemont）

    bounded（Waley）

    courage（Lau）

    bravery（Leys）

8.10 好勇疾贫

    daring（Legge，Soothill，Waley）

    courage（Lau）

    brave（Leys）

    boldness（Ames/Rosemont）

9.29 勇者不惧

    bold（Legge）

    brave（Soothill，Waley，Leys）

    courage（Lau）

    courageous（Ames/Rosemont）

11.24 可使有勇

bold（Legge）

brave（Soothill）

courage（Waley，Lau，Ames/Rosemont）

spirits（Leys）

14.4 仁者必有勇,勇者不必有仁

bold（Legge）

courageous（Soothill）

courage（Waley，Lau）

brave（Leys）

bold（Ames/Rosemont）

14.12 卞庄子之勇

bravery（Legge）

courage（Soothill）

valour（Waley，Leys）

courageous（Lau）

bold（Ames/Rosemont）

14.28 勇者不惧

bold（Legge）

courageous（Soothill，Ames/Rosemont）

brave（Waley）

courage（Lau，Leys）

17.7 好勇不好学

boldness（Legge，Ames/Rosemont）

daring（Soothill）

courge（Waley，Lau）

valour（Leys）

17.21 君子尚勇乎……君子有勇而无义为乱,小人有勇而无义为盗

valour（Legge）

courage（Soothill，Waley，Lau，Leys）

boldness（Ames/Rosemont）

17.22 恶勇而无礼者……恶不孙以为勇者

valour（Legge）

bold（Soothill，Ames/Rosemont）

daring（Waley）

courage（Lau，Leys）

# 友（27）

1.4 与朋友交而不信乎

friend（Legge，Soothill，Waley，Lau，Leys，Ames/Rosemont）

1.7 与朋友交言而有信

friend（Legge，Soothill，Waley，Lau，Leys，Ames/Rosemont）

1.8 无友不如己者

friend（Legge，Soothill，Lau，Ames/Rosemont）

friendship（Waley）

befriend（Leys）

2.21 友于兄弟

discharge duties（Legge）

friendliness（Soothill）

friendly（Waley，Lau）

kind（Leys）

befriend（Ames/Rosemont）

4.26 朋友数,斯疏矣

friend（Legge，Soothill，Lau）

friendly（Leys）

friendship（Waley，Ames/Rosemont）

5.25　匿怨而友其人

friendly（Legge，Soothill，Waley，Lau）

friend（Leys）

friendship（Ames/Rosemont）

5.26　与朋友共敝之而无憾……朋友信之

friend（Legge，Soothill，Waley，Lau，Leys，Ames/Rosemont）

8.5　昔者吾友尝从事于斯矣

friend（Legge，Soothill，Waley，Lau，Leys，Ames/Rosemont）

9.25　毋友不如己者

friend（Legge，Soothill，Lau）

friendship（Waley）

befriend（Leys，Ames/Rosemont）

10.16　朋友死

friend（Legge，Soothill，Waley，Lau，Leys，Ames/Rosemont）

10.17　朋友之馈

friend（Legge，Soothill，Waley，Lau，Leys，Ames/Rosemont）

12.23　子贡问友

friendship（Legge，Soothill）

friend（Waley，Lau，Leys，Ames/Rosemont）

12.24　君子以文会友，以友辅仁

friend（Legge，Soothill，Waley，Lau，Leys，Ames/Rosemont）

13.28　朋友切切偲偲

friend（Legge，Soothill，Waley，Lau，Leys，Ames/Rosemont）

15.10　友其士之仁者

make friends with（Legge，Soothill，Waley，Lau）

befriend（Leys）

befriend（Ames/Rosemont）

16.4 益者三友,损者三友。友直,友谅,友多闻……友便辟,友善柔,友便佞

friendship（Legge，Waley，Leys）

friend（Soothill，Waley，Leys，Ames/Rosemont）

make friends with（Soothill，Lau）

16.5 乐多贤友

friend（Legge，Soothill，Waley，Lau，Leys，Ames/Rosemont）

19.15 吾友张也为难能也

friend（Legge，Soothill，Waley，Lau，Leys，Ames/Rosemont）

# 有道(14)

1.14 就有道而正焉

principle（Legge）

high principled（Soothill）

possess the way（Waley）

possess of the way（Lau）

virtuous（Leys）

know the way（Ames/Rosemont）

5.2 邦有道,不废

well governed（Legge，Soothill）

rule according to the way（Waley）

way prevails（Lau，Leys，Ames/Rosemont）

5.21 邦有道,则知

good order prevails（Legge，Soothill）

way prevails（Waley，Lau，Leys，Ames/Rosemont）

8.13 天下有道则见……邦有道

　　well governed（Legge）

　　law and order prevails（Soothill）

　　way prevails（Waley，Lau，Ames/Rosemont）

　　follow the way（Leys）

12.19 以就有道何如

　　principled（Legge）

　　law abiding（Soothill）

　　have the way（Waley）

　　possess the way（Lau）

　　the good（Leys）

　　on the way（Ames/Rosemont）

14.1 邦有道，谷

　　good government prevails（Legge）

　　well governed（Soothill）

　　rule according to the way（Waley）

　　way prevails（Lau，Leys，Ames/Rosemont）

14.3 邦有道，危言危行

　　good government prevails（Legge）

　　law and order prevails（Soothill）

　　way prevails（Waley，Lau，Leys，Ames/Rosemont）

15.7 邦有道……邦有道

　　good government prevails（Legge）

　　well governed（Soothill）

　　way prevails（Waley，Lau，Ames/Rosemont）

　　under a good government（Leys）

16.2 天下有道……天下有道……天下有道

　　good government prevails（Legge，Soothill）

right principles prevail（Legge）

way prevails（Waley，Lau，Ames/Rosemont）

follow the way（Leys）

18.6 天下有道

right principles prevail（Legge）

right rule prevails（Soothill）

way prevails（Waley，Ames/Rosemont）

way is to be found（Lau）

follow the way（Leys）

# 诱(1)

9.11 夫子循循然善诱人

lead（Legge，Lau）

lure（Soothill，Waley）

entrap（Leys）

draw forward（Ames/Rosemont）

# 愚(9)

2.9 不违,如愚……回也不愚

stupid（Legge，Soothill，Waley，Lau，Leys）

slow（Ames/Rosemont）

5.21 邦无道,则愚……其愚不可及也

stupid（Legge，Lau，Leys，Ames/Rosemont）

fool（Soothill）

folly（Waley）

11.18　柴也愚

　　simple（Legge）

　　simple minded（Soothill）

　　stupid（Waley，Lau，Leys，Ames/Rosemont）

17.2　唯上知与下愚不移

　　stupid（Legge，Soothill，Waley，Lau，Leys，Ames/Rosemont）

17.7　其蔽也愚

　　foolish simplicity（Legge）

　　foolishness（Soothill，Lau）

　　silliness（Waley，Leys）

　　dupe（Ames/Rosemont）

17.14　古之愚也直，今之愚也诈而已矣

　　stupidity（Legge）

　　simple mindedness（Soothill，Waley）

　　foolish（Lau）

　　naiveté（Leys）

　　stupid（Ames/Rosemont）

# 欲(44)

2.4　七十而从心所欲

　　desire（Legge，Soothill，Lau，Leys）

　　dictate（Waley）

　　free rein（Ames/Rosemont）

3.10　吾不欲观之矣

　　wish（Legge，Soothill，Lau，Leys）

far rather（Waley）

desire（Ames/Rosemont）

3.17 子贡欲去告朔之饩羊

wish（Legge，Soothill，Leys）

want（Waley，Lau，Ames/Rosemont）

4.5 是人之所欲也

desire（Legge，Soothill，Waley，Lau）

crave（Leys）

want（Ames/Rosemont）

4.24 君子欲讷于言而敏于行

wish（Legge）

desire（Soothill）

covet（Waley）

desirable（Lau）

should（Leys）

want（Ames/Rosemont）

5.11 枨也欲，焉得刚

passion（Legge，Soothill）

desire（Waley，Lau，Leys）

acquisitive（Ames/Rosemont）

5.12 我不欲人之加诸我也,吾亦欲无加诸人

wish（Legge，Soothill，Lau）

want（Waley，Leys，Ames/Rosemont）

6.6 虽欲勿用

wish（Legge，Soothill）

want（Ames/Rosemont）

6.30 己欲立而立人,己欲达而达人

wish（Legge，Lau，Leys）

　　　　　desire（Soothill，Waley）

　　　　　seek（Ames/Rosemont）

7.30　我欲仁

　　　　　wish（Legge）

　　　　　crave（Soothill）

　　　　　want（Waley）

　　　　　desire（Lau）

　　　　　long for（Leys）

　　　　　seek（Ames/Rosemont）

9.11　欲罢不能……虽欲从之

　　　　　wish（Legge，Soothill）

　　　　　want（Waley，Lau，Leys，Ames/Rosemont）

9.14　子欲居九夷

　　　　　wish（Legge）

　　　　　propose（Soothill）

　　　　　want（Waley，Lau，Leys，Ames/Rosemont）

11.11　门人欲厚葬之

　　　　　wish（Legge）

　　　　　propose（Soothill）

　　　　　want（Waley，Lau，Leys，Ames/Rosemont）

12.2　己所不欲

　　　　　wish（Legge，Leys）

　　　　　would like（Soothill，Waley）

　　　　　desire（Lau）

　　　　　want（Ames/Rosemont）

12.10　爱之欲其生，恶之欲其死。既欲其生，又欲其死

　　　　　wish（Legge，Soothill）

　　　　　want（Soothill，Waley，Lau，Ames/Rosemont）

wish（Leys）

12.18 苟子之不欲

covetous（Legge，Leys）

love of wealth（Soothill）

desire（Waley，Lau）

greedy（Ames/Rosemont）

12.19 子欲善而民善矣

desire（Legge，Waley，Lau，Leys）

aspiration（Soothill）

want（Ames/Rosemont）

13.17 无欲速，无见小利。欲速，则不达

desirous（Legge）

intent（Soothill）

try（Waley，Leys，Ames/Rosemont）

14.1 克、伐、怨、欲不行焉

covetousness（Legge，Waley，Leys）

desire（Soothill）

covetous（Lau）

greed（Ames/Rosemont）

14.12 公绰之不欲

covetousness（Legge，Waley）

desire（Lau，Ames/Rosemont）

14.25 夫子欲寡其过而未能也

anxious（Legge）

seek（Soothill，Lau）

try（Waley，Ames/Rosemont）

wish（Leys）

14.44 欲速成者也

wish（Legge）

want（Soothill）

bend upon（Waley）

be after（Lau）

intent on（Ames/Rosemont）

15.10 工欲善其事

wish（Legge，Lau，Leys）

want（Soothill，Ames/Rosemont）

mean（Waley）

15.24 己所不欲

want（Legge，Ames/Rosemont）

would like（Soothill，Waley）

desire（Lau）

wish（Leys）

16.1 夫子欲之,吾二臣者皆不欲也……君子疾夫舍曰欲之而必为之辞

wish（Legge，Soothill，Lau，Leys）

want（Soothill，Lau，Leys，Ames/Rosemont）

desire（Waley）

in favour of（Waley，Lau）

17.1 阳货欲见孔子

wish（Legge）

want（Soothill，Waley，Lau，Leys，Ames/Rosemont）

17.4 子欲往

incline（Legge，Soothill）

would have liked to（Waley）

want（Lau，Ames/Rosemont）

tempt（Leys）

17.6 子欲往

incline（Legge，Soothill）

would have liked to（Waley）

want（Lau，Ames/Rosemont）

tempt（Leys）

17.17 予欲无言

would prefer（Legge）

wish（Soothill，Leys）

would much rather（Waley）

think（Lau，Ames/Rosemont）

17.18 孺悲欲见孔子

wish（Legge，Soothill）

want（Waley，Lau，Leys）

seek（Ames/Rosemont）

18.5 欲与之言

wish（Legge）

desire（Soothill，Waley）

intention（Lau）

want（Leys，Ames/Rosemont）

18.7 欲洁其身

wish（Legge）

desire（Soothill，Waley，Lau）

think（Ames/Rosemont）

19.24 人虽欲自绝

wish（Legge，Leys）

desire（Soothill）

try（Waley）

want（Lau）

20.2 欲而不贪……欲仁而得仁

desire (Legge, Soothill, Lau, Ames/Rosemont)

long for (Waley)

ambition (Leys)

## 喻(2)

4.16 君子喻于义,小人喻于利

conversant with (Legge)

inform (Soothill)

discover (Waley)

verse in (Lau)

consider (Leys)

understand (Ames/Rosemont)

## 怨(20)

4.12 放于利而行,多怨

murmur (Legge)

animosity (Soothill)

discontent (Waley)

ill will (Lau)

resentment (Leys, Ames/Rosemont)

4.18 劳而不怨

murmur (Legge)

complain (Soothill, Lau)

resentful (Waley)

bitterness(Leys)

resentment(Ames/Rosemont)

5.23 怨是用希

resentment(Legge, Soothill, Leys)

rancor(Waley)

ill will(Lau, Ames/Rosemont)

5.25 匿怨而友其人

resentment(Legge, Soothill)

indignation(Waley)

grievance(Lau)

resent(Leys)

ill will(Ames/Rosemont)

7.15 怨乎……又何怨

repine(Legge, Soothill, Waley)

complain(Lau, Leys)

ill will(Ames/Rosemont)

12.2 在邦无怨,在家无怨

murmur(Legge)

ill will(Soothill, Lau, Ames/Rosemont)

feelings of opposition(Waley)

resentment(Leys)

14.1 克、伐、怨、欲不行焉

resentment(Legge, Soothill, Waley, Leys)

grudge(Lau)

ill will(Ames/Rosemont)

14.9 没齿无怨言

murmur(Legge)

complain(Soothill)

resentment（Waley）

complaint（Lau，Leys）

ill（Ames/Rosemont）

14.10 贫而无怨难

murmur（Legge）

complain（Soothill，Lau）

resent（Waley）

resentment（Leys）

ill will（Ames/Rosemont）

14.34 以德报怨……以直报怨

injury（Legge，Lau）

enmity（Soothill）

resentment（Waley）

hatred（Leys）

ill will（Ames/Rosemont）

14.35 不怨天

murmur（Legge）

complaint（Soothill）

accuse（Waley，Leys）

complain（Lau）

ill will（Ames/Rosemont）

15.15 则远怨矣

resentment（Legge，Soothill）

discontent（Waley，Leys）

ill will（Lau，Ames/Rosemont）

17.8 可以怨

resentment（Legge）

modify the vexations of life（Soothill）

grievance (Waley, Lau)

vehicle for grief (Leys)

sharpen one's critical skills (Ames/Rosemont)

17.23 远之则怨

discontent (Legge)

resent (Soothill, Waley, Leys)

feel badly done by (Lau)

complain (Ames/Rosemont)

18.10 不使大臣怨乎不以

repine (Legge)

discontent (Soothill)

chafe (Waley)

complaint (Lau)

complain (Leys)

ill will (Ames/Rosemont)

20.2 劳而不怨……又谁怨

repine (Legge)

dissatisfaction (Soothill)

resentment (Waley)

complain (Lau)

groan (Leys)

ill will (Ames/Rosemont)

\* 愿(6)

A.

8.16 侗而不愿

attentive (Legge)

honest (Soothill, Waley)

cautious (Lau)

prudent (Leys)

caution (Ames/Rosemont)

B.

5.26 愿车马……愿无伐善……愿闻子之志

should like (Legge, Soothill, Waley, Lau)

wish (Leys)

would like to (Ames/Rosemont)

11.24 愿学焉……愿为小相焉

wish (Legge)

should like (Soothill, Waley)

be ready to (Lau)

would like (Leys)

willing (Ames/Rosemont)

# 约(6)

4.2 不仁者不可以久处约

poverty and hardship (Legge)

adversity (Soothill, Waley, Leys)

straitened circumstance (Lau)

hardship (Ames/Rosemont)

4.23 以约失之者鲜矣

cautious (Legge)

self restrained (Soothill)

    side of strictness (Waley)

    keep to essentials (Lau)

    self control (Leys)

    personal restraint (Ames/Rosemont)

6.27 约之以礼

    restraint (Legge, Waley)

    restrain (Soothill, Leys)

    bring back to essentials (Lau)

    discipline (Ames/Rosemont)

7.26 约而为泰

    straitened (Legge, Lau)

    in strait (Soothill)

    penury (Waley, Leys)

    poverty (Ames/Rosemont)

9.11 约我以礼

    restraint (Legge)

    restrain (Soothill, Waley, Leys)

    bring back to essentials (Lau)

    discipline (Ames/Rosemont)

12.15 约之以礼

    restraint (Legge, Waley)

    restrain (Soothill, Leys)

    bring back to essentials (Lau)

    discipline (Ames/Rosemont)

# 贼(5)

11.23　贼夫人之子

　　　injure（Legge）

　　　do an ill turn（Soothill，Waley）

　　　ruin（Lau）

　　　bad turn（Leys）

　　　harm（Ames/Rosemont）

14.43　是为贼

　　　pest（Legge，Lau）

　　　rogue（Soothill）

　　　useless pest（Waley）

　　　parasite（Leys）

　　　thief（Ames/Rosemont）

17.7　其蔽也贼

　　　injurious disregard of consequence（Legge）

　　　harmful candour（Soothill）

　　　degenerate into villainy（Waley）

　　　harmful behavior（Lau）

　　　banditry（Leys）

　　　harm（Ames/Rosemont）

17.11　德之贼也

　　　thief（Legge）

　　　spoiler（Soothill）

　　　spoil（Waley）

　　　ruin（Lau，Leys）

false pretense(Ames/Rosemont)

20.2　慢令致期谓之贼

　　　injury(Legge，Lau)

　　　robbery(Soothill)

　　　tormentor(Waley)

　　　extortion(Leys)

　　　injurious(Ames/Rosemont)

# 贞(1)

15.37　君子贞而不谅

　　　correctly firm(Legge)

　　　intelligently(Soothill)

　　　consistency is expected(Waley)

　　　steadfast in purpose(Lau)

　　　principled(Leys)

　　　proper(Ames/Rosemont)

# 争(3)

3.7　君子无所争……其争也君子

　　　contention(Legge)

　　　contend(Soothill，Lau)

　　　compete(Waley)

　　　competition(Leys)

　　　competitive(Ames/Rosemont)

15.22 君子矜而不争
　　　wrangle（Legge）
　　　striving（Soothill）
　　　quarrelsome（Waley）
　　　contentious（Lau）
　　　aggressive（Leys）
　　　contentious（Ames/Rosemont）

# 正（24）

1.14 就有道而正焉
　　　rectify（Legge，Soothill）
　　　correct（Waley）
　　　right（Lau）
　　　straighten（Leys）
　　　repair（Ames/Rosemont）

7.34 正唯弟子不能学也
　　　just（Legge，Soothill）
　　　precisely（Lau，Leys，Ames/Rosemont）

8.4 正颜色
　　　regulate（Legge）
　　　order（Soothill）
　　　betake good faith（Waley）
　　　proper（Lau，Ames/Rosemont）
　　　cling to good faith（Leys）

9.15 然后乐正
　　　reform（Legge）

revise（Soothill，Waley，Ames/Rosemont）

put right（Lau）

put back in order（Leys）

10.6 　割不正

properly（Legge，Soothill，Lau，Leys，Ames/Rosemont）

proper（Waley）

10.7 　席不正

straight（Legge，Soothill，Waley，Lau，Leys）

properly placed in accord with custom（Ames/Rosemont）

10.12 　必正席先尝之

adjust（Legge，Soothill，Lau）

straighten（Waley，Leys）

invariably place（Ames/Rosemont）

10.20 　升车，必正立

straight（Legge，Leys）

correctly（Soothill）

squarely（Waley，Lau）

upright（Ames/Rosemont）

12.17 　政者，正也。子帅以正，孰敢不正

rectify（Legge）

correctness（Legge）

correct（Legge，Lau）

aright（Soothill）

right（Soothill）

straighten（Waley）

straight（Leys）

proper（Ames/Rosemont）

13.3 　必也正名乎……奚其正……名不正

rectify (Legge)

correction (Soothill)

correct (Waley)

rectification (Lau)

rectify (Leys)

properly (Ames/Rosemont)

13.6 其身正……其身不正

correct (Legge, Lau)

upright (Soothill, Waley)

straight (Leys)

proper (Ames/Rosemont)

13.13 苟正其身矣……不能正其身, 如正人何

correct (Legge, Soothill, Lau)

aright (Waley)

straight (Leys)

proper (Ames/Rosemont)

14.15 晋文公谲而正, 齐桓公正而不谲

upright (Legge)

honourable (Soothill)

carry out the plain dictates of ritual (Waley)

integrity (Lau)

straight (Leys)

proper (Ames/Rosemont)

15.5 恭己正南面而已矣

gravely (Legge, Waley)

maintain the correct imperial attitude (Soothill)

in a respectful posture (Lau)

reverently (Leys)

due（Ames/Rosemont）

17.8 其犹正墙面而立也与

right against（Legge）

right up（Soothill）

press against（Waley）

squarely（Lau）

20.2 君子正其衣冠

adjust（Legge）

array oneself properly（Soothill）

straight（Waley）

adjust（Lau）

correctly（Leys，Ames/Rosemont）

# 政(41)

1.10 必闻其政

government（Legge，Lau）

administration（Soothill）

policy（Waley）

politics（Leys）

govern（Ames/Rosemont）

2.1 为政以德

government（Legge）

govern（Soothill）

rule（Waley，Lau，Leys）

govern（Ames/Rosemont）

2.3 道之以政

law (Legge，Soothill)

regulation (Waley)

edict (Lau)

political maneuver (Leys)

administrative (Ames/Rosemont)

2.21　子奚不为政……施于有政。是亦为政，奚其为为政

government (Legge，Lau，Leys)

public service (Soothill，Waley)

govern (Ames/Rosemont)

5.19　旧令尹之政

government (Legge)

policy (Soothill)

administration (Waley)

office (Lau，Leys)

affairs of state (Ames/Rosemont)

6.8　仲由可使从政也与……于从政乎何有……赐也可使从政也与……求也可使从政也与……于从政乎何有

government (Legge)

administration (Soothill)

office (Waley，Lau，Ames/Rosemont)

minister (Leys)

8.14　不谋其政

administration (Legge)

policy (Soothill，Waley，Leys，Ames/Rosemont)

office (Lau)

12.7　子贡问政

government (Legge，Soothill，Waley，Lau，Leys)

govern (Ames/Rosemont)

12.11 齐景公问政于孔子

　　government (Legge, Soothill, Waley, Lau, Leys)

　　govern (Ames/Rosemont)

12.14 子张问政

　　government (Legge, Soothill, Lau, Leys)

　　public (Waley)

　　govern (Ames/Rosemont)

12.17 季康子问政于孔子……政者

　　government (Legge, Soothill, Lau, Leys)

　　govern (Legge, Soothill, Leys)

　　art of ruling (Waley)

　　rule (Waley)

　　govern (Ames/Rosemont)

12.19 季康子问政于孔子曰……子为政

　　government (Legge, Soothill, Waley, Lau, Leys)

　　administration (Soothill)

　　rule (Waley)

　　govern (Leys, Ames/Rosemont)

13.1 子路问政

　　government (Legge, Waley, Lau, Leys)

　　art of government (Soothill)

　　govern effectively (Ames/Rosemont)

13.2 仲为季氏宰,问政

　　government (Legge, Waley, Lau, Leys)

　　art of government (Soothill)

　　govern effectively (Ames/Rosemont)

13.3 卫君待子而为政

　　government (Legge, Leys)

administration (Soothill，Lau，Ames/Rosemont)

administer (Waley)

13.5 授之以政

government (Legge，Waley)

administration (Soothill)

administrative (Lau)

official (Leys，Ames/Rosemont)

13.7 鲁、卫之政

government (Legge，Soothill，Ames/Rosemont)

politics (Waley，Leys)

state (Lau)

13.13 于从政乎何有

government (Legge，Waley，Leys)

public service (Soothill)

office (Lau)

govern (Ames/Rosemont)

13.14 有政……如有政

business (Legge)

affairs of state (Soothill，Waley，Lau，Leys，Ames/Rosemont)

13.16 叶公问政

government (Legge，Soothill，Waley，Lau，Leys)

govern (Ames/Rosemont)

13.17 子夏为莒父宰，问政

government (Legge，Waley，Lau)

policy (Soothill)

politics (Leys)

govern (Ames/Rosemont)

13.20 今之从政者何如

government (Legge, Soothill, Waley, Ames/Rosemont)

public life (Lau)

politician (Leys)

14.26 不谋其政

administration (Legge)

policy (Soothill, Waley, Ames/Rosemont)

government (Lau)

official policy (Leys)

16.2 则政不在大夫

government (Legge)

policy (Soothill, Waley, Lau)

political initiative (Leys)

govern (Ames/Rosemont)

16.3 政逮于大夫四世矣

government (Legge, Soothill, Waley, Lau)

political power (Leys)

governance (Ames/Rosemont)

18.5 今之从政者殆而

government (Legge)

office (Soothill, Waley, Lau, Leys, Ames/Rosemont)

19.18 其不改父之臣与父之政

government (Legge)

administration (Soothill)

domestic policy (Waley)

policy (Lau, Leys, Ames/Rosemont)

20.1 四方之政行焉

government (Legge, Soothill, Leys, Ames/Rosemont)

polity (Waley)

government (Lau)

20.2　何如斯可以从政矣……斯可以从政矣

　　　government (Legge, Soothill, Lau, Ames/Rosemont)

　　　administrator (Soothill)

　　　govern (Waley, Leys)

## 政事(1)

11.3　政事：冉有，季路

　　　administrative (Legge)

　　　administrative ability (Soothill)

　　　government (Lau, Leys)

　　　public business (Waley)

　　　statesmanship (Ames/Rosemont)

## *知(118)(zhī, zhì)

A. zhī

1.1　人不知而不愠

　　　take note of (Legge)

　　　recognize (Soothill, Waley)

　　　appreciate one's ability (Lau)

　　　acknowledge (Ames/Rosemont)

1.12　知和而和

　　　know (Legge, Soothill, Waley, Lau, Leys)

　　　realize (Ames/Rosemont)

1.15 告诸往而知来者

　　know（Legge，Soothill，Ames/Rosemont）

　　see（Waley，Lau）

　　figure out（Leys）

1.16 不患人之不己知,患不知人也

　　know（Legge，Soothill）

　　recognize one's merit（Waley）

　　appreciate one's ability（Lau）

　　recognize（Leys）

　　acknowledge（Ames/Rosemont）

2.4 五十而知天命

　　know（Legge，Waley，Leys）

　　understand（Soothill，Lau）

　　realize（Ames/Rosemont）

2.11 温故而知新

　　acquire（Legge，Soothill）

　　gain（Waley）

　　know（Lau，Leys）

　　realize（Ames/Rosemont）

2.22 不知其可也

　　know（Legge，Soothill，Leys）

　　see（Waley，Lau）

　　sure（Ames/Rosemont）

2.23 十世可知也……可知也……可知也……虽百世可知也

　　know（Legge，Lau，Leys，Ames/Rosemont）

　　foreknow（Soothill）

　　foretell（Waley）

3.11 不知也。知其说者之于天下也

know (Legge，Soothill，Waley，Leys，Ames/Rosemont)

understand（Lau）

3.15 孰谓鄹人之子知礼乎

know (Legge，Soothill，Ames/Rosemont)

be expert in（Waley）

understand（Lau）

be expert on（Leys）

3.22 然则管仲知礼乎……管氏而知礼,孰不知礼

know (Legge，Leys)

understand (Soothill，Lau，Ames/Rosemont)

have a great knowledge of（Waley）

3.23 乐其可知也

know (Legge，Lau，Leys)

understand (Soothill)

find out（Waley）

realize（Ames/Rosemont）

4.1 焉得知

wise (Legge, Soothill, Waley, Lau, Leys, Ames/Rosemont)

4.7 斯知仁矣

know (Legge，Soothill, Lau，Leys, Ames/Rosemont)

recognize（Waley）

4.14 不患莫己知,求为可知也

know (Legge，Soothill)

recognition（Waley）

appreciation（Lau）

famous（Leys）

acknowledge（Ames/Rosemont）

4.21 不可不知也

keep in the memory（Legge）

keep in mind（Soothill，Leys）

know（Waley）

aware of（Lau）

know（Ames/Rosemont）

5.5　不知其仁

know（Legge，Soothill，Waley，Leys）

say（Lau，Ames/Rosemont）

5.8　不知也……不知其仁也……不知其仁也……不知其仁也

know（Legge，Soothill，Waley，Leys）

say（Lau）

sure（Ames/Rosemont）

5.9　回也闻一以知十……赐也闻一以知二

know（Legge，Ames/Rosemont）

apprehend（Soothill）

understand（Waley，Lau）

deduce（Leys）

5.19　未知……未知

know（Legge，Soothill，Leys）

sure（Waley，Ames/Rosemont）

wise（Lau）

5.22　不知所以裁之

know（Legge，Soothill，Lau，Leys，Ames/Rosemont）

idea（Waley）

6.20　知之者不如好之者

know（Legge，Soothill，Waley，Lau，Leys）

understand（Ames/Rosemont）

7.14　三月不知肉味

know (Legge，Waley，Ames/Rosemont)

conscious（Soothill）

notice（Lau）

7.19 不知老之将至云尔

perceive（Legge）

observe（Soothill）

realize（Waley，Ames/Rosemont）

notice（Lau）

7.20 我非生而知之者

in the possession of knowledge（Legge）

knowledge（Soothill，Waley，Lau，Leys，Ames/Rosemont）

7.31 陈司败问昭公知礼乎……知礼……君而知礼,孰不知礼……人必知之

know（Legge，Soothill，Waley，Leys，Ames/Rosemont）

notice（Lau）

8.3 吾知免夫

know（Legge，Soothill，Leys）

get through（Waley）

sure（Lau，Ames/Rosemont）

8.9 不可使知之

understand（Legge，Soothill，Waley，Lau，Leys）

realize（Ames/Rosemont）

8.16 吾不知之矣

understand（Legge，Ames/Rosemont）

acquaintance（Soothill）

recognition（Waley）

understanding（Lau，Leys）

9.6 太宰知我乎

know (Legge, Soothill, Lau, Leys, Ames/Rosemont)

quite right about (Waley)

9.23 焉知来者之不如今也

know (Legge, Soothill, Waley, Lau, Leys, Ames/Rosemont)

9.28 然后知松柏之后彫也

know (Legge, Leys)

realize (Soothill, Ames/Rosemont)

see (Waley)

11.12 未知生,焉知死

know (Legge, Waley, Leys)

underatand (Soothill, Lau, Ames/Rosemont)

11.24 不吾知也!如或知尔……且知方也

know (Legge, Soothill)

recognize (Waley, Leys, Ames/Rosemont)

appreciate (Lau)

13.2 焉知贤才而举之……举尔所知;尔所不知

know (Legge, Waley)

recognize (Soothill, Lau, Leys, Ames/Rosemont)

13.3 君子于其所不知

know (Legge)

understand (Soothill, Waley, Ames/Rosemont)

competent (Leys)

13.15 如知为君之难也

know (Legge)

perceive (Soothill)

understand (Waley, Lau, Leys, Ames/Rosemont)

14.1 仁则吾不知也

know (Legge, Soothill, Waley, Lau, Leys, Ames/Rosemont)

14.17 自经于沟渎而莫之知也

　　　know（Legge）

　　　wiser（Soothill，Waley，Ames/Rosemont）

　　　notice（Lau，Leys）

14.30 不患人之不己知

　　　know（Legge，Soothill）

　　　recognize（Waley，Ames/Rosemont）

　　　appreciate（Lau）

14.35 莫我知也夫……何为其莫知子也……知我者其天乎

　　　know（Legge，Soothill，Waley）

　　　understand（Lau，Leys）

　　　appreciate（Ames/Rosemont）

14.38 是知其不可而为之者与

　　　know（Legge，Soothill，Waley，Lau，Leys，Ames/Rosemont）

14.39 莫己知也

　　　notice（Legge）

　　　recognize（Waley）

　　　understand（Lau）

　　　appreciate（Ames/Rosemont）

15.4 知德者鲜矣

　　　know（Legge）

　　　understand（Soothill，Waley，Lau，Leys）

　　　realize（Ames/Rosemont）

15.8 知者不失人

　　　wise（Legge，Waley，Lau，Leys，Ames/Rosemont）

　　　intelligent（Soothill）

15.14 知柳下惠之贤而不与立也

　　　know（Legge，Soothill，Waley，Lau，Leys，Ames/Rosemont）

15.19 不病人之不己知也
　　　know（Legge）
　　　recognize（Waley）
　　　appreciate（Lau）
　　　acknowledge（Ames/Rosemont）

15.34 君子不可小知而可大受也，小人不可大受而可小知也
　　　know（Legge）
　　　distinguishable（Soothill）
　　　knowledge（Waley）
　　　value（Lau）
　　　see（Leys）

16.8 小人不知天命而不畏也
　　　know（Legge，Soothill，Waley，Leys，Ames/Rosemont）
　　　[not] ignorant of（Lau）

16.9 生而知之者上也，学而知之者次也
　　　possession of knowledge（Legge）
　　　wisdom（Soothill）
　　　wise（Waley）
　　　knowledge（Lau，Leys，Ames/Rosemont）

17.22 恶徼以为知者
　　　wisdom（Legge，Soothill，Waley，Lau，Ames/Rosemont）
　　　learned（Leys）

18.6 是知津矣
　　　know（Legge，Soothill，Waley，Leys，Ames/Rosemont）

18.7 已知之矣
　　　aware（Legge，Soothill）
　　　know（Waley，Lau，Ames/Rosemont）
　　　foresee（Leys）

19.5　日知其所亡

　　recognise（Legge）

　　find out（Soothill）

　　conscious（Waley，Lau）

　　remember（Leys）

　　aware（Ames/Rosemont）

19.24　多见其不知量也

　　know（Legge，Waley，Lau，Ames/Rosemont）

　　have idea of（Soothill）

20.3　不知命……不知礼……不知言,无以知人也

　　acquaintace（Legge）

　　know（Legge）

　　recognise（Legge）

　　know（Soothill，Waley）

　　understand（Waley，Lau，Leys，Ames/Rosemont）

B. zhì

2.17　是知也

　　knowledge（Legge，Soothill，Waley，Lau，Leys）

　　wisdom（Ames/Rosemont）

4.2　知者利仁

　　wise（Legge，Soothill，Waley，Lau，Leys）

　　wise person（Ames/Rosemont）

5.18　何如其知也

　　wisdom（Legge，Soothill）

　　sure（Waley）

　　intelligence（Lau）

　　mind（Leys）

　　think（Ames/Rosemont）

5.21 邦有道,则知……其知可及也

　　　know（Legge, Soothill）

　　　wisdom（Waley, Ames/Rosemont）

　　　intelligence（Lau, Leys）

6.22 樊迟问知……可谓知矣

　　　wisdom（Legge, Soothill, Waley, Lau, Leys, Ames/Rosemont）

6.23 知者乐水……知者动……知者乐

　　　wise（Legge, Waley, Lau, Leys, Ames/Rosemont）

　　　clever（Soothill）

7.28 知之次也

　　　know（Legge, Soothill）

　　　knowledge（Waley, Lau, Leys）

　　　understand（Ames/Rosemont）

9.8 吾有知乎哉？无知也

　　　knowledge（Legge, Soothill, Lau）

　　　wisdom（Waley, Ames/Rosemont）

　　　knowledgeable（Leys）

9.29 知者不惑

　　　wise（Legge, Waley, Leys, Ames/Rosemont）

　　　enlighten（Soothill）

　　　wisdom（Lau）

12.22 问知。子曰:知人……乡也吾见于夫子而问知

　　　knowledge（Legge, Soothill, Leys）

　　　know（Legge, Soothill, Waley, Lau, Leys）

　　　wise（Waley）

　　　wisdom（Lau）

　　　realize（Ames/Rosemont）

14.12 若臧武仲之知

knowledge（Legge）

sagacity（Soothill）

wisdom（Waley，Leys）

wise（Lau，Ames/Rosemont）

14.28　知者不惑

wise（Legge，Waley，Ames/Rosemont）

knowledge（Soothill）

wisdom（Lau，Leys）

15.33　知及之……知及之……知及之

knowledge（Legge，Leys）

intellectually（Soothill）

wisdom（Waley）

understanding（Lau）

realization（Ames/Rosemont）

17.1　可谓知乎

wise（Legge，Soothill，Waley，Lau，Leys，Ames/Rosemont）

17.2　唯上知与下愚不移

wise（Legge，Ames/Rosemont）

wisest（Soothill，Waley，Leys）

intelligent（Soothill，Lau）

17.7　好知不好学

know（Legge）

knowledge（Soothill）

wisdom（Waley）

cleverness（Lau）

intelligence（Leys）

wisely（Ames/Rosemont）

19.25　君子一言以为知，一言以为不知

wise（Legge，Soothill，Waley，Lau，Ames/Rosemont）

wisdom（Leys）

# 直(22)

2.19　举直错诸枉……举枉错诸直
　　　upright（Legge，Soothill）
　　　straight（Waley，Lau，Leys）
　　　true（Ames/Rosemont）

5.24　孰谓微生高直
　　　upright（Legge，Soothill，Waley）
　　　straight（Lau，Leys）
　　　true（Ames/Rosemont）

6.19　人之生也直
　　　uprightness（Legge，Soothill）
　　　honesty（Waley）
　　　straight（Lau）
　　　integrity（Leys）
　　　true（Ames/Rosemont）

8.2　直而无礼则绞
　　　straightforwardness（Legge）
　　　frankness（Soothill，Leys）
　　　inflexibility（Waley）
　　　courage（Lau）
　　　candor（Ames/Rosemont）

8.16　狂而不直
　　　upright（Legge）

　　　　straightforward（Soothill）

　　　　honest（Waley）

　　　　straight（Lau）

　　　　sincere（Leys）

　　　　discipline（Ames/Rosemont）

12.20　质直而好义

　　　　straightforward（Legge，Waley）

　　　　upright（Soothill）

　　　　straight（Lau，Leys）

　　　　true（Ames/Rosemont）

12.22　举直错诸枉，能使枉者直……举直错诸枉，能使枉者直

　　　　upright（Legge）

　　　　straight（Soothill，Waley，Lau，Leys）

　　　　true（Ames/Rosemont）

13.18　吾党有直躬者……吾党之直者异于是……直在其中矣

　　　　uprightness（Legge，Waley）

　　　　honesty（Soothill）

　　　　straightness（Lau）

　　　　integrity（Leys）

　　　　true（Ames/Rosemont）

14.34　以直报怨

　　　　justice（Legge，Leys）

　　　　just treatment（Soothill）

　　　　upright（Waley）

　　　　straightness（Lau）

　　　　true（Ames/Rosemont）

15.7　直哉史鱼

　　　　straightforward（Legge）

straight (Soothill, Lau, Leys)

straight and upright (Waley)

true (Ames/Rosemont)

15.25 三代之所以直道而行也

    straightforwardness (Legge)

    straight (Soothill, Waley, Lau, Leys)

    true (Ames/Rosemont)

16.4 友直,友谅,友多闻

    upright (Legge, Soothill, Waley)

    straight (Lau, Leys)

    true (Ames/Rosemont)

17.7 好直不好学,其蔽也绞

    straightforwardness (Legge, Soothill)

    uprightness (Waley)

    forthrightness (Lau)

    frankness (Leys)

    candor (Ames/Rosemont)

17.14 古之愚也直

    straightforwardness (Legge, Soothill)

    straightforward (Waley)

    straight (Lau, Leys)

    frank and direct (Ames/Rosemont)

17.22 恶讦以为直者

    straightforward (Legge)

    straightforwardness (Soothill)

    honesty (Waley)

    forthrightness (Lau)

    frank (Leys)

　　　　true (Ames/Rosemont)

18.2　直道而事人

　　　　upright (Legge)

　　　　honest (Soothill，Waley)

　　　　not prepared to bend (Lau)

　　　　honestly (Leys)

　　　　straight (Ames/Rosemont)

# 志(17)

1.11　观其志

　　　　will (Legge)

　　　　tendency (Soothill)

　　　　intention (Waley)

　　　　mind (Lau)

　　　　aspiration (Leys)

　　　　intend (Ames/Rosemont)

2.4　吾十有五而志于学

　　　　mind (Legge, Soothill, Leys)

　　　　heart (Waley, Lau)

　　　　heart and mind (Ames/Rosemont)

4.4　苟志于仁矣

　　　　will (Legge，Ames/Rosemont)

　　　　mind (Soothill)

　　　　heart (Lau，Waley)

　　　　seek to achieve (Leys)

4.9　士志于道

mind (Legge)

aim at (Soothill)

heart (Waley, Lau, Leys)

purpose (Ames/Rosemont)

4.18 见志不从

advice (Legge, Lau, Leys)

opinion (Waley)

suggestion (Ames/Rosemont)

5.26 盍各言尔志……愿闻子之志

wish (Legge, Soothill, Waley, Leys)

heart (Lau)

would like to do (Ames/Rosemont)

7.6 志于道

will (Legge)

mind (Soothill)

heart (Waley, Lau, Leys)

sight (Ames/Rosemont)

9.26 匹夫不可夺志也

will (Legge, Soothill, Leys)

opinion (Waley)

purpose (Lau, Ames/Rosemont)

11.24 亦各言其志也……亦各言其志也已矣

wish (Legge, Waley)

aspiration (Soothill, Leys)

desire (Soothill, Waley)

heart (Lau)

mind (Ames/Rosemont)

14.36 夫子固有惑志于公伯寮

mind (Soothill, Waley, Leys)

sign (Lau)

15.9　志士仁人

determined scholar (Legge)

resolute scholar (Soothill)

truly the heart of a knight (Waley)

purpose (Lau)

righteous (Leys)

resolute scholar apprentice (Ames/Rosemont)

16.11　隐居以求其志

aim (Legge, Soothill, Waley)

purpose (Lau)

aspiration (Leys)

ends (Ames/Rosemont)

18.8　不降其志……降志辱身矣

will (Legge)

high purpose (Soothill)

high resolve (Waley)

purpose (Lau, Ames/Rosemont)

19.6　博学而笃志

aim (Legge)

will (Soothill)

purpose (Waley, Lau, Leys, Ames/Rosemont)

# 质(8)

6.18　质胜文则野,文胜质则史。文质彬彬

solid quality（Legge）

nature（Soothill，Leys）

natural substance（Waley）

native substance（Lau）

disposition（Ames/Rosemont）

12.8 君子质而已矣……文犹质也，质犹文也

substance（Legge）

nature（Soothill，Leys）

stuff（Waley，Lau）

inborn quality（Waley）

disposition（Ames/Rosemont）

12.20 质直而好义

solid（Legge）

nature（Soothill，Waley，Lau）

timber（Leys）

disposition（Ames/Rosemont）

15.18 君子义以为质

essential（Legge）

foundation principle（Soothill）

material to work（Waley）

basic stuff（Lau）

basis（Leys）

disposition（Ames/Rosemont）

# 治(6)

5.8 可使治其赋也

　　　　manage (Legge)

　　　　administration (Soothill)

　　　　carry out (Waley)

　　　　manage (Lau)

　　　　ministry (Leys)

　　　　in charge of (Ames/Rosemont)

8.20　舜有臣五人而天下治

　　　　well governed (Legge, Lau)

　　　　well ruled (Soothill, Waley)

　　　　rule (Leys)

　　　　properly governed (Ames/Rosemont)

14.19　仲叔圉治宾客,祝鮀治宗庙,王孙贾治军旅

　　　　superintendence (Legge)

　　　　management (Legge)

　　　　direction (Legge)

　　　　charge (Soothill)

　　　　command (Soothill, Waley, Ames/Rosemont)

　　　　deal (Waley)

　　　　regulate (Waley)

　　　　responsible (Lau)

　　　　in charge of (Leys)

　　　　take care of (Ames/Rosemont)

　　　　conduct (Ames/Rosemont)

15.5　无为而治者其舜也与

　　　　govern (Legge, Leys)

　　　　well governed (Soothill)

　　　　rule (Waley)

　　　　achieve order (Lau)

effect proper order (Ames/Rosemont)

# 致(9)

1.7 事君能致其身
   devote (Legge)
   lay down (Soothill, Waley)
   exert (Lau)
   give (Leys, Ames/Rosemont)

8.21 而致孝乎鬼神;恶衣服,而致美乎黻冕
   utmost (Legge, Waley, Lau)
   scrupulous (Soothill)
   unspare (Soothill)
   spare no effort (Lau)
   utter (Leys)
   generous (Ames/Rosemont)
   lavish (Ames/Rosemont)

19.1 士见危致命
   sacrifice (Legge)
   offer (Soothill)
   lay down (Waley, Lau)
   give (Leys)
   put (Ames/Rosemont)

19.4 致远恐泥
   carry out (Legge)
   go (Soothill, Ames/Rosemont)
   pursue (Waley)

19.7 君子学以致其道

　　reach（Legge，Leys）

　　carry one's wisdom to（Soothill）

　　improve（Waley）

　　perfect（Lau）

　　promote（Ames/Rosemont）

19.14 丧致乎哀而止

　　utmost（Legge）

　　suffice as its highest expression（Soothill）

　　dictate（Waley）

　　give full expression（Lau）

　　express（Leys）

　　expression（Ames/Rosemont）

19.17 人未有自致者也

　　show（Legge，Soothill，Waley）

　　realize（Lau）

　　reveal（Leys）

　　give（Ames/Rosemont）

20.2 慢令致期谓之贼

　　insist on with severity（Legge）

　　demand for（Soothill）

　　expect（Waley）

　　insist（Lau）

　　enforce（Ames/Rosemont）

* **中**(25)(zhōng, zhòng)

A. zhōng

2.18 禄在其中矣

in (Legge, Soothill, Lau)

5.1 虽在缧绁之中

in (Legge, Soothill, Lau, Leys, Ames/Rosemont)

6.12 中道而废

middle (Legge)

half (Soothill, Leys)

during (Waley)

among (Lau)

along (Ames/Rosemont)

6.21 中人以上……中人以下

mediocrity (Legge)

average (Soothill, Lau, Leys)

middle (Waley)

common (Ames/Rosemon)

7.16 乐亦在其中矣

midst (Legge)

in (Soothill, Ames/Rosemont)

10.3 立不中门

middle (Legge, Soothill, Waley, Leys, Ames/Rosemont)

centre (Lau)

10.20 车中不内顾

in (Legge, Soothill, Lau, Lau, Leys, Ames/Rosemont)

13.18　直在其中矣

　　in（Legge, Soothill, Lau, Leys, Ames/Rosemont）

　　involve（Waley）

13.21　不得中行而与之

　　medium（Legge）

　　media（Soothill）

　　middle（Waley, Leys）

　　moderate（Lau）

　　temperate（Ames/Rosemont）

15.32　馁在其中矣……禄在其中矣

　　in（Legge, Soothill）

16.1　且在邦域之中矣……龟玉毁于椟中

　　in the midst of（Legge）

　　within（Soothill, Waley, Lau, Ames/Rosemont）

　　in（Soothill, Waley, Lau, Leys）

17.6　佛肸以中牟畔

　　chung（Legge, Soothill, Waley, Lau）

　　zhong（Leys, Ames/Rosemont）

19.6　仁在其中矣

　　in（Legge, Soothill, Ames/Rosemont）

20.1　允执其中

　　due mean（Legge）

　　golden mean（Soothill）

　　centre（Waley）

　　middle way（Lau, Leys）

　　without deviation（Ames/Rosemont）

B. zhòng

11.14　言必有中

hit the point（Legge）

hit the mark（Soothill，Waley，Leys）

to the point（Lau）

on the mark（Ames/Rosemont）

11.18 亿则屡中

correct（Legge）

hit the mark（Soothill，Waley）

right（Lau，Leys）

on the mark（Ames/Rosemont）

13.3 则刑罚不中；刑罚不中

properly awarded（Legge）

right（Lau）

target（Leys）

on the mark（Ames/Rosemont）

18.8 言中伦，行中虑……身中清，废中权

correspond with（Legge）

preserve（Legge）

according to（Legge）

make for（Soothill）

hit off（Soothill）

sustain（Soothill）

consonant with（Waley）

secure（Waley）

maintain（Waley）

in accord with（Lau）

preserve（Leys）

remain（Leys）

shrewd（Leys）

# 中庸(1)

6.29　中庸之为德也
　　　　constant mean (Legge)
　　　　golden mean (Soothill)
　　　　mark in the everyday (Ames/Rosemont)
　　　　mean (Lau)
　　　　middle use (Waley)
　　　　middle way (Leys)

# 忠(18)

1.4　为人谋而不忠乎
　　　　faithful (Legge)
　　　　conscientiousness (Soothill)
　　　　loyal to one's interest (Waley)
　　　　do one's best (Lau)
　　　　trustworthy (Leys)
　　　　utmost (Ames/Rosemont)
1.8　主忠信
　　　　faithfulness (Legge)
　　　　conscientiousness (Soothill)
　　　　faithful (Waley)
　　　　do one's best (Lau)
　　　　loyalty (Leys)

utmost (Ames/Rosemont)

2.20 忠以劝……孝慈则忠

faithful (Legge)

loyalty (Soothill)

loyal (Waley, Leys)

do one's utmost (Lau, Ames/Rosemont)

3.19 臣事君以忠

faithfulness (Legge)

loyalty (Soothill, Leys)

devotion to one's cause (Waley)

do one's utmost (Lau, Ames/Rosemont)

4.15 忠恕而已矣

true to the principles of one's nature (Legge)

conscientiousness (Soothill)

loyalty (Waley, Leys)

do one's best (Lau, Ames/Rosemont)

5.19 子曰:"忠矣。"

loyal (Legge, Leys)

conscientious (Soothill)

faithful (Waley)

do one's best (Lau, Ames/Rosemont)

5.28 必有忠信如丘者焉

honourable (Legge)

conscientious (Soothill)

loyal (Waley, Leys)

do one's best (Lau)

do one's utmost (Ames/Rosemont)

7.25 文,行,忠,信

devotion of soul (Legge)

conscientiousness (Soothill)

loyalty to superior (Waley)

do one's best (Lau, Ames/Rosemont)

loyalty (Leys)

9.25　主忠信

faithfulness (Legge)

conscientiousness (Soothill)

faithful (Waley)

do one's best (Lau)

loyalty (Leys)

do one's utmost (Ames/Rosemont)

12.10　主忠信

faithfulness (Legge)

conscientiousness (Soothill)

loyalty (Waley, Leys)

do one's best (Lau)

utmost (Ames/Rosemont)

12.14　行之以忠

consistency (Legge)

conscientiously (Soothill)

loyally (Waley, Leys)

do one's best (Lau, Ames/Rosemont)

12.23　忠告而善道之

faithfully (Legge)

conscientiously (Soothill)

loyally (Waley)

to the best of one's ability (Lau)

loyal（Leys）

utmost（Ames/Rosemont）

13.19　与人忠

intercourse（Legge）

conscientious（Soothill）

loyal（Waley，Leys）

give of one's best（Lau）

do one's utmost（Ames/Rosemont）

14.7　忠焉,能勿诲乎

loyalty（Legge，Soothill，Leys）

loyal（Waley）

do one's best（Lau，Ames/Rosemont）

15.6　言忠信……言不忠信

sincere（Legge，Soothill）

loyal（Waley）

conscientious（Lau）

loyalty（Leys）

utmost（Ames/Rosemont）

16.10　言思忠

sincere（Legge）

conscientious（Soothill，Lau）

loyal（Waley，Leys）

utmost（Ames/Rosemont）

# 终(11)

1.9　慎终追远

funeral rites to parent (Legge)

decease of parent (Soothill)

dead (Waley, Leys)

funeral of one's parent (Lau)

funerary service (Ames/Rosemont)

2.9 吾与回言终日

whole (Legge, Soothill, Waley)

all (Lau, Leys)

entire (Ames/Rosemont)

4.5 君子无终食之间违仁

（没有对应的译文）

9.27 子路终身诵之

continually (Legge, Waley, Leys)

perpetually (Soothill)

constantly (Lau)

over and over again (Ames/Rosemont)

15.17 群居终日

whole (Legge, Waley, Leys)

lifelong (Soothill)

all (Lau, Ames/Rosemont)

15.24 有一言而可以终身行之者乎

all (Legge, Waley)

lifelong (Soothill)

throughout (Lau)

entire (Leys)

end (Ames/Rosemont)

15.31 吾尝终日不食,终夜不寝

whole (Legge, Soothill, Waley, Leys, Ames/Rosemont)

all (Lau)

17.20 饱食终日

whole (Legge，Ames/Rosemont)

lifelong (Soothill)

all (Waley, Lau，Leys)

17.24 其终也已

continue (Legge)

end (Soothill，Waley，Leys)

no hope (Lau)

hopeless (Ames/Rosemont)

20.1 天禄永终

perpetual end (Legge)

forever end (Soothill)

last forever (Waley)

terminated for ever (Lau)

withdraw forever (Leys)

severed utterly (Ames/Rosemont)

# 众(13)

1.6 泛爱众

all (Legge)

all men (Soothill)

everyone (Waley)

multitude (Lau，Ames/Rosemont)

people (Leys)

2.1 居其所而众星共之

all (Legge, Soothill, Waley, Leys)

multitude (Lau, Ames/Rosemont)

6.30　如有博施于民而能济众

　　all (Legge)

　　multitude (Soothill, Lau, Leys, Ames/Rosemont)

　　whole state (Waley)

9.3　吾从众……虽违众

　　common practice (Legge)

　　general usage (Soothill, Leys)

　　general practice (Waley)

　　majority (Lau)

　　accepted practice (Ames/Rosemont)

12.22　选于众……选于众

　　all the people (Legge)

　　multitude (Soothill, Waley, Lau, Leys, Ames/Rosemont)

15.28　众恶之……众好之

　　multitude (Legge, Lau)

　　all (Soothill)

　　everyone (Waley, Leys, Ames/Rosemont)

17.5　宽则得众

　　all (Legge, Soothill)

　　multitude (Waley, Lau)

　　all hearts (Leys)

　　the many (Ames/Rosemont)

19.3　异乎吾所闻:君子尊贤而容众

　　all (Legge, Soothill, Waley)

　　the mediocre (Leys)

　　multitude (Lau)

everyone (Ames/Rosemont)

20.1 宽则得众

all (Legge, Soothill)

multitude (Waley, Lau)

mass (Leys)

many (Ames/Rosemont)

20.2 君子无众寡

many people (Legge)

many (Soothill, Lau, Leys, Ames/Rosemont)

many persons (Waley)

# 重(4)

1.8 君子不重则不威

grave (Legge, Soothill)

[not] frivolous (Waley)

gravity (Lau, Leys, Ames/Rosemont)

8.7 任重而道远……不亦重乎

heavy (Legge, Soothill, Waley, Lau, Leys, Ames/Rosemont)

20.1 所重:民、食、丧、祭

attach chief importance to (Legge)

lay stress on (Soothill)

care for most (Waley)

consider of importance (Lau)

matter (Leys)

priority (Ames/Rosemont)

# 周(4)

2.14 君子周而不比，小人比而不周
    catholic（Legge）
    broad minded（Soothill）
    see a question from all side（Waley）
    association（Lau）
    whole（Leys）
    associate openly with（Ames/Rosemont）

6.4 君子周急不继富
    help（Legge，Waley，Lau，Leys，Ames/Rosemont）
    succour（Soothill）

20.1 虽有周亲
    near（Legge）
    closely（Soothill）
    close（Lau）
    own（Leys）
    immediate（Ames/Rosemont）

# 周南(2)

17.8 《周南》……《周南》
    châu nan（Legge）
    chou nan（Soothill，Waley，Lau）
    first part of *the Poems*（Leys）

zhounan(Ames/Rosemont)

# 庄(4)

2.20 临之以庄则敬

gravity(Legge)

dignity(Soothill, Waley, Lau, Leys, Ames/Rosemont)

11.19 色庄者乎

gravity(Legge)

seriousness(Soothill)

solemnity(Waley)

dignified(Lau)

solemn(Leys)

serious(Ames/Rosemont)

15.33 不庄以莅之……庄以莅之

dignity(Legge, Soothill, Waley, Lau, Leys, Ames/Rosemont)

# 宗庙(5)

10.1 其在宗庙

ancestorial temple(Legge)

temple(Soothill)

ancestral temple(Waley, Lau, Leys, Ames/Rosemont)

11.24 宗庙之事……宗庙会同

ancestral temple(Legge, Soothill, Waley, Lau, Leys, Ames/Rosemont)

14.19 祝鮀治宗庙

ancestral temple (Legge, Soothill, Waley, Lau, Ames/Rosemont)

ancestors cult (Leys)

19.23 不见宗庙之美

ancestral temple (Legge, Waley, Lau, Leys, Ames/Rosemont)

temple (Soothill)

## 宗族(1)

13.20 宗族称孝焉

circle of one's relative (Legge)

relative (Soothill, Waley, Leys)

clan (Lau)

family (Ames/Rosemont)

## 罪(6)

3.13 获罪于天

offend (Legge, Lau, Leys, Ames/Rosemont)

sin (Soothill)

put oneself in the wrong (Waley)

5.1 非其罪也

guilty (Legge)

wrongdoing (Soothill, Lau)

fault (Waley, Ames/Rosemont)

20.1 有罪不敢赦……朕躬有罪……万方有罪,罪在朕躬

offence (Legge)

sin（Soothill）

guilty（Waley, Lau, Leys，Ames/Rosemont）

# 作(11)

1.2 　而好作乱者

　　　　stir up（Legge）

　　　　create（Soothill）

　　　　start（Lau，Waley）

　　　　foment（Leys）

　　　　initiate（Ames/Rosemont）

3.23 　始作,翕如也

　　　　commencement（Legge）

　　　　proceed（Soothill）

　　　　begin（Waley, Lau，Ames/Rosemont）

7.1 　述而不作

　　　　maker（Legge）

　　　　originator（Soothill）

　　　　make up anything of one's own（Waley）

　　　　innovate（Lau）

　　　　invent（Leys）

　　　　forge new paths（Ames/Rosemont）

7.28 　盖有不知而作之者

　　　　act（Legge，Leys）

　　　　do（Soothill，Waley）

　　　　innovate（Lau）

　　　　initiate（Ames/Rosemont）

9.10 虽少,必作

rise（Legge，Waley，Lau，Ames/Rosemont）

arise（Soothill）

stand up（Leys）

10.19 必变色而作

rise up（Legge）

stand up（Soothill）

rise to one's feet（Waley，Lau，Leys，Ames/Rosemont）

10.21 三嗅而作

rise（Legge，Soothill，Waley）

flow away（Lau，Leys）

take to the air（Ames/Rosemont）

11.14 何必改作

make（Legge）

construct（Soothill）

build（Waley，Lau，Leys，Ames/Rosemont）

11.24 舍瑟而作

rise（Legge，Waley，Ames/Rosemont）

arise（Soothill）

stand up（Lau）

13.22 不可以作巫医

be（Legge）

make（Soothill，Waley，Lau，Leys，Ames/Rosemont）

14.37 作者七人矣

do（Legge，Soothill，Leys）

make（Waley）

get up（Lau）

take initiative（Ames/Rosemont）

# 以译者姓名索引

## 爱(9)

| | |
|---|---|
| Ames/Rosemont | grudge 3.17 |
| | love 1.5, 1.6, 12.10, 12.22, 14.7, 17.3 |
| | loving care 17.19 |
| Lau | be loath to 3.17 |
| | love 1.5, 1.6, 12.10, 12.22, 14.7, 17.3, 17.19 |
| Legge | love 1.5, 1.6, 3.17, 12.10, 12.22, 14.7, 17.3, 17.19 |
| Leys | love 1.5, 1.6, 3.17, 12.10, 12.22, 14.7, 17.3, 17.19 |
| Soothill | affection 17.19 |
| | care for 3.17 |
| | love 1.5, 1.6, 12.10, 12.22, 14.7, 17.3 |
| Waley | affection 1.5 |
| | be all the tenderer towards 17.3 |
| | darling 17.19 |
| | grudge 3.17 |
| | kindly feeling 1.6 |
| | love 12.10, 12.22, 14.7 |

# 安(17)

| | |
|---|---|
| Ames/Rosemont | *adv.* 11. 26 |
| | at ease 7. 38 |
| | bring accord to 14. 42 |
| | comfort 17. 19 |
| | comfort and contentment 1. 14 |
| | comfortable 17. 19 |
| | content 1. 14，2. 10，4. 2 |
| | peace and contentment 5. 26 |
| | secure 16. 1 |
| Lau | *adv.* 11. 26 |
| | at ease 7. 38 |
| | attract 4. 2 |
| | bring peace and security 14. 42 |
| | comfort 17. 19 |
| | comfortable 1. 14 |
| | enjoy 17. 19 |
| | feel at home 2. 10 |
| | make them content 16. 1 |
| | peace 5. 26 |
| | stability 16. 1 |
| Legge | *adv.* 11. 26 |
| | appliances of ease 1. 14 |
| | comfortably 17. 19 |
| | contented and tranquil 16. 1 |

|  |  |
|---|---|
| | easy 7.38 |
| | feel at ease 17.19 |
| | give rest to 14.42 |
| | repose 16.1 |
| | rest 2.10, 4.2, 5.26 |
| Leys | *adv.* 11.26 |
| | comfort 1.14, 17.19 |
| | easy to approach 7.38 |
| | feel at ease 17.19 |
| | make them enjoy 16.1 |
| | peace 2.10, 5.26, 16.1 |
| | rest 4.2 |
| | spread one's peace 14.42 |
| Soothill | *adv.* 11.26 |
| | at rest 4.2 |
| | comfort 5.26 |
| | comfortable 17.19 |
| | contentment reign 16.1 |
| | ease 14.42 |
| | easy 7.38 |
| | feel at ease 17.19 |
| | make them contented 16.1 |
| | rest 2.10 |
| | solicitous of comfort 1.14 |
| Waley | *adv.* 11.26 |
| | comfort 1.14, 5.26 |
| | comfortable 17.19 |
| | content 2.10, 4.2, 16.1 |

|   |   |
|---|---|
|   | ease 14.42 |
|   | easy 7.38 |
|   | feel at ease 17.19 |

## 霸(1)

| | |
|---|---|
| Ames/Rosemont | become leader of 14.17 |
| Lau | become the leader of 14.17 |
| Legge | make leader of 14.17 |
| Leys | impose one's authority over 14.17 |
| Soothill | make the duke leader of 14.17 |
| Waley | become leader of 14.17 |

## 百姓(5)

| | |
|---|---|
| Ames/Rosemont | household 12.9 |
| | people 14.42, 20.1 |
| Lau | people 12.9, 14.42, 20.1 |
| Legge | all the people 14.42 |
| | people 12.9, 20.1 |
| Leys | all the people 14.42 |
| | people 12.9, 20.1 |
| Soothill | people 12.9, 14.42, 20.1 |
| Waley | many families 20.1 |
| | the hundred families 12.9 |
| | people 14.42 |

# 邦(48)

| | |
|---|---|
| Ames/Rosemont | barbarian 15.6 |
| | country 17.1 |
| | govern 13.11 |
| | land 5.2, 5.21 |
| | political 12.2 |
| | public 12.20 |
| | state 1.10, 3.22, 5.19, 8.13, 10.9, 11.24, 13.15, 14.1, 15.7, 15.10, 15.11, 16.1, 16.14, 17.16, 18.2, 19.25 |
| Lau | boundary 16.1 |
| | country 18.2 |
| | land 15.6 |
| | state 1.10, 3.22, 5.2, 5.19, 5.21, 8.13, 10.9, 11.24, 12.2, 12.20, 13.11, 13.15, 14.1, 14.3, 15.7, 15.10, 15.11, 16.1, 16.14, 17.1, 17.16, 19.25 |
| Legge | country 1.10, 5.2, 5.21, 8.13, 12.2, 12.20, 13.11, 13.15, 15.11, 17.1, 18.2 |
| | government 15.7 |
| | kingdom 17.16 |
| | state 3.22, 5.19, 8.13, 10.9, 11.24, 12.20, 14.1, 14.3, 15.10, 16.1, 16.14, 19.25 |
| | territory 16.1 |
| | tribe 15.6 |
| Leys | abroad 10.9 |

|  | barbarian 15.6 |
|---|---|
|  | country 1.10, 5.2, 5.19, 5.21, 13.11, 13.15, 15.10, 17.1, 19.25 |
|  | government 15.7 |
|  | kingdom 17.16 |
|  | land 16.1, 18.2 |
|  | province 16.1 |
|  | public 12.2, 12.20 |
|  | state 3.22, 8.13, 11.24, 14.1, 14.3, 15.11 |
|  | territory 16.1 |
| Soothill | abroad 12.20 |
|  | country 5.2, 13.11, 13.15, 14.1, 15.7, 17.1, 19.25 |
|  | land 14.3, 15.6, 18.2 |
|  | public 12.2 |
|  | state 1.10, 3.22, 5.19, 5.21, 8.13, 10.9, 11.24, 15.10, 15.11, 16.1, 16.14, 17.16 |
| Waley | barbarian 15.6, |
|  | country 1.10, 5.2, 5.19, 5.21, 10.9, 13.11, 13.15, 14.1, 16.14, 17.1 |
|  | kingdom 11.24, 17.16 |
|  | land 14.3, 15.7, 16.1, 18.2 |
|  | state 3.22, 8.13, 12.2, 12.20, 15.10, 15.11, 16.1, 16.14, 19.25 |

# 报(4)

| Ames/Rosemont | repay 14.34 |
|---|---|

| | |
|---|---|
| Lau | repay 14.34 |
| Legge | recompense 14.34 |
| Leys | repay 14.34 |
| Soothill | reward 14.34 |
| Waley | meet 14.34 |

## 本(5)

| | |
|---|---|
| Ames/Rosemont | root 1.2, 3.4, 19.12 |
| Lau | basis 3.4 |
| | root 1.2 |
| | what is basic 19.12 |
| Legge | what is radical 1.2 |
| | root 1.2 |
| | the first thing 3.4 |
| | what is essential 19.12 |
| Leys | fundamental matter 19.12 |
| | root 1.2, 3.4 |
| Soothill | chief principle 3.4 |
| | foundation 1.2 |
| | fundamental 1.2 |
| | radical principles 19.12 |
| Waley | anything important 19.12 |
| | main principles 3.4 |
| | trunk 1.2 |

# 辟(10)

| | |
|---|---|
| Ames/Rosemont | avoid 14.37, 18.5, 18.6 |
| | biased 11.18 |
| | ingratiate 16.4 |
| | various nobles 3.2 |
| Lau | avoid 18.5 |
| | great lord 3.2 |
| | ingratiate 16.4 |
| | onesided 11.18 |
| | run away 18.6 |
| | shun 14.37 |
| Legge | hasten away 18.5 |
| | prince 3.2 |
| | retire from 14.37 |
| | specious 11.18, 16.4 |
| | withdraw 18.6 |
| Leys | avoid 14.37 |
| | away and disappear 18.5 |
| | devious 16.4 |
| | extreme 11.18 |
| | feudal lord 3.2 |
| | forsake 18.6 |
| Soothill | avoid 18.5 |
| | flee 18.6 |
| | plausible 16.4 |

| | |
|---|---|
| | prince and nobleman 3.2 |
| | surface 11.18 |
| | withdraw 14.37 |
| Waley | flee 18.6 |
| | formal 11.18 |
| | get away 18.5 |
| | obsequious 16.4 |
| | ruler and lord 3.2 |
| | withdraw 14.37 |

# 蔽(9)

| | |
|---|---|
| Ames/Rosemont | cover 2.2 |
| | shield 20.1 |
| Lau | attendant fault 17.7 |
| | sum up 2.2 |
| Legge | becloud 17.7 |
| | embrace 2.2 |
| | keep in obscurity 20.1 |
| Leys | degeneration 17.7 |
| | hide 21.1 |
| | sum up 2.2 |
| Soothill | cover 2.2 |
| | keep in obscurity 20.1 |
| | obscure 17.7 |
| Waley | cover 2.2 |
| | degeneration 17.7 |

slay 20.1

# 博(7)

| | |
|---|---|
| Ames/Rosemont | broaden 9.11 |
| | broad 9.2 |
| | broadly 6.27, 6.30, 12.15, 19.6 |
| Lau | broaden 9.11 |
| | extensively 6.30 |
| | wide 9.2 |
| | widely 6.27, 12.15, 19.6 |
| | po 17.20 |
| Legge | chessplayer 17.20 |
| | enlarge 9.11 |
| | extensive 9.2 |
| | extensively 6.27, 6.30, 12.15, 19.6 |
| Leys | enlarge 6.27, 12.15 |
| | extend 19.6 |
| | play chess 17.20 |
| | stimulate 9.11 |
| | vast 9.2 |
| Soothill | broad 19.6 |
| | broaden 9.11 |
| | chessplayer 17.20 |
| | far and wide 6.30 |
| | vast 9.2 |
| | widely 6.27, 12.15 |

| | |
|---|---|
| Waley | broaden 9.11 |
| | vastly 9.2 |
| | wide 6.30 |
| | widely 6.27, 19.6 |

## 才(7)

| | |
|---|---|
| Ames/Rosemont | ability 9.11 |
| | all one can 9.11 |
| | gifted 8.11 |
| | talent 8.11, 8.20, 11.8 |
| | those with superior character and ability 13.2 |
| Lau | all I can 9.11 |
| | gifted 8.11 |
| | man of talent 13.2 |
| | talent 8.20, 11.8 |
| Legge | ability 8.11, 9.11 |
| | man of virtue and talent 13.2 |
| | talent 8.20, 11.8 |
| Leys | man of talent 13.2 |
| | resource 9.11 |
| | talent 8.11, 8.20, 11.8 |
| Soothill | gift 8.11 |
| | gifted 11.8 |
| | power 9.11 |
| | talent 8.20 |
| | those who are worthy and capable 13.2 |

| | |
|---|---|
| Waley | gift 8.11 |
| | gifted 11.8 |
| | man of superior capacity 13.2 |
| | resource 9.11 |
| | right material 8.20 |

## 藏(2)

| | |
|---|---|
| Ames/Rosemont | hold oneself in reserve 7.11 |
| | safekeep 9.13 |
| Lau | put it away safely 9.13 |
| | stay out of sight 7.11 |
| Legge | keep 9.13 |
| | lie retired 7.11 |
| Leys | hide 7.11 |
| | hide it safely 9.13 |
| Soothill | dwell in retirement 7.11 |
| | keep 9.13 |
| Waley | hide 7.11 |
| | wrap it up 9.13 |

## 彻(3)

| | |
|---|---|
| Ames/Rosemont | at the conclusion of their sacrifices as the implements are gathered 3.2 |
| | levy a tithe 12.9 |

| | |
|---|---|
| Lau | tax the people one part in ten 12.9 |
| | when the sacrificial offerings are being cleared away 3.2 |
| Legge | tithe 12.9 |
| | while the vessels are being removed at the condusion of the sacrifice 3.2 |
| Leys | at the end of their ancestral sacrifices 3.2 |
| | tithe 12.9 |
| Soothill | at the removal of the sacrifices 3.2 |
| | tithe 12.9 |
| Waley | during the removal of the sacrificial vessels 3.2 |
| | tithe 12.9 |

## 乘(9)

| | |
|---|---|
| Ames/Rosemont | chariot 1.5, 5.8, 5.19, 11.24 |
| | drive 6.4 |
| | ride 15.11, 15.26 |
| | scribe 15.26 |
| | take 5.7 |
| Lau | chariot 1.5, 5.8, 11.24 |
| | drive 15.26 |
| | horse 5.19 |
| | in a carriage drawn by 6.4 |
| | put to sea 5.7 |
| | ride 15.11 |
| Legge | chariot 1.5, 5.8, 11.24 |
| | get upon 5.7 |

|  |  |
|---|---|
|  | have ... to carriage 6.4 |
|  | horse 5.19 |
|  | ride 15.11, 15.26 |
| Leys | ride 15.11 |
|  | take 5.7 |
|  | test 15.26 |
|  | travel with 6.4 |
| Soothill | chariot 1.5, 5.8, 5.19, 11.24 |
|  | drive 6.4 |
|  | get upon 5.7 |
|  | ride 15.11, 15.26 |
| Waley | chariot 1.5 |
|  | drive 6.4, 15.26 |
|  | get upon 5.7 |
|  | use 15.11 |
|  | war chariot 5.8, 5.19, 11.24 |

# 耻(17)

|  |  |
|---|---|
| Ames/Rosemont | ashamed 5.15 |
|  | be ashamed of 4.9 |
|  | be ashamed 4.22 |
|  | disgrace 1.13, 8.13 |
|  | feel shame 14.27 |
|  | shame 2.3, 9.27, 13.20 |
|  | shameful 14.1 |

| | |
|---|---|
| Lau | shameless 5.25 |
| | ashamed 5.15, 9.27, 14.27 |
| | be ashamed 4.22 |
| | be ashamed of 4.9 |
| | disgrace 1.13 |
| | shame 2.3, 13.20 |
| | shameful 4.22, 5.25, 8.13, 14.1 |
| Legge | ashamed 5.15, 5.25, 9.27 |
| | be ashamed of 4.9, 8.13 |
| | fear 4.22 |
| | modest 14.27 |
| | shame 1.13, 2.3, 13.20 |
| | shameful 14.1 |
| Leys | ashamed 5.15, 14.27 |
| | be ashamed of 4.9 |
| | despise 5.25 |
| | disgrace 13.20 |
| | fear 4.22 |
| | shame 1.13, 2.3, 14.1 |
| | shameful 8.13 |
| Soothill | abashed 9.27 |
| | ashamed 5.15, 5.25, 8.13 |
| | be ashamed of 4.9 |
| | dishonour 13.20, 14.1 |
| | modest 14.27 |
| | out of shame 4.22 |
| | shame 1.13, 2.3 |
| Waley | abashed 9.27 |

ashamed 5.15, 14.27

be ashamed of 4.9

compunction 14.1

disgrace 4.22, 8.13, 13.20

dishonor 1.13

incapable of stooping 5.25

never stoop 5.25

## 辞(5)

| | |
|---|---|
| Ames/Rosemont | decline 6.9, 17.18 |
| | excuse 16.1 |
| | express oneself 15.41 |
| | refuse 6.5 |
| Lau | decline 6.5, 6.9, 17.18 |
| | language 15.41 |
| | plausible pretext 16.1 |
| Legge | decline 6.5, 6.9, 17.18 |
| | explanation 16.1 |
| | language 15.41 |
| Leys | decline 6.5, 17.18 |
| | excuse 16.1 |
| | regret 6.9 |
| | word 15.41 |
| Soothill | decline 6.5, 6.9 |
| | excuse 16.1, 17.18 |
| | language 15.41 |

| Waley | condone 16.1 |
|---|---|
| | decline 6.5 |
| | excuse 17.18 |
| | official speech 15.41 |

## 辞气(1)

| Ames/Rosemont | language 8.4 |
|---|---|
| Lau | speak in proper tone 8.4 |
| Legge | words and tone 8.4 |
| Leys | speech 8.4 |
| Soothill | tone of conversation 8.4 |
| Waley | every word he utters 8.4 |

## 慈(1)

| Ames/Rosemont | kind 2.20 |
|---|---|
| Legge | kind 2.20 |
| Leys | kind father 2.20 |
| Soothill | kind 2.20 |
| Waley | kindness 2.20 |

## 达(18)

| Ames/Rosemont | achieve your end 13.17 |
|---|---|

|     |     |
| --- | --- |
|     | aspire 14.35 |
|     | extend 16.11 |
|     | get the point across 15.41 |
|     | get there 6.30 |
|     | know 10.10 |
|     | perform effectively 13.5 |
|     | prominent 12.20 |
|     | promote 6.30 |
|     | road 14.23 |
|     | talented 6.8 |
|     | understand 12.22 |
| Lau | exercise one's own initiative 13.5 |
|     | get the point across 15.41 |
|     | get there 6.30 |
|     | get through 12.20, 14.23, 14.35 |
|     | good enough 6.8 |
|     | grasp 12.22 |
|     | know 10.10 |
|     | reach one's goal 13.17 |
|     | realize 16.11 |
| Legge | carry out 16.11 |
|     | convey the meaning 15.41 |
|     | distinction 12.20 |
|     | distinguished 12.20 |
|     | do thoroughly 13.17 |
|     | enlarge 6.30 |
|     | fit 6.8 |
|     | know 10.10, 13.5 |

| | |
|---|---|
| | rise 14.35 |
| | understand 12.22 |
| Leys | acquaint 10.10 |
| | hear 14.35 |
| | merely for communication 15.41 |
| | reach 16.11 |
| | reach up 14.23 |
| | reach one's goal 13.17 |
| | obtain 6.30 |
| | perception 12.20 |
| | sagacious 6.8 |
| | understand 12.22 |
| | up to the task 13.5 |
| Soothill | accomplish 13.17 |
| | comprehend 12.22 |
| | develop 6.30 |
| | esteem 12.20 |
| | extend 16.11 |
| | general estimation 12.20 |
| | perspicuity 15.41 |
| | practical ability 13.5 |
| | suitable 6.8 |
| | soar 14.35 |
| | well acquainted 10.10 |
| Waley | acquaint 10.10 |
| | capable 6.8 |
| | come into play 13.17 |
| | extend 16.11 |

feel 14.35

get one 15.41

influence 14.23

influential 12.20

turn one's merits to account 6.30, 13.5

understand 12.22

# 党(12)

Ames/Rosemont　at home 5.22

clique 15.22

fall into group 4.7

fellow villagers 13.20

neighbors 6.5

partisan 7.31

village 9.2, 10.1, 13.18, 14.44

Lau　at home 5.22

community 10.1

form clique 15.22

in the village 13.20

neighborhood 6.5

partiality 7.31

Tang 14.44

type 4.7

village 9.2, 13.18

Legge　partizan 7.31

fellow villagers and neighbours 13.20

|   |   |
|---|---|
| | partizan 15. 22 |
| | the class to which they belong 4. 7 |
| | school 5. 22 |
| | us 13. 18 |
| | village 6. 5, 9. 2, 10. 1, 14. 44 |
| Leys | of his village 13. 20 |
| | one's people 13. 18 |
| | partial 7. 31 |
| | partisan 15. 22 |
| | village 6. 5, 10. 1, 14. 44 |
| Soothill | at home 5. 22 |
| | enter any clique 15. 22 |
| | neighbours 13. 20 |
| | one's type of mind 4. 7 |
| | part of the country 13. 18 |
| | partisan 7. 31 |
| | village 6. 5, 9. 2, 10. 1, 14. 44 |
| Waley | at home 5. 22 |
| | belong to a set 4. 7 |
| | country 13. 18 |
| | fellow villagers 13. 20 |
| | partial 7. 31 |
| | party 15. 22 |
| | village 6. 5, 9. 2, 10. 1, 14. 44 |

# 祷(4)

| | |
|---|---|
| Ames/Rosemont | pray 3.13, 7.35 |
| Lau | offer a prayer 7.35 |
| | pray 7.35 |
| | prayer 3.13, 7.35 |
| Legge | pray 3.13, 7.35 |
| | prayer 7.35 |
| Leys | pray 7.35 |
| | prayer 3.13 |
| Soothill | have prayers offered 7.35 |
| | pray 7.35 |
| | prayer 3.13 |
| Waley | expiation 3.13 |
| | perform the rite of expiation 7.35 |

# 道(90)

| | |
|---|---|
| Ames/Rosemont | byway 19.4 |
| | lead 2.3, 12.23, 19.23 |
| | path 9.30, 14.28, 18.2, 19.12 |
| | remark 9.27 |
| | roadside 9.12 |
| | streets and alleyway 17.12 |
| | talk about 16.5 |

the way to lead 1.5

traditional way 15.42

way 1.2, 1.11, 1.12, 1.14, 3.16, 3.24, 4.5, 4.8, 4.9, 4.15, 4.20, 5.2, 5.7, 5.13, 5.16, 6.12, 6.17, 6.24, 7.6, 8.4, 8.7, 8.13, 11.19, 11.22, 12.19, 13.25, 14.1, 14.3, 14.19, 14.36, 15.7, 15.25, 15.29, 15.32, 15.40, 15.42, 16.2, 16.11, 17.3, 18.6, 18.7, 19.2, 19.7, 19.19, 19.22

Lau

art 19.4

guide 1.5, 2.3, 12.23, 19.25

path 15.25

principle 14.19

quote 14.28

right way 4.5

road 8.7

sing the praise 16.5

thing 14.28

way 1.2, 1.11, 1.12, 1.14, 1.15, 3.16, 3.24, 4.8, 4.9, 4.15, 4.20, 5.2, 5.7, 5.13, 5.16, 5.21, 6.12, 6.17, 6.24, 7.6, 8.4, 8.13, 9.27, 9.30, 11.19, 11.22, 12.19, 13.25, 14.1, 14.3, 14.36, 15.7, 15.29, 15.32, 15.40, 15.42, 16.2, 16.11, 17.3, 18.2, 18.6, 18.7, 19.2, 19.7, 19.12, 19.19, 19.22

wayside 9.12

Legge

all practical courses 1.2

characteristic 5.16

characteristics 11.19

course 8.7, 15.40

doctrine 4.15, 5.7, 6.12, 19.22

duty 19.19

govern 5.2, 14.1, 14.3, 15.7, 16.2

instruct 17.3

lead 2.3, 12.23, 19.25

mean 9.27

order 5.21

path 7.6, 15.25

principle 1.14, 6.24, 8.4, 8.13, 9.30, 12.19, 14.19, 14.36, 15.29, 16.11, 19.7

principle of truth and right 3.24

proper way 4.5

right 11.22, 19.2

right principle 18.6, 18.7, 19.7

right way 4.8

road 9.12

rule 1.5, 15.42

say 14.28

speak of 16.5

studies and employment 19.4

true principle 6.24

truth 4.9, 15.32

way 1.11, 1.12, 3.16, 4.20, 5.13, 6.17, 13.25, 14.28, 17.12, 18.2, 19.12

Leys  conscious 18.2

course 15.25

discipline 19.4

doctrine 4.15, 19.12

draw 14.28

govern 1.5, 15.7

guide 12.23

journey 8.7

lead 2.3, 19.25

line 9.27

mean 13.25

praise 16.5

principle 4.5, 14.19, 14.28

thing 8.4

truth 14.36, 19.7

view 3.16

virtuous 1.14

way 1.2, 1.11, 1.12, 3.24, 4.8, 4.9, 4.20, 5.2, 5.7, 5.13, 5.16, 5.21, 6.12, 6.17, 6.24, 7.6, 8.13, 9.30, 11.19, 11.22, 14.1, 14.3, 15.29, 15.32, 15.40, 15.42, 16.2, 16.11, 17.3, 18.6, 18.7, 19.2, 19.19, 19.22

wayside 9.12

Soothill

art 19.4

characteristic 5.16, 14.28

characterize the way 11.19

conduct 1.5

course 15.25

discuss 16.5

doctrine 5.7, 19.22

duty 15.32

govern 2.3, 5.2, 14.1, 15.7, 16.2

guide 12.23

high-principled 1.14

law 5.13, 12.19

law and order 8.13, 14.3

lead 19.25

light and leading 3.24

order 5.21

point 9.27

principle 14.19, 14.36, 15.29, 16.11, 19.19

proper thing 15.42

public service 18.2

regulation 1.12

right 11.22

right course 1.2

right principle 18.7

right rule 18.6

right way 4.5, 7.6

road 8.7, 17.12

roadside 9.12

rule 3.16, 8.4

say 14.28

teaching 4.15, 6.12, 6.24, 19.12

truth 4.8, 9.30, 19.2

way 1.11, 4.20, 6.17, 6.24, 13.25, 15.40

wisdom 4.9, 17.3, 19.7

Waley

administer 1.5

discuss 16.5

govern 2.3

guide 12.23

highroad 17.12

household 1.11, 4.20

journey 8.7

lead 19.25

recognized way 15.42

roadside 9.12

virtue 5.16

walk 19.4

way 1.2, 1.12, 1.14, 1.15, 3.16, 3.24, 4.5, 4.8, 4.9, 4.15, 5.2, 5.7, 5.13, 5.21, 6.12, 6.17, 6.24, 7.6, 8.4, 8.13, 9.30, 11.19, 11.22, 12.19, 13.25, 14.1, 14.3, 14.19, 14.28, 14.36, 15.7, 15.25, 15.29, 15.32, 15.40, 15.42, 16.2, 16.11, 17.3, 18.2, 18.6, 19.2, 19.7, 19.12, 19.19, 19.22

wisdom 9.27

# 盗(3)

| | |
|---|---|
| Ames/Rosemont | house burglar 17.10 |
| | thief 12.18, 17.21 |
| Lau | brigand 17.21 |
| | burglar 17.10 |
| | thief 12.18 |
| Legge | robbery 17.21 |
| | thief 12.18, 17.10 |
| Leys | bandit 17.21 |

| | |
|---|---|
| | burglar 12.18 |
| | cutpurse 17.10 |
| Soothill | robber 12.18, 17.21 |
| | thief 17.10 |
| Waley | burglar 12.18 |
| | thief 17.21 |

# 德(38)

| | |
|---|---|
| Ames/Rosemont | beneficence 14.34 |
| | character 13.22 |
| | excellence 2.1, 2.3, 4.11, 6.29, 7.3, 7.6, 7.23, 8.1, 8.20, 9.18, 12.10, 12.19, 12.21, 14.4, 14.5, 14.33, 15.4, 15.13, 15.27, 17.11, 17.12, 18.5, 19.2, 19.11 |
| | excellent person 4.25 |
| | fairness 4.11 |
| | gratitude 14.34 |
| | sense of gratitude 16.12 |
| | virtue 1.9 |
| Lau | benign rule 4.11 |
| | good turn 14.34 |
| | moral virtue 6.29 |
| | nature 12.19 |
| | strength 14.33 |
| | the highest virtue 8.1 |
| | virtue 1.9, 2.1, 2.3, 4.25, 7.3, 7.6, 7.23, 8.20, 9.18, 12.10, 12.21, 13.22, 14.4, 14.5, 15.4, 15.13, |

| | |
|---|---|
| Legge | 15. 27, 17. 11, 17. 12, 18. 5, 19. 2 |
| | good 7. 6 |
| | good quality 14. 33 |
| | kindness 14. 34 |
| | virtue 1. 9, 2. 1, 2. 3, 4. 11, 4. 25, 6. 29, 7. 3, 7. 23, 8. 20, 9. 18, 12. 10, 12. 21,13. 22, 14. 5, 15. 4, 15. 13, 15. 27, 16. 12, 17. 11, 17. 12, 18. 5, 19. 2, 19. 11 |
| | virtuous 8. 1, 14. 4 |
| Leys | inner force 14. 33 |
| | justice 4. 11 |
| | kindness 14. 34 |
| | moral 8. 1, 8. 20, 12. 10, 12. 19, 12. 21, 13. 22 |
| | moral power 6. 29, 7. 3, 7. 6, 7. 23, 15. 4 |
| | principle 19. 11 |
| | virtue 1. 9, 2. 1, 2. 3, 4. 11, 4. 25, 9. 18, 14. 5, 15. 13, 15. 27, 17. 11, 17. 12, 19. 2 |
| | virtuous 14. 4 |
| Soothill | character 7. 3, 12. 10, 12. 19, 12. 21, 14. 33 |
| | one's character 4. 11 |
| | kindness 14. 34 |
| | moral 1. 9, 2. 1, 15. 27, 17. 11 |
| | moral character 7. 6, 12. 19, 13. 22 |
| | moral excellence 2. 3 |
| | noblest 8. 1 |
| | principle 14. 4 |
| | virtue 4. 25, 6. 29, 7. 23, 8. 20, 9. 18, 14. 5, 15. 4, 15. 13, 16. 12, 17. 12, 19. 2, 19. 11 |
| Waley | essence 12. 19 |

good deed 16.12

inner power 14.34

inner quality 14.33

moral 8.1, 8.20, 12.10, 12.21, 19.11

moral force 1.9, 2.1, 2.3, 4.11, 4.25, 15.4, 15.27, 19.2

moral power 6.29, 7.3, 9.18, 14.4, 15.13

power 7.6, 7.23, 18.5

te 13.22

true virtue 17.11

virtue 14.5

## 德行(1)

| | |
|---|---|
| Ames/Rosemont | excel in conduct 11.3 |
| Lau | virtuous conduct 11.3 |
| Legge | virtuous principles and practice 11.3 |
| Leys | virtue 11.3 |
| Soothill | moral character 11.3 |
| Waley | moral power 11.3 |

## 弟(14)

Ames/Rosemont   brother 2.21, 12.5, 13.28

deferential 1.6, 13.20

respectful 14.43

|  |  |
|---|---|
|  | sibling 11.5 |
|  | the young 2.8 |
|  | xiaodi (孝弟, filial and fraternal responsibility) 1.2 |
|  | young brother 1.6, 13.7 |
| Lau | brother 2.21, 11.5, 12.5, 13.28 |
|  | deferential 14.43 |
|  | obedient 1.2, 1.6 |
|  | respectful young man 13.20 |
|  | the young 2.8 |
|  | young brother 13.7 |
|  | young man 1.6 |
| Legge | befit a junior 14.43 |
|  | brethren 13.28 |
|  | brother 11.5, 12.5 |
|  | brotherly 2.21 |
|  | fraternal 1.2, 13.20 |
|  | respectful 1.6 |
|  | the young 2.8 |
|  | young brother 13.7 |
|  | youth 1.6 |
| Leys | brother 11.5, 12.5, 13.7, 13.28 |
|  | brotherly 2.21 |
|  | respect 1.2, 1.6, 14.43 |
|  | respect the elder 13.20 |
|  | young brother 13.7 |
|  | young man 1.6 |
|  | young people 2.8 |
| Soothill | brethren 2.21 |

|  |  |
|---|---|
| | brother 11.5, 12.5, 13.28 |
| | brotherly 13.20 |
| | respect 1.2, 14.43 |
| | respectful 1.2, 1.6 |
| | the young 2.8 |
| | young brother 13.7 |
| | youth 1.6 |
| Waley | behave well 1.2, 1.6 |
| | brother 2.21, 11.5, 12.5, 13.28 |
| | deference to one's elder 13.20 |
| | elder 13.20 |
| | elder brothers 1.2 |
| | proper behaviour 1.2 |
| | respect 14.43 |
| | young brother 13.7 |
| | young man 1.6 |
| | young people 2.8 |

## 帝(3)

| | |
|---|---|
| Ames/Rosemont | ancestor 20.1 |
| Lau | lord 20.1 |
| Legge | god 20.1 |
| Leys | god 20.1 |
| Soothill | god 20.1 |
| Waley | god 20.1 |

## 禘(2)

| | |
|---|---|
| Ames/Rosemont | di imperial ancestral sacrifice 3.10, 3.11 |
| Lau | ti sacrifice 3.10, 3.11 |
| Legge | great sacrifice 3.10, 3.11 |
| Leys | the sacrifice to the ancestor of the dynasty 3.10, 3.11 |
| Soothill | quinquennial sacrifice 3.10, 3.11 |
| Waley | ancestral sacrifice 3.10, 3.11 |

## 独(3)

| | |
|---|---|
| Ames/Rosemont | alone 16.13 |
| Lau | alone 12.5 |
| | by himself 16.13 |
| Legge | alone 16.13 |
| | only 12.5 |
| Leys | alone 12.5, 16.13 |
| Soothill | alone 12.5, 16.13 |
| Waley | alone 12.5, 16.13 |

## 笃(7)

| | |
|---|---|
| Ames/Rosemont | earnest 8.13, 11.19, 15.6, 19.2 |
| | earnestly commit to 8.2 |

| | |
|---|---|
| | focuse 19.6 |
| Lau | feel profound affection for 8.2 |
| | firm 8.13 |
| | hold on 19.2 |
| | single minded 15.6 |
| | steadfast 19.6 |
| | tenacious 11.19 |
| Legge | firm and sincere 19.6 |
| | honourable 15.6 |
| | perform well all their duties 8.2 |
| | sincere 8.13 |
| | sincerity 19.2 |
| | solid and sincere 11.19 |
| Leys | dedication 15.6 |
| | determination 19.2 |
| | hold fast to 19.6 |
| | sound 11.19 |
| | treat generously 8.2 |
| | uphold 8.13 |
| Soothill | earnest 19.6 |
| | pay generous regard 8.2 |
| | sincerity 8.13 |
| | solid and reliable 11.19 |
| | steadfastness 19.2 |
| | trustworthy 15.6 |
| Waley | deal generously with 8.2 |
| | earnestly 19.6 |
| | serious 15.6 |

sound 11.19

unwavering 8.13

## 端(3)

| | |
|---|---|
| Ames/Rosemont | doctrine 2.16 |
| | don 11.24 |
| | end 9.8 |
| Lau | dress 11.24 |
| | end 2.16 |
| | side 9.8 |
| Legge | doctrine 2.16 |
| | dress 11.24 |
| | end 9.8 |
| Leys | end 2.16 |
| | side 9.8 |
| | wear 11.24 |
| Soothill | in (gown) 11.24 |
| | pros and cons 9.8 |
| | speculation 2.16 |
| Waley | in (gown) 11.24 |
| | pros and cons 9.8 |
| | strand 2.16 |

# 夺(5)

| | |
|---|---|
| Ames/Rosemont | be deprived of 9.26 |
| | seize 14.9 |
| | steal the place of 17.16 |
| | perturb 8.6 |
| Lau | be deprived of 9.26 |
| | deflect 8.6 |
| | displace 17.16 |
| | take 14.9 |
| Legge | be carried off 9.26 |
| | drive 8.6 |
| | take 14.9 |
| | take away 17.16 |
| Leys | deprive 9.26 |
| | replace 17.16 |
| | take 14.9 |
| Soothill | despoil 14.9 |
| | rob 9.26, 17.16 |
| | shake 8.6 |
| Waley | kill 17.16 |
| | rob 9.26 |
| | seize 14.9 |
| | upset 8.6 |

恶(38)

Ames/Rosemont
abhor 4.6
avoid 4.5
coarse 4.9，8.21
depravity 12.21
despise 13.24，15.28
detest 17.16，17.22
discriminate 4.3
dislike 17.24
grudge 5.23
hate 12.10，19.20
off(colour) 10.6
rude 4.9
vice 20.2
worst 12.16
wrong 4.4

Lau
bad 12.16
coarse 8.21
detest 17.16
dislike 4.3，4.5，11.23，13.24，15.28，17.22，17.24
evil 4.4，12.21
hate 12.10，19.20
off(colour) 10.6
poor 4.9
repulsive 4.6

| | |
|---|---|
| Legge | score 5.23 |
| | wicked 20.2 |
| | bad 4.9, 20.2 |
| | bad quality 12.16 |
| | dis(colour) 10.6 |
| | dislike 4.5, 17.24 |
| | hate 4.3, 4.6, 11.23, 12.10, 13.24, 15.28, 17.16, 17.22, 17.23, 19.20 |
| | hatred 17.22 |
| | poor 8.21 |
| | wickedness 4.4, 5.23, 12.21 |
| Leys | bad 12.16 |
| | coarse 4.9, 8.21 |
| | detest 17.16 |
| | dislike 13.24, 15.28, 17.24 |
| | evil 4.4, 12.21, 20.2 |
| | grievance 5.23 |
| | hate 4.3, 4.5, 4.6, 11.23, 12.10, 17.22, 19.20 |
| | hatred 17.22 |
| | off(colour) 10.6 |
| | shabby 4.9 |
| Soothill | abhor 19.20 |
| | bad 20.2 |
| | detest 4.5, 17.22 |
| | dis(colour) 10.6 |
| | dislike 17.24 |
| | evil 4.4, 12.16 |
| | fail 12.21 |

| | |
|---|---|
| Waley | hate 4.3, 4.6, 11.23, 12.10, 13.24, 15.28, 17.16 |
| | ill 5.23 |
| | poor 4.9 |
| | shabby 4.9, 8.21 |
| | smell 10.6 |
| | abhor 4.6 |
| | coarse 4.9 |
| | defect 12.16 |
| | detest 4.5 |
| | dis(colour) 10.6 |
| | dislike 4.3, 4.4, 15.28, 17.24 |
| | evil 12.21 |
| | hate 11.23, 12.10, 13.24, 17.16, 17.22, 19.20 |
| | hatred 17.22 |
| | ill 5.23 |
| | plainest 8.21 |
| | shabby 4.9 |
| | ugly 20.2 |

# 法度(1)

| | |
|---|---|
| Ames/Rosemont | laws and statutes 20.1 |
| Lau | government measures 20.1 |
| Legge | the body of the laws 20.1 |
| Leys | authority of the government 20.1 |
| Soothill | laws and regulations 20.1 |
| Waley | statutes and laws 20.1 |

# 法语(1)

| | |
|---|---|
| Ames/Rosemont | model saying 9.24 |
| Lau | exemplary word 9.24 |
| Legge | words of strict admonition 9.24 |
| Leys | words of admonition 9.24 |
| Soothill | words of just admonition 9.24 |
| Waley | words of the far 9.24 |

# 方(14)

| | |
|---|---|
| Ames/Rosemont | *adv.* 16.7 |
| | everywhere 20.1 |
| | judge 14.29 |
| | method 6.30 |
| | quarter 13.4, 13.5, 13.20 |
| | specific destination 4.19 |
| | square 11.24 |
| | state 20.1 |
| | sure direction 11.24 |
| Lau | abroad 13.20 |
| | *adv.* 16.7 |
| | foreign states 13.5 |
| | everywhere 20.1 |
| | grade 14.29 |

|         |                                       |
|---------|---------------------------------------|
|         | method 6. 30                          |
|         | quarter 13. 4                         |
|         | sense of direction 11. 24             |
|         | state 20. 1                           |
|         | whereabouts 4. 19                     |
| Legge   | *adv.* 16. 7                          |
|         | art 6. 30                             |
|         | compare 14. 29                        |
|         | fixed place 4. 19                     |
|         | government of the kingdom 20. 1       |
|         | myriad regions 20. 1                  |
|         | quarter 1. 1, 13. 4, 13. 5, 13. 20    |
|         | righteous conduct 11. 24              |
|         | square 11. 24                         |
| Leys    | abroad 13. 5                          |
|         | address 4. 19                         |
|         | *adv.* 16. 7                          |
|         | corner of the world 13. 20            |
|         | criticize 14. 29                      |
|         | everywhere 20. 1                      |
|         | fief 20. 1                            |
|         | recipe 6. 30                          |
|         | set back on one's feet 11. 24         |
| Soothill| *adv.* 16. 7                          |
|         | anywhere 13. 5                        |
|         | country 20. 1                         |
|         | make comparison 14. 29                |
|         | quarter 13. 4                         |

|  |  |
|---|---|
| Waley | right course 11.24 |
|  | rule 6.30 |
|  | square 11.24 |
|  | stated destination 4.19 |
|  | universal 20.1 |
|  | wheresoever 13.20 |
|  | *adv.* 16.7 |
|  | criticize 14.29 |
|  | direction 6.30 |
|  | land 20.1 |
|  | league 11.24 |
|  | quarter 20.1 |
|  | right conduct 11.24 |
|  | side 13.4 |
|  | where 4.19 |

## 放(3)

|  |  |
|---|---|
| Ames/Rosemont | abolish 15.11 |
|  | act with an eye to 4.12 |
|  | say 18.8 |
| Lau | banish 15.11 |
|  | give free rein 18.8 |
|  | guide by 4.12 |
| Legge | a constant view to 4.12 |
|  | banish 15.11 |
|  | give licence to 18.8 |

| | |
|---|---|
| Leys | act out of 14.22 |
| | give up 18.8 |
| | proscribe 15.11 |
| Soothill | banish 15.11 |
| | immoderate 18.8 |
| | work for 4.12 |
| Waley | dictate by 4.12 |
| | do away 15.11 |
| | refrain 18.8 |

## 富(17)

| | |
|---|---|
| Ames/Rosemont | enrich 20.1 |
| | fortune 12.10 |
| | lavishness 19.23 |
| | prospered 13.8 |
| | prosperous 13.9 |
| | rich 1.15, 6.4, 12.22 |
| | wealth 4.5, 7.12, 7.16, 12.5 |
| | wealthy 8.13, 11.17, 14.10 |
| Lau | enrich 20.1 |
| | greater 11.17 |
| | improve 13.9 |
| | rich 6.4, 8.13, 12.10, 12.22, 14.10 |
| | sumptuous 13.8 |
| | sumptuousness 19.23 |
| | wealth 4.5, 6.4, 7.12, 7.16, 12.5 |

|          |                                                              |
|----------|--------------------------------------------------------------|
|          | wealthy 1.15                                                 |
| Legge    | enrich 13.9, 20.1                                            |
|          | rich 1.15, 4.5, 6.4, 7.12, 7.16, 8.13, 12.5, 12.10, 12.22, 13.8, 14.10 |
|          | rich array 19.23                                             |
|          | richer 11.17                                                 |
| Leys     | considerable 13.8                                            |
|          | enrich 13.9                                                  |
|          | prosper 20.1                                                 |
|          | rich 1.15, 4.5, 6.4, 7.12, 7.16, 8.13, 12.5, 12.22, 14.10    |
|          | richer 11.17                                                 |
|          | wealth 12.10, 19.23                                          |
| Soothill | affluence 8.13                                               |
|          | enrich 13.9, 20.1                                            |
|          | have amassed plenty 13.8                                     |
|          | rich 1.15, 6.4, 12.22, 14.10                                 |
|          | richer 11.17                                                 |
|          | richness 19.23                                               |
|          | wealth 4.5, 7.12, 7.16, 12.5, 12.10                          |
| Waley    | enrich 13.9, 20.1                                            |
|          | rich 1.15, 6.4, 8.13, 13.8, 14.10                            |
|          | richer 11.7                                                  |
|          | wealth 4.5, 7.12, 7.16, 12.5, 12.10, 12.22, 19.23            |

# 刚(5)

| | |
|---|---|
| Ames/Rosemont | at its height 16.7 |
| | firm 13.27 |
| | firmness 17.7 |
| | steadfast 5.11 |
| Lau | unbending strength 5.11, 13.27, 17.7 |
| | unyielding 16.7 |
| Legge | firm 13.27 |
| | firm and unbending 5.11 |
| | firmness 17.7 |
| | **full of vigour 16.7** |
| Leys | at its full 16.7 |
| | firmness 13.27 |
| | force 17.7 |
| | steadfast 5.11 |
| Soothill | firm of spirit 13.27 |
| | mature strength 16.7 |
| | of strong character 5.11 |
| | strength of character 17.7 |
| Waley | courage 17.7 |
| | hardened 16.7 |
| | imperturbable 13.27 |
| | steadfast 5.11 |

# 格(1)

| | |
|---|---|
| Ames/Rosemont | order 2.3 |
| Lau | reform 2.3 |
| Legge | good 2.3 |
| Leys | participation 2.3 |
| Soothill | standard 2.3 |
| Waley | accord 2.3 |

# 公(38)

Ames/Rosemont　ducal 16.3

duke 2.19, 3.19, 3.21, 6.3, 7.5, 7.19, 7.31, 8.11, 10.3, 11.17, 12.9, 12.11, 13.8, 13.15, 13.16, 14.15, 14.16, 14.17, 14.18, 14.19, 14.21, 15.1, 16.3, 16.12, 18.3, 18.10

governor 13.18

impartial 20.1

noble 3.2

public 6.14, 10.6

Lau　ducal 16.12

duke 2.19, 3.19, 3.21, 6.3, 7.5, 7.31, 8.11, 11.17, 12.9, 12.11, 13.15, 13.16, 14.15, 14.16, 14.17, 14.18, 14.19, 14.21, 15.1, 16.3, 18.3, 18.10

great lord 3.2

|  |  |
|---|---|
| Legge | governor 7.19, 13.18 |
|  | impartial 20.1 |
|  | lord 10.6 |
|  | official 6.14 |
|  | Lord's 10.3 |
|  | prince 13.8 |
|  | ducal 13.8, 16.12 |
|  | duke 2.19, 3.19, 3.21, 6.3, 7.5, 7.19, 7.31, 8.11, 11.17, 12.9, 12.11, 13.15, 13.16, 13.18, 14.15, 14.16, 14.17, 14.18, 14.19, 14.21, 15.1, 16.3, 18.3, 18.10 |
|  | justice 20.1 |
|  | palace 10.3 |
|  | prince 3.2, 10.6 |
|  | public 6.14 |
| Leys | ducal 16.12 |
|  | duke 2.19, 3.19, 3.21, 6.3, 7.5, 7.31, 8.11, 10.3, 11.17, 12.9, 12.11, 13.15, 13.16, 14.15, 14.16, 14.17, 14.18, 14.19, 14.21, 15.1, 16.3, 18.3, 18.10 |
|  | feudal lord 3.2 |
|  | governor 7.19, 13.18 |
|  | justice 20.1 |
|  | official 6.14 |
|  | prince 13.8 |
|  | state 10.6 |
| Soothill | ducal 10.6, 13.8, 16.12 |
|  | duke 2.19, 3.19, 3.21, 6.3, 7.5, 7.19, 7.31, 8.11, 11.17, 12.9, 12.11, 13.15, 13.16, 13.18, 14.15, |

|  | 14.16, 14.17, 14.18, 14.19, 14.21, 15.1, 16.3, 18.3, 18.10 |
|---|---|
|  | justice 20.1 |
|  | palace 10.3 |
|  | prince and nobleman 3.2 |
|  | public 6.14 |
| Waley | ducal 10.6, 16.12 |
|  | duke 2.19, 3.19, 3.21, 6.3, 7.5, 7.31, 8.11, 11.17, 12.9, 12.11, 13.15, 13.16, 13.18, 14.15, 14.16, 14.17, 14.18, 14.19, 14.21, 15.1, 16.3, 18.3, 18.10 |
|  | governor 7.19 |
|  | grandee 13.8 |
|  | just 20.1 |
|  | ruler and lord 3.2 |
|  | palace 10.3 |
|  | public 6.14 |

# 恭(13)

| Ames/Rosemont | deference 8.2, 16.10, 17.5 |
|---|---|
|  | deferential 1.10, 1.13, 7.38, 12.5, 13.19, 17.5, 19.25 |
|  | gracious 5.16 |
|  | reverently 15.5 |
|  | solicitude 5.25 |
| Lau | respectful 1.10, 1.13, 5.16, 7.38, 12.5, 16.10, 17.5, 19.25 |
|  | respectful attitude 13.19 |

|  |  |
|---|---|
|  | respectful posture 15. 5 |
|  | respectfulness 17. 5 |
|  | servility 5. 25 |
|  | spirit 8. 2 |
| Legge | courteous 1. 10 |
|  | grave 17. 5 |
|  | gravity 17. 5 |
|  | humble 5. 16 |
|  | modest 19. 25 |
|  | respect 1. 13, 5. 25 |
|  | respectful 7. 38, 12. 5, 16. 10 |
|  | respectfulness 8. 2 |
|  | reverently 15. 5 |
|  | sedately grave 13. 19 |
| Leys | conform 1. 13 |
|  | courteous 1. 10, 13. 19, 17. 5 |
|  | courtesy 8. 2, 12. 5, 17. 5 |
|  | deferential 16. 10 |
|  | dignified 5. 16, 7. 38 |
|  | hold 15. 5 |
|  | modest 19. 25 |
|  | obsequiousness 5. 25 |
| Soothill | courteous 1. 10, 7. 38, 12. 5, 13. 19 |
|  | courtesy 8. 2 |
|  | modest 19. 25 |
|  | respect 1. 13, 5. 25, 17. 5 |
|  | respectful 16. 10 |
|  | serious 5. 16 |

| | |
|---|---|
| Waley | seriousness 15.5 |
| | courteous 1.10, 5.16, 13.19, 17.5 |
| | courtesy 8.2, 12.5, 17.5 |
| | modesty 19.25 |
| | obeisance 1.13 |
| | polite 7.38 |
| | respectful 16.10 |
| | reverence 5.25 |
| | reverently 15.5 |

# 躬(11)

| | |
|---|---|
| Ames/Rosemont | bend 10.3 |
| | body 13.18 |
| | bow 10.3, 10.4 |
| | live the life 7.33 |
| | oneself 15.15 |
| | person 20.1 |
| | personally 14.5 |
| Lau | draw in 10.3, 10.4 |
| | oneself 15.15 |
| | person 20.1 |
| | practice 7.33 |
| | take 14.5 |
| Legge | bend one's body 10.3, 10.4 |
| | carry out in one's conduct 7.33 |
| | conduct 13.18 |

| | |
|---|---|
| | oneself 15.15 |
| | one's action 4.22 |
| | person 20.1 |
| | personally 14.5 |
| Leys | bow 10.3, 10.4 |
| | discreetly 10.3 |
| | drive 14.5 |
| | integrity 13.18 |
| | live 7.33 |
| | person 20.1 |
| | oneself 15.15 |
| | one's deed 4.22 |
| Soothill | bow 10.4 |
| | deed 4.22 |
| | oneself 15.15 |
| | live 7.33 |
| | stoop 10.3 |
| | take a personal interest in 14.5 |
| | person 20.1 |
| Waley | carry out the duties 7.33 |
| | devote themselves to 14.5 |
| | double up 10.3, 10.4 |
| | Kung 13.18 |
| | oneself 15.15 |
| | person 20.1 |
| | shrink 10.3 |

# 古(12)

| | |
|---|---|
| Ames/Rosemont | ancient 3.16, 4.22, 7.1, 12.7, 14.40 |
| | antiquity 7.20 |
| | bygone day 7.15 |
| | old 14.24, 17.14 |
| | old day 17.14 |
| Lau | antiquity 3.16, 4.22, 7.1, 7.20, 14.24, 17.14 |
| | man of antiquity 14.40 |
| | old 7.15 |
| | the beginning of time 12.7 |
| Legge | ancient 4.22, 7.1, 7.15, 14.40 |
| | anciently 17.14 |
| | ancient time 14.24 |
| | antiquity 7.20, 17.14 |
| | old 3.16, 12.7 |
| Leys | ancient 3.16, 4.22, 14.40, 17.14 |
| | old 7.15 |
| | old day 14.24 |
| | past 7.1, 7.20 |
| Soothill | antiquity 7.1, 7.20 |
| | in olden time 17.14 |
| | man of old 14.40 |
| | old 4.22, 7.15, 12.7, 14.24, 17.14 |
| | yore 3.16 |
| Waley | ancient 3.16, 7.1 |

man of old 14.40

old 7.15, 12.7, 17.14

old day 4.22, 14.24, 17.14

past 7.20

## 固(10)

| | |
|---|---|
| Ames/Rosemont | certainly 14.36 |
| | definitely 9.6 |
| | heavy fortified 16.1 |
| | indeed 15.42 |
| | inflexible 1.8, 9.4 |
| | **inflexibility 14.32** |
| | miserliness 7.36 |
| | steadfast 15.2 |
| Lau | come as no surprise 15.2 |
| | definite 14.36 |
| | inflexible 1.8, 9.4 |
| | inflexibility 14.32 |
| | shabbiness 7.36 |
| | strongly fortified 16.1 |
| | true 9.6 |
| Legge | certainly 9.6, 14.36, 15.42 |
| | may indeed 15.2 |
| | meanness 7.36 |
| | obstinacy 9.4, 14.32 |
| | solid 1.8 |

|  |  |
|---|---|
|  | strong 16.1 |
| Leys | have strong defense 16.1 |
|  | indeed 9.6, 15.2 |
|  | [not] shallow 1.8 |
|  | pigheadedness 14.32 |
|  | stinginess 7.36 |
| Soothill | certainly 14.36 |
|  | fortified 16.1 |
|  | narrow 7.36 |
|  | obduracy 9.4 |
|  | obstinately immovable 14.32 |
|  | of a truth 9.6 |
|  | stability 1.8 |
|  | undoubtedly 15.42 |
| Waley | certainly 9.6, 15.42 |
|  | firm ground 1.8 |
|  | greatly unsettled 14.36 |
|  | meanness 7.36 |
|  | obstinacy 14.32 |
|  | obstinate 9.4 |
|  | strongly fortified 16.1 |
|  | withstand 15.2 |

## 寡(12)

|  |  |
|---|---|
| Ames/Rosemont | few 2.18, 16.1, 19.23, 20.2 |
|  | less 8.5 |

|        |                                      |
| --- | --- |
| Lau    | little 16.14                         |
|        | reduce 14.25                         |
|        | few 2.18, 8.5                        |
|        | little 16.14                         |
|        | reduce 14.25                         |
|        | underpopulation 16.1                 |
| Legge  | few 2.18, 14.25, 16.1, 19.23, 20.2   |
|        | K'WA 16.14                           |
|        | little 8.5                           |
|        | scarcity 16.1                        |
| Leys   | few 14.25, 19.23, 20.2               |
|        | lack of population 16.1              |
|        | little 16.14                         |
|        | seldom 2.18                          |
|        | talentless 8.5                       |
| Soothill | few 8.5, 14.25, 16.1, 19.23, 20.2  |
|        | Kua 16.14                            |
|        | lack of people 16.1                  |
|        | little 2.18                          |
| Waley  | diminish 14.25                       |
|        | few 19.23, 20.2                      |
|        | lack of men 16.1                     |
|        | less 8.5                             |
|        | lonely 16.14                         |
|        | poor 16.1                            |
|        | seldom 2.18                          |

# 怪(1)

| | |
|---|---|
| Ames/Rosemont | strange happening 7.21 |
| Lau | prodigy 7.21 |
| Legge | extraordinary thing 7.21 |
| Leys | miracle 7.21 |
| Soothill | prodigy 7.21 |
| Waley | prodigy 7.21 |

# 官(4)

| | |
|---|---|
| Ames/Rosemont | estate 19.23 |
| | minister 14.40 |
| | office 20.1 |
| | staff member 3.22 |
| Lau | official 14.40 |
| | official buildings 19.23 |
| | official post 20.1 |
| | staff 3.22 |
| Legge | officer 3.22, 14.40, 19.23, 20.1 |
| Leys | apartment 19.23 |
| | office 20.1 |
| | official 14.40 |
| Soothill | office 20.1 |
| | officer 14.40, 19.23 |

| | | |
|---|---|---|
| | | staff member 3.22 |
| Waley | | minister 14.40 |
| | | ministrant 19.23 |
| | | office 20.1 |
| | | state officer 3.22 |

# 贯(3)

| | |
|---|---|
| Ames/Rosemont | bind together 4.15 |
| | likeness 11.14 |
| | pull together 15.3 |
| Lau | bind together 15.3, 4.15 |
| Legge | all pervade 4.15, 15.3 |
| | style 11.14 |
| Leys | line 11.14 |
| | run through 4.15 |
| | string all 15.3 |
| Soothill | all pervade 4.15 |
| | connect 15.3 |
| Waley | line 11.14 |
| | run through 4.15 |
| | string all 15.3 |

# 归 (11)

| | |
|---|---|
| Ames/Rosemont | defer 12.1 |
| | find its way 19.20 |
| | homeward 5.22 |
| | make a gift 18.4 |
| | residence 3.22 |
| | return home 11.24 |
| | send 17.1 |
| | win 20.1 |
| Lau | consider 12.1 |
| | establishment 3.22 |
| | find its way 19.20 |
| | go home 5.22, 11.24 |
| | incline 1.9 |
| | kin 10.16 |
| | make a present 18.4 |
| | send 17.1 |
| | turn to 20.1 |
| Legge | ascribe 12.1 |
| | depend on 10.16 |
| | flow in 19.20 |
| | kwei 3.22 |
| | resume 1.9 |
| | return 5.22 |
| | return home 11.24 |

|  |  |
|---|---|
|  | send 18.4 |
|  | send a present 17.1 |
|  | turn toward 20.1 |
| Leys | drift 19.20 |
|  | go home 5.22, 11.24 |
|  | palace 3.22 |
|  | rally 12.1 |
|  | send 17.1, 18.4 |
|  | win 20.1 |
| Soothill | accord 12.1 |
|  | fall back upon 10.16 |
|  | flow in 19.20 |
|  | give 20.1 |
|  | kuei palace 3.22 |
|  | restoration 1.9 |
|  | return 5.22 |
|  | return home 11.24 |
|  | send 17.1, 18.4 |
| Waley | accumulate 19.20 |
|  | fall back on 10.16 |
|  | give 20.1 |
|  | go back 5.22 |
|  | go home 11.24 |
|  | lots of wives 3.22 |
|  | reach 1.9 |
|  | respond 12.1 |
|  | send 17.1, 18.4 |

# 鬼(5)

| | |
|---|---|
| Ames/Rosemont | ghost 6.22 |
| | spirit 2.24, 8.21, 11.12 |
| Lau | spirit 6.22, 8.21 |
| | spirit of an ancestor 2.24 |
| | spirit of the dead 11.12 |
| Legge | spirit 2.24, 8.21, 11.12 |
| | spiritual being 6.22 |
| Leys | ghost 6.22 |
| | god 2.24 |
| | the ghosts and sprit 8.21 |
| | spirit 11.12 |
| Soothill | spirit 6.22, 8.21 |
| | spirit of an ancestor 2.24 |
| | the dead 11.12 |
| Waley | ancestor 2.24 |
| | ghost 11.12 |
| | spirit 6.22, 8.21 |

# 贵(8)

| | |
|---|---|
| Ames/Rosemont | honor 4.5, 12.5 |
| | most valuable 1.12 |
| | noble 8.13 |

|        |                                    |
|--------|------------------------------------|
|        | position 7.16                      |
|        | utmost 8.4                         |
|        | value 9.24                         |
| Lau    | high station 4.5                   |
|        | honour 12.5                        |
|        | important 9.24                     |
|        | noble 8.13                         |
|        | rank 7.16                          |
|        | valuable 1.12                      |
|        | value 8.4                          |
| Legge  | consider specially important 8.4   |
|        | honour 4.5, 7.16, 8.13, 12.5       |
|        | prize 1.12                         |
|        | valuable 9.24                      |
| Leys   | honour 7.16, 8.13, 12.5            |
|        | main 9.24                          |
|        | matter most 1.12                   |
|        | pay special attention 8.4          |
|        | rank 4.5                           |
| Soothill | honour 7.16, 8.13, 12.5          |
|        | be of value 1.12                   |
|        | place 8.4                          |
|        | rank 4.5                           |
|        | value 9.24                         |
| Waley  | honour 8.13                        |
|        | matter 9.24                        |
|        | place above all the rest 8.4       |
|        | prize 1.12                         |

rank 4.5, 7.16, 12.5

# 国(10)

| | |
|---|---|
| Ames/Rosemont | state 1.5, 4.13, 5.8, 11.24, 16.1, 16.2, 20.1 |
| Lau | state 1.5, 4.13, 5.8, 11.24, 16.1, 16.2, 20.1 |
| Legge | country 1.5 |
| | kingdom 4.13, 5.8 |
| | state 11.24, 16.1, 16.2, 20.1 |
| Leys | country 4.13, 5.8, 16.2 |
| | state 1.5, 11.24, 16.1, 20.1 |
| Soothill | country 4.13, 11.24 |
| | government of a state 1.5 |
| | kingdom 5.8, 11.24, 16.1, 16.2 |
| | power 11.24 |
| | state 20.1 |
| Waley | country 1.5, 4.13, 5.8, 11.24, 16.2 |
| | state 11.24, 16.1, 20.1 |

# 过(32)

| | |
|---|---|
| Ames/Rosemont | across 16.13 |
| | astray 4.7, 9.25 |
| | better 14.27 |
| | blame 16.1 |
| | divergency 4.7 |

err 1.8

exaggerate 14.13

exceed 5.7

excess 5.27

fail 15.30

fault 14.25

go astray 7.31, 15.30, 19.8, 19.21, 20.1

mistake 6.3, 19.12

offense 13.2

oversight 7.17

overstep the mark 11.16

pass 9.10, 10.3, 14.39, 18.5, 18.6

Lau

cross 16.13

err 15.30

error 4.7, 5.27, 7.17, 14.25, 19.21

exaggerate 14.13

fault 16.1

mistake 1.8, 6.3, 7.31, 9.25, 19.8, 19.12

more ... than 5.7

offender 13.2

outstrip 14.27

overshoot the mark 11.16

pass 9.10, 14.39

past 10.3, 18.5, 18.6

transgress 20.1

wrong 16.1

Legge

beyond the truth 14.13

blame 20.1

| | |
|---|---|
| | error 7.31 |
| | exceed 14.27 |
| | fault 1.8, 4.7, 5.27, 6.3, 7.17, 9.25, 13.2, 14.25, 15.30, 16.1, 19.8, 19.21 |
| | go beyond 11.16 |
| | in fault 16.1 |
| | more ... than 5.7 |
| | pass 10.3, 14.39, 16.13, 18.5, 18.6 |
| | pass by 9.10, 10.3 |
| | wrong 19.12 |
| Leys | accountable 16.1 |
| | blame 16.1 |
| | cross 16.13 |
| | exaggerate 14.13 |
| | fault 1.8, 4.7, 5.27, 15.30 |
| | match 14.27 |
| | mistake 6.3, 7.17, 7.31, 9.25, 13.2, 14.25, 19.8, 19.12, 19.21 |
| | more ... than 5.7 |
| | overshoot 11.16 |
| | pass 10.3, 14.39, 18.6 |
| | past 18.5 |
| | wrong 16.1, 20.1 |
| Soothill | across 16.13 |
| | astray 19.12 |
| | err 15.30 |
| | error 7.17, 13.2, 15.30 |
| | exaggeration 14.13 |

exceed 11. 16

fault 4. 7, 5. 27, 6. 3, 14. 25, 16. 1

grievance 20. 1

misdeed 16. 1

mistake 7. 31, 19. 8

more ... than 5. 7

pass 9. 10, 10. 3, 14. 39, 18. 6

past 18. 5

surpass 14. 27

transgression 19. 21

wrong 1. 8, 9. 25, 16. 1

Waley

error 7. 17

exaggerate 14. 13

far too much 5. 7

fail 14. 25

false 16. 1

fault 4. 7, 5. 27, 6. 3, 15. 30, 16. 1, 19. 21

go through 10. 3

go too far 11. 16

go wrong 19. 8

hold responsible for 16. 1

mistake 1. 8, 7. 31, 9. 25, 19. 12

offence 13. 2

outrun 14. 27

pass 14. 39, 18. 6

past 9. 10, 16. 13, 18. 5

wrong 20. 1

# 行(79)

Ames/Rosemont    accomplish 2.13

act 2.18，4.12，4.24，6.2，11.20，16.11

act upon 5.14，13.3，15.24

advance 7.11

afford 7.7

arrival 18.7

behave 1.6

carry into practice 17.5

carry out 20.1

carry 12.14

command 7.11

come back 18.6

conduct 12.20，13.20，14.3，15.6

conduct be proper 15.6

continue 15.25

deed 14.27

deport 5.16

develop 15.18

diplomat 14.8

do 1.11，7.24，18.8

drive 2.22

effect 18.7

follow 13.6，19.25

go on foot 11.8

|  |  |
|---|---|
|  | go well 1.12 |
|  | intent 11.13 |
|  | introduce 15.11 |
|  | leave 15.2, 18.7 |
|  | live ... life 7.33 |
|  | [not] refrain 14.1 |
|  | occupy 15.17 |
|  | prevail 5.7, 14.36, 18.7 |
|  | proper conduct 7.25, 15.6 |
|  | serve 9.12 |
|  | set off 10.14 |
|  | stroll 7.22 |
|  | take action 5.20 |
|  | take one's leave 18.3, 18.4, 18.7 |
|  | turn 17.17 |
|  | walk 14.44 |
|  | waver 12.6 |
|  | what they do 5.10 |
|  | work 1.12 |
| Lau | act 9.12, 14.3, 15.17 |
|  | action 4.12, 4.24, 12.14 |
|  | activity 1.6 |
|  | command 7.11 |
|  | conduct 5.16, 13.20 |
|  | deed 2.13, 5.10, 12.20, 14.27, 15.6, 18.8 |
|  | depart 15.2, 18.3, 18.4 |
|  | do 1.11, 7.24, 18.7 |
|  | enforce 20.1 |

follow 15.11

give 7.7

go 2.22, 17.17, 18.6

go forward 7.11, 15.6

go forward without obstruction 15.6

go on foot 11.8

guide to conduct 15.24

influenced 12.6

keep to 15.25

master of protocol 14.8

measure 6.2

moral conduct 7.25

obedience 13.6

practicable 13.3

practice 2.18, 7.33, 15.18, 16.11

prevail 5.7, 14.36

put into practice 5.14, 11.20, 17.5, 18.7

resume one's journey 18.7

set off 10.14

stand firm 14.1

take action 5.20

unbending 11.13

walk 7.22, 10.3, 14.44, 19.25

work 1.12

Legge　act 2.13, 5.20, 9.12

act with 4.12

action 12.20, 14.3, 14.27, 15.6, 18.8

advance 14.36

bold and soldierly 11.13

bring 7.7

business 6.2

carry into practice 5.14, 11.20

carry out 7.33, 13.3, 15.17

conduct 1.11, 4.24, 5.10, 5.16, 7.11, 13.20, 15.6

departure 15.2

do 1.12, 7.24

effective 13.6

ethic 7.25

follow 15.11, 19.25

go 2.22, 10.14, 18.6, 18.7

go on one's way 18.7

[not] repress 14.1

observe 1.12

pass 10.3

perform 15.18, 18.7

performance 1.6

practice 2.18, 6.2, 12.14, 16.11, 17.5

pursue 15.25, 17.17

require 7.11

serve as a rule of practice 15.24

successful 12.6

take its course 20.1

take one's departure 18.3, 18.4, 18.7

undertake 7.11

walk 6.14, 7.22, 11.8, 14.44

way 5.7

Leys

act 4.12, 4.24, 5.20, 14.3, 15.6

act accordingly 5.10

action 1.11

apply 2.18

behave 12.20, 13.20

carry 12.14

come out 7.11

command 7.11

conduct 5.16, 15.6

deed 14.27, 18.8

display 15.17

do 1.6, 1.12, 7.24, 13.3

enact 15.18

follow 17.17

go 10.14, 18.6, 18.7

go on foot 11.8

guide 15.24

keen 11.13

leave 8.3, 15.2, 18.3, 18.4

life 7.25

live 7.33

march 19.25

master of protocol 14.8

[not] shed 14.1

observe 15.11

offer 7.7

organize 9.12

practice 2.13, 5.14, 11.20

prevail 5. 7, 14. 36, 18. 7

pull 2. 22

reach 20. 1

resume one's journey 18. 7

serve 18. 7

spread 17. 5

steer 15. 25

walk 14. 44, 16. 11

what they do 5. 10

word 14. 27

work out 13. 6

Soothill

act 1. 6, 2. 18, 4. 24, 5. 20, 9. 12

action 12. 20, 14. 3

adopt 15. 11

carry 12. 14

carry into practice 13. 3, 17. 5

conduct 1. 11, 5. 16, 6. 2, 7. 11, 7. 25, 13. 20, 15. 24

deed 5. 10, 15. 17

depart 18. 3

departure 15. 2

do 7. 24, 14. 27, 18. 8

do one's duty 13. 6

follow 19. 25

foreign minister 14. 8

fulfil 18. 7

full of energy 11. 13

get on 15. 6

get on with other 15. 6

go 2.22, 18.6, 18.7

go one's way 18.7

go through 10.3

make progress 18.7

live ... life 7.33

moved 12.6

[not] refrain 14.1

permissible 1.12

practice 2.13, 11.20, 15.18, 16.11

prevail 14.36, 20.1

progress 5.7

pursue 15.25

put into practice 5.14, 11.20

run 17.17

stare 10.14

take one's departure 18.4

walk 6.14, 7.22, 14.44

walk on foot 11.8

what they do 5.10

what you do 15.6

work for 4.12

Waley    act 2.18, 5.20

action 14.3

act upon 15.24

arrive 18.7

bring 7.7

carry 12.14

carry into effect 13.3

carry one out 1.11

carry out 7.33

carry out one's word 5.10

command 7.7

conduct 5.16, 7.25, 12.20

dealing 6.2

deed 4.24, 14.27, 16.11, 18.8

do 1.6, 7.24, 15.6

follow 15.25

get on 15.6

get on with people 15.6

give 20.1

go 1.12, 2.22, 7.7, 13.6, 18.6, 19.25

go away 18.7

go by 15.11

go in for 9.12

Good 14.1

go on foot 11.8

go on one's way 18.7

go straight 10.14

go through 10.3

go well 13.6

impatient energy 11.13

influenced 12.6

leave 18.3, 18.4

measure 4.12

perform 15.17

practice 2.13, 15.18

prevail 14.36, 18.7

progress 5.7

put into practice 5.14, 11.20, 17.5

run 17.17

service 18.7

travel 15.2

walk 6.14, 7.22, 14.44

what they do 5.10

# 和(8)

| | |
|---|---|
| Ames/Rosemont | harmony 1.12, 13.23, 19.25 |
| | harmonious 16.1 |
| | join in 7.32 |
| Lau | agree with other 13.23 |
| | harmony 1.12, 16.1, 19.25 |
| | in agreement 13.23 |
| | join in 7.32 |
| Legge | accompany 7.32 |
| | affable 13.23 |
| | ease 1.12 |
| | manifest 1.12 |
| | natural ease 1.12 |
| | harmony prevail 16.1 |
| | harmonious 19.25 |
| Leys | harmony 1.12, 13.23, 16.1 |
| | join in 7.32 |

| | |
|---|---|
| Soothill | peace 19.25 |
| | concord prevail 16.1 |
| | friendly 13.23 |
| | harmony 19.25 |
| | join 7.32 |
| | natural 1.12 |
| | naturalness 1.12 |
| Waley | attune 1.12 |
| | conciliatory 13.23 |
| | harmony 1.12 |
| | harmoniously 19.25 |
| | join in 7.32 |
| | [not] divided 16.1 |

## 恒(4)

| | |
|---|---|
| Ames/Rosemont | constancy 13.22 |
| | constant 7.26 |
| Lau | constancy 7.26，13.22 |
| Legge | constancy 7.26，13.22 |
| | constant 13.22 |
| Leys | constancy 13.22 |
| | principled 7.26 |
| | steadfastness 13.22 |
| Soothill | constancy 13.22 |
| | constant 13.22 |
| | constant purpose 7.26 |

| | | |
|---|---|---|
| Waley | | fixed principle 7.26 |
| | | stability 13.22 |
| | | stabilize 13.22 |

## 弘(4)

| | | |
|---|---|---|
| Ames/Rosemont | | broaden 15.29 |
| | | strong 8.7 |
| Lau | | broaden 15.29 |
| | | strong 8.7 |
| Legge | | breadth of mind 8.7 |
| | | enlarge 15.29, 19.2 |
| Leys | | enlarge 15.29 |
| | | strong 8.7 |
| Soothill | | capacity 8.7 |
| | | enlarge 15.29, 19.2 |
| Waley | | broad shouldered 8.7 |
| | | enlarge 15.29 |

## 厚(5)

| | | |
|---|---|---|
| Ames/Rosemont | | lavish 11.11 |
| | | much 15.15 |
| | | thick 10.5 |
| | | thrive 1.9 |
| Lau | | fullness 1.9 |

| | |
|---|---|
| | lavish 11.11 |
| | robe 10.5 |
| | strict standard 15.15 |
| | thick 10.5 |
| Legge | great 11.11 |
| | much 15.15 |
| | proper excellence 1.9 |
| | thick 10.5 |
| Leys | fullest 1.9 |
| | grand 11.11 |
| | much 15.15 |
| | thick 10.5 |
| Soothill | abundant 1.9 |
| | imposing 11.11 |
| | much 15.15 |
| | sumptuously 11.11 |
| | thick 10.5 |
| Waley | grand 11.11 |
| | highest point 1.9 |
| | much 15.15 |
| | thicker 10.5 |

## 怀(9)

| | |
|---|---|
| Ames/Rosemont | bosom 17.19 |
| | cherish 4.11, 14.2 |
| | hoard 17.1 |

| | |
|---|---|
| Lau | love and protect 5.26 |
| | tuck away 15.7 |
| | attach 14.2 |
| | cherish 4.11, 5.26 |
| | hoard 17.1 |
| | nurse 17.19 |
| | put away 15.7 |
| Legge | arm 17.19 |
| | cherish 14.2 |
| | keep it in one's bosom 17.1 |
| | keep in one's breast 15.7 |
| | treat tenderly 5.26 |
| | think of 4.11 |
| Leys | bosom 17.19 |
| | care for 14.2 |
| | cherish 5.26 |
| | fold up in one's heart 15.7 |
| | keep 17.1 |
| | seek 4.11 |
| Soothill | arm 17.19 |
| | cherish 5.26 |
| | hide in one's bosom 17.1 |
| | keep in one's bosom 15.7 |
| | regard 14.2 |
| | think of 4.11 |
| Waley | arm 17.19 |
| | cherish 5.26 |
| | hide it in one's bosom 17.1 |

hide it in the folds of one's dress 15. 7

set one's heart upon 4. 11

think 14. 2

think of 4. 11

## 悔(3)

| | |
|---|---|
| Ames/Rosemont | regret 2. 18, 7. 11 |
| Lau | regret 2. 18, 7. 11 |
| Legge | regret 7. 11 |
| | repentance 2. 18 |
| Leys | fear 7. 11 |
| | regret 2. 18 |
| Soothill | regret 2. 18, 7. 11 |
| Waley | undo 2. 18 |

## 诲(5)

| | |
|---|---|
| Ames/Rosemont | instruct 7. 2, 7. 7, 7. 34, 14. 7 |
| | teach 2. 17 |
| Lau | educate 14. 7 |
| | instruction 7. 7 |
| | teach 7. 2, 7. 34 |
| | tell 2. 17 |
| Legge | instruct 7. 2 |
| | instruction 7. 7, 14. 7 |

| | |
|---|---|
| | teach 2.17, 7.34 |
| Leys | admonish 14.7 |
| | teach 2.17, 7.2, 7.7, 7.34 |
| Soothill | admonition 14.7 |
| | instruction 7.2, 7.7 |
| | teach 2.17, 7.34 |
| Waley | admonish 14.7 |
| | instruction 7.7 |
| | teach 2.17, 7.2, 7.34 |

# 惠(8)

| | |
|---|---|
| Ames/Rosemont | generosity 17.5 |
| | generous 5.16, 17.5, 20.2 |
| | kind 14.9 |
| | think of gain 4.11 |
| Lau | generosity 17.5 |
| | generous 5.16, 14.9, 17.5, 20.2 |
| | generous treatment 4.11 |
| Legge | beneficent 20.2 |
| | favour 4.11 |
| | kind 5.16, 14.9, 17.5 |
| | kindness 17.5 |
| Leys | favour 4.11 |
| | generosity 17.5 |
| | generous 5.16, 14.9, 17.5, 20.2 |
| Soothill | benefaction 20.2 |

|  |  |
|---|---|
| | beneficence 20.2 |
| | beneficent 5.16, 20.2 |
| | favour 4.11 |
| | kindly 14.9 |
| | kindness 17.5 |
| Waley | bounteous 20.2 |
| | clemency 17.5 |
| | clement 17.5 |
| | exemption 4.11 |
| | kindly 14.9 |
| | more than one's due 5.16 |

## 货殖(1)

|  |  |
|---|---|
| Ames/Rosemont | have taken to hoarding and speculations 11.18 |
| Lau | money making 11.18 |
| Legge | good 11.18 |
| Leys | go into business 11.18 |
| Soothill | good 11.18 |
| Waley | enrich oneself 11.18 |

## 继(3)

|  |  |
|---|---|
| Ames/Rosemont | continue 20.1 |
| | succeed 2.23 |
| Lau | revive 20.1 |

| | |
|---|---|
| | successor 2.23 |
| Legge | add to 6.4 |
| | follow 2.23 |
| | restore 20.1 |
| Leys | revive 20.1 |
| | successor 2.23 |
| Soothill | add to 6.4 |
| | restore 20.1 |
| | succeed 2.23 |
| Waley | re-establish 20.1 |
| | successor 2.23 |

# 祭(14)

| | |
|---|---|
| Ames/Rosemont | offering 10.6 |
| | sacrifice 2.5, 2.24, 3.12, 10.6, 10.12, 12.2, 19.1, 20.1 |
| | sacrificial 10.17 |
| Lau | bury 2.5 |
| | offering 10.6, 10.12 |
| | sacrifice 2.24, 3.12, 10.6, 10.17, 12.2, 19.1, 20.1 |
| Legge | offer in sacrifice 10.6 |
| | sacrifice 2.5, 2.24, 3.12, 10.6, 10.12, 10.17, 12.2, 19.1, 20.1 |
| Leys | ceremony 12.2 |
| | sacrifice 2.5, 3.12, 10.6, 19.1, 20.1 |
| | sacrificial 10.17 |

| | |
|---|---|
| Soothill | worship 2.24 |
| | offer in sacrifice 10.6 |
| | sacrifice 2.5, 2.24, 3.12, 10.6, 10.12, 12.2, 19.1, 20.1 |
| | sacrificial 10.17 |
| Waley | offering 10.6 |
| | sacrifice 2.5, 2.24, 3.12, 10.6, 12.2, 19.1, 20.1 |
| | sacrificial 10.12, 10.17 |

## 家(11)

| | |
|---|---|
| Ames/Rosemont | building inside 19.23 |
| | clan 19.25 |
| | family 3.2, 5.8, 17.16 |
| | household 16.1 |
| | personal 12.2 |
| | ruling family 12.20 |
| Lau | family 3.2, 12.2, 12.20, 16.1, 19.25 |
| | house 19.23 |
| | noble family 5.8, 17.16 |
| Legge | apartment 19.23 |
| | clan 5.8, 12.20 |
| | family 3.2, 12.2, 16.1, 17.16, 19.25 |
| Leys | building inside 19.23 |
| | clan 17.16 |
| | family 3.2, 16.1 |
| | private 12.2, 12.20 |

| | | |
|---|---|---|
| Soothill | | family 3.2, 17.16 |
| | | great house 3.2 |
| | | home 12.20, 19.23 |
| | | house 16.1 |
| | | household 5.8 |
| | | private 12.2 |
| Waley | | baronial family 5.8 |
| | | clan 17.16 |
| | | family 12.2, 16.1 |
| | | house 19.23 |
| | | ruling family 12.20 |

## 俭(6)

| | | |
|---|---|---|
| Ames/Rosemont | | frugal 1.10, 3.22 |
| | | frugality 7.36, 9.3 |
| | | modest 3.4 |
| Lau | | frugal 1.10, 3.22 |
| | | frugality 3.4, 7.36 |
| Legge | | economical 9.3 |
| | | parsimonious 3.22 |
| | | parsimony 7.36 |
| | | spear 3.4 |
| | | temperate 1.10 |
| Leys | | convenient 9.3 |
| | | frugal 3.22 |
| | | frugality 7.36 |

| | |
|---|---|
| | simplicity 3.4 |
| | temperate 1.10 |
| Soothill | economical 3.22 |
| | frugal 7.36 |
| | save expense 9.3 |
| | simple 3.4 |
| | temperate 1.10 |
| Waley | economical 9.3 |
| | frugality 3.22, 7.36 |
| | spare 3.4 |
| | temperate 1.10 |

## 贱(3)

| | |
|---|---|
| Ames/Rosemont | disgrace 4.5 |
| | poor 9.6 |
| | without rank 8.13 |
| Lau | humble 8.13, 9.6 |
| | low station 4.5 |
| Legge | a mean condition 8.13 |
| | low 9.6 |
| | meanness 4.5 |
| Leys | poor 9.6 |
| | obscure 8.13 |
| | obscurity 4.5 |
| Soothill | humble 9.6 |
| | obscurity 4.5 |

| | | |
|---|---|---|
| Waley | | of no account 8.13 |
| | | humble 9.6 |
| | | obscure 8.13 |
| | | obscurity 4.5 |

# 教(7)

| | |
|---|---|
| Ames/Rosemont | educate 20.2 |
| | instruct 2.20, 13.29, 13.30 |
| | instruction 13.30, 15.39 |
| | teach 7.25, 13.9 |
| | train 13.30 |
| Lau | instruct 2.20, 7.25 |
| | instruction 15.39 |
| | reform 20.2 |
| | train 13.9, 13.29 |
| Legge | instruct 20.2 |
| | teach 2.20, 7.25, 13.9, 13.29, 15.39 |
| Leys | educate 13.9 |
| | teach 7.25, 13.29, 13.30, 15.39 |
| | train 2.20 |
| Soothill | educate 13.9 |
| | teach 2.20, 7.25, 15.39, 20.2 |
| | train 13.29, 13.30 |
| Waley | instruct 13.9, 13.29, 13.30 |
| | instruction 15.39 |
| | teach 7.25, 20.2 |

train 2.20

## 节(6)

| | |
|---|---|
| Ames/Rosemont | attune 16.5 |
| | column divider 5.18 |
| | differentiation 18.7 |
| | frugal 1.5 |
| | matter 8.6 |
| | regulate 1.12 |
| Lau | correct regulation 16.5 |
| | crisis 8.6 |
| | keep expenditure under proper regulation 1.5 |
| | pillar 5.18 |
| | regulation 18.7 |
| | regulate 1.12 |
| Legge | discriminating study of 16.5 |
| | economy 1.5 |
| | emergency 8.6 |
| | pillar 5.18 |
| | regulate 1.12 |
| | relation 18.7 |
| Leys | difference 18.7 |
| | perform 16.5 |
| | pillar 5.18 |
| | subordinated 1.12 |
| | test 8.6 |

|  |  |
|---|---|
| Soothill | thrifty 1.5 |
|  | economy 1.5 |
|  | emergency 8.6 |
|  | pillar top 5.18 |
|  | refinement 16.5 |
|  | regulation 18.7 |
|  | restraint 1.12 |
| Waley | due ordering 16.5 |
|  | economical 1.5 |
|  | emergency 8.6 |
|  | modulated 1.12 |
|  | pillar top 5.18 |
|  | laws 18.7 |

## 矜(5)

|  |  |
|---|---|
| Ames/Rosemont | proud 17.14 |
|  | self possessed 15.22 |
|  | sympathetic 19.3 |
|  | take pity on and show sympathy 19.19 |
| Lau | conceited 17.14 |
|  | conscious of one's own superiority 15.22 |
|  | compassion 19.19 |
|  | take pity on 19.3 |
| Legge | dignified 15.22 |
|  | pity 19.3, 19.19 |
|  | stern dignity 17.14 |

| Leys | compassion 19.19 |
| | have compassion for 19.3 |
| | pride 17.14 |
| | proud 15.22 |
| Soothill | commiserate 19.3, 19.19 |
| | dignity 15.22, 17.14 |
| Waley | pity 19.3, 19.19 |
| | proud 15.22, 17.14 |

## 谨(3)

| Ames/Rosemont | carefully calibrate 20.1 |
| | cautious 1.6 |
| | deliberation 10.1 |
| Lau | decide on standard 20.1 |
| | speak lightly 10.1 |
| | spare of speech 1.6 |
| Legge | carefully attended 20.1 |
| | cautiously 10.1 |
| | earnest 1.6 |
| Leys | circumspect 10.1 |
| | set standard 20.1 |
| | talk little 1.6 |
| Soothill | careful attention 20.1 |
| | circumspect 1.6 |
| | a measure of reserve 10.1 |
| Waley | cautious 1.6 |

choose one's words with care 10.1

pay strict attention 20.1

# 敬(21)

| | |
|---|---|
| Ames/Rosemont | deferential 5.16 |
| | full attention 15.38 |
| | respect 2.7, 6.2, 6.22, 16.10, 19.1 |
| | respectful 2.20, 3.26, 4.18, 12.5, 13.4, 13.19, 14.42, 15.6 |
| | respectfully 1.5 |
| | treat with respect 5.17, 11.15 |
| Lau | reverence 1.5, 2.7, 3.26, 5.17, 6.2, 6.22, 14.42, 15.38, 19.1 |
| | reverent 2.20, 4.18, 5.16, 12.5, 13.4, 13.19, 15.6, 15.33, 16.10 |
| | treat with respect 11.15 |
| Legge | careful 15.6, 16.10 |
| | respect 5.17, 6.22, 11.15, 15.33 |
| | respectful 5.16 |
| | reverence 2.7, 2.20, 3.26, 4.18 |
| | reverent 13.4 |
| | reverent attention 1.5 |
| | reverential 6.2, 19.1 |
| | reverential carefulness 14.42 |
| | reverentially 12.5 |
| | reverently 15.38 |

| | |
|---|---|
| Leys | reverently attentive 13.19 |
| | devotion 15.38 |
| | dignity 1.5, 14.42 |
| | good faith 15.6 |
| | never turn to familiarity 5.17 |
| | obedient 13.4 |
| | piety 19.1 |
| | respect 2.7, 6.22, 11.15, 15.33 |
| | respectful 2.20, 4.18, 5.16, 16.10 |
| | reverence 3.26, 12.5 |
| | reverent 13.19 |
| | strict 6.2 |
| Soothill | careful attention 15.38 |
| | consideration 5.17 |
| | circumspect 15.6 |
| | deferential 5.16 |
| | earnest 16.10 |
| | religious attention 1.5 |
| | respect 2.20, 6.22, 11.15, 15.33 |
| | respectful 4.18, 13.4 |
| | reverence 2.7, 3.26, 19.1 |
| | self respect 12.5 |
| | serious 13.19 |
| | strict 6.2 |
| | unfailingly respectful 14.42 |
| Waley | attend strictly 1.5 |
| | attend to business 12.5 |
| | careful 15.6 |

deference 4.18

diligent 13.19, 14.42, 16.10

intent 15.38

punctilious 5.16

respect 2.7, 6.22, 11.15, 15.33

respectful 2.20, 13.4

reverence 3.26, 19.1

scrupulous 6.2

scrupulous courtesy 5.17

# 静(1)

| Ames/Rosemont | still 6.23 |
| --- | --- |
| Lau | still 6.23 |
| Legge | tranquil 6.23 |
| Leys | quiet 6.23 |
| Soothill | calm 6.23 |
| Waley | still 6.23 |

# 举(14)

Ames/Rosemont　lift up 20.1

promote 12.22, 13.2, 15.23

raise 2.19, 2.20

select 12.22

show 7.8

| | |
|---|---|
| | take flight 10.21 |
| Lau | point 7.8 |
| | promote 13.2 |
| | raise 2.19, 2.20, 12.22, 20.1 |
| | recommend 15.23 |
| | rise 10.21 |
| Legge | advance 2.19, 2.20 |
| | call 20.1 |
| | employ 12.22 |
| | present 7.8 |
| | promote 15.23 |
| | raise to office 13.2 |
| | rise 10.21 |
| Leys | approve 15.23 |
| | lift 7.8 |
| | promote 13.2 |
| | raise 2.19, 2.20, 12.22 |
| | reinstate 20.1 |
| | rise 10.21 |
| Soothill | appreciate 15.23 |
| | call 20.1 |
| | demonstrate 7.8 |
| | promote 2.19, 2.20, 12.22, 13.2 |
| | rise 10.21 |
| Waley | accept 15.23 |
| | hold 7.8 |
| | promote 2.20, 13.2 |
| | raise 12.22 |

|  |  |
|---|---|
|  | raise up 2.19 |
|  | rise 10.21 |
|  | summon 20.1 |

# 狷(2)

| Ames/Rosemont | the timid 13.21 |
|---|---|
| Lau | the over scrupulous 13.21 |
| Legge | the cautiously decided 13.21 |
| Leys | the pure 13.21 |
| Soothill | the discreet 13.21 |
| Waley | the hasty 13.21 |

# 君子(107)

| Ames/Rosemont | distinguished person 3.24 |
|---|---|
|  | exemplary person 1.1, 1.2, 1.8, 1.14, 2.12, 2.13, 2.14, 3.7, 4.5, 4.10, 4.11, 4.16, 4.24, 5.3, 5.16, 6.4, 6.13, 6.18, 6.26, 6.27, 7.26, 7.31, 7.33, 7.37, 8.2, 8.4, 8.6, 9.6, 9.14, 11.19, 11.24, 12.4, 12.5, 12.8, 12.16, 12.19, 12.24, 13.3, 13.23, 13.25, 13.26, 14.5, 14.6, 14.23, 14.26, 14.27, 14.28, 14.42, 15.2, 15.7, 15.18, 15.19, 15.20, 15.21, 15.22, 15.23, 15.32, 15.34, 15.37, 16.1, 16.7, 16.8, 16.10, 16.13, 17.3, 17.6, 17.19, 17.21, 18.7, 18.10, 19.3, 19.4, 19.7, 19.9, 19.10, 19.12, 19.20, |

19.21, 19.25, 20.2, 20.3

gentleman 12.8

nobility 11.1

one's lord 16.6

persons of nobility 10.5

Lau

abler gentleman 11.24

gentleman 1.2, 1.8, 1.14, 2.12, 2.13, 2.14, 3.7, 3.24, 4.5, 4.10, 4.11, 4.16, 4.24, 5.3, 5.16, 6.4, 6.13, 6.26, 6.27, 7.26, 7.31, 7.33, 7.37, 8.2, 8.4, 8.6, 9.6, 9.14, 10.5, 11.1, 11.19, 12.4, 12.5, 12.8, 12.16, 12.19, 12.24, 13.3, 13.23, 13.25, 13.26, 14.6, 14.23, 14.26, 14.27, 14.28, 14.42, 15.2, 15.18, 15.19, 15.20, 15.21, 15.22, 15.23, 15.32, 15.34, 15.37, 16.1, 16.6, 16.7, 16.8, 16.10, 16.13, 17.3, 17.6, 17.19, 17.21, 17.22, 18.7, 18.10, 19.3, 19.4, 19.7, 19.9, 19.10, 19.12, 19.20, 19.21, 19.25, 20.2, 20.3

gentlemanliness 6.18

gentlemanly 1.1, 3.7, 14.5, 15.7

Legge

accomplished gentleman 11.1

accomplished scholar 2.12

Chün tsze 3.7

man 19.25

man of complete virtue 1.1, 1.14

man of high rank 8.4

man of high station 17.3

man of superior virtue 3.24

man of virtue 6.18, 16.6

man of real talent and virtue 7.26

person in authority 20.2

scholar 1.8

student of virtue 3.7

superior 2.13, 2.14, 5.16, 6.13, 6.26, 7.33, 10.5, 12.19, 13.3

superior man 1.2, 4.5, 4.10, 4.11, 4.16, 4.24, 6.4, 6.27, 7.31, 7.37, 8.6, 9.6, 9.14, 11.19, 11.24, 12.4, 12.5, 12.8, 12.16, 12.24, 13.23, 13.25, 13.26, 14.5, 14.6, 14.23, 14.26, 14.27, 14.28, 14.42, 15.2, 15.7, 15.18, 15.19, 15.20, 15.21, 15.22, 15.23, 15.32, 15.34, 15.37, 16.1, 16.7, 16.8, 16.10, 16.13, 17.6, 17.19, 17.21, 17.22, 18.7, 19.3, 19.4, 19.7, 19.9, 19.10, 19.12, 19.20, 19.21, 20.3

superior virtue 5.3

those who are in old stations 8.2

virtuous man 5.3

virtuous prince 18.10

Leys    gentleman 1.1, 1.2, 1.8, 1.14, 2.12, 2.13, 2.14, 3.7, 3.24, 4.5, 4.10, 4.11, 4.16, 4.24, 5.3, 5.16, 6.4, 6.13, 6.18, 6.26, 6.27, 7.26, 7.31, 7.33, 7.37, 8.2, 8.4, 8.6, 9.6, 9.14, 10.5, 11.19, 12.4, 12.5, 12.8, 12.16, 12.19, 12.24, 13.3, 13.23, 13.25, 13.26, 14.6, 14.23, 14.26, 14.27, 14.28, 14.42, 15.2, 15.7, 15.18, 15.19, 15.20, 15.21, 15.22, 15.23, 15.32, 15.34, 15.37, 16.1, 16.6, 16.7, 16.8, 16.10, 16.13, 17.3, 17.6, 17.19,

17. 21, 17. 22, 18. 7, 18. 10, 19. 3, 19. 4, 19. 7, 19. 9, 19. 10, 19. 12, 19. 20, 19. 21, 19. 25, 20. 2, 20. 3

gentlemanly 14. 5

nobleman 11. 1

noble scholar 6. 13

true gentleman 5. 3, 11. 24

Soothill　　chün tzǔ 12. 5, 12. 8

cultured gentleman 11. 1

educated man 19. 25

gentleman 3. 7

he 10. 5

higher 6. 26

higher type of man 2. 12, 6. 18, 14. 27, 16. 7

highly placed 8. 2

honourable man 5. 3

ideal man 5. 16

man of high rank 8. 4

man of the higher type 11. 19, 14. 6, 15. 34

man of honour 4. 5, 4. 11, 5. 3, 16. 1, 17. 6

man of noble 7. 31, 12. 16

man of noble character 9. 14, 12. 8

man of noble mind 12. 4, 12. 5, 16. 8

man of rank 17. 3

man of superior order 15. 2, 17. 22

man of the superior class 17. 21

man of virtue 3. 24

noble life 7. 33

noble man 7. 26, 12. 4, 14. 28, 15. 7, 15. 18, 15. 19,

15.21, 15.22, 20.3

nobleness 9.6

nobler 6.13

nobler man 7.37, 11.24, 15.20

nobler minded man 14.23

nobler order 8.6, 14.42

nobler type of man 2.13, 2.14

scholar 1.8, 1.14, 6.27, 14.5

superior 16.6

superior man 15.2

true philosopher 1.1, 1.2

those in high position 12.19

true gentleman 13.23, 13.25, 14.26, 14.28

well bred 13.26

well bred man 17.19

wise man 4.10, 4.16, 4.24, 6.4, 12.24, 13.3, 14.26, 15.23, 15.32, 15.37, 16.10, 16.13, 18.7, 19.3, 19.4, 19.7, 19.9, 19.10, 19.12, 19.20, 19.21

wise price 18.10

wise ruler 20.2

Waley gentleman 1.1, 1.2, 1.8, 1.14, 2.12, 2.13, 2.14, 3.7, 3.24, 4.5, 4.10, 4.11, 4.16, 4.24, 5.3, 6.4, 6.13, 6.26, 6.27, 7.26, 7.31, 7.33, 7.37, 8.2, 8.4, 8.6, 9.6, 9.14, 10.5, 11.1, 12.4, 12.5, 12.8, 12.16, 12.19, 12.24, 13.3, 13.23, 13.25, 13.26, 14.23, 14.26, 14.27, 15.2, 15.7, 15.18, 15.19, 15.20, 15.21, 15.22, 15.23, 15.32, 15.34, 15.37, 16.6, 16.7, 16.8, 16.10, 16.13, 17.3, 17.6, 17.19,

17.21, 17.22, 18.7, 18.10, 19.3, 19.4, 19.7, 19.9, 19.10, 19.12, 19.20, 19.21, 19.25, 20.2, 20.3

real gentleman 11.24

true gentleman 5.16, 6.18, 9.14, 11.19, 13.23, 14.5, 14.6, 14.28, 14.42, 16.1

## 克(3)

| | |
|---|---|
| Ames/Rosemont | discipline 12.1 |
| | intimidation 14.1 |
| Lau | overcome 12.1 |
| | press one's advantage 14.1 |
| Legge | subdue 12.1 |
| | superiority 14.1 |
| Leys | ambition 14.1 |
| | tame 12.1 |
| Soothill | ambition 14.1 |
| | denial 12.1 |
| | deny 12.1 |
| Waley | mastery 14.1 |
| | submit 12.1 |

## 宽(4)

| | |
|---|---|
| Ames/Rosemont | tolerance 17.5 |
| | tolerant 3.26, 20.1 |

| | |
|---|---|
| Lau | tolerance 3.26, 17.5 |
| | tolerant 20.1 |
| Legge | generosity 3.26, 17.5, 20.1 |
| Leys | generosity 3.26, 20.1 |
| | tolerance 17.5 |
| Soothill | magnanimity 3.26, 17.5, 20.1 |
| Waley | breadth 17.5 |
| | broad 20.1 |
| | [not] narrow 3.2b |

# 狂(7)

| | |
|---|---|
| Ames/Rosemont | impetuous 8.16 |
| | madman 18.5 |
| | proud 17.14 |
| | rash 13.21, 17.14 |
| | rashness 17.7 |
| Lau | indiscipline 17.7 |
| | madman 18.5 |
| | reject 8.16 |
| | undisciplined 13.21 |
| | wild 17.14 |
| Legge | ardent 8.16, 13.21 |
| | extravagant conduct 17.7 |
| | high mindedness 17.14 |
| | madman 18.5 |
| Leys | anarchy 17.7 |

| | |
|---|---|
| | crazy 13.21 |
| | impetuous 8.16 |
| | madman 18.5 |
| | pride 17.14 |
| Soothill | ambitious 13.21 |
| | eccentric man 18.5 |
| | high spirit 17.14 |
| | impulsive 8.16 |
| | intractability 17.7 |
| Waley | impetuous 8.16, 13.21, 17.14 |
| | madman 18.5 |
| | recklessness 17.7 |

## 狂简(1)

| | |
|---|---|
| Ames/Rosemont | rash and ambitions 5.22 |
| Lau | wildly ambitions 5.22 |
| Legge | ambitions and hasty 5.22 |
| Leys | full of fire 5.22 |
| Soothill | ambitions and hasty 5.22 |
| Waley | headstrong and careless 5.22 |

## 劳(10)

| | |
|---|---|
| Ames/Rosemont | accomplishment 5.26 |
| | concerned 4.18 |

| | |
|---|---|
| Lau | energy 2.8 |
| | lethargy 8.2 |
| | project 20.2 |
| | urge 13.1 |
| | urge on 14.7 |
| | work 19.10, 20.2 |
| | burden 2.8, 20.2 |
| | distressed 4.18 |
| | onerous tasks 5.26 |
| | wear out 8.2 |
| | work 13.1, 19.10, 20.2 |
| | work hard 14.7 |
| Legge | impose labour 19.10 |
| | labour 20.2 |
| | labourious 13.1 |
| | laborious bustle 8.2 |
| | meritorious deeds 5.26 |
| | punish 4.18 |
| | strictness 14.7 |
| | task 20.2 |
| | toil 2.8 |
| Leys | efforts 4.18 |
| | encourage 13.1 |
| | good deeds 5.26 |
| | mobilize 19.10 |
| | service 2.8 |
| | [not] spare 14.7 |
| | task 20.2 |

|  |  |
|---|---|
| Soothill | tiresome 8.2 |
|  | work 20.2 |
|  | task 20.2 |
|  | burden 2.8 |
|  | deal hardly with 4.18 |
|  | exacting 14.7 |
|  | impose burden 19.10 |
|  | labour efforts 8.2 |
|  | merits 5.26 |
|  | service 20.2 |
|  | work 13.1, 20.2 |
| Waley | discouraged 4.18 |
|  | exact effort 14.7 |
|  | encourage 13.1 |
|  | trouble 5.26 |
|  | hard work 2.8 |
|  | perform 20.2 |
|  | put burden 19.10 |
|  | tiresome 8.2 |
|  | work 20.2 |

# 乐(48)

|  |  |
|---|---|
| Ames/Rosemont | Book of Music 9.15 |
|  | court music 17.16 |
|  | enjoy 6.20, 6.23 |
|  | enjoy oneself 7.19 |

|     |     |
| --- | --- |
|     | enjoy the way 1.15 |
|     | enjoyment 1.1, 6.11, 6.23, 16.5 |
|     | happy 14.13 |
|     | happy circumstance 4.2 |
|     | music 3.23, 7.14, 8.8, 11.1, 11.24, 15.11, 16.2, 16.5, 17.9, 17.19 |
|     | play music 14.12 |
|     | playing of music 3.3, 13.3 |
|     | pleased 11.13 |
|     | pleasing 3.20 |
|     | pleasure 7.16, 13.15, 17.19 |
|     | singing and dancing 18.4 |
| Lau | delighting 1.15 |
|     | easy circumstance 4.2 |
|     | enjoy 13.15 |
|     | feeling 14.13 |
|     | find joy 6.20 |
|     | happy 11.13 |
|     | joy 1.1, 3.20, 6.11, 6.23, 7.16, 7.19 |
|     | joyful 6.23 |
|     | music 3.3, 3.23, 7.14, 8.8, 9.15, 11.1, 11.24, 13.3, 14.12, 15.11, 16.2, 17.9, 17.16, 17.19 |
|     | pleasure 13.15, 16.5, 17.19 |
|     | singing and dancing 18.4 |
| Legge | cheerful 1.15 |
|     | delight 6.20 |
|     | delightful 1.1 |
|     | enjoyment 3.20, 4.2, 16.5 |

|  |  |
|---|---|
|  | joy 6.11, 7.16, 7.19 |
|  | joyful 6.23, 14.13 |
|  | music 3.3, 3.23, 7.14, 8.8, 9.15, 11.1, 11.24, 13.3, 14.12, 15.11, 16.2, 16.5, 17.9, 17.19 |
|  | musician 18.4 |
|  | pleased 11.13 |
|  | pleasure 6.23, 13.15, 16.5, 17.19 |
|  | song 17.16 |
| Leys | cheerful 1.15 |
|  | delight 1.1 |
|  | enjoyment 17.19 |
|  | gay 3.20 |
|  | happy 7.16 |
|  | joy 4.2, 6.11, 6.23, 7.19 |
|  | joyful 6.23 |
|  | merry 14.13 |
|  | music 3.3, 3.23, 7.14, 8.8, 9.15, 11.1, 13.3, 14.12, 15.11, 16.2, 16.5, 17.9, 17.16 |
|  | musical performance 17.19 |
|  | pleasure 13.15, 16.5 |
|  | pleased 11.13 |
|  | rejoice 6.20 |
|  | singing and dancing 18.4 |
|  | spiritual wellbeing 11.24 |
| Soothill | arts of civilization 9.15, 11.24 |
|  | cheerfulness 6.11 |
|  | civil ordinances 15.11 |
|  | delight 6.20, 6.23 |

delightful 1.1

enjoy 6.23, 17.19

enjoyment 16.5

gratification 13.15

gratified 11.13

happiness 4.2

happy 1.15, 7.16, 7.19

harmony 13.3, 14.12

music 3.3, 3.23, 7.14, 8.8, 9.15, 11.1, 15.11, 16.2, 16.5, 17.9, 17.16, 17.19

musician 18.4

passionate 3.20

pleased 14.13

pleasure 16.5

Waley

cheerfulness 6.11

delight 6.20, 6.23

delighted 14.13

delightful 1.1

delighting 1.15

enjoyment 16.5

happiness 7.16

happy 6.23, 7.19

music 3.3, 3.23, 7.14, 8.8, 9.15, 11.1, 11.24, 13.3, 14.12, 15.11, 16.2, 16.5, 17.9, 17.16, 17.19

musician 18.4

please 17.19

pleased 11.13

pleasure 3.20, 13.15, 16.5

prosperity 4.2

# 类(1)

| Ames/Rosemont | such thing as social class 15.39 |
| Lau | grade into category 15.39 |
| Legge | distinction of class 15.39 |
| Leys | all 15.39 |
| Soothill | class distinction 15.39 |
| Waley | kind 15.39 |

# 礼(75)

Ames/Rosemont credential 10.4

observances of ritual propriety 2.23, 3.8, 3.15, 13.3, 13.4

observe 3.19, 7.18, 7.31

observe ritual propriety 3.3, 3.4, 3.8, 3.15, 3.19, 7.18, 7.31

propriety 9.3, 11.24, 12.15

rite 16.13

ritual 3.17, 3.18, 3.22

ritual propriety 1.12, 1.13, 1.15, 2.3, 2.5, 3.9, 3.26, 4.13, 6.27, 8.2, 8.8, 9.11, 11.1, 11.24, 12.1, 12.5, 14.12, 14.41, 15.18, 15.33, 16.2, 16.5, 17.9, 17.19, 17.22, 20.3

| | |
|---|---|
| Lau | rules are able to effect order 4.13 |
| | gift 10.4 |
| | observant of the rite 1.13 |
| | practice of the rites 3.8 |
| | respectful 8.2 |
| | rite 1.12, 1.15, 2.3, 2.5, 2.23, 3.3, 3.4, 3.9, 3.15, 3.17, 3.18, 3.19, 3.22, 3.26, 4.13, 6.27, 7.18, 7.31, 8.8, 9.3, 9.11, 11.1, 11.24, 12.1, 12.5, 12.15, 13.3, 13.4, 14.12, 14.41, 15.18, 15.33, 16.2, 16.5, 16.13, 17.9, 17.19, 17.22, 20.3 |
| Legge | ceremony 3.4, 3.8, 3.9, 3.17, 3.26, 11.1, 16.2, 16.5 |
| | observance of propriety 17.19 |
| | observant of propriety 17.22 |
| | present 10.4 |
| | propriety 2.5, 7.31, 9.11, 11.24, 12.1, 12.5, 12.15, 13.3, 13.4 |
| | regulation 2.23 |
| | rule 9.3 |
| | rules of propriety 1.12, 1.15, 2.3, 3.15, 3.18, 3.19, 3.22, 3.26, 4.13, 6.27, 7.18, 8.2, 8.2, 8.8, 14.12, 14.41, 15.18, 15.33, 16.13, 17.9, 20.3 |
| | the rites of propriety 3.3 |
| | what is proper 1.13 |
| Leys | ceremony 3.17, 3.26, 7.18 |
| | civility 14.41 |
| | considerate 1.15 |
| | courtesy 3.19, 12.5 |

Soothill

gift 10.4

knowledge of rite 11.1

manner 17.22

rite 12.1, 13.3,13.4, 14.12, 16.2, 16.5, 17.9, 20.3

ritual 1.12, 1.13, 2.3, 2.5, 2.23, 3.3, 3.4, 3.8, 3.9, 3.15, 3.18, 3.22, 4.13, 6.27, 7.31, 8.2, 8.8, 9.3, 9.11, 12.15, 15.18, 15.33, 16.13

ritual practice 17.19

ritual restraint 11.24

spiritual wellbeing 11.24

arts of civilization 11.1, 11.24

arts of courtesy 14.12

bounds of good taste 6.27

ceremonial observance 3.4

ceremony 3.17

civil ordinances 16.2

civilization 2.23, 3.9

correct form 3.15

courtesy 1.15, 3.19, 15.18

decorum 1.12, 2.5

decorous conduct 2.3

etiquette 3.22

forms of courtesy 4.13

good manner 13.4

good taste 1.13, 12.15

homage 3.18

law 8.2, 8.8

laws of right demeanour 20.3

manner 3.8, 15.33, 16.5, 17.19, 17.22

observances of decorum 7.18

offering 17.9

order 13.3

orderly behaviour 14.41

present 10.4

regulation 7.31

religious observance 3.26

reverence 9.11

right and proper 12.1

right bearing 11.24

rules of ceremony 9.3, 16.13

well behaved 12.5

worship 3.3

Waley     gift 10.4

orders concerning ritual 16.2

prescriptions of ritual 3.19, 15.33

rite 7.31, 11.24, 13.3, 17.19, 20.3

ritual 1.12, 1.13, 1.15, 2.3, 2.5, 2.23, 3.3, 3.4, 3.8, 3.9, 3.15, 3.17, 3.18, 3.22, 3.26, 4.13, 6.27, 7.18, 8.2, 8.8, 9.3, 9.11, 11.1, 11.24, 12.1, 12.5, 13.4, 14.12, 14.41, 15.18, 15.33, 16.5, 16.13, 17.9, 17.22

rules of ritual 12.15

## 历数(1)

| | |
|---|---|
| Ames/Rosemont | lines of succession 20.1 |
| Lau | succession 20.1 |
| Legge | order of succession 20.1 |
| Leys | succession 20.1 |
| Soothill | lineage 20.1 |
| Waley | succession 20.1 |

## 厉(5)

| | |
|---|---|
| Ames/Rosemont | exploit 19.10 |
| | serious 7.38 |
| | stern 19.9 |
| | stern firmness 17.10 |
| | take the plunge 14.39 |
| Lau | brave 17.10 |
| | go across by wading 14.39 |
| | stern 7.38, 19.9 |
| | ill-used 19.10 |
| Legge | cross with the clothes on 14.39 |
| | dignified 7.38 |
| | firm and decided 19.9 |
| | oppress 19.10 |
| | stern firmness 17.10 |

| | | |
|---|---|---|
| Leys | | fierce 17. 10 |
| | | ill-used 19. 10 |
| | | incisive 19. 9 |
| | | stern 7. 38 |
| | | wade through it with one's cloth 14. 39 |
| Soothill | | decided 19. 9 |
| | | dignified 7. 38 |
| | | oppress 19. 10 |
| | | stern firmness 17. 10 |
| | | strip up to the waist 14. 39 |
| Waley | | exploit 19. 10 |
| | | fierceness 17. 10 |
| | | firm 7. 38 |
| | | incisive 19. 9 |
| | | use the stepping stone 14. 39 |

## 立(26)

| | |
|---|---|
| Ames/Rosemont | endure 12. 7 |
| | establish 6. 30 |
| | give one a place 15. 14 |
| | rise up 9. 11 |
| | stand 8. 8, 9. 27, 9. 30, 10. 2, 10. 3, 10. 8, 10. 20, 15. 6, 16. 13, 18. 7, 20. 3 |
| | take hold 1. 2 |
| | take stand 17. 8, 19. 25 |
| | take one's stance 2. 4 |

| | |
|---|---|
| | take one's place 5. 8 |
| | what it takes to have one 4. 14 |
| Lau | establish 1. 2 |
| | give one an appropriate position 15. 14 |
| | stand 18. 7 |
| | rise sheer 9. 11 |
| | stand 8. 8, 9. 27, 9. 30, 10. 2, 10. 3, 10. 8, 10. 20, 12. 7, 15. 6, 16. 13, 17. 8, 18. 7, 19. 25 |
| | take one's place 5. 8 |
| | take one's stand 2. 4, 16. 13, 20. 3 |
| | take stand 6. 30 |
| | what would earn one a position 4. 14 |
| Legge | establish 1. 2, 6. 30, 8. 8, 9. 30, 16. 13, 20. 3 |
| | fit oneself for one 4. 14 |
| | plant 19. 25 |
| | stand 5. 8, 9. 11, 9. 27, 10. 2, 10. 3, 10. 8, 10. 20, 12. 7, 15. 6, 15. 14, 16. 13, 17. 8, 18. 7, 19. 25 |
| | stand firm 2. 4 |
| Leys | achieve 6. 30 |
| | commitment 9. 30 |
| | deserve a position 4. 14 |
| | raise 19. 25 |
| | secure 1. 2 |
| | share one's position 15. 14 |
| | stand 5. 8, 9. 27, 10. 2, 10. 3, 10. 8, 10. 20, 12. 7, 15. 6, 16. 13, 19. 25 |
| | steady 8. 8 |
| | stick 17. 8 |

|  |  |
|---|---|
|  | take one's stand 2.4, 16.13, 20.3 |
|  | tower right above 9.11 |
| Soothill | appoint 15.14 |
|  | establish 1.2, 8.8 |
|  | fit one to occupy it 4.14 |
|  | form one's character 20.3 |
|  | maintain 6.30 |
|  | stand 5.8, 9.11, 9.27, 10.2, 10.3, 10.8, 10.20, 12.7, 15.6, 16.13, 17.8, 18.7, 19.25 |
|  | stand firm 2.4 |
|  | sustain 6.30 |
|  | take such a firm 9.30 |
| Waley | give a firm footing 8.8 |
|  | halt 10.3 |
|  | have one as one's colleague 15.14 |
|  | indeed 12.7 |
|  | plant one's feet firm upon the ground 2.4 |
|  | qualities that entitle one to office 4.14 |
|  | raise 19.25 |
|  | set up 1.2 |
|  | stand 5.8, 6.30, 9.11, 9.27, 10.8, 10.20, 15.6, 16.13, 17.8, 18.7, 20.3 |
|  | take one's stand 9.30, 16.13 |

# 利(11)

| | |
|---|---|
| Ames/Rosemont | advantage 4.16, 9.1 |

|  |  |
|---|---|
|  | beneficial 20.2 |
|  | benefit 20.2 |
|  | flourish 4.2 |
|  | glib tongued 17.16 |
|  | opportunity 13.17 |
|  | profit 4.12, 14.12 |
|  | sharpen 15.10 |
| Lau | advantage 4.2 |
|  | beneficial 20.2 |
|  | clever 17.16 |
|  | gain 13.17 |
|  | profit 4.12, 9.1, 14.12 |
|  | profitable 4.16 |
|  | sharpen 15.10 |
|  | take advantage of 20.2 |
| Legge | advantage 4.12, 13.17 |
|  | beneficial 20.2 |
|  | benefit 20.2 |
|  | desire 4.2 |
|  | derive benefit 20.2 |
|  | gain 4.16, 14.12 |
|  | profitableness 9.1 |
|  | sharp 17.16 |
|  | sharpen 15.10 |
| Leys | advantage 13.17 |
|  | beneficial 20.2 |
|  | expedient 4.16 |
|  | glib 17.16 |

|  |  |
|---|---|
| | let 20.2 |
| | profit 4.2, 9.1, 14.12 |
| | interest 4.12 |
| | sharpen 15.10 |
| Soothill | advantage 13.17, 14.12 |
| | benefit 20.2 |
| | covet 4.2 |
| | interest 4.12 |
| | natural resource 20.2 |
| | profit 9.1 |
| | sharp 17.16 |
| | sharpen 15.10 |
| | what will pay 4.16 |
| Waley | advantage 20.2 |
| | advantageous 20.2 |
| | consideration 13.17 |
| | chance 14.12 |
| | expediency 4.12 |
| | gain 14.12 |
| | profit 9.1 |
| | sharp 17.16 |
| | sharpen 15.10 |
| | what is right 4.16 |

# 廉(1)

| | |
|---|---|
| Ames/Rosemont | smug 17.14 |

| | |
|---|---|
| Lau | uncompromising 17.14 |
| Legge | grave reserve 17.14 |
| Leys | blunt 17.14 |
| Soothill | reserve 17.14 |
| Waley | stiff and formal 17.14 |

# 谅(3)

| | |
|---|---|
| Ames/Rosemont | earnestness 14.17 |
| | fastidious 15.37 |
| | make good on one's word 16.4 |
| Lau | inflexible 15.37 |
| | petty faithfulness 14.17 |
| | trustworthy 16.4 |
| Legge | fidelity 14.17 |
| | firm merely 15.37 |
| | sincere 16.4 |
| Leys | rigid 15.37 |
| | trustworthy 16.4 |
| | wits' end 14.17 |
| Soothill | blindly loyal 15.37 |
| | faithful 16.4 |
| | fidelity 14.17 |
| Waley | blind fidelity 15.37 |
| | true constancy 14.17 |
| | true to death 16.4 |

# 陋(3)

| | |
|---|---|
| Ames/Rosemont | crudeness 9.14 |
| | hovel 6.11 |
| Lau | mean 6.11 |
| | uncouthness 9.14 |
| Legge | mean narrow 6.11 |
| | rudeness 9.14 |
| Leys | a hovel for one's shelter 6.11 |
| | wild 9.14 |
| Soothill | lack of civilization 9.14 |
| | mean 6.11 |
| Waley | lack of refinement 9.14 |
| | mean 6.11 |

# 禄(5)

| | |
|---|---|
| Ames/Rosemont | charge 20.1 |
| | official salary 15.32 |
| | ranks and emolument 16.3 |
| | take office 2.18 |
| Lau | honour 20.1 |
| | official career 2.18 |
| | patronage 16.3 |

| | |
|---|---|
| Legge | salary of an official 15.32 |
| | emolument 15.32 |
| | official emolument 2.18 |
| | revenue 20.1 |
| | revenue of the state 16.3 |
| Leys | authority 16.3 |
| | career 2.18，15.32 |
| | gift 20.1 |
| | official position 2.18 |
| Soothill | bounty 20.1 |
| | emolument 15.32 |
| | preferment 2.18 |
| | revenue 16.3 |
| Waley | gift 20.1 |
| | han lu 2.18 |
| | high pay 15.32 |
| | power over the exchequer 16.3 |
| | reward 2.18 |

## 乱(15)

| | |
|---|---|
| Ames/Rosemont | come to naught 15.27 |
| | corrupt 17.16 |
| | crescendo 8.15 |
| | disorder 7.21 |
| | drunk 10.6 |
| | in revolt 8.13 |

| | |
|---|---|
| | rebellion 1.2 |
| | rowdiness 8.2 |
| | trouble 8.10 |
| | turmoil 18.7 |
| | undermine 15.27 |
| | unruliness 17.7 |
| | unruly 17.21 |
| Lau | capable 8.20 |
| | come to its end 8.15 |
| | confuse 10.6 |
| | confusion 18.7 |
| | corrupt 17.16 |
| | disorder 7.21 |
| | in danger 8.13 |
| | insubordination 8.10, 17.7 |
| | make trouble 17.21 |
| | rebellion 1.2 |
| | timid 8.2 |
| | ruin 15.27 |
| Legge | able 8.20 |
| | confound 15.27, 17.16 |
| | confusion 1.2, 18.7 |
| | confuse 10.6 |
| | disorder 7.21 |
| | disorganized 8.13 |
| | insubordination 8.2, 8.10, 17.7, 17.21 |
| | magnificent 8.15 |
| Leys | corrupt 17.16 |

|   |   |
|---|---|
|   | degenerate 17. 7 |
|   | discard 18. 7 |
|   | disorder 7. 21 |
|   | finale 8. 15 |
|   | in turmoil 8. 13 |
|   | [not] clear 10. 6 |
|   | quarrelsome 8. 2 |
|   | rebel 8. 10, 17. 21 |
|   | rebellion 1. 2 |
|   | ruin 15. 27 |
| Soothill | able 8. 20 |
|   | closing strains 8. 15 |
|   | confound 15. 27 |
|   | confusion 10. 6 |
|   | desperate deed 8. 10 |
|   | disorder 1. 2 |
|   | insubordination 17. 7 |
|   | lawlessness 7. 21 |
|   | pervert 17. 16 |
|   | rebel 17. 21 |
|   | rebellious 8. 13 |
|   | recklessness 8. 2 |
|   | subvert 18. 7 |
| Waley | confound 15. 27 |
|   | corrupt 17. 16 |
|   | disorder 7. 21 |
|   | disorderly 10. 6 |
|   | flood 8. 15 |

|   |   |
|---|---|
|   | into turbulence 17.7 |
|   | [not] law abiding 8.10 |
|   | rebel 8.13 |
|   | revolution 1.2 |
|   | subvert 18.71 |
|   | timidity 8.2 |
|   | turbulent 17.21 |

## 伦(2)

|   |   |
|---|---|
| Ames/Rosemont | reasonable 18.8 |
|   | relationship 18.7 |
| Lau | human relationship 18.7 |
|   | station 18.8 |
| Legge | reason 18.8 |
|   | relation 18.7 |
| Leys | decency 18.8 |
|   | human relationship 18.7 |
| Soothill | principle 18.7 |
|   | social order 18.8 |
| Waley | relationship 18.7，18.8 |

## 慢(3)

|   |   |
|---|---|
| Ames/Rosemont | neglect 20.2 |
|   | rancorous conduct 8.4 |

|   |   |
|---|---|
| | slow 20.2 |
| Lau | neglect 20.2 |
| | tardy 20.2 |
| Legge | disrespect 20.2 |
| | heedlessness 8.4 |
| | without urgency 20.2 |
| Soothill | remissness 8.4, 20.2 |
| | slight 20.2 |
| Waley | arrogance 8.4 |
| | dilatory 20.2 |
| | slight 20.2 |

## 貌(3)

|   |   |
|---|---|
| Ames/Rosemont | bearing and attitude 16.10 |
| | demeanor 8.4 |
| | respect 10.19 |
| Lau | countenance 8.4 |
| | demeanour 16.10 |
| | respect 10.19 |
| Legge | ceremonious manner 10.19 |
| | demeanour 16.10 |
| | deportment and manner 8.4 |
| Leys | attitude 8.4, 16.10 |
| | respect 10.19 |
| Soothill | bear 8.4 |
| | manner 16.10 |

| | |
|---|---|
| Waley | respect 10.19 |
| | attitude 8.4，10.19 |
| | manner 16.10 |

# 美(14)

| | |
|---|---|
| Ames/Rosemont | admirable 8.11，8.21 |
| | beautiful 3.25 |
| | best 12.16 |
| | countenance 6.16 |
| | dazzling 3.8 |
| | elegant 1.12 |
| | exquisite 9.13 |
| | greatest attraction 4.1 |
| | luxurious 13.8 |
| | magnificence 19.23 |
| | virtue 20.2 |
| Lau | beautiful 1.12，3.8，3.25，4.1，9.13 |
| | excellent practice 20.2 |
| | gifted 8.11 |
| | good 12.16 |
| | good look 6.16 |
| | grand 13.8 |
| | magnificence 19.23 |
| | sacrificial 8.21 |
| Legge | admirable 8.11，13.8 |
| | admirable quality 12.16 |

|  |  |
|---|---|
|  | beautiful 3. 25，9. 13 |
|  | beauty 6. 16，19. 23 |
|  | elegance 8. 21 |
|  | excellence 4. 1 |
|  | excellent 20. 2 |
|  | excellent quality 1. 12 |
|  | excellent thing 20. 2 |
|  | pretty 3. 8 |
| Leys | beautiful 3. 8，3. 25，4. 1 |
|  | beauty 1. 12，6. 16 |
|  | good 12. 16 |
|  | magnificence 8. 21 |
|  | precious 9. 13 |
|  | splendid 8. 11，13. 8 |
|  | splendor 19. 23 |
|  | treasure 20. 2 |
| Soothill | admirable 8. 11 |
|  | admirable feature 1. 12 |
|  | beauty 6. 16，19. 23 |
|  | beautiful 3. 25 |
|  | bewitching 3. 8 |
|  | elegance 8. 21 |
|  | excellence 4. 1 |
|  | fine 13. 8 |
|  | good 12. 16 |
|  | lovely 9. 13 |
|  | treasure 20. 2 |
| Waley | beauty 1. 12，3. 25，4. 1，6. 16，19. 23 |

beautiful 13.8

good 12.16

lovely 3.8, 9.13

lovely thing 20.2

magnificence 8.21

wonderful 8.11

## 猛(3)

| | |
|---|---|
| Ames/Rosemont | fierce 20.2 |
| | severe 7.38 |
| Lau | fierce 7.38, 20.2 |
| Legge | fierce 7.38, 20.2 |
| Leys | fierce 20.2 |
| | overbearing 7.38 |
| Soothill | domineering 20.2 |
| | overbearing 7.38 |
| Waley | ferocious 20.2 |
| | ferocity 20.2 |
| | harsh 7.38 |

## 民(48)

| | |
|---|---|
| Ames/Rosemont | common people 1.5, 1.9, 5.16, 12.2, 12.7, 13.4, 14.41, 15.33, 15.35, 16.12, 17.14, 19.10, 19.19, 20.1, 20.2 |

| | |
|---|---|
| | people 2.3, 2.19, 2.20, 3.21, 6.2, 6.22, 6.29, 6.30, 8.1, 8.2, 8.9, 8.19, 11.24, 12.19, 13.3, 13.29, 13.30, 14.17, 15.25, 18.8 |
| | they 16.9 |
| Lau | common people 1.9, 2.3, 2.19, 2.20, 3.21, 5.16, 6.2, 6.22, 6.29, 6.30, 8.1, 12.2, 12.7, 12.19, 13.3, 13.4, 13.29, 13.30, 14.17, 14.41, 15.25, 15.33, 15.35, 16.9, 16.12, 17.14, 19.10, 19.19, 20.1, 20.2 |
| | labour of the common people 1.5 |
| | man 18.8 |
| | people 8.2, 8.9, 8.19 |
| | population 11.24 |
| Legge | man 6.22, 15.35, 17.14, 18.8 |
| | people 1.5, 1.9, 2.3, 2.19, 2.20, 3.21, 5.16, 6.2, 6.29, 6.30, 8.1, 8.2, 8.9, 8.19, 11.24, 12.2, 12.7, 12.19, 13.3, 13.4, 13.29, 13.30, 14.17, 14.41, 15.25, 15.33, 16.9, 16.12, 19.10, 19.19, 20.1, 20.2 |
| Leys | ancient 17.14 |
| | common people 16.9 |
| | man 15.35 |
| | people 1.5, 1.9, 2.3, 2.19, 2.20, 3.21, 5.16, 6.2, 6.22, 6.29, 6.30, 8.1, 8.2, 8.9, 8.19, 11.24, 12.2, 12.7, 12.19, 13.3, 13.4, 13.29, 13.30, 14.17, 14.41, 15.25, 15.33, 16.12, 19.10, 19.19, 20.1, 20.2 |
| | world 18.8 |
| Soothill | humanity 6.22 |

|  |  |
|---|---|
| | man 15.35, 16.9, 18.8 |
| | people 1.9, 2.3, 2.19, 2.20, 3.21, 5.16, 6.2, 6.30, 8.1, 8.2, 8.9, 8.19, 11.24, 12.2, 12.7, 12.19, 13.3, 13.4, 13.29, 13.30, 14.17, 14.41, 15.25, 15.33, 16.12, 17.14, 19.10, 19.19, 20.1, 20.2 |
| | public work 1.5 |
| Waley | common people 2.19, 2.20, 3.21, 6.29, 6.30, 11.24, 12.2, 12.7, 13.4, 15.25, 15.33, 16.9, 17.14, 19.19 |
| | peasantry 1.5 |
| | people 1.9, 2.3, 5.16, 6.2, 8.1, 8.2, 8.9, 8.19, 12.7, 12.19, 13.3, 13.29, 13.30, 14.17, 14.41, 15.35, 16.12, 20.1, 20.2 |
| | subject 6.22, 18.8 |

## 民人(1)

|  |  |
|---|---|
| Ames/Rosemont | people 11.23 |
| Lau | common people and one 11.23 |
| Legge | common people and officer 11.23 |
| Leys | local people 11.23 |
| Soothill | people and officer 11.23 |
| Waley | peasant 11.23 |

## 敏(9)

|  |  |
|---|---|
| Ames/Rosemont | action 1.14 |

|  |  |
|---|---|
|  | clever 12.1, 12.2 |
|  | diligence 17.5 |
|  | diligent 5.15, 20.1 |
|  | earnest 7.20 |
|  | quick 4.24 |
| Lau | quick 1.14, 4.24, 5.15, 7.20, 12.1, 12.2, 20.1 |
|  | quickness 17.5 |
| Legge | active nature 5.15 |
|  | earnest 1.14, 4.24, 7.20, 20.1 |
|  | earnestness 17.5 |
|  | intelligence and vigour 12.1, 12.2 |
| Leys | agile mind 5.15 |
|  | clever 12.1, 12.2 |
|  | diligent 1.14, 7.20 |
|  | industriousness 20.1 |
|  | prompt 4.24 |
| Soothill | clever 5.15, 12.1, 12.2 |
|  | diligence 20.1 |
|  | diligent 1.14, 7.20 |
|  | earnestness 17.5 |
|  | quick 4.24 |
| Waley | clever 12.1, 12.2 |
|  | diligence 17.5 |
|  | diligent 1.14, 5.15, 7.20, 20.1 |
|  | prompt 4.24 |

# 名(8)

| | |
|---|---|
| Ames/Rosemont | accomplishment 8.19 |
| | name 4.5, 13.3, 15.20 |
| | put a name to 13.3 |
| | renowned 9.2 |
| Lau | name 4.5, 8.19, 9.2, 13.3, 15.20, 17.8 |
| Legge | name 4.5, 8.19, 9.2, 13.3, 15.20, 17.8 |
| Leys | bounty 8.19 |
| | conceive of 13.3 |
| | name 4.5, 9.2, 13.3, 15.20, 17.8 |
| Soothill | denominate 13.3 |
| | express 8.19 |
| | name 4.5, 15.20, 17.8 |
| | reputation 9.2 |
| | term 13.3 |
| Waley | language 13.3 |
| | name 4.5, 8.19 |
| | reputation 9.2, 15.20 |

# 命(22)

| | |
|---|---|
| Ames/Rosemont | carry message 14.44 |
| | cede throne 20.1 |
| | circumstance 14.36, 20.3 |

|       |                                              |
| ----- | -------------------------------------------- |
|       | command 16.2                                 |
|       | commission 8.6，13.20                        |
|       | diplomatic treaty 14.8                       |
|       | life 19.1                                    |
|       | live 14.12                                   |
|       | lot 11.18，12.5                              |
|       | message 17.18                                |
|       | propensity 2.4                               |
|       | propensity of circumstance 9.1               |
|       | report 10.2                                  |
|       | summon 10.14                                 |
| Lau   | allotted span 6.3，11.7                      |
|       | command 20.1                                 |
|       | commission 13.20                             |
|       | decree 2.4                                   |
|       | destiny 6.10，9.1，12.5，14.36，20.3          |
|       | fate 8.6                                     |
|       | life 14.12，19.1                             |
|       | lot 11.18                                    |
|       | message 17.18                                |
|       | prerogative to command 16.2                  |
|       | report 10.2                                  |
|       | summon 10.14                                 |
|       | text of a treaty 14.8                        |
|       | visitor 14.44                                |
| Legge | appointment of Heaven 6.10，9.1，11.18       |
|       | appointed time 6.3，11.7                     |
|       | authority 8.6                                |

call 10.14

carry the message 14.44

charge 20.1

commission 13.20

decree 2.4

determined appointment 12.5

governmental notification 14.8

life 14.12, 19.1

message 17.18

order 14.36, 16.2

ordinances of heaven 20.3

report 10.2

Leys     affair 16.2

allotted span 6.2

announce 10.2

call 10.14

commission 13.20

edict 14.8

fate 6.10, 9.1, 12.5, 20.3

government 8.6

heaven 14.36

life 11.7, 14.12, 19.1

lot 11.18

message 17.18

messenger 14.44

pass the message 20.1

summoned 10.14

will 2.4

| | |
|---|---|
| Soothill | act as messenger 14.44 |
| | charge 20.1 |
| | command 8.6, 10.14, 16.2 |
| | commission 13.20 |
| | divine 20.3 |
| | divine dispensation 12.5 |
| | fated 14.36 |
| | law 2.4 |
| | life 6.3, 11.7, 14.12, 19.1 |
| | lot 11.18 |
| | message 17.18 |
| | ordering of providence 9.1 |
| | state document 14.8 |
| | will of heaven 6.10 |
| Waley | allotted span 11.7 |
| | bidding 2.4 |
| | charge 20.1 |
| | command 10.14 |
| | commission 13.20, 16.2 |
| | ducal mandate 14.8 |
| | fate 9.1 |
| | heaven 12.5 |
| | life 14.12, 19.1 |
| | lot 11.18 |
| | message 14.44, 17.18 |
| | ordained 6.10 |
| | report 10.2 |
| | sovereignty 8.6 |

span of life 6.3

will of heaven 14.36, 20.3

# 末(6)

Ames/Rosemont
do not 9.24
no road 9.11
nothing that one can do 15.16
nowhere 17.4
tip of the branch 19.12

Lau
do nothing 9.24
no 14.39
no way 9.11
nothing one can do 15.16
nowhere 17.4
trifling matter 19.12

Legge
branch 19.12
can indeed do nothing 15.16
do nothing 9.24
no way 9.11
not 14.39, 17.4

Leys
cannot 9.11
do not 9.24, 15.16
nowhere 17.4
trifle 19.12

Soothill
branch 19.12
do nothing 9.24

|  |  |
|---|---|
| Waley | never 9.11 |
|  | not 14.39 |
|  | nothing whatever one can do 15.16 |
|  | nowhere 17.4 |
|  | do nothing 9.24 |
|  | minor matter 19.12 |
|  | no possibility of one's doing anything 15.16 |
|  | no way 9.11 |

# 难(22)

|  |  |
|---|---|
| Ames/Rosemont | difficult 6.16, 7.26, 7.29, 12.3, 13.15, 13.25, 14.10, 17.23, 19.16, 19.18 |
|  | difficulty 6.22, 13.15 |
|  | hard 14.1, 14.20, 15.17 |
|  | laudable in ability 19.15 |
|  | problem 17.20 |
|  | questions to ask 16.10 |
| Lau | difficult 2.8, 6.16, 7.29, 8.20, 12.3, 13.15, 13.25, 14.1, 14.10, 14.20, 17.23, 19.15, 19.16, 19.18 |
|  | difficulty 6.22, 13.15, 15.17, 17.20 |
|  | hard 7.26 |
|  | in doubt 16.10 |
| Legge | difficult 6.16, 7.26, 7.29, 8.20, 13.15, 13.25, 14.1, 14.10, 14.20, 14.39, 17.23 |
|  | difficulty 2.8, 6.22, 12.3, 13.15 |
|  | hard 15.17, 17.20, 19.15, 19.16, 19.18 |

| | |
|---|---|
| Leys | question other 16. 10 |
| | content 7. 26 |
| | deaf 7. 29 |
| | difficult 12. 3, 13. 15, 14. 1, 14. 10, 17. 23 |
| | difficulty 13. 15 |
| | matter 2. 8 |
| | [not] easy 13. 25, 19. 16 |
| | not enough 6. 16 |
| | hard 7. 26, 14. 20 |
| | question 16. 10 |
| | rare ability 19. 15 |
| | trials 6. 22 |
| Soothill | difficult 6. 22, 12. 3, 13. 25, 14. 1, 14. 10, 14. 39 |
| | difficulty 2. 8, 13. 15, 14. 20 |
| | hard 6. 16, 7. 26, 7. 29, 8. 20, 13. 25, 15. 17, 17. 20, 17. 23, 19. 16 |
| | hardly possible 19. 15, 19. 18 |
| | seek information 16. 10 |
| Waley | ask for information 16. 10 |
| | beyond one's power 14. 20 |
| | difficult 2. 8, 6. 22, 7. 29, 12. 3, 13. 25, 14. 1, 15. 17, 17. 20 |
| | hard 6. 16, 8. 20, 13. 15, 14. 10, 17. 23, 19. 15, 19. 16, 19. 18 |

# 佞(10)

| | |
|---|---|
| Ames/Rosemont | authoritative conduct 6.16 |
| | eloquence 5.5 |
| | eloquent talker 14.32 |
| | glib 11.23 |
| | glib talker 15.11, 16.4 |
| Lau | facile tongue 5.5 |
| | flattery 14.32 |
| | plausible 11.23 |
| | plausible in speech 16.4 |
| | plausible man 15.11 |
| | smooth tongue 6.16 |
| Legge | be ready with the tongue 5.5 |
| | glib tongued 11.23, 16.4 |
| | insinuating talker 14.32 |
| | readiness of the tongue 5.5 |
| | specious talker 15.11 |
| Leys | agile tongue 6.16 |
| | clever talker 15.11 |
| | clever tongue 14.32 |
| | eloquence 5.5 |
| | glib 16.4 |
| | wit 11.23 |
| Soothill | adcaptandum talker 14.32 |
| | glib 11.23, 16.4 |

| | |
|---|---|
| Waley | ready of speech 5.5 |
| | ready speech 5.5 |
| | specious men 15.11 |
| | clever at talk 16.4 |
| | clever talker 14.32, 15.11 |
| | glib 11.23 |
| | good talker 5.5 |

## 怒(1)

| | |
|---|---|
| Ames/Rosemont | anger 6.3 |
| Lau | anger 6.3 |
| Legge | anger 6.3 |
| Leys | frustration 6.3 |
| Soothill | anger 6.3 |
| Waley | wrath 6.3 |

## 虐(1)

| | |
|---|---|
| Ames/Rosemont | cruel 20.2 |
| Lau | cruel 20.2 |
| Legge | cruelty 20.2 |
| Leys | terror 20.2 |
| Soothill | cruelty 20.2 |
| Waley | savagery 20.2 |

## 朋(1)

| | |
|---|---|
| Ames/Rosemont | friend 1.1 |
| Lau | like minded friend 1.1 |
| Legge | friend 1.1 |
| Leys | friend 1.1 |
| Soothill | man of kindred spirit 1.1 |
| Waley | friend 1.1 |

## 朋友(8)

| | |
|---|---|
| Ames/Rosemont | colleague and friend 1.7 |
| | friend 1.4, 5.26, 10.16, 10.17, 13.28 |
| | friendship 4.26 |
| Lau | friend 1.4, 1.7, 4.26, 5.26, 10.16, 10.17, 13.28 |
| Legge | friend 1.4, 1.7, 4.26, 5.26, 10.16, 10.17, 13.28 |
| Leys | friend 1.4, 1.7, 5.26, 10.16, 10.17, 13.28 |
| | friendly 4.26 |
| Soothill | friend 1.4, 1.7, 4.26, 5.26, 10.16, 10.17, 13.28 |
| Waley | friend 1.4, 1.7, 5.26, 10.16, 10.17, 13.28 |
| | friendship 4.26 |

# 贫(9)

| | |
|---|---|
| Ames/Rosemont | poor 1.15, 8.13, 14.10, 16.1 |
| | poverty 4.5, 8.10, 15.32, 16.1 |
| Lau | poor 1.15, 8.13, 14.10 |
| | poverty 4.5, 8.10, 15.32, 16.1 |
| Legge | poor 1.15, 14.10 |
| | poverty 4.5, 8.10, 8.13, 15.32, 16.1 |
| Leys | poor 1.15, 8.13, 14.10, 15.32 |
| | poverty 4.5, 8.10, 16.1 |
| Soothill | needy 8.13 |
| | poor 1.15, 14.10 |
| | poverty 4.5, 8.10, 15.32, 16.1 |
| Waley | few 16.1 |
| | needy 8.13 |
| | poor 1.15, 14.10 |
| | poverty 4.5, 8.10, 15.32, 16.1 |

# 齐(10)

| | |
|---|---|
| Ames/Rosemont | fasting 7.13 |
| | hem of skirt 10.3 |
| | keep orderly 2.3 |
| | mourn 9.10, 10.19 |
| | purification 10.5, 10.6 |

| | |
|---|---|
| Lau | solemnity 10.6 |
| | stand shoulder to shoulder with 4.17 |
| | as good as 4.17 |
| | bereaved 10.19 |
| | fasting 7.13 |
| | keep in line 2.3 |
| | mourn 9.10, 10.19 |
| | purification 10.5, 10.6 |
| | robe 10.3 |
| | solemnly 10.6 |
| Legge | equal 4.17 |
| | fasting 7.13, 10.5, 10.6 |
| | grave 10.6 |
| | mourn 9.10, 10.19 |
| | robe 10.3 |
| | uniformity 2.3 |
| Leys | abstinence 10.5, 10.6 |
| | devoutly 10.6 |
| | emulate 4.17 |
| | fasting 7.13 |
| | hem of gown 10.3 |
| | mourn 9.10, 10.19 |
| | restrain 2.3 |
| Soothill | fasting 7.13, 10.5, 10.6 |
| | keep in order 2.3 |
| | mourn 9.10, 10.19 |
| | rise to one's level 4.17 |
| | skirt 10.3 |

| | |
|---|---|
| Waley | solemnity 10.6 |
| | equal 4.17 |
| | keep order 2.3 |
| | mourn 9.10, 10.19 |
| | prepare oneself for sacrifice 10.5, 10.6 |
| | purification before sacrifice 7.13 |
| | skirt 10.3 |
| | solemnly 10.6 |

## 祇(1)

| | |
|---|---|
| Ames/Rosemont | gods 7.35 |
| Lau | gods 7.35 |
| Legge | spirits 7.35 |
| Leys | spirits 7.35 |
| Soothill | spirits 7.35 |
| Waley | spirits 7.35 |

## 器(6)

| | |
|---|---|
| Ames/Rosemont | according to one's ability 13.25 |
| | capacity 3.22 |
| | tool 15.10 |
| | vessel 2.12, 5.4 |
| Lau | capacity 3.22 |
| | tool 15.10 |

| | |
|---|---|
| Legge | vessel 2.12, 5.4 |
| | within the limits of one's capacity 13.25 |
| | according to one's capacity 13.25 |
| | capacity 3.22 |
| | tool 15.10 |
| | utensil 2.12, 5.4 |
| Leys | caliber 3.22 |
| | never demand anything that is beyond one's capacity 13.25 |
| | pot 2.12, 5.4 |
| | tool 15.10 |
| Soothill | calibre 3.22 |
| | tool 15.10 |
| | machine 2.12 |
| | regard to one's capacity 13.25 |
| | vessel 5.4 |
| Waley | capacity 3.22 |
| | tool 15.10 |
| | implement 2.12 |
| | vessel 5.4 |
| | what one is capable of performing 13.25 |

# 亲(9)

| | |
|---|---|
| Ames/Rosemont | close 1.13 |
| | family relation 18.10 |
| | immediate relatives 20.1 |

|   |   |
|---|---|
| | intimate 1. 6 |
| | parent 8. 2, 12. 21, 19. 17 |
| | personally 17. 6 |
| Lau | cultivate the friendship 1. 6 |
| | in one's own person 17. 6 |
| | kinsman 1. 13, 20. 1 |
| | parent 8. 2, 12. 21, 19. 17 |
| | those closely related to 18. 10 |
| Legge | cultivate the friendship 1. 6 |
| | one's 10. 20 |
| | in one's own person 17. 6 |
| | intimate 1. 13 |
| | parent 12. 21, 19. 17 |
| | relation 8. 2, 18. 10 |
| | relative 20. 1 |
| Leys | associate 1. 6 |
| | closely relatives 20. 1 |
| | kin 8. 2, 12. 21 |
| | kinsman 1. 13 |
| | parent 19. 17 |
| | personally 17. 6 |
| | relative 18. 10 |
| Soothill | ally 1. 6 |
| | closely related 20. 1 |
| | family 8. 2 |
| | friend 1. 13 |
| | one's 10. 20 |
| | parent 19. 17 |

| | |
|---|---|
| Waley | personally 17.6 |
| | relative 12.21, 18.10 |
| | father or mother 19.17 |
| | one's 10.20 |
| | in one's own person 17.6 |
| | intimacy 1.6 |
| | kin 1.13, 8.2 |
| | kinsman 18.10, 20.1 |
| | kith and kin 12.21 |

# 清(2)

| | |
|---|---|
| Ames/Rosemont | flawless 18.8 |
| | incorruptible 5.19 |
| Lau | pure 5.19 |
| | purity 18.8 |
| Legge | pure 5.19 |
| | purity 18.8 |
| Leys | pure 5.19, 18.8 |
| Soothill | clean handed 5.19 |
| | purity 18.8 |
| Waley | integrity 18.8 |
| | scrupulous 5.19 |

# 情(2)

| | |
|---|---|
| Ames/Rosemont | [not] duplicitous 13.4 |
| | what really happens 19.19 |
| Lau | true colour 13.4 |
| | truth 19.19 |
| Legge | sincere 13.4 |
| | truth 19.19 |
| Leys | [not] mendacious 13.4 |
| Soothill | discovery 19.19 |
| | sincere 13.4 |
| Waley | evidence 19.19 |
| | [not] depart from facts 13.4 |

# 穷(4)

| | |
|---|---|
| Ames/Rosemont | adversity 15.2 |
| | dire strait 20.1 |
| Lau | dire strait 20.1 |
| | in extreme strait 15.2 |
| Legge | endure want 15.2 |
| | want 15.2, 20.1 |
| Leys | distress 15.2 |
| | penury 20.1 |
| Soothill | in want 15.2 |

| | | |
|---|---|---|
| Waley | lean 20.1 | |
| | dry 20.1 | |
| | hardship 15.2 | |

## 权(3)

| | |
|---|---|
| Ames/Rosemont | discretion 18.8 |
| | scale 20.1 |
| | weigh things up 9.30 |
| Lau | measure 18.8 |
| | exercise of moral discretion 9.30 |
| | weight 20.1 |
| Legge | exigency of the times 18.8 |
| | weight 20.1 |
| | weigh occurring event 9.30 |
| Leys | self-effacement 18.8 |
| | share counsel 9.30 |
| | weight 20.1 |
| Soothill | associate in judgment 9.30 |
| | weighty cause 18.8 |
| | weight 20.1 |
| Waley | due balance 18.8 |
| | join in counsel 9.30 |
| | weight 20.1 |

# 群(4)

| | |
|---|---|
| Ames/Rosemont | gather together 15.22 |
| | get together 15.17 |
| | get on with others 17.8 |
| | run with 18.6 |
| Lau | associate with 18.6 |
| | come together 15.22 |
| | live in a community 17.8 |
| | together 15.17 |
| Legge | associate with 18.6 |
| | a number of people 15.17 |
| | sociability 17.8 |
| | sociable 15.22 |
| Leys | associate with 18.6 |
| | communion 17.8 |
| | sociable 15.22 |
| | together 15.17 |
| Soothill | associate together 15.17 |
| | herd with 18.6 |
| | sociable 15.22 |
| | social intercourse 17.8 |
| Waley | ally 15.22 |
| | herd with 18.6 |
| | keep company 17.8 |
| | together 15.17 |

# 让(7)

| | |
|---|---|
| Ames/Rosemont | defer to other 4.13 |
| | deference 11.24 |
| | make way for 3.7 |
| | renounce 8.1 |
| | unassuming 1.10 |
| | yield 15.36 |
| Lau | abdicate 8.1 |
| | deference 4.13 |
| | deferential 1.10 |
| | make way for 3.7 |
| | modesty 11.24 |
| | yield 15.36 |
| Legge | complaisant 1.10 |
| | complaisantly 3.7 |
| | declined 8.1 |
| | humble 11.24 |
| | yield 15.36 |
| Leys | be afraid to 15.36 |
| | deference 4.13 |
| | deferential 1.10 |
| | exchange civility 3.7 |
| | renounce 8.1 |
| | [not] swagger 11.24 |
| Soothill | deference 4.13 |

Waley

deferential 1.10

give way 15.36

leave 8.1

modesty 11.24

yield 3.7

avoid competing with 15.36

cession 11.24

deferential 1.10

make way for 3.7

renounce 8.1

yield 4.13

# 仁(109)

Ames/Rosemont

authoritative 3.3, 4.2, 4.3, 4.6, 4.7, 5.5, 5.8, 5.19, 6.7, 6.22, 6.23, 6.26, 6.30, 7.34, 9.29, 12.1, 12.20, 12.22, 14.1, 14.4, 14.6, 14.16, 14.17, 14.28, 15.9, 15.33, 15.36, 17.1, 17.5, 17.7, 19.15, 20.2

authoritative conduct 1.2, 1.3, 4.4, 4.5, 5.19, 6.22, 6.30, 7.6, 7.30, 8.2, 8.7, 9.1, 12.2, 12.3, 12.24, 13.12, 13.19, 13.27, 15.35, 17.15, 19.6, 19.16

authoritative in one's conduct 7.15, 19.16

authoritative person 4.1, 5.8, 15.9, 18.1, 20.1

conduct 1.6, 15.10, 15.36

ren 17.19

scholar apprentice 15.10

| | |
|---|---|
| Lau | benevolence 4.1, 4.2, 4.4, 4.5, 4.6, 6.7, 6.22, 6.30, 7.6, 7.15, 7.30, 8.2, 8.7, 9.1, 9.29, 12.1, 12.2, 12.3, 12.20, 12.22, 12.24, 13.12, 13.19, 13.27, 14.16, 14.28, 15.9, 15.10, 15.33, 15.35, 15.36, 17.5, 17.7, 19.6, 19.15, 19.16, 20.2 |
| | benevolent 1.3, 3.3, 4.2, 4.3, 4.6, 5.5, 5.8, 5.19, 6.22, 6.23, 6.26, 6.30, 7.34, 8.10, 14.1, 14.4, 14.6, 14.17, 17.1, 17.5, 17.15, 18.1, 20.1 |
| | benevolent gentleman 15.10 |
| | character 1.2 |
| | one's fellow man 1.6 |
| | human 17.19 |
| Legge | benevolence 12.22 |
| | benevolent 6.26, 17.1, 17.7, 20.2 |
| | benevolent action 1.2 |
| | good 1.6 |
| | man of virtue 15.9, 18.1 |
| | perfect 9.1 |
| | perfect virtue 6.22, 7.6, 7.34, 8.7, 12.1, 12.3, 13.19, 17.5 |
| | perfectly virtuous 5.8 |
| | principle 14.4 |
| | true virtue 1.3 |
| | truly virtuous 5.5 |
| | virtue 3.3, 4.2, 4.4, 4.5, 4.6, 6.7, 6.22, 6.30, 7.30, 8.2, 12.2, 12.20, 12.24, 13.12, 13.27, 14.16, 14.17, 15.9, 15.10, 15.33, 15.35, 15.36, 17.15, 17.19, 19.6, 19.16, 20.1 |

| | |
|---|---|
| Leys | virtuous 4.2, 4.3, 4.6, 4.7, 5.19, 6.23, 6.30, 8.10, 9.29, 14.6, 14.28, 15.10, 19.15 |
| | virtuous manner 4.1 |
| | virtuously 7.15 |
| | good 4.2, 4.3, 5.5, 5.8, 5.19, 6.22, 6.23, 6.26, 6.30, 9.29, 14.4 |
| | goodness 1.3, 4.6, 6.7, 6.22, 6.30, 7.6, 7.15, 7.30, 8.2, 15.33, 17.15 |
| | gentlemen 15.10 |
| | human perfection 7.34 |
| | human quality 14.16 |
| | humanity 1.2, 3.3, 4.1, 4.4, 4.5, 8.7, 9.1, 12.1, 12.2, 12.3, 12.22, 12.24, 13.12, 13.19, 13.27, 14.1, 14.6, 14.28, 15.9, 15.10, 15.35, 17.5, 17.7, 17.19, 19.6, 19.15, 19.16, 20.2 |
| | models of humanity 18.1 |
| | morality 8.10 |
| | principle 4.5, 14.17 |
| | virtue 12.20, 15.36 |
| | virtuous 1.6, 17.1, 20.1 |
| | trust 20.1 |
| | one's quality 4.7 |
| Soothill | altruist 6.26 |
| | feelingness 17.19 |
| | good 1.6, 20.2 |
| | goodness of character 12.24 |
| | kindness 7.6, 8.2, 17.7 |
| | lover of fellow man 17.1 |

magnanimity 12.20

moral 4.1

moral character 4.1, 8.10, 15.33

moral duty 15.36

perfect 19.16

perfection 9.1

philanthropist 6.30

philanthropy 6.30

virtue 1.3, 4.2, 4.4, 4.5, 4.6, 4.7, 5.5, 5.8, 5.19, 6.7, 6.22, 7.15, 7.30, 7.34, 8.7, 12.1, 12.2, 12.3, 12.22, 13.12, 13.19, 13.27, 14.1, 14.16, 14.17, 15.9, 15.10, 15.35, 17.5, 17.15, 18.1, 19.6, 19.15, 20.1

virtuous 3.3, 4.2, 4.3, 4.6, 5.5, 6.23, 9.29, 14.4, 14.6, 14.28, 15.9, 15.10

virtuous man 15.9

unselfish life 1.2

Waley

feeling 17.19

good 1.3, 1.6, 3.3, 4.1, 4.2, 4.3, 4.6, 5.5, 5.8, 5.19, 6.22, 6.23, 6.26, 6.30, 7.34, 9.29, 12.22, 12.3, 14.1, 14.4, 14.17, 14.28, 15.9, 15.10, 17.1, 17.5, 17.15, 19.15, 19.16, 20.1

good man 18.1

goodness 1.2, 4.1, 4.4, 4.5, 4.6, 4.7, 6.7, 6.22, 6.30, 7.6, 7.15, 8.2, 8.7, 9.1, 12.1, 12.2, 12.3, 12.20, 12.24, 13.12, 13.19, 13.27, 14.6, 14.16, 15.9, 15.33, 15.35, 15.36, 17.5, 17.7, 19.6, 20.2

truly good 8.10

virtue 7.30

## 忍(3)

| | |
|---|---|
| Ames/Rosemont | condone 3.1 |
| | impatient 15.27 |
| Lau | self restraint 15.27 |
| | tolerate 3.1 |
| Legge | bear 3.1 |
| | forbearance 15.27 |
| Leys | capable of 3.1 |
| | impatience 15.27 |
| Soothill | bear 3.1 |
| | impatience 15.27 |
| Waley | endure 3.1 |
| | impatient 15.27 |

## 任(4)

| | |
|---|---|
| Ames/Rosemont | charge 8.7 |
| | rely upon 17.5, 20.1 |
| Lau | burden 8.7 |
| | entrust 17.5, 20.1 |
| Legge | burden 8.7 |
| | sustain 8.7 |
| | trust 17.5, 20.1 |

以译者姓名索引

| | |
|---|---|
| Leys | burden 8.7 |
| | trust 17.5, 20.1 |
| Soothill | confidence 20.1 |
| | load 8.7 |
| | trust 17.5 |
| Waley | burden 8.7 |
| | trust 17.5, 20.1 |

## 容(6)

| | |
|---|---|
| Ames/Rosemont | countenance 10.4 |
| | demeanor 8.4 |
| | high enough 10.3 |
| | kneel in a formal posture as though entertaining guests 10.18 |
| | tolerant 19.3 |
| Lau | admit 10.3 |
| | countenance 8.4 |
| | expression 10.4 |
| | sit in the formal manner of a guest 10.18 |
| | tolerant 19.3 |
| Legge | admit 10.3 |
| | appearance 10.4 |
| | bear with 19.3 |
| | deportment 8.4 |
| | put on any formal deportment 10.18 |
| Leys | attitude 8.4 |

|  |  |
|---|---|
|  | expression 10. 4 |
|  | sit stiffly like a guest 10. 18 |
|  | tolerate 19. 3 |
| Soothill | admit 10. 3 |
|  | bear 8. 4 |
|  | look 10. 4 |
|  | tolerate 19. 3 |
|  | wear formal air 10. 18 |
| Waley | attitude 8. 4 |
|  | expression 10. 4 |
|  | have room 10. 3 |
|  | find room 19. 3 |
|  | use ritual attitudes 10. 18 |

## 儒(2)

|  |  |
|---|---|
| Ames/Rosemont | counselor 6. 13 |
| Lau | ju 6. 13 |
| Legge | scholar 6. 13 |
| Leys | noble scholar 6. 13 |
| Soothill | scholar 6. 13 |
| Waley | ju 6. 13 |

## 辱(6)

|  |  |
|---|---|
| Ames/Rosemont | bring disgrace 18. 8 |

| | |
|---|---|
| | disgrace 4. 26, 12. 23, 13. 20 |
| | insult 1. 13 |
| Lau | disgrace 1. 13, 13. 20 |
| | humiliation 4. 26 |
| | humiliate 18. 8 |
| | snub 12. 23 |
| Legge | disgrace 1. 13, 4. 26, 12. 23, 13. 20 |
| | taint 18. 8 |
| Leys | disgrace 1. 13, 4. 26, 13. 20 |
| | insult 18. 8 |
| | rebuff 12. 23 |
| Soothill | abase 18. 8 |
| | disgrace 1. 13, 4. 26, 13. 20 |
| | humiliation 12. 23 |
| Waley | bring humiliation upon 18. 8 |
| | disgrace 13. 20 |
| | dishonor 1. 13 |
| | humiliation 12. 23 |
| | loss of favour 4. 26 |

## 丧(22)

| | |
|---|---|
| Ames/Rosemont | destroy 9. 5 |
| | funerary 9. 16 |
| | funeral 10. 5, 19. 1 |
| | loss 3. 24 |
| | mourning 3. 4, 7. 9, 17. 19, 19. 14, 19. 17, 20. 1 |

| | |
|---|---|
| Lau | mourning rite 3.26 |
| | ruin 11.9, 13.15, 14.19 |
| | bereaved 7.9 |
| | bereft 11.9 |
| | destroy 9.5 |
| | funeral 9.16 |
| | lose 14.19 |
| | loss of office 3.24 |
| | mourning 3.4, 3.26, 10.5, 17.19, 19.1, 19.14, 19.17, 20.1 |
| | ruin 13.15 |
| Legge | destroy 11.9 |
| | duties to the dead 9.16 |
| | lose 14.19 |
| | loss of office 3.24 |
| | mourner 7.9 |
| | mourning 3.4, 3.26, 10.5, 17.19, 19.1, 19.14, 19.17, 20.1 |
| | perish 9.5 |
| | ruin 13.15 |
| Leys | bury the dead 9.16 |
| | destroy 9.5, 11.9 |
| | dismissal 3.24 |
| | funeral 3.4, 10.5 |
| | lose 14.19 |
| | mourn 19.1 |
| | mourning 3.26, 7.9, 17.19, 19.14, 19.17, 20.1 |
| | ruin 13.15 |

| | |
|---|---|
| Soothill | bereft 11.9 |
| | destroy 9.5 |
| | duties to one's fathers and brethren 9.16 |
| | lose 14.19 |
| | loss of office 3.24 |
| | mourn 19.17 |
| | mourner 7.9 |
| | mourning 3.4, 3.26, 10.5, 17.19, 19.1, 19.14, 20.1 |
| | ruin 13.15 |
| Waley | bereft 11.9 |
| | grief 14.19 |
| | destroy 9.5 |
| | disappear 9.5 |
| | failure 3.24 |
| | mourning 3.4, 3.26, 7.9, 9.16, 10.5, 17.19, 19.1, 19.14, 19.17, 20.1 |
| | ruin 13.15 |

## 色(27)

| | |
|---|---|
| Ames/Rosemont | appearance 1.3, 10.19, 12.20, 17.10, 17.15 |
| | approach 10.21 |
| | beauty 1.7 |
| | color 10.6 |
| | countenance 2.8, 5.25, 8.4, 10.2, 16.6, 16.10 |
| | decadent manner 14.37 |
| | demeanor 10.4, 12.20 |

| | |
|---|---|
| | expression 10.3 |
| | face 5.19 |
| | final touches 14.8 |
| | licentiousness 16.7 |
| | physical beauty 9.18, 15.13 |
| | pretend 11.19 |
| Lau | appearance 5.19, 11.19 |
| | attraction of feminine beauty 16.7 |
| | beauty 15.13 |
| | beauty in woman 9.18 |
| | colour 10.6 |
| | countenance 1.3, 1.7, 5.25, 16.10, 17.15 |
| | embellish 14.8 |
| | expression 2.8, 8.4, 10.2, 10.3, 10.4, 10.19, 12.20, 16.6 |
| | facade 12.20 |
| | front 17.10 |
| | hostile look 14.37 |
| Legge | appearance 1.3, 5.25, 11.19, 12.20, 17.10, 17.15 |
| | beauty 9.18, 15.13 |
| | colour 10.6 |
| | countenance 2.8, 5.19, 8.4, 10.2, 10.3, 10.4, 10.19, 10.21, 12.20, 16.6, 16.10 |
| | disrespectful look 14.37 |
| | elegance 14.8 |
| | love of beauty 1.7 |
| | lust 16.7 |
| Leys | affectation 5.25 |

|  | air 12. 20 |
|  | attitude 2. 8, 14. 37 |
|  | colour 10. 6 |
|  | countenance 10. 19 |
|  | expression 8. 4, 10. 3, 10. 4, 12. 20, 16. 6, 16. 10 |
|  | look 1. 7, 17. 10 |
|  | lust 16. 7 |
|  | manner 1. 3, 17. 15 |
|  | polish 14. 8 |
|  | pretense 11. 19 |
|  | sex 9. 18, 15. 13 |
| Soothill | air 12. 20 |
|  | appearance 11. 19, 16. 10, 17. 10 |
|  | beauty 15. 13 |
|  | colour 10. 6 |
|  | demeanour 1. 3, 2. 8, 5. 25, 17. 15 |
|  | embellish 14. 8 |
|  | expression 10. 2, 10. 3, 10. 4, 10. 19, 12. 20, 16. 6 |
|  | face 10. 21 |
|  | feminine allurement 1. 7 |
|  | look 8. 4 |
|  | lust 16. 7 |
|  | sign 5. 19 |
|  | uncongenial look 14. 37 |
|  | woman 9. 18 |
| Waley | air of respect 1. 7 |
|  | colour 10. 6 |
|  | demeanour 2. 8 |

expression 10.4, 10.19, 12.20, 16.6

look 8.4, 10.2, 10.3, 14.37, 16.10

lust 16.7

manner 1.3, 5.25, 17.15

outward 11.19, 12.20, 17.10

sexual desire 9.18, 15.13

sign 5.19, 10.21

# 杀(9)

| | |
|---|---|
| Ames/Rosemont | execute 20.2 |
| | give up 15.9 |
| | kill 12.19, 13.11, 14.16, 14.17, 18.7 |
| | tailor 10.5 |
| Lau | accept death 15.9 |
| | cut 10.5 |
| | death penalty 20.2 |
| | kill 12.19, 13.11, 14.16, 14.17, 18.7 |
| Legge | capital punishment 13.11 |
| | cut 10.5 |
| | death 20.2 |
| | kill 12.19, 14.16, 14.17, 18.7 |
| | sacrifice 15.9 |
| Leys | cut 10.5 |
| | give one's life 15.9 |
| | kill 12.19, 14.16, 14.17, 18.7 |
| | murder 13.11, 20.2 |

| | |
|---|---|
| Soothill | capital punishment 13.11 |
| | death 20.2 |
| | execute 12.19 |
| | kill 18.7 |
| | put to death 14.16, 14.17 |
| | sacrifice 15.9 |
| | shape 10.5 |
| Waley | death 20.2 |
| | give one's life 15.9 |
| | put to death 14.16, 14.17 |
| | slaughter 13.11 |
| | slay 12.19 |

## 善(37)

| | |
|---|---|
| Ames/Rosemont | ability 5.26, 16.11 |
| | adept 2.20, 12.19 |
| | adeptly 12.23 |
| | apt 13.22 |
| | best 6.9, 13.24 |
| | efficacious 8.13, 13.15, 13.29, 19.3 |
| | excellent 12.11 |
| | felicitous 3.25, 8.4 |
| | fine 12.21 |
| | good 5.17, 9.13, 15.33, 17.6 |
| | good at 9.11, 15.10 |
| | make the most of 13.8 |

|  |  |
|---|---|
| | master 14.5 |
| | [not] perversity (bushan) 19.20 |
| | productive 7.3 |
| | strength 7.22 |
| | what others do well 16.5 |
| | what works well 7.28 |
| | well 7.32 |
| Lau | attractive 7.32 |
| | excel 5.17 |
| | good 2.20, 3.25, 5.26, 7.28, 8.4, 8.13, 9.13, 12.19, 13.15, 13.24, 16.11, 17.6, 19.3 |
| | good at 9.11, 14.5 |
| | goodness 16.5 |
| | good point 7.22 |
| | laudable 13.8 |
| | [not] wicked 19.20 |
| | practise one's craft well 15.10 |
| | perfection 15.33 |
| | properly 12.23 |
| | splendid 12.11, 12.21 |
| | tactfully 6.9 |
| | well 13.22 |
| Legge | excellence 5.26, 8.13, 15.33 |
| | good 2.20, 3.25, 7.3, 7.28, 8.4, 9.13, 12.11, 12.19, 12.21, 13.15, 13.22, 13.24, 16.11, 19.3 |
| | goodness 16.5 |
| | good quality 7.22 |
| | know well 5.17 |

|  |  |
|---|---|
| | [not] wickedness 19.20 |
| | polite 6.9 |
| | skillfully 9.11, 12.23, 14.5 |
| | well 7.32, 13.8 |
| | work well 15.10 |
| Leys | best 7.28 |
| | do good work 15.10 |
| | excellent 12.11, 12.21 |
| | good 2.20, 3.25, 5.26, 7.3, 8.13, 9.13, 12.19, 13.24, 14.5, 16.11, 19.3 |
| | know 5.17, 9.11, 13.8 |
| | kindly 6.9 |
| | like 7.32 |
| | [not] wickedness 19.20 |
| | quality 7.22, 16.5 |
| | right 13.15 |
| | right sort of power 15.33 |
| | true 8.4, 13.22 |
| | tactfully 12.23 |
| Soothill | courteously 6.9 |
| | discreetly 12.23 |
| | excel 2.20, 14.5 |
| | excellence 8.13, 15.33, 16.5 |
| | excellent 12.11, 12.21 |
| | gifted 5.17 |
| | good 3.25, 5.26, 7.28, 7.32, 9.13, 12.19, 13.15, 13.24, 16.11, 19.3 |
| | good quality 7.22 |

Waley

[not] iniquity 19. 20

perfection 7. 3

skillfully 9. 11

worth listening to 8. 4

well 13. 8, 13. 22

work well 15. 10

be of note 8. 4

best 9. 13

discreetly 12. 23

do good work 15. 10

excellent 12. 21

good 5. 26, 7. 28, 8. 13, 12. 19, 13. 15, 13. 24, 16. 11, 19. 3

good at 16. 4

good example 5. 17

goodness 3. 25

good point 16. 5

good quality 7. 22

like 7. 32

mighty 14. 5

[not] wicked 19. 20

polite 6. 9

skillfully 9. 11

true 12. 11

well 13. 22

worthy 2. 20

# 善人(5)

| Ames/Rosemont | efficacious person 7.26, 11.19, 13.29, 20.1 |
| --- | --- |
| | efficacious people 13.11 |
| Lau | good man 7.26, 11.19, 13.11, 13.29, 20.1 |
| Legge | good man 7.26, 11.19, 13.11, 13.29 |
| | the good 20.1 |
| Leys | good man 11.19, 13.11, 13.29 |
| | good people 20.1 |
| | perfect man 7.26 |
| Soothill | good man 7.26, 13.11, 13.29 |
| | man of natural goodness 11.19 |
| | the good 20.1 |
| Waley | faultless man 7.26 |
| | good people 11.19 |
| | man of the right sort 13.29 |
| | right sort of people 13.11 |
| | the good 20.1 |

# 伤(4)

| Ames/Rosemont | damage 19.24 |
| --- | --- |
| | harm 11.24 |
| | hurt 10.11 |
| | injurious 3.20 |

| | |
|---|---|
| Lau | detract 19.24 |
| | hurt 10.11 |
| | harm 11.24 |
| | self injury 3.20 |
| Legge | harm 11.24, 19.24 |
| | hurt 10.11 |
| | hurtfully excessive 3.20 |
| Leys | affect 19.24 |
| | bitterness 3.20 |
| | harm 11.24 |
| | hurt 10.11 |
| Soothill | harm 11.24, 19.24 |
| | hurt 10.11 |
| | morbid 3.20 |
| Waley | harm 11.24, 19.24 |
| | hurt 10.11 |
| | self injury 3.20 |

## 韶(3)

| | |
|---|---|
| Ames/Rosemont | Shao 3.25, 7.14, 15.11 |
| Lau | Shao 3.25, 7.14, 15.11 |
| Legge | Shâo 3.25, 7.14, 15.11 |
| Leys | coronation hymn of shun 7.14 |
| | coronation Hymn of Shun and Victory Hymn of Wu 15.11 |
| | hymn of peaceful coronation 3.25 |

| | |
|---|---|
| Soothill | Shao 3.25, 7.14, 15.11 |
| Waley | succession 7.14, 15.11 |
| | succession dance 3.25 |

## 召南(1)

| | |
|---|---|
| Ames/Rosemont | shaonan 17.8 |
| Lau | shao nan 17.8 |
| Legge | Shâo nan 17.8 |
| Leys | second part of the poem 17.8 |
| Soothill | Chao Nan 17.8 |
| Waley | shao nan 17.8 |

## 摄(3)

| | |
|---|---|
| Ames/Rosemont | lift 10.3 |
| | responsibility 3.22 |
| | set 11.24 |
| Lau | lift 10.3 |
| | situate 11.24 |
| Legge | hold up 10.3 |
| | perform 3.22 |
| | straiten 11.24 |
| Leys | lift 10.3 |
| | service 3.22 |
| | squeeze 11.24 |

| | | |
|---|---|---|
| Soothill | | hem 11.24 |
| | | hold up 10.3 |
| | | perform 3.22 |
| Waley | | hem 11.24 |
| | | hold up 10.3 |
| | | perform 3.22 |

# 身(17)

| | | |
|---|---|---|
| Ames/Rosemont | | body 10.5 |
| | | itself to one 4.6 |
| | | one 15.24 |
| | | one's life 15.9 |
| | | one's own person 18.8 |
| | | one's whole person 1.7 |
| | | over and over again 9.27 |
| | | own 12.21 |
| | | own conduct 13.13 |
| | | person 1.4 |
| | | personal 18.7 |
| | | personal conduct 13.6 |
| | | personally 17.6 |
| Lau | | character 18.7 |
| | | constantly 9.27 |
| | | one 13.6, 15.24 |
| | | oneself 1.4, 1.7, 13.13, 18.8 |
| | | one's person 4.6 |

| | |
|---|---|
| Legge | own 12.21 |
| | own person 13.6, 17.6 |
| | body 10.5 |
| | continually 9.27 |
| | life 1.7, 12.21 |
| | one 15.24 |
| | oneself 1.4 |
| | one's life 15.9 |
| | one's person 4.6, 18.8 |
| | own conduct 13.13 |
| | own person 17.6 |
| | personal 18.7 |
| | personal conduct 13.6 |
| Leys | continually 9.27 |
| | life 1.7, 15.24 |
| | oneself 1.4, 12.21 |
| | one 4.6, 13.6, 18.7 |
| | one's life 15.9 |
| | own life 13.13 |
| | personally 17.6 |
| Soothill | body 10.5 |
| | life 1.7, 15.24 |
| | personal 18.7 |
| | personally 17.6 |
| | one 4.6 |
| | one's live 15.9 |
| | oneself 1.4, 13.6, 13.13, 18.8 |
| | own 12.21 |

| Waley | continually 9.27 |
| --- | --- |
| | life 1.7 |
| | man 10.5 |
| | one 4.6 |
| | oneself 1.4, 13.6, 13.13, 18.8 |
| | one's life 15.9 |
| | one's own 18.7 |
| | own 12.21 |
| | own person 17.6 |

# 神(7)

| Ames/Rosemont | god 11.12 |
| --- | --- |
| | gods of the heaven 7.35 |
| | spirit 3.12, 6.22, 7.21, 8.21 |
| Lau | ancestral 8.21 |
| | god 3.12, 6.22, 7.21 |
| | gods above 7.35 |
| | spirit 11.12 |
| Legge | spirit 3.12, 8.21, 11.12 |
| | spiritual being 6.22, 7.21 |
| | spirits of the upper 7.35 |
| Leys | god 3.12, 6.22, 11.12 |
| | spirit 7.21, 7.35, 8.21 |
| Soothill | god 3.12 |
| | spirit 6.22, 8.21, 11.12 |
| | spirits celestial 7.35 |

| | |
|---|---|
| Waley | supernatural 7.21 |
| | sky spirit 7.35 |
| | spirit 3.12, 6.22, 7.21, 8.21, 11.12 |

# 慎(7)

| | |
|---|---|
| Ames/Rosemont | care 7.13 |
| | careful 19.25 |
| | caution 8.2 |
| | cautious 1.14, 2.18 |
| | circumspect 1.9 |
| Lau | careful 7.13, 8.2, 19.25 |
| | cautious 1.14, 2.18 |
| | meticulous care 1.9 |
| Legge | careful 1.9, 1.14, 19.25 |
| | carefulness 8.2 |
| | caution 7.13 |
| | cautious 2.18 |
| Leys | careful 19.25 |
| | cautious 2.18 |
| | circumspection 7.13 |
| | honored 1.9 |
| | prudence 8.2 |
| | prudent 1.14 |
| Soothill | caution 8.2 |
| | guarded 1.14 |
| | guardedly 2.18 |

| | |
|---|---|
| Waley | heed 19.25 |
| | solicitude 1.9, 7.13 |
| | attention 7.13 |
| | careful 19.25 |
| | caution 8.2 |
| | cautious 1.14, 2.18 |
| | proper respect 1.9 |

## 圣(4)

| | |
|---|---|
| Ames/Rosemont | sage 6.30, 7.34, 9.6 |
| Lau | sage 6.30, 7.34, 9.6 |
| Legge | sage 6.30, 7.34, 9.6 |
| Leys | saint 6.30, 9.6 |
| | wisdom 7.34 |
| Soothill | inspiration 9.6 |
| | sage 6.30, 7.34 |
| Waley | divine sage 6.30, 7.34, 9.6 |

## 圣人(4)

| | |
|---|---|
| Ames/Rosemont | sage 7.26, 16.8, 19.12 |
| Lau | sage 7.26, 16.8, 19.12 |
| Legge | sage 7.26, 16.8, 19.12 |
| Leys | saint 7.26, 16.8, 19.12 |
| Soothill | inspired man 7.26 |

| | |
|---|---|
| | sage 16.8, 19.12 |
| Waley | divine sage 7.26, 16.8, 19.12 |

## 诗(14)

| | |
|---|---|
| Ames/Rosemont | book of song 1.15, 8.3 |
| | song 2.2, 3.8, 7.18, 8.8, 13.5, 16.13, 17.8 |
| Lau | ode 1.15, 2.2, 3.8, 7.18, 8.3, 8.8, 13.5, 16.13, 17.8 |
| Legge | book of poetry 1.15, 2.2, 8.3, 17.8 |
| | ode 3.8, 7.18, 8.8, 13.5, 16.13 |
| Leys | poem 1.15, 2.2, 3.8, 7.18, 8.3, 8.8, 13.5, 16.13, 17.8 |
| Soothill | ode 1.15, 2.2, 7.18, 8.3, 13.5, 16.13 |
| | poet 3.8, 8.8 |
| | poetry 17.8 |
| Waley | song 1.15, 2.2, 3.8, 7.18, 8.3, 8.8, 13.5, 16.13, 17.8 |

## 识(6)

| | |
|---|---|
| Ames/Rosemont | broad vocabulary 17.8 |
| | grasp 19.22 |
| | persevere in storing up what is learned 7.2 |
| | remember 7.28, 15.3 |
| Lau | acquire a wide knowledge of 17.8 |

| | |
|---|---|
| | learn in one's mind 15. 3 |
| | retain 7. 28 |
| | get hold of 19. 22 |
| | store up knowledge 7. 2 |
| Legge | acquaint 17. 8 |
| | keep in memory 7. 28，15. 3 |
| | remember 19. 22 |
| | treasure up of knowledge 7. 2 |
| Leys | learn 17. 8 |
| | keep a record of 7. 28 |
| | retain 19. 22 |
| | store all up 15. 3 |
| | store up knowledge 7. 2 |
| Soothill | acquaint 17. 8 |
| | keep in mind 19. 22 |
| | retain all in mind 15. 3 |
| | treasure up 7. 28 |
| | treasure up of knowledge 7. 2 |
| Waley | acquaintance 17. 8 |
| | note what is said 7. 2 |
| | record 19. 22 |
| | take due note of 7. 28 |
| | retain in mind 15. 3 |

## 实(2)

| | |
|---|---|
| Ames/Rosemont | fruit 9. 22 |

| | |
|---|---|
| | much 8.5 |
| Lau | fruit 9.22 |
| | full 8.5 |
| Legge | fruit 9.22 |
| | full 8.5 |
| Leys | fruit 9.22 |
| | full 8.5 |
| Soothill | fruit 9.22 |
| | full 8.5 |
| Waley | fruit 9.22 |
| | full 8.5 |

## 食(41)

| | |
|---|---|
| Ames/Rosemont | cereal 10.6 |
| | compensation 15.38 |
| | diet 10.5，10.6 |
| | dine 7.9 |
| | dish 10.6 |
| | eat 7.16，7.19，10.6，15.31，17.6，17.19 |
| | eating 15.31 |
| | eclipse 19.21 |
| | food 2.8，4.9，8.21，10.6，10.12，12.7，12.11 |
| | meal 4.5，10.6 |
| | millet 18.7 |
| | rice 6.11，14.9 |
| | sufficient 20.1 |

| | |
|---|---|
| Lau | sustenance 15.32 |
| | diet 10.5, 10.6 |
| | eat 4.5, 8.21, 7.9, 7.16, 7.19, 8.21, 10.6, 17.6, 17.19, 18.7 |
| | eclipse 19.21 |
| | food 2.8, 4.9, 10.12, 12.7, 12.11, 15.31, 15.32, 20.1 |
| | meal 10.6 |
| | reward 15.38 |
| | rice 6.11, 14.9 |
| Legge | cook meat 10.12 |
| | eat 7.9, 7.16, 10.6, 15.31, 17.6, 17.19 |
| | eating 15.31 |
| | eclipse 19.21 |
| | emolument 15.38 |
| | feast 18.7 |
| | food 1.14, 2.8, 4.9, 7.19, 8.21, 10.5, 10.6, 12.7, 12.11, 15.32, 17.20, 20.1 |
| | meal 4.5 |
| | rice 6.11, 10.6, 14.9 |
| Leys | diet 10.5, 10.6 |
| | eat 1.14, 7.9, 7.19, 8.21, 10.6, 17.6, 17.19 |
| | eclipse 19.21 |
| | food 2.8, 4.9, 7.16, 10.12, 12.7, 12.11, 14.9, 15.31, 17.20, 20.1 |
| | living 15.32 |
| | meal 10.6 |
| | millet 18.7 |

|  |  |
| --- | --- |
| Soothill | reward 15.38 |
|  | rice 6.11, 10.6 |
|  | diet 10.5, 10.6 |
|  | dine 7.9 |
|  | eat 7.16, 10.6, 17.6, 17.19, 18.7 |
|  | eclipse 19.21 |
|  | food 1.14, 2.8, 4.9, 7.19, 8.21, 10.6, 10.12, 12.7, 12.11, 14.9, 15.31, 17.20, 20.1 |
|  | living 15.32 |
|  | meal 4.5 |
|  | meat 10.6 |
|  | millet 6.11 |
|  | pay 15.38 |
|  | rice 10.6 |
| Waley | eat 1.14, 7.16, 10.6, 17.6, 17.19 |
|  | eclipse 19.21 |
|  | food 2.8, 4.9, 8.21, 10.5, 10.6, 10.12, 12.7, 12.11, 14.9, 15.31, 17.20, 20.1 |
|  | hunger 7.19 |
|  | make a living 15.32 |
|  | meal 7.9 |
|  | millet 18.7 |
|  | rice 6.11, 10.6 |
|  | pay 15.38 |

# 史(3)

| Ames/Rosemont | officious scribe 6.18 |
| | scribe 15.26 |
| Lau | pedantry 6.18 |
| | shih 15.7 |
| | scribe 15.26 |
| Legge | historiographer 15.7, 15.26 |
| | manners of a clerk 6.18 |
| Leys | pedantry 6.18 |
| | shi 15.7 |
| | scribe 15.26 |
| Soothill | clerk 6.18 |
| | recorder 15.7, 15.26 |
| Waley | pedantry 6.18 |
| | recorder 15.7 |
| | scribe 15.26 |

# 士(18)

| Ames/Rosemont | groom 7.12 |
| | magistrate 18.2, 19.19 |
| | scholar apprentice 4.9, 8.7, 12.20, 13.20, 13.28, 14.2, 15.9, 15.10, 18.11, 19.1 |
| | teacher 18.6 |

| | |
|---|---|
| Lau | gentleman 4.9, 8.7, 12.20, 13.20, 13.28, 14.2, 15.9, 15.10, 18.6, 18.11, 19.1 |
| | guard 7.12 |
| | judge 18.2, 19.19 |
| Legge | chief criminal judge 18.2, 19.19 |
| | groom 7.12 |
| | officer 8.7, 12.20, 13.20, 18.11 |
| | scholar 4.9, 13.28, 14.2, 15.9, 15.10, 19.1 |
| | one 18.6 |
| Leys | ganitor 7.12 |
| | gentleman 13.20, 13.28, 15.10, 18.6, 19.1 |
| | judge 19.19 |
| | knight 18.11 |
| | magistrate 18.2 |
| | man 15.9 |
| | scholar 4.9, 8.7, 12.20, 14.2 |
| Soothill | chief criminal judge 18.2, 19.19 |
| | educated man 13.28 |
| | groom 7.12 |
| | leader 18.6 |
| | man 12.20 |
| | officer 13.20 |
| | scholar 8.7, 14.2, 15.9, 15.10 |
| | servant of the State 19.1 |
| | student 4.9 |
| | valiant men 18.11 |
| Waley | gentleman 7.12 |
| | leader of the knight 18.2, 19.19 |

knight 4.9, 12.20, 13.20, 15.9, 15.10, 18.11, 19.1

knight of the way 8.7, 13.28, 14.2

one 18.6

# 世 (14)

Ames/Rosemont
descendent 16.1

generation 2.23, 13.12, 16.2, 16.3

lineage 20.1

office 14.37

one's day 15.20

world 6.16, 18.6

Lau
descendant 16.1

generation 2.23, 13.12, 16.2, 16.3

lines 20.1

world 14.37, 18.6

Legge
age 2.23, 6.16

descendant 16.1

families whose line of succession 20.1

generation 13.12, 16.2, 16.3

world 14.37, 18.6

Leys
age 6.16

children and grandchildren 16.1

dynastic line 20.1

generation 2.23, 13.12, 16.2, 16.3

world 14.37, 15.20, 18.6

Soothill
age 2.23

|  |  |
|---|---|
|  | descendant 16.1 |
|  | generation 6.16, 13.12, 16.2, 16.3 |
|  | one's day 15.20 |
|  | succession 20.1 |
|  | world 14.37, 18.6 |
| Waley | generation 2.23, 13.12, 14.37, 16.2, 16.3, 18.6 |
|  | lines of succession 20.1 |
|  | one's day 15.20 |
|  | son or grandson 16.1 |

## 仕(8)

|  |  |
|---|---|
| Ames/Rosemont | give of one's service 15.7 |
|  | prime minster 5.19 |
|  | public office 19.13 |
|  | seek office 5.6 |
|  | serve in office 17.1, 18.7 |
| Lau | enter public life 18.7 |
|  | prime minister 5.19 |
|  | take office 5.6, 15.7, 17.1, 19.13 |
| Legge | enter on official employment 5.6 |
|  | go into office 17.1 |
|  | in office 15.7 |
|  | office 5.19, 15.7 |
|  | officer 19.13 |
|  | take office 15.7, 18.7 |
| Leys | accept the office 17.1 |

| | |
|---|---|
| Soothill | display one's talents 15. 7 |
| | official position 5. 6 |
| | politics 19. 13 |
| | prime minister 5. 19 |
| | public life 18. 7 |
| | hold office 15. 7 |
| | in office 5. 6 |
| | office 19. 13 |
| | serve one's country 18. 7 |
| | take office 5. 19，17. 1 |
| Waley | duty to the state 19. 13 |
| | office 5. 19 |
| | serve 17. 1 |
| | serve one's country 18. 7 |
| | serve the state 15. 7 |
| | take office 5. 6 |

## 守(5)

| | |
|---|---|
| Ames/Rosemont | shore up 16. 1 |
| | steadfast 8. 13 |
| | sustain 15. 33 |
| Lau | abide 8. 13 |
| | keep 15. 33 |
| | preserve 16. 1 |
| Legge | hold 8. 13，15. 33 |
| | preserve 16. 1 |

| | |
|---|---|
| Leys | defend 8.13 |
| | hold it together 16.1 |
| | retain 15.33 |
| Soothill | keep 8.13 |
| | live up to 15.33 |
| | preserve 16.1 |
| Waley | attack 8.13 |
| | save 16.1 |
| | secure that power 15.33 |

## 寿(1)

| | |
|---|---|
| Ames/Rosemont | long enduring 6.23 |
| Lau | long lived 6.23 |
| Legge | long lived 6.23 |
| Leys | live long 6.23 |
| Soothill | prolong life 6.23 |
| Waley | secure 6.23 |

## 述(3)

| | |
|---|---|
| Ames/Rosemont | accomplish 14.43 |
| | find the proper way 17.17 |
| | follow the proper way 7.1 |
| Lau | transmit 7.1, 17.17 |
| | worthwhile 14.43 |

| Legge | record 17.17 |
| | transmit 7.1 |
| | worthy of being handed down 14.43 |
| Leys | achieve 14.43 |
| | hand down 17.17 |
| | transmit 7.1 |
| Soothill | pass on 17.17 |
| | transmit 7.1 |
| | worthy of mentioning 14.43 |
| Waley | hand down 17.17 |
| | transmit 7.1 |
| | worth mentioning 14.43 |

## 恕(2)

| Ames/Rosemont | put oneself in the other's place 4.15 |
| | Shu 15.24 |
| Lau | use oneself as a measure to gauge the likes and dislikes of others 4.15 |
| | Shu 15.24 |
| Legge | benevolent 4.15 |
| | reciprocity 15.24 |
| Leys | reciprocity 4.15, 15.24 |
| Soothill | consideration 4.15 |
| | sympathy 15.24 |
| Waley | consideration 4.15, 15.24 |

## 说(21)

**Ames/Rosemont**
discuss 3.21
explanation 3.11
happy 6.28, 20.1
like 11.4
[not] upset 17.4
pleased 5.6, 9.24, 13.16, 13.25
pleasure 1.1, 9.24
rejoice 6.12
repeat 17.12
speak 12.8

**Lau**
explain away 3.21
gossip 17.12
pleased 5.6, 6.12, 6.28, 9.24, 11.4, 13.16, 13.25, 17.4, 20.1
pleasure 1.1
speak 12.8
theory 3.11

**Legge**
delighted 20.1
delight 6.12, 11.4
happy 13.16
meaning 3.11
pleasant 1.1
pleased 5.6, 6.28, 9.24, 13.25, 17.4
speak out 3.21

| | |
|---|---|
| Leys | tell 17. 12 |
| | word 12. 8 |
| | argue 3. 21 |
| | delight 5. 6, 9. 24 |
| | enjoy 6. 12 |
| | happy 13. 16 |
| | joy 1. 1, 20. 1 |
| | meaning 3. 11 |
| | [not] dismayed 17. 4 |
| | pleased 6. 28, 11. 4, 13. 25 |
| | say 12. 8, 17. 12 |
| Soothill | discuss 3. 21 |
| | gratified 20. 1 |
| | happy 13. 16 |
| | meaning 3. 11 |
| | pleased 5. 6, 9. 24, 13. 25, 17. 4 |
| | pleasure 1. 1, 6. 12, 6. 28 |
| | proclaim 17. 12 |
| | satisfied 11. 4 |
| | word 12. 8 |
| Waley | accept 11. 4 |
| | approve 9. 24, 13. 16, 17. 4 |
| | delight 5. 6 |
| | discuss 3. 21 |
| | explanation 3. 11 |
| | joy 20. 1 |
| | pleased 6. 28, 13. 25 |
| | pleasure 1. 1 |

|  | speak 12.8 |
|  | tell 17.12 |

## 私(2)

| Ames/Rosemont | on one's own 2.9 |
|  | private 10.4 |
| Lau | in private 2.9 |
|  | private 10.4 |
| Legge | conduct when away from one 2.9 |
|  | private 10.4 |
| Leys | on one's own 2.9 |
|  | private 10.4 |
| Soothill | conduct when not with one 2.9 |
|  | private 10.4 |
| Waley | private 10.4 |
|  | private conduct 2.9 |

## 思(24)

| Ames/Rosemont | concern oneself with 19.1 |
|  | go 2.2 |
|  | reflect 19.6 |
|  | reflection 2.15 |
|  | think 4.17, 5.20, 9.30, 14.12 |
|  | think about 16.10 |

|          |                                                          |
|----------|----------------------------------------------------------|
| Lau      | thought 14. 26, 15. 31                                   |
|          | [not] forget 19. 1                                       |
|          | reflect 19. 6                                            |
|          | remember 14. 12                                          |
|          | think 2. 15, 4. 17, 9. 30, 15. 31                        |
|          | thought 5. 20, 14. 26                                    |
|          | turn one's thought to 16. 10                             |
| Legge    | anxious 16. 10                                           |
|          | reflect with self application 19. 6                      |
|          | subjects with one of thoughtful consideration 16. 10     |
|          | think 4. 17, 9. 30, 14. 12, 15. 31, 16. 10               |
|          | think of 19. 1                                           |
|          | thought 2. 2, 2. 15, 5. 20, 14. 26, 19. 1                |
|          | thoughtful consideration 16. 10                          |
| Leys     | contemplate 14. 26                                       |
|          | meditate 15. 31, 19. 6                                   |
|          | not make one forget 19. 1                                |
|          | seek to 4. 17                                            |
|          | sense 14. 12                                             |
|          | take 16. 10                                              |
|          | think 2. 2, 2. 15, 9. 30                                 |
|          | thought 5. 20                                            |
| Soothill | care 16. 10                                              |
|          | reflection 19. 6                                         |
|          | point of thoughtful care 16. 10                          |
|          | think 2. 15, 4. 17, 5. 20, 9. 31, 14. 12, 15. 31         |
|          | thought 2. 2, 14. 26, 19. 1                              |
| Waley    | care 16. 10                                              |

careful 16.10

love 9.31

meditate 15.31

think 2.15, 4.17, 5.20, 14.12, 16.10

think of 19.1

think for oneself 19.6

thought 2.2, 14.26

## 死(38)

Ames/Rosemont

dead 2.5, 9.5, 11.21

death 4.8, 7.11, 8.7, 8.13, 11.12, 11.13, 12.5, 12.7, 19.25

die 6.3, 9.12, 10.16, 11.7, 11.8, 11.9, 11.10, 11.11, 11.21, 12.10, 14.16, 14.17, 14.43, 16.12

dying 8.4

lose one's life 15.35, 18.1

meet an unnatural end 14.5

Lau

dead 9.5

death 8.7, 8.13, 11.12, 11.13, 12.5, 12.7, 16.12, 19.25

die 2.5, 4.8, 6.3, 7.11, 9.12, 10.16, 11.7, 11.8, 11.9, 11.10, 11.11, 11.21, 12.10, 14.16, 14.17, 14.43, 15.35

dying 8.4

lose one's life 18.1

meet violent deaths 14.5

| | |
|---|---|
| Legge | dead 2.5 |
| | death 8.7, 8.13, 9.5, 11.12, 11.13, 12.5, 12.7, 16.12 |
| | die 4.8, 6.3, 8.4, 9.12, 10.16, 11.7, 11.8, 11.9, 11.10, 11.11, 11.21, 12.10, 14.16, 14.17, 15.35, 18.1, 19.25 |
| | die a natural death 14.5 |
| | dying 7.11 |
| Leys | dead 6.3, 9.5, 11.7, 11.21 |
| | death 7.11, 8.7, 11.12, 11.13, 12.5, 12.7, 14.43, 16.12, 19.25 |
| | die 2.5, 4.8, 8.4, 9.12, 10.16, 11.8, 11.9, 11.10, 11.11, 11.21, 12.10, 14.16 |
| | die a natural death 14.5 |
| | execute 18.1 |
| | life 8.13 |
| | lose one's life 15.35 |
| Soothill | dead 2.5, 11.21, 12.10 |
| | death 8.7, 8.13, 11.12, 11.13, 12.5, 12.7, 16.12, 18.1, 19.25 |
| | die 4.8, 6.3, 9.12, 10.16, 11.7, 11.8, 11.9, 11.10, 11.11, 11.21, 14.16, 15.35 |
| | die a natural death 14.5 |
| | dying 7.11, 8.4, 14.17, 14.43 |
| | mortal 9.5 |
| Waley | come to a bad end 14.5 |
| | dead 11.12, 11.21 |
| | death 8.7, 12.5, 12.7, 16.12, 19.25 |

die 2.5, 4.8, 6.3, 7.11, 8.4, 8.13, 9.12, 10.16, 11.7, 11.8, 11.9, 11.10, 11.11, 11.13, 11.21

dying 14.17

give one's life 14.16

lose one's life 15.35

mortal 9.5

perish 12.10

slay 18.1

## 四海(2)

| | |
|---|---|
| Ames/Rosemont | four seas 20.1 |
| | world 12.5 |
| Lau | empire 20.1 |
| | four seas 12.5 |
| Legge | four seas 12.5, 20.1 |
| Leys | four seas 12.5, 20.1 |
| Soothill | four seas 12.5 |
| | land 20.1 |
| Waley | four seas 12.5, 20.1 |

## 肆(3)

| | |
|---|---|
| Ames/Rosemont | display 14.36 |
| | reckless 17.14 |
| | shop 19.7 |

| Lau | expose 14. 36 |
| | impatient of restraint 17. 14 |
| | workshop 19. 7 |
| Legge | disregard of small thing 17. 14 |
| | expose 14. 36 |
| | shop 19. 7 |
| Leys | carefree 17. 14 |
| | expose 14. 36 |
| | workshop 19. 7 |
| Soothill | expose 14. 36 |
| | liberty in detail 17. 14 |
| | workshop 19. 7 |
| Waley | expose 14. 36 |
| | impatient of small restraint 17. 14 |
| | workshop 19. 7 |

## 绥(2)

| Ames/Rosemont | bring peace 19. 25 |
| | cord 10. 20 |
| Lau | bring peace 19. 25 |
| | mounting cord 10. 20 |
| Legge | cord 10. 20 |
| | make one happy 19. 25 |
| Leys | handrail 10. 20 |
| | offer one peace 19. 25 |
| Soothill | give one tranquility 19. 25 |

| | |
|---|---|
| Waley | mounting cord 10.20 |
| | mounting cord 10.20 |
| | steady one as with a rope 19.25 |

## 泰(6)

| | |
|---|---|
| Ames/Rosemont | comfort 7.26 |
| | distinguished 13.26 |
| | hubris 9.3 |
| | proud 20.2 |
| Lau | at ease 13.26, 20.2 |
| | casual 9.3 |
| | comfortable 7.26 |
| Legge | at ease 7.26 |
| | arrogant 9.3 |
| | dignified ease 13.26, 20.2 |
| Leys | affluence 7.26 |
| | authority 20.2 |
| | rude 9.3 |
| | shows authority 13.26 |
| Soothill | dignified 13.26, 20.2 |
| | too far 9.3 |
| | prosperous 7.26 |
| Waley | affluence 7.26 |
| | dignified 13.26 |
| | presumptuous 9.3 |
| | proud 20.2 |

## 贪(2)

| Ames/Rosemont | covetous 20.2 |
|---|---|
| Lau | greedy 20.2 |
| Legge | covetous 20.2 |
| Leys | rapacity 20.2 |
| Soothill | greedy 20.2 |
| Waley | covetous 20.2 |

## 天(22)

| Ames/Rosemont | sky 19.25<br>tian 3.13, 3.24, 6.28, 7.23, 8.19, 9.5, 9.6, 9.12, 11.9, 12.5, 14.35, 17.17, 20.1 |
|---|---|
| Lau | heaven 3.13, 3.24, 6.28, 7.23, 8.19, 9.5, 9.6, 9.12, 11.9, 12.5, 14.35, 17.17, 20.1<br>sky 19.25 |
| Legge | heaven 3.2, 3.13, 3.24, 6.28, 7.23, 8.19, 9.5, 9.6, 9.12, 11.9, 12.5, 14.35, 16.2, 17.17, 19.25<br>heavenly 20.1 |
| Leys | heaven 3.2, 3.13, 3.24, 6.28, 7.23, 8.19, 9.5, 9.6, 9.12, 11.9, 12.5, 14.35, 16.2, 17.17<br>heavenly 20.1<br>sky 19.25 |
| Soothill | celestial 20.1 |

| | |
|---|---|
| | heaven 3.2, 3.13, 3.24, 6.28, 7.23, 8.19, 9.5, 9.6, 9.12, 11.9, 12.5,14.35, 17.17, 20.1 |
| | sky 19.25 |
| Waley | heaven 3.2, 3.13, 3.24, 6.28, 7.23, 8.19, 9.5, 9.6, 9.12, 11.9, 12.5,14.35, 16.2, 17.17 |
| | heavenly 20.1 |
| | sky 19.25 |

## 天道(1)

| | |
|---|---|
| Ames/Rosemont | the way of tian 5.13 |
| Lau | the way of heaven 5.13 |
| Legge | the way of heaven 5.13 |
| Leys | the way of heaven 5.13 |
| Soothill | the laws of heaven 5.13 |
| Waley | the way of heaven 5.13 |

## 天命(3)

| | |
|---|---|
| Ames/Rosemont | propensities of tian 2.4, 16.8 |
| Lau | decrees of heaven 2.4, 16.8 |
| Legge | decrees of heaven 2.4 |
| | ordinances of heaven 16.8 |
| Leys | will of heaven 2.4, 16.8 |
| Soothill | divine will 16.8 |
| | laws of heaven 2.4 |

| | | |
|---|---|---|
| Waley | biddings of heaven 2.4 | |
| | will of heaven 16.8 | |

## 天下(23)

| | |
|---|---|
| Ames/Rosemont | all under tian 3.24 |
| | empire 3.11, 8.1, 14.17, 17.19 |
| | land 12.22 |
| | throughout the land 20.1 |
| | whole empire 12.1 |
| | world 4.10, 8.13, 8.18, 8.20, 14.5, 16.2, 17.5, 18.6, 19.20 |
| Lau | empire 3.11, 3.24, 8.1, 8.13, 8.18, 8.20, 12.22, 14.5, 14.17, 16.2, 17.5, 17.19, 18.6, 19.20, 20.1 |
| | whole empire 12.1 |
| | world 4.10 |
| Legge | all under heaven 12.1 |
| | empire 8.18, 8.20, 16.2, 17.19, 18.6 |
| | kingdom 3.11, 3.24, 8.1, 8.13, 12.22, 14.5, 16.2 |
| | throughout the kingdom 20.1 |
| | whole empire 17.5 |
| | world 4.10, 19.20 |
| | whole kingdom 14.17 |
| Leys | all over the world 20.1 |
| | entire world 8.1, 8.20 |
| | entire world in order 14.17 |
| | everywhere in the world 17.5, 17.19 |

|   |   |
|---|---|
| Soothill | heaven 8. 18 |
| | whole world 12. 1 |
| | world 3. 11, 3. 24, 4. 10, 8. 13, 12. 22, 14. 5, 16. 2, 18. 6, 19. 20 |
| | all 20. 1 |
| | empire 3. 24, 8. 13, 8. 18, 8. 20, 12. 22, 14. 5, 14. 17, 16. 2 |
| | everybody 12. 1 |
| | everywhere 17. 5, 17. 19 |
| | imperial 8. 1 |
| | whole empire 3. 11 |
| | world 4. 10, 18. 6, 19. 20 |
| Waley | all that is under heaven 12. 22, 14. 5, 14. 17 |
| | all things under heaven 3. 11, 8. 1 |
| | everyone under heaven 12. 1 |
| | everywhere under heaven 17. 5, 17. 19 |
| | heaven 8. 18 |
| | under heaven 8. 13, 8. 20, 16. 2, 18. 6, 19. 20, 20. 1 |
| | world 3. 24, 4. 10 |

# 同(9)

|   |   |
|---|---|
| Ames/Rosemont | alliance 11. 24 |
| | [not] different 15. 4 |
| | run with 18. 6 |
| | same 7. 31 |
| | sameness 13. 23 |

| | |
|---|---|
| Lau | together 14. 18 |
| | echo 13. 23 |
| | gathering 11. 24 |
| | [not] different 15. 4 |
| | same 7. 31 |
| | side by side 14. 18 |
| Legge | adulatory 13. 23 |
| | associate with 18. 6 |
| | audience 11. 24 |
| | equal 3. 16 |
| | in company with 14. 18 |
| | [not] different 15. 4 |
| | same 7. 31 |
| Leys | associate with 18. 6 |
| | conformity 13. 23 |
| | even 3. 16 |
| | gathering 11. 24 |
| | [not] different 15. 4 |
| | together 14. 18 |
| Soothill | audience 11. 24 |
| | equal 3. 16 |
| | familiar 13. 23 |
| | herd with 18. 6 |
| | in company with 14. 18 |
| | [not] different 15. 4 |
| | same 7. 31 |
| Waley | accommodating 13. 23 |
| | general gathering 11. 24 |

herd with 18.6

[not] different 15.4

same 7.31, 14.18

## 偷(1)

| | |
|---|---|
| Ames/Rosemont | indifferent 8.2 |
| Lau | shirk obligation 8.2 |
| Legge | meanness 8.2 |
| Leys | fickle 8.2 |
| Soothill | meanly 8.2 |
| Waley | fickle 8.2 |

## 退(13)

| | |
|---|---|
| Ames/Rosemont | back 10.11 |
| | rein in 11.20 |
| | retire 7.29, 10.2 |
| | return 13.14 |
| | take one's leave 16.13 |
| | withdraw 2.9, 7.31, 12.22 |
| Lau | go 7.31 |
| | hold back 11.20 |
| | retire 16.13 |
| | return 10.11, 13.14 |
| | withdraw 2.9, 7.29, 12.22, 19.12 |

| | |
|---|---|
| Legge | withdrawal 10.2 |
| | keep back 11.20 |
| | recede 19.12 |
| | retire 2.9, 7.29, 7.31, 10.2, 12.22, 16.13 |
| | retire and slow 11.20 |
| | return 10.11, 13.14 |
| Leys | beside 7.29 |
| | depart 10.2 |
| | go away 16.13 |
| | hold back 11.20 |
| | leave 10.11 |
| | return 13.14 |
| | say goodbye 19.12 |
| | slow 11.20 |
| | withdraw 7.31, 12.22, 16.13 |
| Soothill | come from 13.14 |
| | come forth from 10.11 |
| | depart 10.2 |
| | go out 16.13 |
| | hold back 11.20 |
| | lag behind 11.20 |
| | retire 19.12 |
| | withdraw 2.9, 7.29, 7.31, 12.22 |
| Waley | backward 11.20 |
| | come away 16.13 |
| | come back 13.14 |
| | go 10.2 |
| | hold back 11.20 |

retire 7.29, 16.13, 19.12

return 10.11

when one is not with 2.9

withdraw 7.31, 12.22

## 万方(2)

| Ames/Rosemont | many states 20.1 |
| Lau | ten thousand states 20.1 |
| Legge | the people of the myriad regions 20.1 |
| Leys | ten thousand fiefs 20.1 |
| Soothill | the country 20.1 |
| Waley | many lands 20.1 |

## 罔(3)

| Ames/Rosemont | crook 6.19 |
| | dupe 6.26 |
| | perplexity 2.15 |
| Lau | bewildered 2.15 |
| | dupe 6.26, 6.19 |
| Legge | befool 6.26 |
| | labour lost 2.15 |
| | lose one's uprightness 6.19 |
| Leys | futile 2.15 |
| | lead astray 6.26 |

| | |
|---|---|
| Soothill | without 6.19 |
| | hoodwink 6.26 |
| | useless 2.15 |
| | without 6.19 |
| Waley | lead astray 6.26 |
| | lost 2.15 |
| | without 6.19 |

# 威(4)

| | |
|---|---|
| Ames/Rosemont | command 7.38 |
| | dignify 20.2 |
| | dignity 1.8 |
| Lau | awe 1.8 |
| | awe inspiring 7.38, 20.2 |
| Legge | majestic 7.38, 20.2 |
| | veneration 1.8 |
| Leys | authority 1.8, 7.38 |
| | stern 20.2 |
| Soothill | command 7.38, 20.2 |
| | respect 1.8 |
| Waley | awe 20.2 |
| | command 7.38 |
| | respect 1.8 |

# 违(14)

| | |
|---|---|
| Ames/Rosemont | abandon 4.5 |
| | belie 12.20 |
| | contrary 2.5, 4.18, 9.3 |
| | depart 6.7 |
| | objection 2.9 |
| | take exception to 13.15 |
| | take one's leave 5.19 |
| Lau | against 9.3, 13.15 |
| | belie 12.20 |
| | disagree 2.9 |
| | disobedient 4.18 |
| | fail to comply 2.5 |
| | forsake 4.5 |
| | lapse 6.7 |
| | leave 5.19 |
| Legge | abandon 4.5, 4.18 |
| | contrary 6.7 |
| | disobedient 2.5 |
| | leave 5.19 |
| | objection 2.9 |
| | oppose 9.3 12.20 |
| | opposition 13.15 |
| Leys | against 9.3 |
| | contradict 4.18 |

|  |  |
|---|---|
|  | contradiction 13. 15 |
|  | contrary 12. 20 |
|  | disobey 2. 5 |
|  | forsake 4. 5 |
|  | go against 4. 5 |
|  | interruption 6. 7 |
|  | leave 5. 19 |
|  | objection 2. 9 |
| Soothill | belie 12. 20 |
|  | depart 6. 7 |
|  | desist 4. 18 |
|  | disobedient 2. 5 |
|  | disregard 4. 5 |
|  | leave 5. 19 |
|  | infringe 9. 3 |
|  | objection 2. 9 |
|  | oppose 13. 15 |
| Waley | belie 12. 20 |
|  | contrary 6. 7, 9. 3 |
|  | differ 2. 9 |
|  | disobey 2. 5 |
|  | go away 5. 19 |
|  | oppose 13. 15 |
|  | quit 4. 5 |
|  | thwart 4. 18 |

# 畏(10)

| | |
|---|---|
| Ames/Rosemont | awe 16.8, 20.2 |
| | esteem 9.23 |
| | surround 9.5, 11.21 |
| Lau | awe 9.23, 16.8, 20.2 |
| | meet with danger 9.5, 11.21 |
| Legge | awe 16.8, 20.2 |
| | fear 11.21 |
| | put in fear 9.5 |
| | respect 9.23 |
| Leys | awe 9.23, 20.2 |
| | fear 16.8 |
| | trap 9.5, 11.21 |
| Soothill | awe 16.8, 20.2 |
| | intimidate 9.5 |
| | peril 11.21 |
| | respect 9.23 |
| Waley | awe 20.2 |
| | fear 16.8 |
| | respect 9.23 |
| | trap 9.5, 11.21 |

# 温(5)

| | |
|---|---|
| Ames/Rosemont | cordial 1.10, 19.9 |
| | cordiality 16.10 |
| | gracious 7.38 |
| | review 2.11 |
| Lau | cordial 1.10, 7.38, 16.10, 19.9 |
| | keep fresh 2.11 |
| Legge | benign 1.10, 16.10 |
| | cherish 2.11 |
| | mild 7.38, 19.9 |
| Leys | affable 7.38 |
| | amiable 16.10, 19.9 |
| | cordial 1.10 |
| | revise 2.11 |
| Soothill | affable 7.38 |
| | benign 1.10 |
| | kindly 16.10 |
| | gracious 19.9 |
| | review 2.11 |
| Waley | affable 7.38 |
| | cordial 1.10 |
| | kindly 16.10 |
| | mild 19.9 |
| | reanimate 2.11 |

# 文(25)

| | |
|---|---|
| Ames/Rosemont | culture 6.27, 7.25, 7.33, 9.11, 12.15 |
| | gloss 19.8 |
| | improve yourself 1.6 |
| | refine 5.15, 14.12, 14.18 |
| | refinement 6.18, 12.8, 12.24 |
| | text 15.26 |
| | wen 9.5, 19.22 |
| Lau | acquired refinement 6.18 |
| | cultivate 1.6, 12.24 |
| | culture 3.14, 6.27, 7.25, 9.5, 9.11, 12.15 |
| | gloss 19.8 |
| | refine 14.12 |
| | refinement 12.8, 15.26 |
| | wen 5.15, 14.18, 19.22 |
| Legge | accomplishment 6.18 |
| | add to 14.12 |
| | all learning 6.27 |
| | cause of truth 9.5 |
| | culture 12.24 |
| | gloss 19.8 |
| | learning 9.11, 12.15 |
| | letters 7.25, 7.33 |
| | ornamental 12.8 |
| | one's text 15.26 |

|  |  |
|---|---|
|  | polite study 1.6 |
|  | regulation 3.14 |
|  | WĂN 5.15, 14.18, 19.22 |
| Leys | civilization 3.14, 9.5 |
|  | civilized 5.15, 14.18 |
|  | cover up 19.8 |
|  | culture 6.18, 12.8, 12.24 |
|  | grace 14.12 |
|  | literature 1.6, 6.27, 7.25, 9.11, 12.15 |
|  | wen 19.22 |
| Soothill | art 12.8 |
|  | culture 3.14, 7.25, 9.11, 12.24, 14.18 |
|  | cultured 5.15 |
|  | embellish 19.8 |
|  | enlightenment 9.5 |
|  | letters 6.27, 7.33, 12.15 |
|  | polite study 1.6 |
|  | one's record 15.26 |
|  | refine 14.12 |
|  | training 6.18 |
|  | wên 19.22 |
| Waley | culture 3.14, 7.25, 9.5, 9.11, 12.8, 12.24 |
|  | cultured 5.15 |
|  | grace 14.12 |
|  | letters 6.27, 12.15 |
|  | ornamentation 6.18 |
|  | over elaboration 19.8 |
|  | polite arts 1.6 |

wên 14.18, 19.22

## 文德(1)

| | |
|---|---|
| Ames/Rosemont | refinement 16.1 |
| Lau | moral quality 16.1 |
| Legge | civil culture and virtue 16.1 |
| Leys | moral power of civilization 16.1 |
| Soothill | culture and morality 16.1 |
| Waley | prestige 16.1 |

## 文献(1)

| | |
|---|---|
| Ames/Rosemont | documentation 3.9 |
| Lau | record 3.9 |
| Legge | record 3.9 |
| Leys | record 3.9 |
| Soothill | record 3.9 |
| Waley | document 3.9 |

## 文学(1)

| | |
|---|---|
| Ames/Rosemont | study of culture 11.3 |
| Lau | culture and learning 11.3 |
| Legge | literary 11.3 |

| | |
|---|---|
| Leys | culture 11.3 |
| Soothill | literature and learning 11.3 |
| Waley | culture and learning 11.3 |

## 文章(2)

| | |
|---|---|
| Ames/Rosemont | cultural achievement 8.19 |
| | cultural refinement 5.13 |
| Lau | accomplishment 5.13 |
| | civilized accomplishment 8.19 |
| Legge | elegant regulation 8.19 |
| | personal displays of one's principles and ordinary descriptions of them 5.13 |
| Leys | institution 8.19 |
| | view 5.13 |
| Soothill | civilising regulation 8.19 |
| | culture and refinement 5.13 |
| Waley | culture 8.19 |
| | views concerning culture and the outward insignia of goodness 5.13 |

## 无道(12)

| | |
|---|---|
| Ames/Rosemont | abandon the way 12.19 |
| | lose one's way 3.24 |
| | lose the way 14.19 |

以译者姓名索引 609

|         |                                                          |
|---------|----------------------------------------------------------|
|         | way does not prevail 5. 2, 16. 2                         |
|         | way not prevail 8. 13, 14. 1, 14. 3, 15. 7               |
|         | without the way 5. 21                                    |
| Lau     | lack of moral principle 14. 19                           |
|         | not follow the way 12. 19                                |
|         | way does not prevail 8. 13, 14. 3, 16. 2                 |
|         | way falls into disuse 5. 2, 15. 7                        |
|         | way no longer prevails 5. 21                             |
|         | way not prevail 14. 1                                    |
|         | without the way 3. 24                                    |
| Legge   | bad government prevail 14. 1, 14. 3, 15. 7, 16. 2        |
|         | disorder 5. 21                                           |
|         | ill governed 5. 2, 8. 13                                 |
|         | unprincipled 12. 19                                      |
|         | unprincipled course 14. 19                               |
|         | without the principles 3. 24                             |
| Leys    | bad 12. 19                                               |
|         | bad government 15. 7                                     |
|         | lose the way 5. 21, 8. 13, 14. 1, 14. 3, 16. 2           |
|         | without principle 14. 19                                 |
|         | without the way 3. 24, 5. 2                              |
| Soothill| disorder 5. 21                                           |
|         | good government fail 16. 2                               |
|         | ill governed 5. 2, 14. 1, 15. 7                          |
|         | lack law and order 14. 3                                 |
|         | law and order fail 8. 13                                 |
|         | lawless 12. 19                                           |
|         | unprincipled character 14. 19                            |

| | |
|---|---|
| Waley | without light and leading 3.24 |
| | have not the way 12.19 |
| | no follower of the true way 14.19 |
| | not rule according to the way 5.2, 14.1 |
| | way no longer prevails 3.24, 5.21 |
| | way ceased 15.7 |
| | way does not prevail 8.13, 14.3, 16.2 |
| | way no longer prevailed 5.21 |

## 武(1)

| | |
|---|---|
| Ames/Rosemont | wu 3.25 |
| Lau | wu 3.25 |
| Legge | wû 3.25 |
| Leys | hymn of military conquest 3.25 |
| Soothill | wu 3.25 |
| Waley | war dance 3.25 |

## 习(3)

| | |
|---|---|
| Ames/Rosemont | apply 1.1 |
| | practice 1.4 |
| | virtue of one's habit 17.2 |
| Lau | behavior 17.2 |
| | practice 1.4 |
| | try out 1.1 |

| | |
|---|---|
| Legge | application 1.1 |
| | master and practice 1.4 |
| | practice 17.2 |
| Leys | habit 17.2 |
| | practice 1.4 |
| | put into practice 1.1 |
| Soothill | exercise 1.1 |
| | practice 1.4, 17.2 |
| Waley | practice 17.2 |
| | repeat 1.1, 1.4 |

# 贤(25)

| | |
|---|---|
| Ames/Rosemont | better 17.20, 19.23 |
| | care for 1.7 |
| | character 1.7, 6.11, 7.15 |
| | highest character 14.37 |
| | ministers who are of the highest character 15.10 |
| | person of exceptional character 4.17 |
| | superior 19.3, 19.25 |
| | superior character 11.16, 14.29, 14.31, 15.14, 16.5, 19.22, 19.24 |
| | those with superior character 13.2 |
| Lau | admirable 6.11 |
| | better 17.20, 19.3 |
| | distinguished counsellor 15.10 |
| | excellence 15.14, 19.24 |

| | |
|---|---|
| | excellent 7.15, 16.5 |
| | man of excellence 1.7 |
| | man of talent 13.2 |
| | show deference 1.7 |
| | someone better than oneself 4.17 |
| | superior 11.16, 14.29, 14.31, 19.3, 19.22, 19.23, 19.25 |
| Legge | admirable 6.11 |
| | apply as sincerely to the love of 1.7 |
| | better 17.20 |
| | excellence 14.29 |
| | great officer 15.10 |
| | man of virtue and talent 13.2 |
| | man of worth 4.17 |
| | superior 11.16, 19.23, 19.25 |
| | superior worth 14.31 |
| | talented and virtuous 19.3 |
| | talents and virtue 19.22, 19.24 |
| | virtue 15.14 |
| | virtuous 1.7 |
| | worth 14.37 |
| | worthy 7.15, 16.5 |
| Leys | admirable 6.11 |
| | better 11.16, 17.20, 19.23 |
| | better qualified 15.14 |
| | highest wisdom 14.37 |
| | man of talent 13.2 |
| | merit 19.24 |

|         |                                       |
|---------|---------------------------------------|
|         | perfection 14. 29                     |
|         | sagacity 14. 31                       |
|         | superior 19. 25                       |
|         | talented 16. 5                        |
|         | value 1. 7                            |
|         | virtue 1. 7                           |
|         | virtuous 7. 15                        |
|         | virtuous minister 15. 10              |
|         | wisdom 19. 3                          |
|         | wise 19. 3, 19. 22                    |
|         | worthy man 4. 17                      |
| Soothill | better 11. 16, 17. 20                |
|         | excellence 19. 24                     |
|         | excel 1. 7                            |
|         | gifted 19. 22                         |
|         | good 14. 37                           |
|         | man of worth 4. 17                    |
|         | minister 15. 10                       |
|         | moral excellence 1. 7                 |
|         | real worth 14. 31                     |
|         | superior 19. 23, 19. 25               |
|         | superiority 15. 14                    |
|         | those who are worthy and capable 13. 2 |
|         | worth 19. 3                           |
|         | worthy 6. 11, 7. 15, 14. 29, 16. 5, 19. 3 |
| Waley   | best man 15. 14                       |
|         | best of all 14. 37                    |
|         | better 1. 7, 11. 16, 17. 20, 19. 23   |

excel 19.3

good 7.15, 19.24

good man 4.17

incomparable 6.11

man of superior capacity 13.2

officers as are worthy 15.10

perfect 14.29

sage 14.31

superior 19.25

those of great understanding 19.22

those that excel 19.3

treat better 1.7

wise 16.5

# 小人(24)

| | |
|---|---|
| Ames/Rosemont | petty person 2.14, 4.11, 4.16, 6.13, 7.37, 12.16, 12.19, 13.4, 13.23, 13.25, 13.26, 14.6, 14.23, 15.2, 15.21, 15.34, 16.8, 17.3, 17.10, 17.21, 17.23, 19.8 |
| Lau | petty 6.13, 13.4 |
| | small man 2.14, 4.11, 4.16, 6.13, 7.37, 12.16, 12.19, 13.23, 13.25, 13.26, 14.6, 14.23, 15.2, 15.21, 15.34, 16.8, 17.3, 17.10, 17.21, 17.23, 19.8 |
| | stubborn petty mindedness 13.20 |
| Legge | inferior 12.19 |
| | little man 13.20 |

|  |  |
|---|---|
|  | man of low station 17.3 |
|  | mean man 2.14, 4.16, 6.13, 7.37, 12.16, 13.23, 13.25, 13.26, 14.6, 14.23, 15.2, 15.21, 16.8, 19.8 |
|  | one of lower people 17.21 |
|  | small mean people 17.10 |
|  | small man 4.11, 13.4, 15.34 |
|  | servant 17.23 |
| Leys | common man 12.19 |
|  | coward 17.10 |
|  | small man 2.14, 4.11, 4.16, 14.6 |
|  | small people 17.3 |
|  | underling 17.23 |
|  | vulgar man 6.13, 7.37, 12.16, 13.4, 13.20, 13.23, 13.25, 13.26, 14.23, 15.2, 15.21, 15.34, 16.8, 17.21, 19.8 |
| Soothill | baser man 16.8 |
|  | common herd 17.10 |
|  | common people 17.3 |
|  | ill bred 13.26 |
|  | inferior man 2.14, 4.11, 4.16, 6.13, 7.37, 13.23, 13.25, 14.23, 15.2, 15.21, 15.34, 19.8 |
|  | little minded man 12.16, 13.4 |
|  | man of grit 13.20 |
|  | man of the lower order 17.21 |
|  | one of the lower type 14.6 |
|  | servant 17.23 |
|  | those below 12.19 |
| Waley | commoner 4.11 |

common people 6.13, 13.23, 13.25, 13.26

lesser man 4.16

low walks of life 17.10

no gentleman 13.4

not a gentleman 14.6

people of low birth 17.23

small man 2.14, 7.37, 12.16, 14.23, 15.2, 15.21, 15.34, 16.8, 17.3, 17.21, 19.8

small people 12.19

such a one 13.20

# 亵(3)

| | |
|---|---|
| Ames/Rosemont | casual clothing 10.5 |
| | frequent acquaintance 10.19 |
| | night coat 10.5 |
| Lau | lapels and cuff 10.5 |
| | night shirt 10.5 |
| | well known to one 10.19 |
| Legge | sleeping dress 10.5 |
| | undress 10.19 |
| Leys | lapel 10.5 |
| | low condition 10.19 |
| | nightgown 10.5 |
| Soothill | not in public 10.19 |
| | sleeping garment 10.5 |
| | undress 10.5 |

| | |
|---|---|
| Waley | bedcloth 10.5 |
| | informally 10.19 |
| | undress 10.5 |

## 心(6)

| | |
|---|---|
| Ames/Rosemont | heart and mind 2.4, 17.20, 20.1 |
| | moving 14.39 |
| | thoughts and feelings 6.7 |
| Lau | frustrated purpose 14.39 |
| | heart 2.4, 6.7, 17.20 |
| | mind, 20.1 |
| Legge | heart 2.4, 14.39 |
| | mind 6.7, 17.20, 20.1 |
| Leys | heart 2.4, 20.1 |
| | mind 6.7, 17.20 |
| | real heart 14.39 |
| Soothill | feeling 14.39 |
| | heart 2.4, 6.7, 20.1 |
| | mind 17.20 |
| Waley | heart 2.4, 20.1 |
| | mind 6.7, 17.20 |
| | passionately 14.39 |

# 新(3)

| | |
|---|---|
| Ames/Rosemont | incoming 5.19 |
| | new 2.11, 17.19 |
| Lau | new 2.11, 17.19 |
| | successor 5.19 |
| Legge | new 2.11, 17.19, 5.19 |
| Leys | new 2.11, 17.19 |
| | successor 5.19 |
| Soothill | new 2.11, 17.19, 5.19 |
| Waley | new 2.11, 17.19 |
| | successor 5.19 |

# 信(38)

| | |
|---|---|
| Ames/Rosemont | believe 5.10, 14.13, 14.14 |
| | commitment 8.13 |
| | confidence 7.1, 12.7, 19.10 |
| | honesty 8.16, 14.31 |
| | indeed 12.11 |
| | earnest 19.2 |
| | make good on one's word 1.4, 1.5, 1.6, 1.7, 1.8, 1.13, 2.22, 5.28, 7.25, 9.25, 12.10, 13.4, 13.20, 15.6, 15.18, 17.5, 17.7, 20.1 |
| | sure 5.6 |

| | |
|---|---|
| Lau | trust and confidence 5.26, 8.4 |
| | believe 14.14, 19.2 |
| | faith 8.13, 14.31 |
| | keep one's word 13.20 |
| | true 14.13 |
| | truly 12.11 |
| | trust 5.10, 5.26, 8.4, 12.7, 19.10 |
| | trust oneself 5.6 |
| | trustworthy 1.4, 1.5, 1.6, 1.7, 1.8, 1.13, 2.22, 5.28, 7.25, 8.16, 9.25, 12.10, 15.6, 15.18, 20.1 |
| | trustworthiness 13.4, 17.5, 17.7 |
| | truthful 7.1 |
| Legge | agreement 1.13 |
| | assurance 5.6 |
| | believe 7.1, 14.14, 14.31 |
| | confidence 12.7, 19.10 |
| | faith 8.13 |
| | give one credit 5.10 |
| | good faith 13.4 |
| | indeed 12.11 |
| | make the people repose 20.1 |
| | sincere 1.4, 1.7, 5.28, 8.16, 13.20, 17.7 |
| | sincerity 1.5, 1.8, 5.26, 8.4, 9.25, 12.10, 15.18, 17.5, 19.2 |
| | true 14.13 |
| | truthful 1.6, 15.6 |
| | truthfulness 2.22, 7.25 |
| Leys | believe 14.14 |

chivalry 17. 7

conviction 19. 2

faith 8. 4, 8. 13, 12. 10, 14. 31, 15. 18

faithful 1. 4, 5. 28

faithfulness 1. 8

good faith 1. 5, 1. 6, 7. 25, 13. 4, 15. 6, 17. 5, 20. 1

indeed 12. 11

promise 1. 13

reliable 8. 16

true 1. 7, 14. 13

trust 2. 22, 5. 10, 5. 26, 7. 1, 12. 7, 13. 20, 19. 10

trust above everything else 9. 25

up to the task 5. 6

Soothill

believe 7. 1, 14. 14, 19. 2

confidence 5. 6, 12. 7, 19. 10

faithful 5. 26

give one credit 5. 10

good faith 1. 5, 2. 22, 7. 25, 13. 4, 20. 1

honesty 17. 7

not doubt one's word 14. 31

promise 1. 13

sincere 1. 4, 1. 7, 5. 28

sincerity 1. 8, 8. 4, 8. 13, 9. 25, 12. 10, 15. 18, 17. 5

stand by one's word 13. 20

true 14. 13

truly 12. 11

truthful 1. 6, 8. 16, 15. 6

Waley

believe 14. 14, 19. 2

confidence 12.7, 19.10

fact 14.13

faith 5.6, 5.26, 8.13, 12.10

faithful 7.1, 15.18

good faith 8.4, 13.4, 17.5

indeed 12.11

keep all promise 9.25

keep one's word 20.1

keep promise 1.8, 17.7

keeping of promise 7.25

promise 1.13, 14.31

punctual 1.6

punctually observe one's promise 1.5

simple minded 8.16

stand by one's word 13.20

take for granted 5.10

true 1.7, 5.28, 15.6

true to one's word 1.4

trust 2.22, 12.7

## 兴(9)

Ames/Rosemont
arise one's sensibilities 17.8

aspire 8.2

flourish 13.3

inspiration 8.8

prosper 13.15

|  |  |
|---|---|
| Lau | restore 20.1 |
|  | stand up 15.2 |
|  | flourish 13.3 |
|  | get to one's feet 15.2 |
|  | prosper 13.15 |
|  | restore 20.1 |
|  | stimulate 8.8 |
|  | stir 8.2 |
|  | stimulate the imagination 17.8 |
| Legge | arouse 8.2, 8.8 |
|  | flourish 13.3 |
|  | prosperous 13.15 |
|  | revive 20.1 |
|  | rise 15.2 |
|  | stimulate the mind 17.8 |
| Leys | attract 8.2 |
|  | draw inspiration 8.8 |
|  | prosperity 13.15 |
|  | restore 20.1 |
|  | rise to one's feet 15.2 |
|  | stimulation 17.8 |
|  | [not] wither 13.3 |
| Soothill | flourish 13.3 |
|  | form 8.8 |
|  | prosperous 13.15 |
|  | re-establish 20.1 |
|  | stand 15.2 |
|  | stimulate the mind 17.8 |

| | |
|---|---|
| Waley | stir 8.2 |
| | drag oneself on to one's feet 15.2 |
| | flourish 13.3 |
| | incite people's emotions 17.8 |
| | incite 8.2, 8.8 |
| | raise up 20.1 |
| | save 13.15 |

## 行人(1)

| | |
|---|---|
| Ames/Rosemont | the diplomat 14.8 |
| Lau | the master of protocol 14.8 |
| Legge | the manager of Foreign intercourse 14.8 |
| Leys | the master of protocol 14.8 |
| Soothill | the Foreign Minister 14.8 |
| Waley | the receriver of Envoys 14.8 |

## 省(4)

| | |
|---|---|
| Ames/Rosemont | examine 1.4, 2.9, 4.17, 12.4 |
| Lau | examine 1.4, 4.17 |
| | find 12.4 |
| | look 2.9 |
| Legge | examine 1.4, 2.9, 4.17 |
| | examination 12.4 |
| Leys | conscience 12.4 |

|  |  |
|---|---|
| | examine 1.4, 4.17 |
| | observe 2.9 |
| Soothill | examine 1.4, 2.9, 4.17 |
| | find 12.4 |
| Waley | examine 1.4 |
| | enquire 2.9 |
| | look 12.4 |
| | turn one's gaze within 4.17 |

# 性(2)

|  |  |
|---|---|
| Ames/Rosemont | natural tendency 17.2 |
| | natural disposition 5.13 |
| Lau | human nature 5.13 |
| | nature 17.2 |
| Legge | man 5.13 |
| | nature 17.2 |
| Leys | nature 17.2 |
| | nature of thing 5.13 |
| Soothill | nature 17.2 |
| | nature of man 5.13 |
| Waley | man 5.13 |
| | nature 17.2 |

## 兄弟(6)

| | |
|---|---|
| Ames/Rosemont | brother 2.21, 12.5, 13.7, 13.28 |
| Lau | brother 2.21, 12.5, 13.7, 13.28 |
| Legge | brethren 13.28 |
| | brother 12.5, 13.7 |
| | brotherly 2.21 |
| Leys | brother 2.21, 12.5, 13.7, 13.28 |
| Soothill | brethren 2.21 |
| | brother 12.5, 13.7, 13.28 |
| Waley | brother 2.21, 12.5, 13.7, 13.28 |

## 修(11)

| | |
|---|---|
| Ames/Rosemont | cultivate 7.3, 14.42 |
| | cultivation 16.1 |
| | dried meat 7.7 |
| | reform 12.21 |
| | revise 14.8 |
| | revive 20.1 |
| Lau | cultivate 7.3, 14.42, 16.1 |
| | dried meat 7.7 |
| | re-establish 20.1 |
| | reform 12.21 |
| | reformation 12.21 |

| | |
|---|---|
| Legge | touch up 14. 8 |
| | correct 12. 21 |
| | cultivate 16. 1 |
| | cultivation 7. 3, 14. 42 |
| | dried flesh 7. 7 |
| | polish 14. 8 |
| | restore 20. 1 |
| Leys | cultivate 7. 3 |
| | cultivation 14. 42, 16. 1 |
| | edit 14. 8 |
| | neutralize 12. 21 |
| | re-establish 20. 1 |
| | token 7. 7 |
| Soothill | amend 14. 8 |
| | correct 12. 21 |
| | cultivate 14. 42 |
| | cultivation 7. 3 |
| | dried flesh 7. 7 |
| | promotion 16. 1 |
| | remedy 12. 21 |
| | restore 20. 1 |
| Waley | amend 14. 8 |
| | cultivate 14. 42 |
| | dried flesh 7. 7 |
| | enhance 16. 1 |
| | repair 12. 21 |
| | restore 20. 1 |
| | tend 7. 3 |

## 羞(1)

| | |
|---|---|
| Ames/Rosemont | shame 13.22 |
| Lau | shame 13.22 |
| Legge | disgrace 13.22 |
| Leys | disgrace 13.22 |
| Soothill | disgrace 13.22 |
| Waley | evil 13.22 |

## 虚(2)

| | |
|---|---|
| Ames/Rosemont | emptiness 7.26 |
| | empty 8.5 |
| Lau | empty 7.26, 8.5 |
| Legge | empty 7.26, 8.5 |
| Leys | emptiness 7.26 |
| | empty 8.5 |
| Soothill | empty 7.26, 8.5 |
| Waley | emptiness 7.26 |
| | empty 8.5 |

## 学(64)

| | |
|---|---|
| Ames/Rosemont | educate 1.7 |

learn 6.27, 7.34, 11.23, 11.24, 12.15, 13.4, 15.3, 16.9, 19.6

learning 1.14, 2.4, 2.15, 5.15, 5.28, 6.3, 8.13, 9.2, 11.7, 15.31, 17.7, 19.5

scholar 14.24

study 1.1, 1.6, 1.8, 7.17, 8.12, 8.17, 9.30, 14.35, 15.1, 16.9, 16.13, 17.3, 17.8, 19.7, 19.13, 19.22

studying 2.18, 7.2, 15.32

what one learns 7.3

Lau

learn 1.1, 1.14, 2.15, 5.15, 5.28, 6.3, 7.2, 7.17, 7.34, 9.30, 11.7, 11.23, 11.24, 15.3, 19.5, 19.6, 19.22

learning 2.4, 8.13, 9.2, 15.31, 17.7, 19.7

instruct 17.3

school 1.7

study 1.8, 8.12, 8.17, 14.24, 14.35, 15.1, 15.32, 16.9, 16.13, 17.8, 19.13

studying 2.18

teach 13.4

verse 6.27, 12.15

what one has learned 7.3

Legge

employ 1.6

imitate 7.34

instruct 17.3

learn 1.1, 1.7, 1.14, 6.3, 8.12, 8.17, 11.7, 11.23, 11.24, 14.24, 15.1, 15.3, 16.9, 16.13, 19.5, 19.7, 19.22

learning 1.8, 2.4, 2.15, 2.18, 5.15, 5.28, 7.2,

|  |  |
|---|---|
|  | 8.13, 9.2, 15.31, 15.32, 17.7, 19.6, 19.13 |
|  | study 6.27, 7.17, 9.30, 12.15, 14.35, 17.8 |
|  | teach 13.4 |
|  | what is learned 7.3 |
| Leys | cultivate 17.3 |
|  | derive one's learning 19.22 |
|  | educate 1.7 |
|  | emulate 7.34 |
|  | information 9.30 |
|  | learn 1.1, 11.23, 11.24, 15.1, 15.3, 19.5 |
|  | learning 1.8, 1.14, 2.4, 5.15, 5.28, 6.3, 6.27, 7.2, 8.17, 9.2, 11.7, 12.15, 14.35, 15.32, 16.9, 17.7, 19.6, 19.7, 19.13 |
|  | study 1.6, 2.15, 7.17, 8.12, 14.24, 15.31, 16.13, 17.8 |
|  | studying 2.18 |
|  | teach 13.4 |
|  | what one has learned 7.3 |
| Soothill | acquire 16.9 |
|  | acquire knowledge 1.1 |
|  | culture 19.6 |
|  | educate 1.7, 11.23 |
|  | employ 1.6 |
|  | learn 7.34, 8.17, 11.24, 15.31, 16.9, 17.3, 17.7 |
|  | learning 1.8, 1.14, 2.15, 5.15, 5.28, 6.3, 9.2, 11.7, 19.5, 19.22 |
|  | moral 8.13 |
|  | pursuit of wisdom 7.2 |

|  | scholarship 15.32 |
|---|---|
|  | study 7.3, 7.17, 8.12, 9.30, 14.24, 14.35, 15.1, 15.3, 16.13, 17.8, 19.7, 19.13 |
|  | studying 2.18 |
|  | teach 13.4 |
|  | verse 6.27, 12.15 |
|  | wisdom 2.4 |
| Waley | derive one's learning 19.22 |
|  | educate 1.7 |
|  | education 1.7, 1.8 |
|  | learn 1.1, 2.15, 7.34, 8.17, 9.2, 15.3, 15.31 |
|  | learning 1.14, 2.4, 5.15, 5.28, 6.3, 7.2, 7.3, 8.13, 11.7, 11.23, 15.32, 16.9, 17.7, 19.5 |
|  | study 1.6, 7.17, 8.12, 9.30, 14.24, 14.35, 15.1, 16.13, 17.3, 17.8, 19.6, 19.7, 19.13 |
|  | studying 2.18 |
|  | teach 13.4 |
|  | train 11.24 |
|  | verse 6.27, 12.15 |

# 血气(3)

| Ames/Rosemont | vigorous 16.7 |
|---|---|
| Lau | blood and ch'i 16.7 |
| Legge | physical power 16.7 |
| Leys | energy of the blood 16.7 |
| Soothill | physical nature 16.7 |

| | | |
|---|---|---|
| Waley | | blood and vital humours 16.7 |

## 雅(4)

| | |
|---|---|
| Ames/Rosemont | classical 17.16 |
| | proper 7.18 |
| | songs of the kingdom 9.15 |
| Lau | classical 17.16 |
| | correct 7.18 |
| | ya 9.15 |
| Legge | royal songs 9.15 |
| | ya 17.16 |
| Leys | classical 17.16 |
| | correct 7.18 |
| | court pieces 9.15 |
| Soothill | correct 17.16 |
| | secular pieces 9.15 |
| Waley | correct 7.18 |
| | court music 17.16 |
| | court pieces 9.15 |

## 厌(9)

| | |
|---|---|
| Ames/Rosemont | abandon 6.28 |
| | object 10.6 |
| | respite 7.2, 7.34 |

| | |
|---|---|
| Lau | tired 14.13 |
| | curse 6.28 |
| | flag 7.2 |
| | tired 7.34, 14.13 |
| Legge | dislike 10.6 |
| | get tired of 14.13 |
| | reject 6.28 |
| | satiety 7.2, 7.34 |
| Leys | confound 6.28 |
| | flag 7.34 |
| | gorge 10.6 |
| | think that one speaks too much 14.13 |
| Soothill | objection 10.6 |
| | reject 6.28 |
| | tire of 14.13 |
| | weary 7.2, 7.34 |
| Waley | avert 6.28 |
| | feel too much 14.13 |
| | objection 10.6 |
| | tired 7.2 |
| | weary 7.34 |

# 野(3)

| | |
|---|---|
| Ames/Rosemont | boorish 6.18 |
| | dense 13.3 |
| | simple folk 11.1 |

| | |
|---|---|
| Lau | boorish 13.3 |
| | churlishness 6.18 |
| | rustic 11.1 |
| Legge | rustic 11.1 |
| | rusticity 6.18 |
| | uncultivated 13.3 |
| Leys | savage 6.18 |
| | boorish 13.3 |
| | common 11.1 |
| Soothill | rustic 6.18 |
| | uncultivated 11.1, 13.3 |
| Waley | boorish 13.3 |
| | boorishness of the rustic 6.18 |
| | common 11.1 |

## 疑(3)

| | |
|---|---|
| Ames/Rosemont | doubt 16.10 |
| | unsure 2.18 |
| Lau | doubt 16.10 |
| | doubtful 2.18 |
| | misgiving 12.20 |
| Legge | doubt 2.18, 12.20, 16.10 |
| Leys | doubt 16.10 |
| | doubtful 2.18 |
| | flappable pretense 12.20 |
| Soothill | doubt 2.18, 16.10 |

| | |
|---|---|
| Waley | misgiving 12.20 |
| | doubt 16.10 |
| | doubtful 2.18 |
| | no self-assurance 12.20 |

## 亿(2)

| | |
|---|---|
| Ames/Rosemont | suspect 14.31 |
| | venture 11.9 |
| Lau | conjecture 11.9 |
| | presume 14.31 |
| Legge | judgment 11.9 |
| | think beforehand 14.31 |
| Leys | judgment 11.9 |
| | suspect 14.31 |
| Soothill | imagine 14.31 |
| | judgment 11.9 |
| Waley | calculation 11.18 |
| | reckon 14.31 |

## 义(24)

| | |
|---|---|
| Ames/Rosemont | appropriate 1.13, 2.24, 4.10, 5.16, 6.22, 7.3, 7.16, 12.10, 12.20, 14.13, 18.7, 19.1 |
| | appropriate conduct 13.4, 14.12, 15.17, 15.18, 16.10, 17.21 |

|       |                                                      |
| ----- | ---------------------------------------------------- |
|       | sense of appropriateness 17.21                       |
|       | what is appropriate 4.16, 16.11                      |
| Lau   | duty 18.7                                            |
|       | just 5.16                                            |
|       | moral 1.13, 7.16                                     |
|       | morality 15.18, 17.21                                |
|       | right 6.22, 7.3, 12.20, 14.13, 16.11, 19.1           |
|       | rightness 12.10                                      |
|       | subject of morality 15.17                            |
|       | what is moral 4.10, 4.16                             |
|       | what is right 13.4, 14.12, 16.10                     |
|       | what ought to be done 2.24                           |
| Legge | duty 6.22                                            |
|       | just 5.16                                            |
|       | right 2.24, 4.10                                     |
|       | righteous 18.7                                       |
|       | righteousness 4.16, 7.3, 7.16 12.20, 13.4, 14.12, 14.13, 15.17, 15.18, 16.10, 16.11, 17.21, 19.1 |
|       | what is right 1.13, 12.10                            |
| Leys  | if it is fair 16.10                                  |
|       | just 5.16, 14.13, 17.21                              |
|       | justice 2.24, 4.10, 7.16, 12.10, 12.20, 13.4, 14.12, 15.18 |
|       | right 6.22, 7.3, 18.7, 19.1                          |
|       | righteousness 16.11                                  |
|       | single truth 15.17                                   |
|       | what is just 4.16                                    |
|       | what is right 1.13                                   |

| | |
|---|---|
| Soothill | duty 6.22 |
| | just 5.16 |
| | justice 12.20, 13.4 |
| | rectitude 17.21 |
| | recognised duty 7.3 |
| | right 2.24, 12.10, 14.12, 14.13, 15.18, 16.10, 16.11, 18.7, 19.1 |
| | what is just and right 15.17 |
| | what is right 1.13, 4.10, 4.16 |
| | worthily 7.16 |
| Waley | consequence 16.10 |
| | just 5.16 |
| | right 2.24, 4.10, 6.22, 7.16, 12.10, 12.20, 13.4, 14.12, 14.13, 15.17, 15.18, 16.10, 17.21, 18.7, 19.1 |
| | righteous 7.3 |
| | righteousness 16.11 |
| | what is right 1.13, 4.16 |

# 艺(4)

| | |
|---|---|
| Ames/Rosemont | art 7.6, 9.7 |
| | cultivated 14.12 |
| | cultivated and refined 6.8 |
| Lau | accomplished 6.8, 14.12 |
| | art 7.6 |
| | jack of all trades 9.7 |

| | |
|---|---|
| Legge | art 7.6, 9.7 |
| | varied talent 14.12 |
| | various ability 6.8 |
| Leys | art 7.6 |
| | skill 14.12 |
| | talented 6.8 |
| | various skills 9.7 |
| Soothill | art 7.6, 9.7 |
| | proficiency 6.8 |
| | skill 14.12 |
| Waley | art 7.6 |
| | dexterity 14.12 |
| | handy 9.7 |
| | versatile 6.8 |

# 易(12)

| | |
|---|---|
| Ames/Rosemont | change 18.6 |
| | easy 8.12, 13.15, 13.25, 14.41, 17.3 |
| | formal details 3.4 |
| Lau | change 18.6 |
| | easy 8.12, 13.15, 13.25, 14.41, 17.3 |
| | indifference 3.4 |
| | put on 1.7 |
| Legge | change 18.6 |
| | easy 8.12, 13.15, 13.25, 14.10 |
| | easily 17.3 |

|            |                                                                 |
|------------|-----------------------------------------------------------------|
|            | minute attention to observances 3. 4                            |
|            | readily 14. 41                                                  |
|            | withdraw one's mind from 1. 7                                   |
|            | Yì 7. 17                                                        |
| Leys       | easy 8. 12, 13. 15, 13. 25, 14. 10, 17. 3                       |
|            | easily 14. 41                                                   |
|            | formality 3. 4                                                  |
|            | reform 18. 6                                                    |
|            | the changes 7. 17                                               |
| Soothill   | easy 8. 12, 13. 15, 13. 25, 14. 10                              |
|            | easily 14. 41, 17. 3                                            |
|            | observance of detail 3. 4                                       |
|            | reform 18. 6                                                    |
|            | the book of change 7. 17                                        |
|            | transfer 1. 7                                                   |
| Waley      | alter 18. 6                                                     |
|            | be dictated by fear 3. 4                                        |
|            | easy 8. 12, 13. 15, 13. 25, 14. 41, 17. 3                       |
|            | wear 1. 7                                                       |

# 逸民(2)

| Ames/Rosemont | examples of those whose talents are lost to the people 18. 8 |
|---------------|--------------------------------------------------------------|
|               | those subjects whose talents have been lost to the people 20. 1 |
| Lau           | man who has withdrawn from society 20. 1                     |

| | |
|---|---|
| | man who withdraws from society 18. 8 |
| Legge | man who has retired to privacy from the world 18. 8 |
| | those who have retired into obscurity 20. 1 |
| Leys | political exile 20. 1 |
| | those who withdraw from the world 18. 8 |
| Soothill | man who has exiled oneself 20. 1 |
| | man noted for withdrawal into private life 18. 8 |
| Waley | lost subject 20. 1 |
| | subjects whose service are lost to the State 18. 8 |

## 意(1)

| | |
|---|---|
| Ames/Rosemont | speculate 9. 4 |
| Lau | entertain conjectures 9. 4 |
| Legge | foregone conclusion 9. 4 |
| Leys | [no] capriciousness 9. 4 |
| Soothill | preconceptions 9. 4 |
| Waley | take something for granted 9. 4 |

## 毅(2)

| | |
|---|---|
| Ames/Rosemont | resoluteness 13. 27 |
| | resolve 8. 7 |
| Lau | resolute 8. 7 |
| | resoluteness 13. 27 |
| Legge | endure 13. 27 |

|  |  |
|---|---|
| Leys | vigorous endurance 8.7 |
|  | resolute 8.7 |
|  | resolution 13.27 |
| Soothill | fortitude 8.7 |
|  | resolute in character 13.27 |
| Waley | resolute 13.27 |
|  | stout of heart 8.7 |

## 淫(2)

|  |  |
|---|---|
| Ames/Rosemont | excessive 3.20 |
|  | lewd 15.11 |
| Lau | wanton 15.11 |
|  | wantonness 3.20 |
| Legge | licentious 3.20, 15.11 |
| Leys | corrupt 15.11 |
|  | lasciviousness 3.20 |
| Soothill | licentious 15.11 |
|  | sensual 3.20 |
| Waley | debauch 3.20 |
|  | licentious 15.11 |

## 隐(9)

|  |  |
|---|---|
| Ames/Rosemont | cover 13.18 |
|  | hidden away 7.24 |

|  |  |
|---|---|
| | hold back 16.6 |
| | recluse 18.7 |
| | remain hidden away 8.13 |
| | seclusion 16.11, 18.8 |
| Lau | cover up 13.18 |
| | evasive 16.6 |
| | hide 7.24 |
| | keep out of sight 8.13 |
| | live as recluses 18.8 |
| | recluse 18.7 |
| | retirement 16.11 |
| Legge | concealment 7.24, 16.6 |
| | conceal the misconduct 13.18 |
| | hide 18.8 |
| | keep concealed 8.13 |
| | recluse 18.7 |
| | retirement 16.11 |
| Leys | covers up 13.18 |
| | hermit 18.7, 18.8 |
| | hide 7.24, 8.13 |
| | secretiveness 16.6 |
| | withdraw 16.11 |
| Soothill | possess something occult 7.24 |
| | recluse 18.7 |
| | reticence 16.6 |
| | screen 13.18 |
| | seclusion 16.11, 18.8 |
| | withdraw 8.13 |

| | |
|---|---|
| Waley | hide 8.13 |
| | keep 7.24 |
| | recluse 18.7 |
| | screen 13.18 |
| | seclusion 16.11,18.8 |
| | secretiveness 16.6 |

## 盈(2)

| | |
|---|---|
| Ames/Rosemont | fill 8.15 |
| | fullness 7.26 |
| Lau | fill 8.15 |
| | full 7.26 |
| Legge | fill 8.15 |
| | full 7.26 |
| Leys | fullness 7.26,8.15 |
| Soothill | fill 8.15 |
| | full 7.26 |
| Waley | fill 8.15 |
| | fullness 7.26 |

## 勇(16)

| | |
|---|---|
| Ames/Rosemont | bold 14.4,14.12,17.22 |
| | boldness 5.7,8.2,8.10,17.7,17.21 |
| | courage 2.24,11.24 |

|  |  |
|---|---|
|  | courageous 9.29, 14.28 |
| Lau | courage 2.24, 8.2, 8.10, 9.29, 11.24, 14.4, 14.28, 17.7, 17.21, 17.22 |
|  | courageous 14.12 |
|  | foolhardy 5.7 |
| Legge | bold 9.29, 11.24, 14.4, 14.28 |
|  | boldness 8.2, 17.7 |
|  | bravery 14.12 |
|  | courage 2.24 |
|  | daring 8.10 |
|  | fonder of daring 5.7 |
|  | valour 17.21, 17.22 |
| Leys | bold 5.7 |
|  | brave 8.10, 9.29, 14.4 |
|  | bravery 8.2 |
|  | courage 14.28, 17.21, 17.22 |
|  | not cowardice 2.24 |
|  | spirits 11.24 |
|  | valor 14.12, 17.7 |
| Soothill | bold 17.22 |
|  | boldness 8.2 |
|  | brave 9.29, 11.24 |
|  | courage 14.12, 17.21 |
|  | courageous 14.4, 14.28 |
|  | daring 8.10, 17.7 |
|  | fonder of daring 5.7 |
|  | not cowardice 2.24 |
| Waley | bounded 8.2 |

brave 9.29, 14.28

courage 11.24, 14.4, 17.7, 17.21

daring 8.10, 17.22

feats of physical daring 5.7

not cowardice 2.24

valour 14.12

# 友(27)

| | |
|---|---|
| Ames/Rosemont | befriend 2.21, 9.25, 15.10 |
| | friend 1.4, 1.7, 1.8, 5.26, 8.5, 10.16, 10.17, 12.23, 12.24, 13.28, 16.4, 16.5, 19.15 |
| | friendship 4.26, 5.25 |
| Lau | friend 1.4, 1.7, 1.8, 4.26, 5.26, 8.5, 9.25, 10.16, 10.17, 12.23, 12.24, 13.28, 16.5, 19.15 |
| | friendly 2.21, 5.25 |
| | make friends with 15.10, 16.4 |
| Legge | discharge duties 2.21 |
| | friend 1.4, 1.7, 1.8, 4.26, 5.26, 8.5, 9.25, 10.16, 10.17, 12.24, 13.28, 16.5, 19.15 |
| | friendly 5.25 |
| | friendship 12.23, 16.4 |
| | make friends with 15.10 |
| Leys | befriend 1.8, 9.25, 15.10 |
| | friend 1.4, 1.7, 5.25, 5.26, 8.5, 10.16, 10.17, 12.24, 13.28, 16.4, 16.5, 19.15 |
| | friendly 4.26 |

| | |
|---|---|
| | friendship 16.4 |
| | kind 2.21 |
| Soothill | friend 1.4, 1.7, 1.8, 4.26, 5.26, 8.5, 9.25, 10.16, 10.17, 12.24, 13.28, 16.4, 16.5, 19.15 |
| | friendliness 2.21 |
| | friendly 5.25 |
| | friendship 12.23 |
| | make friends with 15.10 |
| Waley | friend 1.4, 1.7, 5.26, 8.5, 10.16, 10.17, 12.23, 12.24, 13.28, 16.4, 16.5, 19.15 |
| | friendly 2.21, 5.25 |
| | friendship 1.8, 4.26, 9.25, 16.4 |
| | make friends with 15.10 |

## 有道(14)

| | |
|---|---|
| Ames/Rosemont | on the way 12.19 |
| | way prevails 5.2, 5.21, 8.13, 14.1, 14.3, 15.7, 16.2, 18.6 |
| | know the way 1.14 |
| Lau | possess of the way 1.14 |
| | possess the way 12.19 |
| | way is to be found 18.6 |
| | way prevails 5.2, 5.21, 8.13, 14.1, 14.3, 15,7, 16.2 |
| Legge | good government prevails 14.1, 14.3, 15.7, 16.2 |
| | good order prevails 5.21 |
| | principle 1.14 |

| | |
|---|---|
| | principled 12.19 |
| | right principles prevail 16.2, 18.6 |
| | well governed 5.2, 8.13 |
| Leys | follow the way 8.13, 16.2, 18.6 |
| | the good 12.19 |
| | under a good government 15.7 |
| | virtuous 1.14 |
| | way prevails 5.2, 5.21, 14.1, 14.3 |
| Soothill | good government prevails 16.2 |
| | good order prevails 5.21 |
| | high principled 1.14 |
| | law abiding 12.19 |
| | law and order prevails 8.13, 14.3 |
| | right rule prevails 18.6 |
| | well governed 5.2, 14.1, 15.7 |
| Waley | have the way 12.19 |
| | possess the way 1.14 |
| | rule according to the way 5.2, 14.1 |
| | way prevails 5.21, 8.13, 14.3, 15.7, 16.2, 18.6 |

## 诱(1)

| | |
|---|---|
| Ames/Rosemont | draw forward 9.11 |
| Lau | lead 9.11 |
| Legge | lead 9.11 |
| Leys | entrap 9.11 |
| Soothill | lure 9.11 |

| | |
|---|---|
| Waley | lure 9.11 |

## 愚(9)

| | |
|---|---|
| Ames/Rosemont | dupe 17.7 |
| | slow 2.9 |
| | stupid 5.21, 11.18, 17.2, 17.14 |
| Lau | foolish 17.14 |
| | foolishness 17.7 |
| | stupid 2.9, 5.21, 11.18, 17.2 |
| Legge | foolish simplicity 17.7 |
| | simple 11.18 |
| | stupid 2.9, 5.21, 17.2 |
| | stupidity 17.14 |
| Leys | naiveté 17.14 |
| | stupid 2.9, 5.21, 11.18, 17.2 |
| | silliness 17.7 |
| Soothill | fool 5.21 |
| | foolishness 17.7 |
| | simple minded 11.18 |
| | simple mindedness 17.14 |
| | stupid 2.9, 17.2 |
| Waley | folly 5.21 |
| | silliness 17.7 |
| | simple mindedness 17.14 |
| | stupid 2.9, 11.18, 17.2 |

# 欲(44)

| | |
|---|---|
| Ames/Rosemont | acquisitive 5.11 |
| | desire 3.10, 14.12, 20.2 |
| | free rein 2.4 |
| | greed 14.1 |
| | greedy 12.18 |
| | intent on 14.44 |
| | seek 6.30, 7.30, 17.18 |
| | think 17.17, 18.7 |
| | try 13.17, 14.25 |
| | want 3.17, 4.5, 4.24, 5.12, 6.6, 9.11, 9.14, 11.11, 12.2, 12.10, 12.19, 15.10, 15.24, 16.1, 17.1, 17.4, 17.6, 18.5 |
| Lau | be after 14.44 |
| | covetous 14.1 |
| | desirable 4.24 |
| | desire 2.4, 4.5, 5.11, 7.30, 12.2, 12.18, 12.19, 14.12, 15.24, 18.7, 20.2 |
| | in favour of 16.1 |
| | intention 18.5 |
| | seek 14.25 |
| | think 17.17 |
| | want 3.17, 9.11, 9.14, 11.11, 12.10, 17.1, 17.4, 17.6, 17.18, 19.24 |
| | wish 3.10, 5.12, 6.30, 15.10, 16.1 |

| | |
|---|---|
| Legge | anxious 14.25 |
| | covetous 12.18 |
| | covetousness 14.1, 14.12 |
| | desire 2.4, 4.5, 12.19, 20.2 |
| | desirous 13.17 |
| | incline 17.4, 17.6 |
| | passion 5.11 |
| | want 15.24 |
| | wish 3.10, 3.17, 4.24, 5.12, 6.6, 6.30, 7.30, 9.11, 9.14, 11.11, 12.2, 12.10, 14.44, 15.10, 16.1, 17.1, 17.18, 18.5, 18.7, 19.24 |
| | would prefer 17.17 |
| Leys | ambition 20.2 |
| | covetous 12.18 |
| | covetousness 14.1 |
| | crave 4.5 |
| | desire 2.4, 5.11, 12.19 |
| | long for 7.30 |
| | should 4.24 |
| | tempt 17.4, 17.6 |
| | try 13.17 |
| | want 5.12, 9.11, 9.14, 11.11, 16.1, 17.1, 17.18, 18.5 |
| | wish 3.10, 3.17, 6.30, 12.2, 12.10, 14.25, 15.10, 15.24, 16.1, 17.17, 19.24 |
| Soothill | aspiration 12.19 |
| | crave 7.30 |
| | desire 2.4, 4.5, 4.24, 6.30, 14.1, 18.5, 18.7, |

19. 24, 20. 2

incline 17. 4, 17. 6

intent 13. 17

love of wealth 12. 18

passion 5. 11

propose 9. 14, 11. 11

seek 14. 25

want 14. 44, 15. 10, 16. 1, 17. 1

wish 3. 10, 3. 17, 5. 12, 6. 6, 9. 11, 12. 10, 17. 17, 17. 18

would like 12. 2, 15. 24

Waley  bend upon 14. 44

covet 4. 24

covetousness 14. 1, 14. 12

desire 4. 5, 5. 11, 6. 30, 12. 18, 12. 19, 16. 1, 18. 5, 18. 7

dictate 2. 4

far rather 3. 10

long for 20. 2

mean 15. 10

try 13. 17, 14. 25, 19. 24

want 3. 17, 5. 12, 7. 30, 9. 11, 9. 14, 11. 11, 12. 10, 17. 1, 17. 18

would have liked to 17. 4, 17. 6

would like 12. 2, 15. 24

would much rather 17. 17

## 喻(2)

| | |
|---|---|
| Ames/Rosemont | understand 4.16 |
| Lau | verse in 4.16 |
| Legge | conversant with 4.16 |
| Leys | consider 4.16 |
| Soothill | inform 4.16 |
| Waley | discover 4.16 |

## 怨(20)

| | |
|---|---|
| Ames/Rosemont | complain 17.23 |
| | ill 14.9 |
| | ill will 5.23, 5.25, 7.15, 12.2, 14.1, 14.10, 14.34, 14.35, 15.15, 18.10, 20.2 |
| | resentment 4.12, 4.18 |
| | sharpen one's critical skills 17.8 |
| Lau | complain 4.18, 7.15, 14.10, 14.35, 20.2 |
| | complaint 14.9, 18.10 |
| | feel badly done by 17.23 |
| | grievance 5.25, 17.8 |
| | grudge 14.1 |
| | ill will 4.12, 5.23, 12.2, 15.15 |
| | injury 14.34 |
| Legge | discontent 17.23 |

|  | injury 14.34 |
|---|---|
|  | murmur 4.12, 4.18, 12.2, 14.9, 14.10, 14.35 |
|  | repine 7.15, 18.10, 20.2 |
|  | resentment 5.23, 5.25, 14.1, 15.15, 17.8 |
| Leys | accuse 14.35 |
|  | bitterness 4.18 |
|  | complain 7.15, 18.10 |
|  | complaint 14.9 |
|  | discontent 15.15 |
|  | groan 20.2 |
|  | hatred 14.34 |
|  | resent 5.25, 17.23 |
|  | resentment 4.12, 5.23, 12.2, 14.1, 14.10 |
|  | vehicle for grief 17.8 |
| Soothill | animosity 4.12 |
|  | complain 4.18, 14.9, 14.10 |
|  | complaint 14.35 |
|  | discontent 18.10 |
|  | dissatisfaction 20.2 |
|  | enmity 14.34 |
|  | ill will 12.2 |
|  | modify the vexations of life 17.8 |
|  | repine 7.15 |
|  | resent 17.23 |
|  | resentment 5.23, 5.25, 14.1, 15.15 |
| Waley | accuse 14.35 |
|  | chafe 18.10 |
|  | discontent 4.12, 15.15 |

feelings of opposition 12.2

grievance 17.8

indignation 5.25

rancor 5.23

repine 7.15

resent 14.10, 17.23

resentful 4.18

resentment 14.1, 14.9, 14.34, 20.2

# 愿(6)

| | |
|---|---|
| Ames/Rosemont | caution 8.16 |
| | willing 11.24 |
| | would like to 5.26 |
| Lau | be ready to 11.24 |
| | cautious 8.16 |
| | should like 5.26 |
| Legge | attentive 8.16 |
| | should like 5.26 |
| | wish 11.24 |
| Leys | prudent 8.16 |
| | wish 5.26 |
| | would like 11.24 |
| Soothill | honest 8.16 |
| | should like 5.26, 11.24 |
| Waley | honest 8.16 |
| | should like 5.26, 11.24 |

# 约(6)

| | |
|---|---|
| Ames/Rosemont | discipline 6.27, 9.11, 12.15 |
| | hardship 4.2 |
| | personal restraint 4.23 |
| | poverty 7.26 |
| Lau | bring back to essentials 6.27, 9.11, 12.15 |
| | keep to essentials 4.23 |
| | straitened 7.26 |
| | straitened circumstance 4.2 |
| Legge | cautious 4.23 |
| | poverty and hardship 4.2 |
| | restraint 6.27, 9.11, 12.15 |
| | straitened 7.26 |
| Leys | adversity 4.2 |
| | penury 7.26 |
| | restrain 6.27, 9.11, 12.15 |
| | self control 4.23 |
| Soothill | adversity 4.2 |
| | in strait 7.26 |
| | restrain 6.27, 9.11, 12.15 |
| | self restrained 4.23 |
| Waley | adversity 4.2 |
| | penury 7.26 |
| | restrain 9.11 |
| | restraint 6.27, 12.15 |

side of strictness 4.23

# 贼(5)

| | |
|---|---|
| Ames/Rosemont | false pretense 17.11 |
| | harm 11.23, 17.7 |
| | injurious 20.2 |
| | thief 14.43 |
| Lau | harmful behavior 17.7 |
| | injury 20.2 |
| | pest 14.43 |
| | ruin 11.23, 17.11 |
| Legge | injure 11.23 |
| | injurious disregard of consequence 17.7 |
| | injury 20.2 |
| | pest 14.43 |
| | thief 17.11 |
| Leys | bad turn 11.23 |
| | banditry 17.7 |
| | extortion 20.2 |
| | parasite 14.43 |
| | ruin 17.11 |
| Soothill | do an ill turn 11.23 |
| | harmful candour 17.7 |
| | robbery 20.2 |
| | rogue 14.43 |
| | spoiler 17.11 |

| | |
|---|---|
| Waley | degenerate into villainy 17.7 |
| | do an ill turn 11.23 |
| | spoil 17.11 |
| | tormentor 20.2 |
| | useless pest 14.43 |

## 贞(1)

| | |
|---|---|
| Ames/Rosemont | proper 15.37 |
| Lau | steadfast in purpose 15.37 |
| Legge | correctly firm 15.37 |
| Leys | principled 15.37 |
| Soothill | intelligently 15.37 |
| Waley | consistency is expected 15.37 |

## 争(3)

| | |
|---|---|
| Ames/Rosemont | competitive 3.7 |
| | contentious 15.22 |
| Lau | contend 3.7 |
| | contentious 15.22 |
| Legge | contention 3.7 |
| | wrangle 15.22 |
| Leys | aggressive 15.22 |
| | competition 3.7 |
| Soothill | contend 3.7 |

|  |  |
|---|---|
| Waley | striving 15.22 |
|  | compete 3.7 |
|  | quarrelsome 15.22 |

## 正(24)

|  |  |
|---|---|
| Ames/Rosemont | correctly 20.2 |
|  | due 15.5 |
|  | invariably place 10.12 |
|  | precisely 7.34 |
|  | proper 8.4, 12.17, 13.6, 13.13, 14.15 |
|  | properly 10.6, 13.3 |
|  | properly placed in accord with custom 10.7 |
|  | repair 1.14 |
|  | revise 9.15 |
|  | upright 10.20 |
| Lau | adjust 10.12, 20.2 |
|  | correct 12.17, 13.6, 13.13 |
|  | in a respectful posture 15.5 |
|  | integrity 14.15 |
|  | precisely 7.34 |
|  | proper 8.4 |
|  | properly 10.6 |
|  | put right 9.15 |
|  | rectification 13.3 |
|  | right 1.14 |
|  | squarely 10.20, 17.8 |

| | |
|---|---|
| Legge | straight 10. 7 |
| | adjust 10. 12，20. 2 |
| | correct 12. 17，13. 6，13. 13 |
| | correctness 12. 17 |
| | gravely 15. 5 |
| | just 7. 34 |
| | properly 10. 6 |
| | rectify 1. 14，12. 17，13. 3 |
| | reform 9. 15 |
| | regulate 8. 4 |
| | right against 17. 8 |
| | straight 10. 7，10. 20 |
| | upright 14. 15 |
| Leys | cling to good faith 8. 4 |
| | correctly 20. 2 |
| | precisely 7. 34 |
| | properly 10. 6 |
| | put back in order 9. 15 |
| | rectify 13. 3 |
| | reverently 15. 5 |
| | straight 10. 7，10. 20，12. 17，13. 6，13. 13，14. 15 |
| | straighten 1. 14，10. 12 |
| Soothill | adjust 10. 12 |
| | aright 12. 17 |
| | array oneself properly 20. 2 |
| | correct 13. 13 |
| | correction 13. 3 |
| | correctly 10. 20 |

honourable 14. 15

just 7. 34

maintain the correct imperial attitude 15. 5

order 8. 4

properly 10. 6

rectify 1. 14

revise 9. 15

right 12. 17

right up 17. 8

straight 10. 7

upright 13. 6

Waley　　aright 13. 13

betake good faith 8. 4

carry out the plain dictates of ritual 14. 15

correct 1. 14，13. 3

gravely 15. 5

press against 17. 8

proper 10. 6

revise 9. 15

squarely 10. 20

straight 10. 7，20. 2

straighten 10. 12，12. 17

upright 13. 6

# 政(41)

Ames/Rosemont　administration 13. 3

|       |                                                                 |
| ----- | --------------------------------------------------------------- |
|       | administrative 2. 3                                             |
|       | affairs of state 5. 19, 13. 14                                  |
|       | govern 1. 10, 2. 1, 2. 21, 12. 7, 12. 11, 12. 14, 12. 17,       |
|       | 12. 19, 13. 13, 13. 16, 13. 17, 16. 2                           |
|       | governance 16. 3                                                |
|       | govern effectively 13. 1, 13. 2                                 |
|       | government 13. 7, 13. 20, 20. 1, 20. 2                          |
|       | office 6. 8, 18. 5                                              |
|       | official 13. 5                                                  |
|       | policy 8. 14, 14. 26, 19. 18                                    |
| Lau   | administration 13. 3                                            |
|       | administrative 13. 5                                            |
|       | affairs of state 13. 14                                         |
|       | edict 2. 3                                                      |
|       | government 1. 10, 2. 21, 12. 7, 12. 11, 12. 14, 12. 17,         |
|       | 12. 19, 13. 1, 13. 2, 13. 16, 13. 17, 14. 26, 16. 3, 20. 1,     |
|       | 20. 2                                                           |
|       | office 5. 19, 6. 8, 8. 14, 13. 13, 18. 5                        |
|       | policy 16. 2, 19. 18                                            |
|       | public life 13. 20                                              |
|       | rule 2. 1                                                       |
|       | state 13. 7                                                     |
| Legge | administration 8. 14, 14. 26                                    |
|       | business 13. 14                                                 |
|       | government 1. 10, 2. 1, 2. 21, 5. 19, 6. 8, 12. 7, 12. 11,      |
|       | 12. 14, 12. 17, 12. 19, 13. 1, 13. 2, 13. 3, 13. 5, 13. 7,      |
|       | 13. 13, 13. 16, 13. 17, 13. 20, 16. 2, 16. 3, 18. 5,            |
|       | 19. 18, 20. 1, 20. 2                                            |

| | |
|---|---|
| Leys | law 2.3 |
| | affairs of state 13.14 |
| | govern 12.17, 20.2 |
| | government 2.21, 12.7, 12.11, 12.14, 12.17, 12.19, 13.1, 13.2, 13.3, 13.13, 13.16, 20.1 |
| | minister 6.8 |
| | office 5.19, 18.5 |
| | official 13.5 |
| | official policy 14.26 |
| | policy 8.14, 19.18 |
| | politics 1.10, 13.7, 13.17 |
| | political maneuver 2.3 |
| | political initiative 16.2 |
| | political power 16.3 |
| | politician 13.20 |
| | rule 2.1 |
| Soothill | administration 1.10, 6.8, 13.3, 13.5, 19.18 |
| | administrator 20.2 |
| | affairs of state 13.14 |
| | art of government 13.1, 13.2 |
| | govern 2.1 |
| | government 12.7, 12.11, 12.14, 12.17, 12.19, 13.7, 13.16, 13.20, 16.3, 20.1, 20.2 |
| | law 2.3 |
| | office 18.5 |
| | policy 5.19, 8.14, 13.17, 14.26, 16.2 |
| | public service 2.21, 13.13 |
| Waley | administer 13.3 |

administration 5.19

affairs of state 13.14

art of ruling 12.17

domestic policy 19.18

govern 20.2

government 12.7, 12.11, 12.19, 13.1, 13.2, 13.5, 13.13, 13.16, 13.17, 13.20, 16.3

office 6.8, 18.5

policy 1.10, 8.14, 14.26, 16.2

politics 13.7

polity 20.1

public 12.14

public service 2.21

regulation 2.3

rule 2.1, 12.17, 12.19

# 政事(1)

| | |
|---|---|
| Ames/Rosemont | statesmanship 11.3 |
| Lau | government 11.3 |
| Legge | administrative 11.3 |
| Leys | government 11.3 |
| Soothill | administrative ability 11.3 |
| Waley | public business 11.3 |

# 知(118)

| | |
|---|---|
| Ames/Rosemont | acknowledge 1.1, 1.16, 4.14, 15.19 |
| | appreciate 14.35, 14.39 |
| | aware 19.5 |
| | know 1.15, 2.23, 3.11, 3.15, 4.7, 4.21, 5.9, 5.22, 7.14, 7.31, 9.6, 9.23, 14.1, 14.38, 15.14, 16.8, 18.6, 18.7, 19.24 |
| | knowledge 7.20, 16.9 |
| | realization 15.33 |
| | realize 1.12, 2.4, 2.11, 3.23, 7.19, 8.9, 9.28, 12.22, 15.4 |
| | recognize 11.24, 13.2, 14.30 |
| | say 5.5 |
| | sure 2.22, 5.8, 5.19, 8.3 |
| | think 5.18 |
| | understand 3.22, 6.20, 7.28, 8.16, 11.12, 13.3, 13.15, 20.3 |
| | wisdom 2.17, 5.21, 6.22, 9.8, 17.22 |
| | wise 4.1, 6.23, 9.29, 14.12, 14.28, 15.8, 17.1, 17.2, 19.25 |
| | wisely 17.7 |
| | wise person 4.2 |
| | wiser 14.17 |
| Lau | appreciate 11.24, 14.30, 15.19 |
| | appreciate one's ability 1.1, 1.16 |

appreciation 4.14

aware of 4.21

cleverness 17.7

conscious 19.5

intelligence 5.18, 5.21

intelligent 17.2

know 1.12, 2.11, 2.17, 2.23, 3.23, 4.7, 5.22, 6.20, 9.6, 9.23, 12.22, 14.1, 14.38, 15.14, 18.7, 19.24

knowledge 7.20, 7.28, 9.8, 16.9

[not] ignorant of 16.8

notice 7.14, 7.19, 7.31, 14.17

realize 3.23

recognize 13.2

say 5.5, 5.8

see 1.15, 2.22

sure 8.3

understand 2.4, 3.11, 3.15, 3.22, 5.9, 8.9, 11.12, 13.15, 14.35, 14.39, 15.4, 20.3

understanding 8.16, 15.33

value 15.34

wisdom 6.22, 9.29, 12.22, 14.28, 17.22

wise 4.1, 4.2, 5.19, 6.23, 14.12, 15.8, 17.1, 19.25

Legge

acquaintance 20.3

acquire 2.11

aware 18.7

in the possession of knowledge 7.20

keep in the memory 4.21

know 1.12, 1.15, 1.16, 2.4, 2.22, 2.23, 3.11, 3.15,

3.22, 3.23, 4.7, 4.14, 5.5, 5.8, 5.9, 5.19, 5.21, 5.22, 6.20, 7.14, 7.28, 7.31, 8.3, 9.6, 9.23, 9.28, 11.12, 11.24, 12.22, 13.2, 13.3, 13.15, 14.1, 14.17, 14.30, 14.35, 14.38, 15.4, 15.14, 15.19, 15.34, 16.8, 17.7, 18.6, 19.24, 20.3

knowledge 2.17, 9.8, 12.22, 14.12, 15.33

notice 14.39

perceive 7.19

possession of knowledge 16.9

recognise 19.5, 20.3

take note of 1.1

understand 8.9, 8.16

wisdom 5.18, 6.22, 17.22

wise 4.1, 4.2, 6.23, 9.29, 14.28, 15.8, 17.1, 17.2, 19.25

Leys  be expert on 3.15

competent 13.3

deduce 5.9

famous 4.14

figure out 1.15

foresee 18.7

intelligence 5.21, 17.7

keep in mind 4.21

know 1.12, 2.4, 2.11, 2.22, 2.23, 3.11, 3.22, 3.23, 4.7, 5.5, 5.8, 5.19, 5.22, 6.20, 7.31, 8.3, 9.6, 9.23, 9.28, 11.12, 12.22, 14.1, 14.38, 15.14, 16.8, 18.6

knowledge 2.17, 7.20, 7.28, 12.22, 15.33, 16.9

knowledgeable 9.8

learned 17.22

mind 5.18

notice 14.17

recognize 1.16, 11.24, 13.2

remember 19.5

see 15.34

sure 2.22

understand 8.9, 13.15, 14.35, 15.4, 20.3

understanding 8.16

wisdom 6.22, 14.12, 14.28, 19.25

wise 4.1, 4.2, 6.23, 9.29, 15.8, 17.1

wisest 17.2

Soothill

acquaintance 8.16

acquire 2.11

apprehend 5.9

aware 18.7

clever 6.23

conscious 7.14

distinguishable 15.34

enlighten 9.29

find out 19.5

foreknow 2.23

have idea of 19.24

intellectually 15.33

intelligent 15.8, 17.2

keep in mind 4.21

know 1.12, 1.15, 1.16, 2.22, 3.11, 3.15, 4.7, 4.14,

5.5, 5.8, 5.19, 5.21, 5.22, 6.20, 7.28, 7.31, 8.3, 9.6, 9.23, 11.24, 12.22, 14.1, 14.30, 14.35, 14.38, 15.14, 16.8, 18.6, 20.3

knowledge 2.17, 7.20, 9.8, 12.22, 14.28, 17.7

observe 7.19

perceive 13.15

realize 9.28

recognize 1.1, 13.2

sagacity 14.12

understand 2.4, 3.22, 3.23, 8.9, 11.12, 13.3, 15.4

wisdom 5.18, 6.22, 16.9, 17.22

wise 4.1, 4.2, 17.1, 19.25

wiser 14.17

wisest 17.2

Waley  be expert in 3.15

conscious 19.5

find out 3.23

foretell 2.23

gain 2.11

get through 8.3

have a great knowledge of 3.22

idea 5.22

know 1.12, 2.4, 3.11, 4.21, 5.5, 5.8, 6.20, 7.14, 7.31, 9.23, 11.12, 12.22, 13.2, 14.1, 14.35, 14.38, 15.14, 16.8, 18.6, 18.7, 19.24, 20.3

knowledge 2.17, 7.20, 7.28, 15.34

quite right about 9.6

realize 7.19

recognition 4.14, 8.16

recognize 1.1, 4.7, 11.24, 14.30, 14.39, 15.19

recognize one's merit 1.16

see 1.15, 2.22, 9.28

sure 5.18, 5.19

understand 5.9, 8.9, 13.3, 13.15, 15.4, 20.3

wisdom 5.21, 6.22, 9.8, 14.12, 15.33, 17.7, 17.22

wise 4.1, 4.2, 6.23, 9.29, 12.22, 14.28, 15.8, 16.9, 17.1, 19.25

wiser 14.17

wisest 17.2

# 直(22)

| | |
|---|---|
| Ames/Rosemont | candor 8.2, 17.7 |
| | discipline 8.16 |
| | frank and direct 17.14 |
| | straight 18.2 |
| | true 2.19, 5.24, 6.19, 12.20, 12.22, 13.18, 14.34, 15.7, 15.25, 16.4, 17.22 |
| Lau | courage 8.2 |
| | forthrightness 17.7, 17.22 |
| | not prepared to bend 18.2 |
| | straight 2.19, 5.24, 6.19, 8.16, 12.20, 12.22, 15.7, 15.25, 16.4, 17.14 |
| | straightness 13.18, 14.34 |
| Legge | justice 14.34 |

| | |
|---|---|
| | straightforward 12.20, 15.7, 17.22 |
| | straightforwardness 8.2, 15.25, 17.7, 17.14 |
| | upright 2.19, 5.24, 8.16, 12.22, 16.4, 18.2 |
| | uprightness 6.19, 13.18 |
| Leys | frank 17.22 |
| | frankness 8.2, 17.7 |
| | honestly 18.2 |
| | integrity 6.19, 13.18 |
| | justice 14.34 |
| | sincere 8.16 |
| | straight 2.19, 5.24, 12.20, 12.22, 15.7, 15.25, 16.4, 17.14 |
| Soothill | frankness 8.2 |
| | honest 18.2 |
| | honesty 13.18 |
| | just treatment 14.34 |
| | straight 12.22, 15.7, 15.25 |
| | straightforward 8.16 |
| | straightforwardness 17.7, 17.14, 17.22 |
| | upright 2.19, 5.24, 12.20, 16.4 |
| | uprightness 6.19 |
| Waley | honest 8.16, 18.2 |
| | honesty 6.19, 17.22 |
| | inflexibility 8.2 |
| | straight 2.19, 12.22, 15.25 |
| | straight and upright 15.7 |
| | straightforward 12.20, 17.14 |
| | upright 5.24, 14.34, 16.4 |

uprightness 13.18, 17.7

# 志(17)

Ames/Rosemont
　ends 16.11
　heart and mind 2.4
　intend 1.11
　mind 11.24
　purpose 4.9, 9.26, 18.8, 19.6
　resolute scholar apprentice 15.9
　sight 7.6
　suggestion 4.18
　will 4.4
　would like to do 5.26

Lau
　advice 4.18
　heart 2.4, 4.4, 4.9, 5.26, 7.6, 11.24
　mind 1.11
　purpose 9.26, 15.9, 16.11, 18.8, 19.6
　sign 14.36

Legge
　advice 4.18
　aim 16.11, 19.6
　determined scholar 15.9
　mind 2.4, 4.9, 7.6
　will 1.11, 4.4, 9.26, 18.8
　wish 5.26, 11.24

Leys
　advice 4.18
　aspiration 1.11, 11.24, 16.11

|  |  |
|---|---|
| | heart 4.9, 7.6 |
| | mind 2.4, 14.36 |
| | purpose 19.6 |
| | righteous 15.9 |
| | seek to achieve 4.4 |
| | will 9.26 |
| | wish 5.26 |
| Soothill | aim 16.11 |
| | aim at 4.9 |
| | aspiration 11.24 |
| | desire 11.24 |
| | high purpose 18.8 |
| | mind 2.4, 4.4, 7.6, 14.36 |
| | resolute scholar 15.9 |
| | tendency 1.11 |
| | will 9.26, 19.6 |
| | wish 5.26 |
| Waley | aim 16.11 |
| | desire 11.24 |
| | heart 2.4, 4.4, 4.9, 7.6 |
| | high resolve 18.8 |
| | intention 1.11 |
| | mind 14.36 |
| | opinion 4.18, 9.26 |
| | purpose 19.6 |
| | truly the heart of a knight 15.9 |
| | wish 5.26, 11.24 |

# 质(8)

| | |
|---|---|
| Ames/Rosemont | disposition 6.18，12.8，12.20，15.18 |
| Lau | stuff 12.8，15.18 |
| | native substance 6.18 |
| | nature 12.20 |
| Legge | essential 15.18 |
| | solid 12.20 |
| | solid quality 6.18 |
| | substance 12.8 |
| Leys | basis 15.18 |
| | nature 6.18，12.8 |
| | timber 12.20 |
| Soothill | foundation principle 15.18 |
| | nature 6.18，12.8，12.20 |
| Waley | material to work 15.18 |
| | natural substance 6.18 |
| | nature 12.20 |
| | stuff 12.8 |

# 治(6)

| | |
|---|---|
| Ames/Rosemont | command 14.19 |
| | conduct 14.19 |
| | effect proper order 15.5 |

| | |
|---|---|
| Lau | in charge of 5.8 |
| | properly governed 8.20 |
| | take care of 14.19 |
| | achieve order 15.5 |
| | manage 5.8 |
| | responsible 14.19 |
| | well governed 8.20 |
| Legge | direction 14.19 |
| | govern 15.5 |
| | manage 5.8 |
| | management 14.19 |
| | superintendence 14.19 |
| | well governed 8.20 |
| Leys | govern 15.5 |
| | in charge of 14.19 |
| | ministry 5.8 |
| | rule 8.20 |
| Soothill | administration 5.8 |
| | charge 14.19 |
| | command 14.19 |
| | well governed 15.5 |
| | well ruled 8.20 |
| Waley | carry out 5.8 |
| | command 14.19 |
| | deal 14.19 |
| | regulate 14.19 |
| | rule 15.5 |
| | well ruled 8.20 |

# 致(9)

| | |
|---|---|
| Ames/Rosemont | devotion 8.21 |
| | enforce 20.2 |
| | expression 19.14 |
| | generous 8.21 |
| | give 1.7, 19.17 |
| | go 19.4 |
| | lavish 8.21 |
| | promote 19.7 |
| | put 19.1 |
| Lau | exert 1.7 |
| | give full expression 19.14 |
| | insist 20.2 |
| | lay down 19.1 |
| | perfect 19.7 |
| | realize 19.17 |
| | spare no effort 8.21 |
| | utmost 8.21 |
| Legge | carry out 19.4 |
| | devote 1.7 |
| | insist on with severity 20.2 |
| | reach 19.7 |
| | sacrifice 19.1 |
| | show 19.17 |
| | utmost 8.21, 19.14 |

| | |
|---|---|
| Leys | devotion 8. 21 |
| | express 19. 14 |
| | give 1. 7, 19. 1 |
| | reach 19. 7 |
| | reveal 19. 17 |
| | utter 8. 21 |
| Soothill | carry one's wisdom to 19. 7 |
| | demand for 20. 2 |
| | go 19. 4 |
| | lay down 1. 7 |
| | offer 19. 1 |
| | scrupulous 8. 21 |
| | show 19. 17 |
| | suffice as its highest expression 19. 14 |
| | unspare 8. 21 |
| Waley | dictate 19. 14 |
| | expect 20. 2 |
| | improve 19. 7 |
| | lay down 1. 7, 19. 1 |
| | pursue 19. 4 |
| | show 19. 17 |
| | utmost 8. 21 |

## 中(25)

| | |
|---|---|
| Ames/Rosemont | along 6. 12 |
| | common 6. 21 |

| | |
|---|---|
| | in 5.1, 7.16, 10.20, 13.18, 19.6 |
| | middle 10.3 |
| | on the mark 11.14, 11.18, 13.3 |
| | temperate 13.21 |
| | within 16.1 |
| | without deviation 20.1 |
| | zhong 17.6 |
| Lau | among 6.12 |
| | average 6.21 |
| | centre 10.3 |
| | chung 17.6 |
| | in 2.18, 5.1, 10.20, 13.18 |
| | in accord with 18.8 |
| | middle way 20.1 |
| | moderate 13.21 |
| | right 11.18, 13.3 |
| | to the point 11.14 |
| | within 16.1 |
| | according to 18.8 |
| Legge | chung 17.6 |
| | correct 11.18 |
| | correspond with 18.8 |
| | due mean 20.1 |
| | hit the point 11.14 |
| | in 2.18, 5.1, 10.20, 13.18, 15.32, 19.6 |
| | in the midst of 16.1 |
| | mediocrity 6.21 |
| | middle 6.12, 10.3 |

| | |
|---|---|
| | midst 7.16 |
| | medium 13.21 |
| | pressure 18.8 |
| | properly awarded 13.3 |
| Leys | average 6.21 |
| | half 6.12 |
| | hit the mark 11.4 |
| | in 5.1, 10.20, 13.18, 16.1 |
| | middle 10.3, 13.21 |
| | middle way 20.1 |
| | preserve 18.8 |
| | right 11.18 |
| | target 13.3 |
| | zhong 17.6 |
| Soothill | average 6.21 |
| | chung 17.6 |
| | golden mean 20.1 |
| | half 6.12 |
| | hit the mark 11.14, 11.18 |
| | hit off 18.8 |
| | in 2.18, 5.1, 7.16, 10.20, 13.18, 15.32, 16.1, 19.6 |
| | make for 18.8 |
| | media 13.21 |
| | middle 10.3 |
| | sustain 18.8 |
| | within 16.1 |
| Waley | centre 20.1 |
| | chung 17.6 |

consonant with 18.8

during 6.12

hit the mark 11.14, 11.18

involve 13.18

middle 6.21, 10.3, 13.21

secure 18.8

shrewd 18.8

within 16.1

## 中庸(1)

| | |
|---|---|
| Ames/Rosemont | mark in the everyday 6.29 |
| Lau | mean 6.29 |
| Legge | constant mean 6.29 |
| Leys | middle way 6.29 |
| Soothill | golden mean 6.29 |
| Waley | middle use 6.29 |

## 忠(18)

| | |
|---|---|
| Ames/Rosemont | do one's best 4.15, 5.19, 7.25, 12.14, 14.7 |
| | do one's utmost 2.20, 3.19, 5.28, 9.25, 13.19 |
| | utmost 1.4, 1.8, 12.10, 12.23, 15.6, 16.10 |
| Lau | conscientious 15.6, 16.10 |
| | do one's best 1.4, 1.8, 4.15, 5.19, 5.28, 7.25, 9.25, 12.10, 12.14, 14.7 |

|       |                                                           |
| ----- | --------------------------------------------------------- |
|       | do one's utmost 2.20, 3.19                                |
|       | give of one's best 13.19                                  |
|       | to the best of one's ability 12.23                        |
| Legge | consistency 12.14                                         |
|       | devotion of soul 7.25                                     |
|       | faithful 1.4, 2.20                                        |
|       | faithfully 12.23                                          |
|       | faithfulness 1.8, 3.19, 9.25, 12.10                       |
|       | honourable 5.28                                           |
|       | intercourse 13.19                                         |
|       | loyal 5.19                                                |
|       | loyalty 14.7                                              |
|       | sincere 15.6, 16.10                                       |
|       | true to the principles of one's nature 4.15               |
| Leys  | loyal 2.20, 5.19, 5.28, 12.23, 13.19, 16.10               |
|       | loyalty 1.8, 3.19, 4.15, 7.25, 9.25, 12.10, 14.7, 15.6    |
|       | loyally 12.14                                             |
|       | trustworthy 1.4                                           |
| Soothill | conscientious 5.19, 5.28, 13.19, 16.10                 |
|       | conscientiously 12.14, 12.23                              |
|       | conscientiousness 1.4, 1.8, 4.15, 7.25, 9.25, 12.10       |
|       | loyalty 2.20, 3.19, 14.7                                  |
|       | sincere 15.6                                              |
| Waley | devotion to one's cause 3.19                              |
|       | faithful 1.8, 5.19, 9.25                                  |
|       | loyal 2.20, 5.28, 13.19, 14.7, 15.6, 16.10                |
|       | loyally 12.14, 12.23                                      |

loyal to one's interest 1.4

loyalty 4.15, 12.10

loyalty to superior 7.25

# 终(11)

| | |
|---|---|
| Ames/Rosemont | all 15.17 |
| | end 15.24 |
| | entire 2.9 |
| | funerary service 1.9 |
| | hopeless 17.24 |
| | over and over again 9.27 |
| | severed utterly 20.1 |
| | whole 15.31, 17.20 |
| Lau | all 2.9, 15.17, 15.31, 17.20 |
| | constantly 9.27 |
| | funeral of one's parent 1.9 |
| | no hope 17.24 |
| | terminated for ever 20.1 |
| | throughout 15.24 |
| Legge | all 15.24 |
| | continually 9.27 |
| | continue 17.24 |
| | funeral rites to parent 1.9 |
| | perpetual end 20.1 |
| | whole 2.9, 15.17, 15.31, 17.20 |
| Leys | all 2.9, 17.20 |

|  |  |
|---|---|
| | continually 9.27 |
| | dead 1.9 |
| | end 17.24 |
| | entire 15.24 |
| | whole 15.17，15.31 |
| | withdraw forever 20.1 |
| Soothill | decease of parent 1.9 |
| | end 17.24 |
| | forever end 20.1 |
| | lifelong 15.17，15.24，17.20 |
| | perpetually 9.27 |
| | whole 2.9，15.31 |
| Waley | all 15.24，17.20 |
| | continually 9.27 |
| | dead 1.9 |
| | end 17.24 |
| | last forever 20.1 |
| | whole 2.9，15.17，15.31 |

## 众(13)

|  |  |
|---|---|
| Ames/Rosemont | accepted practice 9.3 |
| | everyone 15.28，19.3 |
| | many 17.5，20.1，20.2 |
| | multitude 1.6，2.1，6.30，12.22 |
| Lau | majority 9.3 |
| | many 20.2 |

| | |
|---|---|
| | multitude 1.6, 2.1, 6.30, 12.22, 15.28, 17.5, 19.3, 20.1 |
| Legge | all 1.6, 2.1, 6.30, 17.5, 19.3, 20.1 |
| | all the people 12.22 |
| | common practice 9.3 |
| | many people 20.2 |
| | multitude 15.28 |
| Leys | all 2.1 |
| | all hearts 17.5 |
| | everyone 15.28 |
| | general usage 9.3 |
| | many 20.2 |
| | mass 20.1 |
| | mediocre 19.3 |
| | multitude 6.30, 12.22 |
| | people 1.6 |
| Soothill | all 2.1, 15.28, 17.5, 19.3, 20.1 |
| | all men 1.6 |
| | general usage 9.3 |
| | many 20.2 |
| | multitude 6.30, 12.22 |
| Waley | all 2.1, 19.3 |
| | everyone 1.6, 15.28 |
| | general practice 9.3 |
| | many persons 20.2 |
| | multitude 12.22, 17.5, 20.1 |
| | whole state 6.30 |

# 重(4)

| | |
|---|---|
| Ames/Rosemont | gravity 1.8 |
| | heavy 8.7 |
| | priority 20.1 |
| Lau | consider of importance 20.1 |
| | gravity 1.8 |
| | heavy 8.7 |
| Legge | attach chief importance to 20.1 |
| | grave 1.8 |
| | heavy 8.7 |
| Leys | gravity 1.8 |
| | heavy 8.7 |
| | matter 20.1 |
| Soothill | grave 1.8 |
| | heavy 8.7 |
| | lay stress on 20.1 |
| Waley | care for most 20.1 |
| | [not] frivolous 1.8 |
| | heavy 8.7 |

# 周(4)

| | |
|---|---|
| Ames/Rosemont | associate openly with 2.14 |
| | help 6.4 |

| | |
|---|---|
| Lau | immediate 20. 1 |
| | association 2. 14 |
| | close 20. 1 |
| | help 6. 4 |
| Legge | catholic 2. 14 |
| | help 6. 4 |
| | near 20. 1 |
| Leys | help 6. 4 |
| | own 20. 1 |
| | whole 2. 14 |
| Soothill | broad minded 2. 14 |
| | closely 20. 1 |
| | succor 6. 4 |
| Waley | help 6. 4 |
| | see a question from all side 2. 14 |

# 周南(2)

| | |
|---|---|
| Ames/Rosemont | zhounan 17. 8 |
| Lau | chou nan 17. 8 |
| Legge | châu nan 17. 8 |
| Leys | first part of *the Poems* 17. 8 |
| Soothill | chou nan 17. 8 |
| Waley | chou nan 17. 8 |

## 庄(4)

| | |
|---|---|
| Ames/Rosemont | dignity 2. 20，15. 33 |
| | serious 11. 19 |
| Lau | dignified 11. 19 |
| | dignity 2. 20，15. 33 |
| Legge | dignity 15. 33 |
| | gravity 2. 20，11. 19 |
| Leys | dignity 2. 20，15. 33 |
| | solemn 11. 19 |
| Soothill | dignity 2. 20，15. 33 |
| | seriousness 11. 19 |
| Waley | dignity 2. 20，15. 33 |
| | solemnity 11. 19 |

## 宗庙(5)

| | |
|---|---|
| Ames/Rosemont | ancestral temple 10. 1，11. 24，14. 19，19. 23 |
| Lau | ancestral temple 10. 1，11. 24，14. 19，19. 23 |
| Legge | ancestorial temple 10. 1 |
| | ancestral temple 11. 24，14. 19，19. 23 |
| Leys | ancestor cult 14. 19 |
| | ancestral temple 10. 1，11. 24，19. 23 |
| Soothill | ancestral temple 11. 24，14. 19 |
| | temple 10. 1，19. 23 |

| | |
|---|---|
| Waley | ancestral temple 10.1, 11.24, 14.19, 19.23 |

## 宗族(1)

| | |
|---|---|
| Ames/Rosemont | family 13.20 |
| Lau | clan 13.20 |
| Legge | circle of one's relative 13.20 |
| Leys | relative 13.20 |
| Soothill | relative 13.20 |
| Waley | relative 13.20 |

## 罪(6)

| | |
|---|---|
| Ames/Rosemont | fault 5.1 |
| | offend 3.13 |
| | guilty 20.1 |
| Lau | guilty 20.1 |
| | offend 3.13 |
| | wrongdoing 5.1 |
| Legge | guilty 5.1 |
| | offence 20.1 |
| | offend 3.13 |
| Leys | guilty 20.1 |
| | offend 3.13 |
| Soothill | sin 3.13, 20.1 |
| | wrongdoing 5.1 |

| | | |
|---|---|---|
| Waley | | fault 5.1 |
| | | guilty 20.1 |
| | | put oneself in the wrong 3.13 |

# 作(11)

| | | |
|---|---|---|
| Ames/Rosemont | | begin 3.23 |
| | | build 11.14 |
| | | forge new paths 7.1 |
| | | initiate 1.2, 7.28 |
| | | rise 9.10, 11.24 |
| | | make 13.22 |
| | | rise to one's feet 10.19 |
| | | take initiative 14.37 |
| | | take to the air 10.21 |
| Lau | | begin 3.23 |
| | | build 11.14 |
| | | flow away 10.21 |
| | | get up 14.3 |
| | | innovate 7.1, 7.28 |
| | | make 13.22 |
| | | rise 9.10 |
| | | rise to one's feet 10.19 |
| | | stand up 11.24 |
| | | start 1.2 |
| Legge | | act 7.28 |
| | | be 13.22 |

| | |
|---|---|
| | commencement 3. 23 |
| | do 14. 37 |
| | make 11. 14 |
| | maker 7. 1 |
| | rise 9. 10, 10. 21, 11. 24 |
| | rise up 10. 19 |
| | stir up 1. 2 |
| Leys | act 7. 28 |
| | build 11. 14 |
| | do 14. 37 |
| | flow away 10. 21 |
| | foment 1. 2 |
| | invent 7. 1 |
| | make 13. 22 |
| | rise to one's feet 10. 19 |
| | stand up 9. 10 |
| Soothill | arise 9. 10, 11. 24 |
| | construct 11. 14 |
| | create 1. 2 |
| | do 7. 28, 14. 37 |
| | make 13. 22 |
| | originator 7. 1 |
| | proceed 3. 23 |
| | rise 10. 21 |
| | stand up 10. 19 |
| Waley | begin 3. 23 |
| | build 11. 14 |
| | do 7. 28 |

make 13.22, 14.37

make up anything of one's own 7.1

rise 9.10, 10.21, 11.24

rise to one's feet 10.19

start 1.2

图书在版编目(CIP)数据

《论语》英译本术语引得 / 张靖，徐建委主编. —
南京：南京大学出版社，2021.3
(《论语》英译本汇释汇校丛书 / 杨慧林主编)
ISBN 978-7-305-21895-8

Ⅰ.①论… Ⅱ.①张… ②徐… Ⅲ.①《论语》—英语—翻译—研究 Ⅳ.①H315.9②B222.25

中国版本图书馆 CIP 数据核字(2019)第 063097 号

| 出版发行 | 南京大学出版社 | | |
|---|---|---|---|
| 社　　址 | 南京市汉口路 22 号 | 邮　编 | 210093 |
| 出 版 人 | 金鑫荣 | | |

丛 书 名　《论语》英译本汇释汇校丛书
丛书主编　杨慧林
书　　名　《论语》英译本术语引得
主　　编　张　靖　徐建委
责任编辑　沈清清

照　　排　南京南琳图文制作有限公司
印　　刷　南京爱德印刷有限公司
开　　本　635×965　1/16　印张 44.25　字数 600 千
版　　次　2021 年 3 月第 1 版　2021 年 3 月第 1 次印刷
ISBN 978-7-305-21895-8
定　　价　188.00 元

网址：http://www.njupco.com
官方微博：http://weibo.com/njupco
官方微信号：njupress
销售咨询热线：(025) 83594756

\* 版权所有,侵权必究

\* 凡购买南大版图书,如有印装质量问题,请与所购
　图书销售部门联系调换